CW01459361

The Security Consultant's Handbook

The Security Consultant's Handbook

RICHARD BINGLEY

it gp™

IT Governance Publishing

Every possible effort has been made to ensure that the information contained in this book is accurate at the time of going to press, and the publisher and the author cannot accept responsibility for any errors or omissions, however caused. Any opinions expressed in this book are those of the author, not the publisher. Websites identified are for reference only, not endorsement, and any website visits are at the reader's own risk. No responsibility for loss or damage occasioned to any person acting, or refraining from action, as a result of the material in this publication can be accepted by the publisher or the author.

Apart from any fair dealing for the purposes of research or private study, or criticism or review, as permitted under the Copyright, Designs and Patents Act 1988, this publication may only be reproduced, stored or transmitted, in any form, or by any means, with the prior permission in writing of the publisher or, in the case of reprographic reproduction, in accordance with the terms of licenses issued by the Copyright Licensing Agency. Enquiries concerning reproduction outside those terms should be sent to the publishers at the following address:

IT Governance Publishing
IT Governance Limited
Unit 3, Clive Court
Bartholomew's Walk
Cambridgeshire Business Park
Ely, Cambridgeshire
CB7 4EA
United Kingdom
www.itgovernance.co.uk

© Richard Bingley 2015

The author has asserted the rights of the author under the Copyright, Designs, and Patents Act, 1988, to be identified as the author of this work.

First published in the United Kingdom in 2015
by IT Governance Publishing

ISBN 978-1-84928-748-7

DEDICATION

For my grandparents, Daphne Hart (1927-2011)
and Ian Harrison

ACKNOWLEDGEMENTS

I would like to thank Antonio Velasco, CEO of Sinersys Technologies and ir. H.L. (Maarten) Souw RE, Enterprise Risk and QA Manager, UVW, for their helpful comments during the review process.

ABOUT THE AUTHOR

Richard Bingley is a senior lecturer in security and organisational resilience at Buckinghamshire New University, in the United Kingdom. Richard is co-founder of CSARN, the popular business security advisory network with offices in the UK and Australia. He has more than 15 years' experience in a range of high-profile security and communications roles, including as a close protection operative at London's 2012 Olympics and in Russia for the 2014 Winter Olympic Games. Richard has previously authored two popular books: *Terrorism: Just the Facts* (2004) and *Arms Trade: Just the Facts* (2003). Richard is a licensed close protection operative in the UK and holds a postgraduate certificate in teaching and learning in higher education.

ABBREVIATIONS

ABH: Actual Bodily Harm
ABI: Association of British Investigators
ACAS: Advisory and Conciliation Service
ACFE: Association of Certified Fraud Examiners
ACPO: Association of Chief Police Officers
ADP: British Army Doctrine Publication
ADS: Aerospace, Defence, Security trade group
AFO: Authorised Firearms Officers
AGM: Annual General Meeting
AIEs: Advanced Industrialised Economies
APICS: Association for Supply Chain and Operations Management
APPF: Afghan Public Protection Force
AS: Anti Surveillance
ASIS: American Society for Industrial Security
BPSS: Baseline Personnel Security Standard
BC: Business Continuity
BCI: Business Continuity Institute
BCM: Business Continuity Management
BG: Bodyguard
BIMCO: Baltic and International Maritime Council
BP: Beyond Petroleum, formerly British Petroleum
BRC: British Retail Consortium
BRIC: Brazil, Russia, India and People's Republic of China
BSI: British Standards Institute
BSIA: British Security Industry Association
CBA: Cost Benefit Analysis
CEO: Chief Executive Officer
CEOP: Child Exploitation and Online Protection Centre
CESG: Communications-Electronic Security Group
CI: Competitive Intelligence
CIA: Central Intelligence Agency, US
CIA (The CIA Triad): Confidentiality, Integrity, Accessibility
CII: Council of International Investigators
CIO: Chief Information Officer
CIR Magazine: Continuity, Insurance and Risk
CISO: Chief Information Security Officer
CLV: Customer Life Value

CM: Crisis Management
CoLCPA: City of London Crime Prevention Association
COSWP: Code of Safe Working Practices for Merchant Seamen
CPNI: Centre for the Protection of National Infrastructure, UK
CPO: Close Protection Operative
CRA: Country Risk Analysis
CRB: Criminal Records Bureau
CS: Counter Surveillance
CSA: Crime Scene Analysis
CSARN: City Security and Resilience Networks
CSF: Comprehensive Soldier Fitness
CT (scan): Computerised Tomography
DHS: Department for Homeland Security
DNA: Deoxyribonucleic Acid
DVLA: Driver Vehicle Licencing Agency
ECHR: European Convention of Human Rights
EDI: Electronic Data Interchange
EHIC: European Health Insurance Card
EISF: European Interagency Security Forum
EM: Emerging Market
EP: Emergency Planning
ERM: Enterprise Risk Management
EU: European Union
EU NAVFOR: European Union Naval Forces
FCO: Foreign and Commonwealth Office (UK)
FEMA: Federal Emergency Management Agency
FSA: Financial Services Authority
GATT: General Agreement on Tariffs and Trade
GPS: Global Positioning System
GBH: Grievous Bodily Harm
G8: Group of eight leading global economies.
G20: G8 plus some of the world's larger emerging national economies
HASAW: Health and Safety at Work
HASE: Health and Safety Executive
HBR: Harvard Business Review
HEA: Higher Education Academy
HEBCON: Higher Education Business Continuity Network
HMG: Her Majesty's Government, United Kingdom
HR: Human Resources
HRA: Health Risk Assessments
HSC: Health and Safety Commission

ICC: International Criminal Court
ICC: International Chamber of Commerce
ICOC: International Code of Conduct for Private Security Service Providers
ICJ: International Court of Justice
ICPEM: Institute of Civil Protection and Emergency Managers
ICT: Information Communications Technology
IPS: Identity and Passport Service
IMF: International Monetary Fund
IoD: Institute of Directors
IOFM: Institute of Financial Management
IPO: Intellectual Property Office (United Kingdom)
IPR: Intellectual Property Rights
ISMS: Information Security Management System Standard ISO27001
ISPS: International Ship and Port Facility Security Code
IT: Information Technology
JIT: Just in Time
JV: Joint Venture
KPI: Key Performance Indicators
KRAs: Key Results Areas
K&R: Kidnap and Ransom
LBC: London's Big Conversation
LEPs: Local Enterprise Partnerships
LLP: Limited Liability Partnership
MDGs: Millennium Development Goals
MENA: Middle East and North Africa
Mispers: Missing Persons
NaCTSO: National Counter Terrorism Security Office
NATO: North Atlantic Treaty Organisation
NAPPS: National Association of Professional Process Servers
NEOUCOM: Northeastern Ohio Universities College of Medicine
NFA: No Further Action
NFA: National Fraud Authority (UK)
NFIB: National Fraud Intelligence Bureau (UK)
NFRC: National Fraud Reporting Centre (UK)
NFSTC: National Forensic Science Technology Centre
NGO: Non-Governmental Organisation
NIAC: National Infrastructure Advisory Council
NOS: National Occupational Standards
NPIA: National Policing Improvement Agency
NSI: National Security Inspectorate
NZ: New Zealand

Abbreviations

OECD: Organisation for Economic Co-operation and Development
OM: Operations Management
OMBOK: Operations Management Body of Knowledge Framework
ONI: Office of Naval Intelligence
OP: Observation Post
OSAC: Overseas Security Advisory Council (US)
OSINT: Open Source Intelligence
OU: Open University
PACE: Police and Criminal Evidence Act (1984)
PACT: Parents & Abducted Children Together
PAS: Publicly Available Specification
PCASP: Privately Contracted Armed Security Personnel
PES: Personal Escort Section
PESTLE: Political, Economic, Social, Technological, Legal, Environmental
PI: Private Investigator
PIN: Personal Identification Number
PIR: Priority Information Request
PLC: Public Limited Company
PMSC: Private Maritime Security Companies
POTUS: President of the United Sates of America
PPE: Personal Protective Equipment
PSCs: Private Security Contractors
PSF: UK Professional Standards Framework
PUB: Personal Unblocking Code
PVS: Passport Validation Service
RDSG: Royal Dutch Shell Group
RIDDOR: Reporting of Injuries, Diseases and Dangerous Occurrences
Regulations (2013)
RIPA: Regulation of Investigatory Powers Act 2000
ROI: Return on Investment
RUF: International Model Set of Maritime Rules for the Use of Force
SAMI: Security Association for the Maritime Industry
SCEG: Security in Complex Environments Group
SIA: Security Industry Authority
SIs: Statutory instruments
SLAs: Service Level Agreements
SMART: Specific, Measurable, Achievable, Relevant and Time-bound
SOLAS: The International Convention for the Safety of Life at Sea
SWOT: Strengths, Weakness, Opportunities, Threats
TGP: Target Group Profiling
TINYg: Terrorist Information New York Group

TRIPS: Agreement on Trade-Related Aspects of Intellectual Property Rights
UN: United Nations
US: United States
USP: Unique Sales Proposition
USTPO: United States Trademark and Patent Office
VoIP: Voice over Internet Protocol
VPS: Victim Personal Statements
WTO: World Trade Organisation

FOREWORD

Welcome to *The Security Consultant's Handbook*.

This book is *not* a training manual about the security industry, or any subdiscipline within it. There are hundreds, or thousands, of specialist security training services and guidance manuals out there that can explain and evaluate their niche and technical specialisms far better than I.

Yet several years have now passed since a range of very decent generalist support books for security managers and practitioners have been produced. A lot has happened since: economic crashes, national security data haemorrhages, nuclear reactor meltdowns, nihilistic international terrorism and a social media revolution that has brought about individual and corporate liberation and tyranny; possibly in equal measure.

My purpose, therefore, is to set out to provide a compendium of business approaches, opportunities and risks that fairly reflect those faced by the modern security entrepreneur and practitioner, at this point in time. I say *entrepreneur* because – whether we are sole contractors, employees, or public authority officials – most of us nowadays are required to innovate and adopt entrepreneurial approaches by our paymasters.

More than ever before, a failure to read and adapt to our operating environments, can leave us short of perceived value. The business world is more accessible, but possibly less forgiving, than ever before.

In this book, I therefore aim to provide a holistic oversight of essential core knowledge, emerging opportunities and approaches to corporate thinking that are being increasingly demanded by employers and buyers in the security market. This book aims to provide options and directions for those who are ambitious to succeed in security, either individually or as part of a team.

I also hope to stimulate some fresh ideas and new routes to market to consider for security professionals who may feel that they are under-appreciated and over-exerted in traditional business domains. I do hope that each of the eight chapters really does help the reader to enjoy a renewed sense of passion and control over their entrepreneurial activity.

This book will therefore unapologetically seek to encourage and facilitate the reader's own lateral thinking in relation to existing markets, management and business approaches. Near the beginning, we provide some foundation knowledge of so-called emerging markets, even though these markets – such as Brazil, India, Russia and China – have now been maturing for several decades.

Moreover, I attempt to encourage the reader's own skills and knowledge, by linking much of our content to further opportunities for training, higher education and longer-term professional development.

Possibly the biggest barrier to our own success is an individual and collective impatience with *reflective learning* techniques. Our inability to sensibly review or admit to various faults, is a fundamental recurring weakness for us information-rich, but knowledge-poor, human beings.

Since time immemorial, *cognitive bias* has been a significant contributor in the causation of wars, industrial-scale accidents and bankruptcies. Being caught in an activity trap, or constricted by tunnel vision, prevents us from exploiting so many nearby opportunities to improve and excel. I therefore very much hope that this book encourages readers to reach beyond their comfort zones, yet still remain within the bounds of law and sanity!

Today's world does unequivocally provide a treasure trove of opportunity for entrepreneurs and innovators, I believe. It's surely the dilemma as to which doors to open or close that tends to vex us entrepreneurs.

This said, I hope that our readers' decision-making capabilities may be well assisted by discovering lots of new facts and case studies across the eight chapters. These sections seek to cover foundation knowledge in the domains of: entrepreneurial practice; management practice; legislation and regulation; private investigations; information and cyber security; protective security; safer business travel; personal and organisational resilience.

For context, I'm a security management lecturer and security contractor. I first conceived the idea for this book as I was travelling from Belorussky railway station northwards towards Moscow's Sheremetyevo Airport, on a sleek, bullet-shaped, Aero Express shuttle train. The 2014 Sochi Winter Olympics had safely concluded a few hours before.

I had taken some time out from university teaching and accepted a brief security contract. My role on this occasion was as a protective security agent for an American client organisation in Russia.

Our company had had some Olympic guests travelling back through Moscow from Sochi, mainly towards the United States. Some were a little apprehensive about their transit. Understandably so. Suicide bombings at Russian rail stations had occurred a few weeks before the Games. Moreover, 100 or so suicide bombings during the last decade and a half had hit the Russian people hard. But our people were safely through and back in various planetary quarters. Job done.

As I boarded the train, a bilingual announcement told us that chemical weapons or firearms were – thankfully – not permitted on this train. Passengers around me curled up into their coats with the same type of melancholic gloom reserved for any pre-dawn, Monday morning, midwinter commute anywhere in the world.

My Wi-Fi connection suddenly kicked in. Emails pulsed through from my own students in Iraq, the UAE, Canada and US. My project bosses in Florida had also pinged me a message or two about returning items. Another colleague sent me an SMS: should we add a brief evaluation of ongoing events in Ukraine to my daily threat assessment? Ukraine's President had been toppled by protestors 48 hours before. 'Nftr' I responded (Nothing further to report). As things stood, all our guests had safely left the region.

Moments later I received a text message from a Chamber of Commerce boss in Russia. Another text streamed in, this time from my mother. My old dog Floyd was asleep by her home hearth. She expressed genuine surprise that I was still alive. Perhaps even a small suspicion that I hadn't been in Russia at all, because I wasn't even slightly incapacitated.

How perspectives can vary. I instantly thought back to the previous night's dinner on Moscow's neon-illuminated boulevard, *Novy Arbat*. A Russian friend recoiled in dismay when I told them that western visitors to Moscow actually required a physical security detail: "We have far less crime than New York", they moaned.

So there we have it. The world *has* closed in, just as the Scorpions sang back in 1991 after the Berlin Wall was hammered down. Today our planet is a global village. We global citizens can talk to one another and see one another, although we may all live in wildly different time zones. We all share the same data sets and read the same news blogs. We are all – I hope – more interested in developing intercontinental business alliances, rather than intercontinental ballistic missiles.

Yet human perspectives can remain poles apart; entrenched by different experiences, cultures, approaches and interpretations.

Knowing in essence who and what to believe, and also what to do if certain scenarios occur, does actually get to the heart of what constitutes working life as a security operative. Beneath the corporate-enshrined authority of an executive boardroom, there really aren't many company roles with such a significant sense of duty and responsibility, than that of a professional security officer.

For those interested in progression within the security profession, the world is your operating environment. Therefore, good subject matter knowledge is not so much a route to power, but a fundamental duty of your day job role, which is to keep your colleagues and assets safe and secure.

This may be quite a daunting statement.

This publication is therefore designed to be a practical and enabling guide for security officers and contractors. Its purpose is to plug information gaps, or provoke new ideas, rather than to be treated as a fully garrisoned academic tome.

My aim was to provide a 'real-world' support tool for those who want to offer safe, proportionate and value-driven security services to their clients.

By carrying out some 50 interviews with leading security practitioners, and reviewing a large range of credible literature, which now supports business security activity, I have tried wherever possible to suspend personal opinions and philosophies. I wanted to let the experts and facts speak for themselves.

Nevertheless, personal leanings and preferences will be evident, such as the choices I have made around chapter topics. These editorial choices tend to reflect my philosophy and my own experiences within the profession, as to what topics have emerged to be significant from a corporate world viewpoint.

I apologise if this book's menu does not suit every reader's taste. Please do let me know if significant areas of interest have been omitted and we will seek to include such omissions in subsequent editions.

In closing, I would like to thank the many interviewees who shared their insights both for open-source and background contexts. Face-to-face interviews were conducted during 2013, 2014 and early 2015 in mainland Britain, Northern Ireland, Lebanon, the US, the Czech Republic and Russian Federation. I also express sincere thanks to a fantastic range of students at Buckinghamshire New University's growing Department of Security and Resilience, based in the UK, where I teach as a senior lecturer.

For context, many, if not all, of my undergraduate and postgraduate students can claim to be officially *mature* because they are over 25 years old. They also work as full-time security consultants and managers in some of the world's most complex and volatile environments. Each student works viscerally hard in their day job. They somehow study in their non-existent 'spare' time. More often than not each learner defeats exceptional life constraints. Their motivation and application continues to inspire me. Some were able to share their own work experiences for learning purposes within this book. I am hugely indebted that so many found the time and patience to teach and support me, when it should of course be the other way around.

Foreword

I would particularly like to thank Phil Wood MBE, former Head of Academic Department at Buckinghamshire New University, for his support when I joined his team of academics. Likewise, a 'thank you' also to our new Head of Academic Department, Emma Parkinson, for her support and endless sympathy as I came to conclude writing this book. I am also indebted to my fellow security management lecturers, Simon King and Gavin Butler, alongside Dianne Cameron, Dianne Dunn and Peter Brown (senior registrar) in our university's Blended Learning Unit. They all bore the brunt of my research and book writing diversions. For context, Simon King also very kindly contributed subsections 4.5 (surveillance techniques) and 4.6 (electronic surveillance, the law and ethics) of this book's Private Investigations chapter. Gavin Butler also very kindly supplied some of the chapter subheadings and was pivotal in shaping the list of contents for this edition. I would like to record my gratitude for all of those who contributed quotes, ideas and interviews to this book. These include: Antoni Bick, Thomas Black, Scott Brant, John Paul Breed, Paul Brown, Lee Caines, Daniel Cogan, James Gess, Jon Hill (Polaris), Tom Hough, Tracey Hough, Simon Hull, Jason Layton, Brett Lovegrove, Seth Martin, Paul Morgan, Chris Phillips, Robert Newman, Lisa Reilly, Thomas Richmond, Rob Scott (SCG Security), Adam Smith, Jason Towse (Mitie Total Security), John Tristram and Andy Williams (ex-Marriott EMEA security director).

Some have chosen to remain uncited.

I do also wish to specifically thank my publishers at IT Governance, including Vicki Utting, for her patience and compassion, as my book deadline did require a couple of extensions, following the passing of my father, Randal Bingley. A big further 'thank you' to my mother, Amanda Bingley, who has provided me with consistent love and support. My final 'thank you' is directed toward PC Milena Bauerova, of London's famous Metropolitan Police Service. PC Bauerova came to my rescue during a sunny afternoon in June 2013, on London's picturesque Hampstead Common. Clearly, without her kind intervention back then, this book may never have witnessed the light of day.

The errors in this material are all mine.

Richard Bingley, London, 2015

CONTENTS

Contents

CHAPTER 1: BECOMING AN ENTREPRENEUR IN THE SECURITY BUSINESS

1.1 Context

"You miss 100% of the shots you don't take." – Wayne Gretzky, NHL Hall of Fame.

Whether as an employee, senior manager, or self-employed consultant, we are all expected to be entrepreneurs. Growing a successful business, your own enterprise or somebody else's, is one of the most satisfying experiences during anybody's working life. Winning new contracts is a thrilling endorsement of conceptual plans, existing skills, prior investment and experiences. On paper, becoming a *successful* entrepreneur within the security sector can be viewed as relatively straightforward by those on the outside of our profession. There is a popular perception that the private security market is awash with money. Especially around high-value assets where niche specialisms and uber-exciting professional backgrounds may well be required by clients. Two recent conversations that I've had spring to mind. The first, with a young law undergraduate at my boxing gym. After sparring me out of the ring, my pal wanted to chat about how he could 'diversify' into security. (Doesn't being a barrister pay enough?) Secondly, a talk with Jason Towse, a managing director at one of the UK's biggest security operators. He told me that margins from manned-guarding had all but evaporated. Success was hard-earned and cumulatively accrued, he said, "from building long-standing strategic relationships". Longer-term relationships enabled the client and vendor to develop a trusted synergy based upon an intuitive understanding of one another. There had to be a 'cross-cultural fit' between both organisations, Towse reflected (1).

The truth is, of course, that security markets are, in essence, volatile. Furthermore they remain vulnerable to changing commercial market conditions, like any other private enterprise. Security markets mirror wider global market conditions, unless specific local incidents or security cultures emerge. That is, if they are lucky! Some three or four years after the noughties banking crisis, major financial institutions in London were still laying-off dozens of security staff, despite the international terrorism threat level either being designated 'severe' or 'substantial' (2). Yet elsewhere, often in fragile spheres of instability and conflict, the private security market has boomed beyond the wildest imagination of most practitioners. For example, after almost a decade of military intervention in Afghanistan, by 2010, the US Department of Defense employed around 20,000 private contractors and licensed 37 companies in

Afghanistan. Circumstances again changed rapidly that year. Afghanistan's President, Hamid Karzai, issued a decree prohibiting private security companies and established an Afghan Public Protection Force (APPF). The APPF was tasked to replace all non-diplomatic private security management functions (3). Yet four years later, following significant security lapses, and consideration for wider national security concerns, the outgoing President revoked his 2010 force nationalisation decree. Thus, market continuity planning, to militate against inconsistent customers and uncertain markets, will be a recurring theme for entrepreneurs as we travel through this book.

Taking on the role of business planner, when the sands of politics and economics are permanently shifting, can absorb and expend a lot of energy and enthusiasm. It may even sap individual and team morale after a while. Chronic uncertainty causes fatigue. Yet, there is a positive side for security practitioners because surrounding instability, even adversity, should really play to our strengths. Uncertainty and adversity are the very reasons why our clients look for our services. After all, if a security consultant does *not* survive and thrive on instability, then why on earth should an external client ever need to have confidence in you?

As we will see in this chapter, and subsequent sections of the Handbook, information is a critical success factor to any enterprise. Knowledge is, de facto, commercial power – a mix of leverage, authority and trust in us to do the right thing, at the right time. Those who take time to properly research, analyse and make sense of surrounding business environments, will reap longer-term dividends. Not least, because a greater sense of authority and resilience will emerge about your enterprise in the eyes of your putative clients and market peers. By positively embracing uncertainty, and shining a torch of leadership in difficult and unpredictable environments, the modern day security practitioner is ideally equipped to add real value to most organisations, including their own. Security practitioners and successful entrepreneurs have many shared characteristics: adaptability, a preference for back-up plans, and, above all, psychological resilience and stamina. "There's no such thing as a setback", said self-help guru business mogul, Tony Robins, who declared this enjoyable truism after his latest TV series was cancelled by producers (4). Just a nudge in another direction, perhaps.

1.2 Competitive intelligence

"Competitive Intelligence is not an invention of the 20th Century." – (Leonard Fuld, 2013)

Enterprises thrive due to many factors; desirable products, effective marketing, blindly optimistic and wealthy investors, dynamic working cultures and, of course, good leadership and motivated employees. Nevertheless, in all likelihood, a business can only survive and prosper in the longer-term by remaining actively aware and adaptive to its operating environment. Such alertness includes keeping a careful and most respectful eye upon similar organisations fishing in the same waters.

Security sector job roles are more fragile than others. Services and consultancies are in many cases contracted out, licensed and regulated by government departments and public authorities. This extra political dimension – sometimes influenced by a swift change in public opinion, or a new ministerial appointment – means that projects or administrative regimes can be uprooted or radically changed with very little notice. Commercial security and risk services are often tasked around delivery into higher-risk domains, where the approach by government agencies could be more volatile and uncertain. The only consistent feature of many higher risk environments is their inherent inconsistency. Governments will often seek to take direct control of a crisis situation or contagion of negative events. Authorities may wish to extend their reach over a perceived, troublesome sector, such as security, by issuing a raft of measures that may be impracticable and toxic to continued business. Security risk management thus attracts a high degree of interest from media and NGOs which makes public authorities even more susceptible to intervening within this sector. Sudden alterations to the operating environment imposed by governments and public authorities, can lead to damaging losses if the new conditions are not quickly anticipated. On the positive side, riskier security or operating environments provide fantastic opportunities for security enterprises to shine and excel. Companies that know their operating environments well, and also uphold professional practices around individual and organisational resilience (those that we delve into across this book's eight chapters), will gain competitive advantage over their commercial peers.

<u>Case studies: Four overnight game-changers to a private security operating environment</u>

1. The introduction of British troops into Northern Ireland in 1969 to separate warring factions, and provide protection for civilians. This UK Government move followed the escalation of widespread sectarian and terrorist violence in Northern Ireland, and concerns in relation to the neutrality of some public services including domestic police functions.
2. The shooting and killing of several citizens in Baghdad by a small handful of employees working for the US security company, Blackwater, during 2007.

> The company was immediately ejected from Iraq by the domestic government. A national and international clamp-down on overseas-based private security contractors followed. This tragic event contributed, somewhat, as a catalyst for 'Montreux Document': also known as the *International Code of Conduct for Private Security Service Providers* (ICoC), a Swiss Government initiative. ICoC was codified into sector guidance by security trade association, ASIS, who later published the widely practiced *Management System for the Quality of Private Security Company Operations* (ANSI/ASIS PSC 2012).
>
> 3. Establishment of the Afghan Public Protection Force (APPF) by President Hamid Karzai's administration, following his declaration in 2010 that all Private Security Contractors (PSCs) will be disbanded and services provided direct by the APPF. Karzai repealed his decision four years later.
> 4. A last-minute decision by UK Government ministers and officials to deploy several thousand Armed Forces personnel to guard the London 2012 Olympics sites, following an admission by the central security contractor, G4S, that there was a significant service delivery shortfall in required security guards. The British Security Industry Authority had warned about significant potential shortfalls more than two years beforehand. Those well-mobilised private companies that anticipated the shortfall were able to pick up the slack and win last-minute contracts, including for specialised services, such as close protection.

What is competitive intelligence?

"Competitive Intelligence is not an invention of the 20th century," reports Leonard Fuld, a pre-eminent expert in the field. It is just another form of intelligence gathering, specifically tasked to gather actionable and high-grade information about activities, strengths and weaknesses of market competition. Fuld points to a historical example of nineteenth century British financier, Nathan Rothschild, who, "managed to corner the market on British government securities by receiving early warning of Napoleon's defeat at Waterloo". Fuld adds: "He used carrier pigeons, the email of his day. He knew the information to watch and how to make sense of it; in the end, he used this intelligence to make a killing in the market" (5).

Competitive intelligence (CI) gained ground in American business journals half a century ago. Competitive intelligence is a process which identifies and researches various important market information sets, which when integrated together, provide a company with insightful information and therefore a 'competitive advantage' over others in the field. We will take some time in the next sub-chapter (1.3) to look at management tools which enable us to build and achieve competitive intelligence products; perhaps the most famous being Harvard Professor Michael Porter's *Five Forces Model*. With Porter's work, CI gained a greater business educational grounding in the US. His 1980 study, *Competitive Strategy: Techniques for*

Analyzing Industries and Competitors, is deemed a seminal paper by corporate strategists. Security planners confidently deploying Porter's modelling will undoubtedly impress potential clients! Porter summarises his findings by saying: "Customers, suppliers, substitutes and potential entrants are all 'competitors' to companies in the industry and may be more or less prominent depending on the circumstances. Competition in this broader sense might be termed *extended rivalry*" (6). An important document emerged in 2008 that attempted to pull together the range of definitions and parameters set by CI practitioners and academics. The Society of Competitive Intelligence Professionals (SCIP) published a definition in its journal: "… a necessary, ethical business discipline for decision making based on understanding the competitive environment" (7). Stephen Miller, formerly an editor of SCIP's journal, describes CI as a *positive* corporate business function: "CI enables managers in companies of all sizes to make decisions about everything from marketing, R&D and investing tactics, to long term business strategies" (8).

Competitive intelligence includes the following traits and focus:

- Its core focus is on the external business environment
- There is some form of process involved, or established business function/s, whereby information and knowledge is gathered and processed into an actionable 'intelligence product'
- CI could also act as a radar-like 'early warning system' for a company to be made aware, sooner rather than later, of possible major market changes or incidents

---

Case Study: Fund's ten principles of competitive intelligence

1. Competitive intelligence is information that has been analysed to the point where you can make a decision.
2. Competitive intelligence is a tool to alert management to an early warning of both threats and opportunities.
3. Competitive intelligence is a means to deliver reasonable assessments.
4. Competitive intelligence comes in many flavours [sic].
5. Competitive intelligence is a way for companies to improve their bottom line.
6. Competitive intelligence is a way of life, a process.
7. Competitive intelligence is part of all best-in-class companies.
8. Competitive intelligence is directed from the executive suite.
9. Competitive intelligence is seeing outside yourself.
10. Competitive intelligence is both short and long term (9).

How can we stay on the right side of the law?

With real-time global interconnectedness, and greater commercial pressures for transparency, Open Source Intelligence gathering (OSINT) has become big business. Decent OSINT briefings can provide real value-added services to clients. OSINT can also provide tangible internal organisational value. Unfortunately, the line between legitimate intelligence activities and unlawful espionage is sometimes crossed. One company, IT hardware manufacturer Hewlett Packard, was made to pay around $14m in fines, and its contracted private investigator was jailed, following unlawful intercepts carried out on senior employees' telephones. The *Fuld Gilad Herring Academy of Competitive Intelligence* runs the Competitive Intelligence Certification Program. Its President, Dr Ben Gilad, stated: "If more companies took care to thoroughly train their managers and executives in how to produce and how to use intelligence in all levels of the organization, fiascos such as those at HP ... would be much less likely to occur" (10). It's a good point and for that reason we more comprehensively cover the laws and regulations which regulate intelligence gathering activities in chapters 3, 4 and 5 of this book.

Pitfalls of competitive intelligence

Despite a huge amount of media and political anxiety around functions associated with intelligence gathering within the security sector, the fact remains that research, monitoring and evaluations of the competitive environment are routinely carried out by all types of organisations, including by the very same newspapers and politicians who may sometimes stoke up political firestorms related to intelligence-topic controversies! If this is the case, it is often under the guise of more benign terminology. Job titles, such as research assistant, or analyst, often do indicate some form of business intelligence role. Nevertheless, the iron-rule is to conduct research and analysis of competitors in a fair and lawful manner. Moreover, you may wish to ask a stack load of questions before accepting or seeking to fulfil an intelligence-related contract. For example, if a client is seeking to buy in CI services, their motivations may be vague: because how do they know what they really need to know? Seek to develop clarity around the task, or project, before you set off launching various lines of inquiry, or commissioning endless investigative reports. Moreover, can external security practitioners really step into other corporate environments and cultures, and credibly tell them what their risk exposure is? Be confident that you and your team can deliver. Before accepting a contract, consider other questions that might also need to be answered. Such as, to what extent is the client's executive team behind this initiative? Or are you being recruited to serve a more personalised or discreet agenda? If so, why? For those individuals and companies undertaking competitive intelligence functions, *The Society of Strategic and Competitive Intelligence Professionals* exists to help you tackle such challenging questions (11).

1.3 Linking business intelligence to our operating environment

Each organisation is different, with a unique culture, mix of employees and a unique combination of incoming events which undoubtedly impact it. Therefore, it may well be that many organisations establish their own ways to read, anticipate and map-out their own operating environments. Management tools which help us to draw a map of our business environment are as critically important to the lives of private companies as navigation charts are to the survival of sailors. It is therefore worth familiarising ourselves with some widely familiar business-environment analysis models. If deployed correctly, these management tools can hugely assist enterprises to harness control of resources and target operations to optimum effect.

Three business management models: PESTLE, Porter's Five Forces and SWOT

A widely favoured business tool is for business researchers and analysts to work to the PESTLE (Political, Economic, Sociological, Technological, Legal and Environmental) model to evaluate important external and internal forces that can impact an organisation. On the positive side PESTLE can provide structured information that can then be exploited by a company, because it has a coherent list of forces at work in its own operating environment. PESTLE, and other variations to this famous mnemonic out there, really does help business planners to dig under the skin of an operating environment. PESTLE challenges organisational autopilot and collective comfort zones. Like all of these business analysis tools that we're looking at in this chapter, PESTLE provides for a crucial episode of corporate *reflective learning*. This management tool also nurtures a sense of belonging and corporate purpose, to all executives who play their part in devising the PESTLE.

Professor Michael Porter's *Five Forces Model* helps companies to summarise the five competitive forces that provide a risk, or opportunities for them, within an industrial sector (12). These can literally be identified and listed under the following categories, Porter suggests:

- Threat of new entrants
- Threat of substitute products or services
- Bargaining power of buyers

- Bargaining power of suppliers
- Competitive rivalry between companies.

However, it might be that a company chooses to look more internally at the Strengths, Weaknesses, Threats and Opportunities (SWOT): the team, product and brand that it has at its disposal to take on the world. SWOT analysis, credited to management academic, Albert Humphrey, has been a very popular management tool deployed for several decades. This model enables teams, and companies, to articulate and address some weaker points in a positive and transformational manner … rather than allocating individual blame to individuals or departments. This is because SWOT analysis tends to be collectivist and can be concluded by focusing on the more positive organisational elements (strengths and opportunities) towards the end of the exercise. This modus operandi should leave the team forum satisfied and reassured, if not entirely exhilarated.

The three management models above can all be considered effective and well-known corporate business tools to provide intelligence-led decision making. If you get five or ten minutes to address a C-suite (senior executive board) officer, give consideration to deploying some, or all of these, in a presentable and engaging manner to your target audience. Moreover, do bear in mind that bad news is best delivered in a sandwich of diplomacy and provisos.

1.4 Examining appropriate intellectual property rights (IPR) in order to protect business ideas and enterprise

As you set about establishing your enterprise, knowledge about how to best protect your expanding corporate intellectual property becomes critical. For security practitioners, familiarity and professionalism in this field is additionally important from a reputational point of view because potential clients and industry peers will expect your company to possess proficiency in this sphere. Information asset protection is a fast-growing business-line, as we shall see later (during the Information and Cyber Security pages of Chapter 5). Therefore, developing advanced capability and expertise in this important sphere may well help you to win new clients, and also expand revenue streams from existing buyers.

Common types of intellectual property rights include: copyright, industrial design rights, patents, trademarks, trade dress, and in some jurisdictions, trade secrets. Common definitions can be found within each country's designated supervising agency. For example, in the United Kingdom, the UK Intellectual Property Office (IPO) is responsible for supporting and advising businesses in this area. All emerging security companies, and those responsible for intellectual property protections, would do well to familiarise themselves with baseline definitions and frameworks helpfully provided by the IPO, or any corresponding agencies in your country of operation (13).

Definitions, laws, protocols and rules can also be made or agreed by supranational organisations, such as the European Union (EU). The UN's World Intellectual Property Organisation (WIPO) based in Geneva is vested with overall global authority and responsibility for issuing guidance and resolving disputes (14). Issues and resolutions can also often be handled by delicate and detailed state-to-state negotiations ('bilaterals') or multinational forums, such as the G8 and G20 groupings on major national and emerging economies (15).

Patents: A patent grants an inventor exclusive rights to make, use, sell and import an invention for a limited period of time, in exchange for the public disclosure of the invention. An invention is a solution to a specific technological problem which may be a product or a process (16).

Copyright: A copyright gives the creator of the original work the exclusive rights to it, usually for a limited time. Copyright may apply to a wide range of creative, intellectual, or artistic forms, or works. Copyright does not cover ideas and information themselves, only the form, or manner, in which they are expressed (17).

Industrial design rights: An industrial design consists of the creation of a shape, configuration or composition of pattern or colour, or combinations thereof, in three dimensional form, containing aesthetic – and thus significant commercial – value. An industrial design can be a two- or three-dimensional pattern used to produce a product, industrial commodity or handicraft (18).

Trademarks: According to the United States Trademark and Patent Office (USTPO): "A trademark is a word, phrase, symbol, and/or design that identifies and distinguishes the source of the goods of one party from those of others" (19).

Trade dress: is "a legal term of art that generally refers to characteristics of the visual appearance of a product or its packaging (or even the design of a building) that signify the source of the product to consumers", explains the University of Princeton website (20).

Trade secrets: according to USTPO, a trade secret is "a formula, practice, process, design, instrument, pattern, or compilation of information which is not generally known or reasonably ascertainable, by which a business can obtain an economic advantage over competitors or customers (21)". In the US, trade secret law is primarily handled at the state level under the Uniform Trade Secrets Act, which most states have adopted, and a federal law, and the Economic Espionage Act 1996, which makes the theft or misappropriation of a trade secret a Federal crime.

IP: International governance and protocols

Patents and trademarks are territorial and must be filed in each country where protection is sought. Since the rights granted by any country's patent office, such as the USPTO in America, extend only throughout the territory of that sovereign territory (or state in some cases), and have no effect in a foreign country, an inventor who wishes patent protection in other countries must apply to the relevant nation state or regional patent offices. Almost every country has its own patent laws. A full list of national authorities responsible for IP is published by the World Intellectual Property Organisation. Specific guidance has been produced for small and medium-sized companies (SMEs) and some of this advice is amplified by interviews carried out with smaller scale security companies by the author in the next section (22).

USPTO usefully provides *toolkits* for IP-related issues as they pertain to specific countries. This provides a mix of general and location-specific guidance and findings including white papers from interest groups, such as the *American Chinese Chamber of Commerce*. A link to USPTO's advice is provided in the end-chapter references list (23).

Difficulties with managing IP for start-ups and partnerships

Intellectual property cases are usually complex, ambiguous and resource-heavy for companies that seek recourse in this area. Public authorities and non-profit organisations in some countries offer mediation services, in order to help resolve issues between organisations and avert them from escalating into costly and very public legal battles. Modern, highly mobilised work patterns can complicate governance and parameters around intellectual property. Employees with expertise and sought-after skills, particularly those at a senior level, often move between new employers or different geographic markets with alacrity. Moreover, directors and executive-level staff or contractors with access to sensitive operational details, can often be employed, or retained, by several different organisations; possibly companies with a conflict of interest.

These are just some of the challenges to sensibly retaining critical information within key groups of collaborators and enterprises. But add in to the mix 'real-time' digital communications, international business collaborations, increased expectations of product scrutiny (at exhibitions, etc.), then intellectual property protection becomes an almost fanciful concept. Trade shows and exhibitions, technology magazines, journals and digital information, and self-publication, have all extensively proliferated in modern times. Dominant trade publications and journals now expect access to all products and employees!

Moreover, sometimes there are cultural barriers which can scupper plans to protect information or designs during business trips. Some cultures tend to reject that knowledge and research should be privately owned. Development and progress is seen as a fraternal human obligation. Lessons for security contractors, which arose from several first-hand experiences of IP fragmentation, do raise the issue of teamwork and trust: "transparency among one another, and an awareness of the value of our information to everybody else, is vital", reports Rob Scott, a UK-based security contractor (24). Tips from a range of security contractors include:

- Be clear from the outset; what information are you providing to the company? Also, be clear in your own mind, what will you retain copyright over?

- Be proactive in registering intellectual property with national authorities. Despite media horror stories, they can actually be helpful and informative.

- Perception is reality. Entrepreneurs sometimes start out in teams or alliances of individuals coming together to fill a market gap. You may all be juggling a variety of commercial interests. Therefore, if you have a perceived *conflict of interest* in the eyes of your team members (remember, you might not think so, but we are talking about *perception*), then be really clear from the outset about your commercial aims and interests. Full disclosure is always better than falling out.

Counterfeiting and piracy

> *"Counterfeiting is the ultimate technology for people who want to get something for nothing."* – (Financial writer, Marshall Brain, *'How Counterfeiting Works'*)

The Organisation for Economic Co-operation and Development (OECD) estimated that up to $200bn (US) of world trade is made up of counterfeit goods. OECD statisticians admit that this figure is magnified to "several hundred billion dollars or more" because they were unable to calculate "domestically produced and consumed" so-called 'knock-off goods'. The OECD is just one high-profile organisation urging national governments and industry sectors to share information in relation to useful anti-counterfeiting strategies, and busily issues various missives upon domestic police agencies and prosecutors to "enhance enforcement" (25).

Counterfeiting and *piracy* are terms used to describe a range of illicit activities at the core of IP infringement. The impact upon business communities has become so severe that the World Trade Organisation (WTO) enshrined provisions relating to fair play and honest business practices when it was established by the Marrakesh

Agreement (1994). Provisions within the *Agreement on Trade-Related Aspects of Intellectual Property Rights* (TRIPS) do form a continuous workstream for some of the WTO's 600 staff in Geneva, Switzerland (26). This body, which has the unenviable task of liberalising trade barriers, replaced the well-known 1948 General Agreement on Tariffs and Trade (GATT). TRIPS brought in provisions of expected standards and dispute resolution procedures. This body attempts to provide global governance, controls and policy direction around: trademarks, copyrights, patents and design rights, as well as a number of related entitlements.

Business impact of IP breaches

Counterfeiting and piracy are longstanding problems which are growing in scope and magnitude, argues the OECD and many likeminded organisations. They are of concern to both government and industrial sectors because of the profound damage that information theft can bring into societal and industrial levels of innovation. Moreover, many IP breaches pose a clear and present danger to the welfare of consumers, such as poor or fake medical products and equipment. Counterfeiting and piracy activity does tend to channel substantial cash and functional resources that can be used by criminal networks and organised crime groups, that profoundly corrode the normal functioning of everyday civilian life, argues the OECD.

Furthermore, companies are also badly disadvantaged by knock-off products and unlicensed goods or operators that can undercut existing, lawful, business enterprises. Moreover, the incentive for companies to invest in their own research and development is massively undermined if they are unable to enjoy the benefits of such effort and expense.

Business and law enforcement responses

Despite international protocols and emerging agreements between international organisations and states, legal recourse against counterfeiting and piracy is usually addressed within the country where suspected offences are committed. Nevertheless, some domestic police forces, such as the UK's City of London Police, and the US's Federal Bureau of Investigation (FBI) are chasing down British and American-based persons and companies involved in large-scale IP criminal activity (27). Action Fraud is the UK's National Fraud Reporting Centre (NFRC). The service is run by the new National Fraud Authority, the "government agency that helps co-ordinate the fight against fraud in the UK" (28). In terms of gathering information, the NFRC is part-supported by the City of London Police's National Fraud Intelligence Bureau. Suspected counterfeiting, and other frauds, can be reported into Action Fraud.

Under the clever strapline '*Fake costs more, I'll buy real*', the International Chamber of Commerce (ICC) launched an impressive research and publications programme, in order to identify and offer solutions in response to counterfeiting activity. Several years on, the ICC-run *Business Action to Stop Counterfeiting and Piracy program* continues to keep business communities well briefed in relation to areas of IP risk. The ICC also provides a toolkit for public authorities, such as policy-makers, police and prosecutors, to strengthen proceeds of crime legislation (29). Should you wish to develop your knowledge in this area, the following report is recommended: *Controlling the Zone: Balancing facilitation and control to combat illicit trade in the world's free trade zones,* produced by the ICC (2013), listed in the references section below (30).

1.5 Emerging markets

> "*The twenty first century may well be the time when the balance of power shifts to Brazil, Russia, India and China, nations collectively referred to as BRICs. These nations constitute the shape of the future, giving rise to a new world economy.*" – William C Hunter, Dean of University of Connecticut Business School (31)

The concept of new *emerging markets* (EMs) does generate much excitement among entrepreneurs. This optimism has been compounded by the global economic downturn from 2007, which has subsequently remained resilient across most of the established, so-called, advanced industrial economies (AIEs). Cost-cutting, which has driven lots more innovation, ICT dependency and efficiency, has occurred across almost all commercial and public sector domains since. So, what is it that is actually driving forward globalisation and an enthusiasm for emerging markets?

- The rapid growth of *middle income* purchasing power for non-essential goods in emerging economies (including Brazil, Russia, India, China … commonly now known as *BRIC* markets). The products include domestic appliances, cars, computers and smartphones. For example, analysts at the *Economist Intelligence Unit* report that by 2020 China will be a larger domestic automotive market than America, and Russia will topple Germany as Europe's biggest car market (32).
- The rapid spread of interactive ICT (Web 2.0) due to accessibility of digital and social media and ecommerce platforms. There is also now instant access to information sources for market and competitor intelligence.

- The untapped markets still to come: at the time of writing, India had 250 million internet users, and ecommerce penetration was relatively low compared to developed markets, such as the UK, where 19 out of 20 citizens now buy online (33). This type and profile of untapped market is hugely exciting to entrepreneurs, who may well reflect upon Ferdinand Porsche's splendid motivational quote: "We build cars that nobody needs but everybody wants to have."
- A rapid 'catch up' of productivity levels in emerging economies to close the 'productivity gap' in comparison to established AIEs.
- Expansion of international and supranational organisations, such as the G8, IMF and World Bank, which marshal trade liberalisation and development strategies within some emerging markets.
- An 'infrastructure boom' led by the BRIC quartet, with India predicted to implement a one trillion dollar investment in national infrastructure between 2013-17 (34).
- The rise of 'city economies'. According to eminent global management consultants' company, McKinsey, the gross domestic product (GDP) of global cities will surge by \$30 trillion during the period between 2010 and 2025. Some 47% will be generated in 440 'emerging market centres'; most of these are to be found in Asia, Africa and Latin America, say McKinsey's researchers (35).

What is an emerging market?

In 1981, World Bank economist, Antoine W Agtmael, coined the phrase 'emerging market economy'. Although parameters around a definition are widely set, Agtmael's thoughts did include reference to, "an economy with low to medium per capita income" (36). Emerging markets are transitional. They are usually perceived to be on the move, from a closed (controlled) economy, surrounded by barriers to entry, towards participation into international markets. Some common features of emerging markets can be expected. In order to achieve greater accessibility and international leverage, leaders in potentially successful emerging markets will often seek to introduce reforms to business and taxation policies, such as promoting fiscal transparency, uniform levels of legal compliance, and also the removal of barriers, such as anti-foreign property laws, as well as the privatisation (sale) of many state-owned enterprises. Such a process will usually displace some of the economic and political *ancien regime*. Thus, do not be tempted to 'put all your eggs in one basket'. Ongoing power struggles and regular changes of influential personnel are hardly uncommon in emerging markets. Some countries have also been able to 'emerge' and flourish due to a decline in armed conflict; for instance, Indonesia and Colombia are fast becoming tigers in Pacific Asia and Latin America respectively.

Where are these 'emerging markets'?

Since Agtmael's definition became broadly accepted, the world's most successful emerging economies were spread quite evenly around the globe. Six of the top 20 markets (also four of the top six) were located in East Asia, as identified by business monitoring organisation, Bloomberg. These being: China (first), South Korea (second), Thailand (third) and Malaysia (sixth) (37). Headline hype around the vitality of certain emerging economies does need to be further examined by potential investors and visitors alike. Seldom do headlines and selected data used by news organisations actually relate back an accurate and actionable picture. For instance, many economists do predict that the impact of the 2007/8 global economic crash upon emerging markets may well have been initially slower, and far less visible, than was the case in advanced industrial economies (AIE), such as the US, UK and Germany. These aftershocks have continued well into the following decade because quantitative easing programmes only came to closure five years later. Hence, emerging markets are not always the commercial 'promised land'. Another concern is that productivity in AIEs has continued to stagnate or fall, almost a decade after the economic crash. To some extent, the fate of emerging markets is intertwined because stagnation of major economic powers will also continue to take orders out of the supply chain in many emerging economies, including Russia, East Europe and Latin America (6). Other age-old economic problems persist in emerging market zones, caused by serious political or military instability, the rise and fall of oil prices, and significant natural disasters. Thus a neutral and open-minded application of sensible business intelligence analysis techniques, such as PESTLE and SWOT, is strongly advised before the establishment security functions and consultancies in emerging markets.

Economic aid

Efforts to open up economies to international trade and to carry out market liberalisation reforms, will often attract international development aid from supportive national states, the IMF and the World Bank. Moreover, in 1970, the United Nations passed Resolution 2626 which stipulated that advanced industrial societies should each contribute at least the equivalent of 0.7% of their GDP directly to international development assistance (38). Development efforts and aid were consolidated by an agreement at the UN of eight millennium development goals (MDG). These MDGs are due for revision in 2015, possibly expanding the range of contributing countries and nature of their contributions. This could expand or reduce investment by aid organisations or government initiatives that directly invest in security management functions related to aid and humanitarian assistance projects.

Networks, such as the European Interagency Security Forum (EISF), ensure that security managers working for NGOs are able to share good practice, mutual aid and educational support between one another, and across many complex and fragile overseas environments, including many officially designated emerging markets (39). According to Lisa Reilly, chairperson of EISF, there are several attributes that will give some security practitioners an advantage over competitors. Reilly stated: "Consultants need to really understand the ethos and mandate of the organisations they wish to work for. Just using the term 'humanitarian' does not mean that training or services to be provided are appropriate in content or approach, and practitioners who do not understand this can cause more security risks than they resolve" (40).

Further information about emerging markets

The website *Emerging Markets: News, Analysis and Opinion (www.emergingmarkets.org)* is an increasingly important hub for financial and political information, even running awards ceremonies for economists and bankers in emerging zones, and employing Nobel Prize winning economists, such as Joseph Stiglitz, as columnists (41). *Forbes Magazine* in the US and London's *Financial Times* (FT) provide upbeat, strategic market information that can be critically examined and corroborated via further in-country reports. Industry forums, such as the Chambers of Commerce and their in-country websites, are often excellent hubs for advice and further decent business contacts. Forbes' does estimate that emerging economies will experience financial growth at some two to three times the pace of AIEs (42). Of the old guard, only Japan and the US are likely to remain as the world's top six largest economies, with India, Russia and Brazil due to usurp Germany, France and Britain in the financial 'pecking order'. According to Forbes' analysis: "… another benefit for investors is the diversification that the EM's provide, because they tend to perform differently than developed markets, and have been successful at decoupling from the greater, longer term woes of the mature economies of the West" (43).

The largest four emerging markets – Brazil, Russia, India and China – were coined as 'BRIC' economies by international investment bank, Goldman Sachs, in a seminal published report in 2001 (44). Another global investment bank, Morgan Stanley, has also reported on the emerging markets and has developed criteria to classify economies based around accessibility, size and liquidity. Morgan Stanley began this now well-known index back in 1988, when only ten economies satisfied their strict economic development criteria; now some 23 cross the threshold of investor opportunity. These are:

Latin America: Brazil; Chile; Mexico; Colombia; Peru

Europe, Middle East and Africa: Czech Republic; Egypt; Greece; Hungary; Poland; Qatar; Russia; South Africa; Turkey; United Arab Emirates

Asia: China; India; Indonesia; Korea; Malaysia; Philippines; Taiwan; Thailand

Source: Morgan Stanley, Emerging Market Index 2014 (45)

Figure 1: Morgan Stanley's emerging market index

Risks of emerging markets

Emerging markets generally do not have the level of market efficiency and strict standards in accounting and securities regulation to be on par with advanced industrialised economies. But emerging markets will typically have developing financial infrastructure including banks, a stock exchange and one unified currency.

Emerging markets can offer decent potential returns for security companies, not just by way of protective security contracts. Often lacking in stability and political certainty, inward investors do turn to physical security providers for employee safety reassurance and, possibly, also to achieve some form of 'force projection' that may act as a deterrent to potential adversaries. Security risk management companies that routinely deploy threat and risk assessment services, as core business for their clients, will also therefore correspondingly develop a very rich knowledge-bank of refined information about the in-country operating environment. The sourcing of local, dependable chaperones, translators, business network organisations, and also the processes of carrying out various reconnaissance and site surveys, does mean that security risk management can diversify beyond protective roles and into business enabling services, such as by launching business and market intelligence and analysis products (either as a value-added service or specifically intended separate revenue stream.)

Understanding what an 'emerging economy' actually is can be most helpful to a security department. Further research and clarity about the specific operating environment that is being targeted is essential; because sometimes a raft of credible assertions that a market is 'emerging' (often backed up by enthusiastic newspaper articles, government promotions and the march of semi-adventurous tourists) can sometimes lead to a disproportionately optimistic news narrative. Such positive terminology may encourage investors to walk blind-sided with their employees into a new market, and assume – quite incorrectly – that risk levels have reduced. Security practitioners should therefore be aware that emerging economies are still very much high-risk political/economic pendulums that can quickly and violently swing backwards, instead of forwards. Clients will undoubtedly expect their security teams to demonstrate strong, forward-thinking awareness around opportunities and threats in less stable markets. Moreover, it should be the case that at times of uncertainty and change, well-prepared security practitioners will actually be in their commercial and personal element.

Traditional markets: the brave old world

Before we close this section, it is worth reminding ourselves that more traditional, established domestic security markets still offer plenty of opportunity. ASIS and the Institute of Financial Management (IOFM) reported in a 2012 report (that interviewed some 400 security industry executives) that the US security market *alone* was worth $350 billion (around £220 billion) (46).

Key findings of the report include:

- $350 billion market breaks down into some $282 billion in private sector spending and $69 billion of federal government spending on homeland security.
- Operational (non-IT) private security spending is estimated to be $202 billion, with expected growth of 5.5% in 2013; IT-related private security market is estimated at $80 billion, with growth of 9% projected for 2013.
- Number of full-time security workers is estimated to be between 1.9 and 2.1 million.
- 42% of respondents indicated spending on training would increase in 2013, with 12% anticipating a rise of 10% or more.
- The private investigator is one of the fastest growing occupations; with anticipated growth of 21% projected through 2020; several IT positions are anticipated to grow 22% through 2020.

1.6 Targeting consumer markets and marketing

"Market intelligence is a must-have tool for all security directors planning their departmental and personnel budgets and resource needs, as well as for

industry suppliers planning their marketing and product growth." – RD Whitney, Executive Director at Institute of Financial Management (47)

Entrepreneurs usually start companies to solve problems. They believe that something necessary is missing from the market and that they provide the unique approach to fix the marketplace. Hopefully, during the initial period of establishing a business, there is clarity of vision and a sense of common purpose. The business has a clear understanding of its competitors, its finances, its goals, and the direction of its own market position. Most successful entrepreneurs write down and communicate their business plan and strategy. Nevertheless, a feature of a successful business start-up, is that it swiftly generates pace and momentum of its own. Hundreds or thousands of decisions must be made, equipment purchased, problems solved, etc. This activity curve is both an immensely rewarding window of opportunity for entrepreneurs, but also a period of substantial risk. A new, uncontrolled project is always at some risk from hurtling off the rails. The power and the velocity of an enterprise that gathers momentum can sometime surprise its founders. The brand may gather a level of momentum and generate a scale of interest that surpasses existing competences and capacity. Or an unexpected revenue stream may come in, which can move the entrepreneur some distance away from their company's original vision. Control and co-ordination of market navigation is critical. Nowhere is this more important than in the sphere of developing a marketing strategy.

The 'marketing mix': the four Ps

Marketing is defined by the *Chartered Institute of Marketing* as the process "responsible for identifying, anticipating and satisfying consumers' requirements profitably" (48). The business leadership company, *Mindtools*, identify marketing as: "putting the right product in the right place, at the right price, at the right time" (49).

A dominant formula within the marketing industry that aims to help enterprises understand their commercial strategy, product development and positioning is known as the *marketing mix*. The mix demands that companies carry out structured analysis around their own products, prices, places and promotions – the four Ps. The marketing mix for every business will be different.

When marketing, companies need to create a successful mix of:

- The right product
- Sold at the right price

- In the right place
- Using the most suitable promotion (50).

Source: Business Case Studies website www.businesscasestudies.co.uk

---

Figure 2: The marketing mix

To create the right marketing mix, businesses have to meet the following conditions:

- **Product:** must have the right features to address market need. For example, it must look good and work well.
- **Price:** the price must be right and build in profit (unless it's a deliberate promotional loss leader). Discounts and margins must be accurately calculated.
- **Place:** the goods must be in the right place at the right time. Ensure on-time storage, delivery and accuracy. Develop channels.
- **Promotion:** the target group needs to be made aware of the existence and availability of the product through promotion.

The *Business Case Studies* website gives some excellent case studies of how the 4Ps formula works within some exciting global enterprises including: Manchester United, supermarket Aldi, Red Bull Formula 1 racing team and the National Trust, a British charity. Integrating the elements, business processes, marketing, sales, finance, compliance, communications, security, and so on, will contribute to more powerful and relevant marketing. Marketing departments, like any other busy office functions, can be prone to slipping into silos. But how on earth can marketing be successful if marketing professionals don't know the nuts and bolts, and strengths and weaknesses, of other business functions? This quandary for marketing professionals, who are often cajoled by boardrooms to 'get to know the business better', is not dissimilar to some complaints levelled against security functions! Thus, here exists an opportunity for security entrepreneurs and managers; explore together what functions are mutually supportive. You may find that synergies exist, such as around sharing business and market intelligence information, providing safety and security bulletins and workshops, or working together to invest and develop the company in exciting new emerging markets.

Much underestimated by some security professionals, marketing and sales strategy is the engine that propels forward any company in any sector. Carefully considered planning, coupled with accurate market analysis, will invariably determine just how successful your company and collaborations become. "Focus on the core problem your business solves and put out lots of content and enthusiasm and ideas about how to solve that problem", is a piece of great advice from Laura Fitton, founder of *oneforty.com* (51). Moreover, beware of launching 'loss leaders'; free or low-cost products or product samples. They can exhaust and bankrupt you as the following case study demonstrates:

Case Study: Free holiday offer cleans out Hoover

The UK company, Hoover, ended up paying out £50m in legal bills including compensation, and being sold off to an Italian competitor, after devising a ruinous marketing campaign that offered customers free flights to Europe (later extended to America), if they bought products worth a minimum of £100. Between 1992 and 1993 a trickle of customers claimed the flights. But soon demand became an avalanche, as this wonderful news spread. Customers could literally fulfil their travel dreams merely by buying an expensive but useful domestic appliance. The marketing tag-line for Hoover was: 'Two Return Seats – Unbelievable'.

It soon was. Hoover quickly appeared to renege on its deal by cancelling the offer to existing customers. The *Hoover Holiday Pressure Group* was formed by one customer, Harry Crichy. Such was the outrage of customers that a Hoover engineer was kidnapped on a call-out after reportedly telling his customer: "If you think buying a washing machine's going to get you two tickets to America, you must be an idiot" (52).

The pressure group estimated that it had 8,000 members at its peak. Questions were asked by MPs in Parliament. Hoover ended up being forced to provide some 220,000 free flights after losing prolonged legal actions by customers which lasted six years in some cases. Hoover's UK division was sold to Italian manufacturer, Candy. The managing director of Hoover Limited and president of Hoover Europe, and the two directors most closely involved with the promotion – the Hoover vice-president of marketing, and the director of marketing services – were dismissed by Hoover. By 1998, the company had paid out £50 million in legal bills.

1.7 Business funding

The success of winning investment involves entrepreneurs 'stepping into the shoes' of potential investors; what will encourage them about your company and vision? Conversely, what avoidable factors may dissuade an investment group away from your enterprise? It is worth accepting from the outset that – as in a job interview – applying for funding and then accepting a potential investor is a mutual, two-way, process. A poor investor match, based on poor information sharing, or divergent business philosophies, can sink an enterprise faster than an unexpected torpedo attack.

Moreover, if your capital investment is endogenous (perhaps derived from your own hard-earned savings), then it is essential for you to apply the same cost-benefit assessment models that others might apply to a decision about whether to invest in you. Imposing strict cost controls and carrying out regular cost benefit and profit and loss monitoring from the outset, will install a habit and, then, a culture of self-discipline and accountability. Further down the line, the benefits of cost control and prudence will be magnified, because it might mean that – thanks to your prudence – you will not be forced to release so much equity in the company, or sign up to unfavourable business finance terms, when it comes to the point that you might need to access extra funding. Being able to choose and carefully select an appropriate investor into your business, can be one of the most exciting and optimistic times for entrepreneurs who wish to expand and drive their business into its next development phase.

Demonstrating to your potential investor your competences and vision for the target marketplace is essential in unlocking investment for any business. But security companies in hazardous environments, or perceived to operate in risky environments, will need to provide extra reassurance to investors as to the legality, security and resilience of their own business. Investors will often look at the security market with a mix of trepidation and excitement around the return on investment (ROI).

As security practitioners, our skills and experience in delivering contingency planning and business continuity strategies for clients, are hopefully second-to-none. But we sometimes take these capabilities for granted. Potential investors, especially those with non-security career backgrounds, are likely to be far more welcoming if security companies demonstrate their own in-house business resilience strategies within any business plan and pitch that is supplied to the investor.

A clear sense of where liabilities and responsibilities exist is absolutely essential in collaborations and joint venture (JV) operations. The report of investigation by Statoil, one of three JV parties who owned the In Amenas oil plant in Algeria at the time of the 2013 terrorist attack, demonstrates just how complex and exhausting the security and legal arrangements of JVs can be in relation to claims for loss and damages (53).

General sources of business finance

Contrary to much media hype, banking institutions can be accessible and the first ports of call for business finance, although, as we will read below, many diverse forms of business finance are steadily coming on stream. Most banks attest to the fact that most applications for business finance do actually receive approval. Moreover, there are tangible reasons behind a banking decision (based upon their own financial risk assessments) to either deny funding, or ask for a business plan or loan application to be revised. The website *yourbusinessmatters.net* offers an excellent synopsis to the post-banking crisis sector approach to finance:

> *"Banks are repeatedly accused of being too cautious when lending to small businesses, yet the likes of RBS, Barclays and Santander routinely claim to approve approximately 90% of applications with the 7-10% of rejections being due to applicants having un-realistic expectations of their business operation and viability. If more businesses produced a sound business plan and could demonstrate their viability and positive use of additional finance for growth then the banks say that the money is there to be lent. Often criticised for only 'backing safe bets', the banks are quite rightly showing due diligence with responsible lending. Anyone being rejected by a bank should first question their own business plan, and then consider alternative forms of finance without running to 'payday lenders'".* (54)

Moreover, the publication *SME Finance Monitor Q1 2013: The Uncertainty of Demand* is just one business publication that shows traditional landscapes of business finance to be changing. Many existing companies are focusing on longer-term resilience; they now seek to reduce debt by making efficiencies and are showing a bigger aversion to borrowing cash for expansion than before. Most start-ups are using personal finances, so that they keep control rather than give away equity in their idea. Furthermore, due to digital media and growth in online investment portfolios, there does seem to be a seismic shift in the amount and diversity of alternative business finance options (55).

Financing options

1. **Investment finance** – Traditionally associated with venture capitalists and more recently identified as 'angel' investors (made high profile by the popular TV series *Dragons Den*), this involves selling part of your business to an/or investor(s). There are several reasons to consider this route to finance. Business 'angels' usually bring a degree of mentoring, necessary new skills and opportunities to a great emerging business that may not have been available before. The benefits are a quick and professional injection of capital and knowledge. The downside is that the investor ultimately takes a substantial equity share. You will also need to consult and persuade your investors before making any sizeable decisions, as they effectively become part of the strategic management team. This form of finance is also usually available to limited companies, as shares will need to be issued.

2. **Crowd or 'peer-to-peer' funding** – Online communities of investors (crowds) are often keen to invest into promising micro-companies, fresh start-ups and

SMEs. There are two types of crowd funding. The most popular being an actual capital loan, with interest repayments paid back to the cluster. A second method is to raise investment in exchange for equity (shareholdings) from the online crowd.

Websites, such as *Funding Circle*, enable businesses to bid for finance by outlining their business plan, completing an initial credit assessment, and then requesting a specified amount of capital. At the time of writing, Funding Circle stated that some 37,000 investors were supporting around 7,000 smaller businesses at terms comparably preferable to traditional banking institutions (56). The website's registered investors are asked to bid in order to contribute to a total sum requested. The money is consequently raised by multiple investors pledging relatively small amounts of money but looking for an agreed percentage return. It is essentially a capital loan, but at a very competitive interest rate.

3. **Credit unions** – many start-ups only need £500-£1,000 to get started. Credit unions usually set a maximum rate of interest of two percent each month. Credit unions are owned by their customers and run as non-profit organisations (such as in the case of British 'building societies'). Each union is made up of 'members' who deposit savings, which are then, in turn, lent out to other members. Regulated by the FSA, members' savings are protected up to £85,000, and following tough credit checks, member businesses can apply for loans at better rates than with many banks. Because many credit unions are locally-based, and membership includes successful local businesses, they can also offer additional support, such as mentoring and member reductions on support services.

4. **Invoice financing** – this can generate a quick injection of cash into your business and can help to reduce your bad debt on invoiced business. According to *Businessmatters.net*, there is a downside: "A viable alternative to running an overdraft, this does need to be approached with caution as the fees will eat into some of your profit margin". If your profit margins are razor thin, or you underestimate costs on a contract, then invoice financing can be a risky proposal (57) Two types of invoice financing exist. Invoice 'factoring', where the debt is sold to a third party who then collect the debt owed by your customer. They give your company a percentage of the cost (usually 85%) up front and then chase down the full debt from your customer. Once they receive the money, the balance is then paid across to your company. Interest rates and fees are then charged to you by the credit control subcontractor. Invoice 'discounting' involves investors, usually banks, lending you money against your unpaid invoices, for a fee and/or interest rate (58). Although another disadvantage to this method is that companies will not then have 'book debts' available as security for further finance. Moreover, if the contracted invoice deals with your customer poorly, then prospects for repeat business diminish.

5. **Leasing and asset finance** – companies often have to invest in machinery and equipment to service customer requirements and expand operations. Leasing enables start-ups and fast growing companies to get access to necessary assets and equipment. Financial planning and budgeting is helped by leasing and asset finance because businesses can spread steep start-up or development costs through leasing, via monthly instalments with fixed interest rates. If companies ultimately default on payments, then they may well lose access to the asset, but not necessarily their entire business.

6. **Grants and government assistance** – the development and growth of small businesses is a priority for many governments and pro-business NGOs. In the UK, The *Department for Business Innovation & Skills* (BIS) run a variety of initiatives to either inform businesses of government-funded schemes, or local and regional programmes to stimulate enterprise and growth. BIS's 2013 Report, *SME access to finance schemes,* is one such portal to help smaller enterprises access funding (59). The UK government has launched a number of initiatives designed to encourage banks to lend and the private sector to lead the economy out of recession, including the new business bank, the finance for lending scheme and requiring LEPs to take the lead on their region's structural and investment fund strategy. Small companies, with a decent business plan and emerging sector footprint, would be well advised to invest some time scanning the Internet and BIS-related websites to stay abreast of various support initiatives which can include; direct assistance for certain sectors and locations; relevant local and regional market advice (through local enterprise partnerships) (60). The *Business is Great* website produced by the UK Government provides a plethora of useful ideas, business finance articles, case studies and a 'My Business Support Tool' to identify what support may be available to UK-based companies (61). The *BusinessUSA* website run by the US State Department is the official government website to help start-ups, growth, exporting and financing for American companies (62). Moreover, several charities and NGOs offer start-up loans and 'seed funding' but these are usually aimed at specific social demographical groups or sector types. In the UK, *The Prince's Trust* charity is perhaps the most well-known and it offers business loans to entrepreneurs aged between 18-30 (63). Likewise, their sister charity, *PRIME*, provides assistance to some companies established by those over 50 (64). Being environmentally conscious and sustainable is a key ethical and reputational concern for responsible companies but proactive initiative around supporting the 'green' agenda may also make your business an attractive investment proposition for some, as the *green wise business* website pointed out in a recent article: *Consider 'Green' routes: £5m Green energy fund to target SMEs* (65). Due to the importance of business funding, a further information section below has been compiled to provide you with key business groups and initiatives within BRIC economies

and the EU, in order to help your company develop links to potential investor bodies.

Case study: A close shave – Avoiding rejection for finance

The prominent UK-based newspaper, *The Daily Telegraph*, runs an excellent advice centre for businesses called *Soapbox*. The following interview with a UK entrepreneur is an adept commentary on why so many start-ups fail to entice investors:

Will King, founder of shaving products business, King of Shaves, warns that large numbers of SMEs are missing out on finance opportunities because alternative funders are failing to shout about what they can offer them.

King said: "Alternative funding providers are really missing a trick. They have come up with a fantastic idea to bypass the banks and give SMEs what they want – but nobody knows what they do because nobody has ever heard of them. Alternative funders really need to market their products to the people who need it, just as any consumer product or service brand needs to do".

He added: "The problem is that all of these alternative funding companies are run by finance people who were previously bankers or accountants. None of them really have a grasp of how to market to people to help them understand what alternative funding is".

King himself raised £627,000 for his own business through alternative means, with the creation of a 'shaving bond' for customers, who received 6% interest a year and shaving products, in return for buying a three year bond.

The past few years has seen the arrival of several alternative funding providers aimed at offering SMEs a real alternative to banks. These include Funding Circle, which amasses small amounts of money from individual lenders to lend to SMEs; Market Invoice, which lends SMEs money against the value of their invoices; Kickstarter and Crowdcube, which enable individuals to invest collectively in a business in return for equity.

However, King argues that so far the only alternative funder to have made a real effort to promote their services is Wonga, the controversial payday lender. As a result of an intensive marketing and promotional campaign, Wonga has become a household name and the number of individuals and businesses using it has increased sharply.

King said: "Other alternative funding providers should look at how successful Wonga has been as a brand. I'm not a supporter of what Wonga's business is, or what it does, but I am impressed by how they've done it. Then the alternative funders should raise some money themselves, get on TV and deliver a virtuous circle".

It is Britain's SMEs who are missing out most, he said. "The big alternative funding providers are aimed at small to medium size enterprises with an established turnover and an established track record. But the SMEs who are supposed to be driving the country out of recession haven't got a clue about what alternative funding options are available to them."

If promoted properly, the new funding models have the potential to become a serious long-term alternative to banks, King said.

> *"I think there is going to be seismic change in the way that companies and individuals, brands, products, services, will be able to access funding in the future because of the Internet and the fact that so many people are globally connected through social media networks. The alternative funders are to banks what Apple was to Nokia. Five years ago Nokia had a 61% share of the worldwide mobile phone market and then along came Steve Jobs with a phone with no buttons and blew Nokia up."* (66)

Top tips: Business finance checklist

In summary of this section, here are checklist items for entrepreneurs to bear in mind as they begin to reach out to investors:

- Ensure that your business plan is a realistic plan-of-action, not a 'tick-box' document to gain investment.
- What analysis have you done, and can you clearly communicate to give investors' confidence in your operating environment?
- Will investment finance be provided by a Financial Conduct Authority-registered company (in the UK) or with the equivalent protection in your country of operation?
- Be flexible, adaptive and ensure that you can diversify.
- Do you need to patent your product and/or protect the intellectual property of your service?

Advice and ideas around business planning and finance: *www.yourbusinessmatters.net*

Business plan writing guides: A range of more than 500 sample business plans at this excellent website: *www.Bplans.co.uk*

Chambers of Commerce: *www.britishchambers.org.uk* or *www.londonchambers.org.uk/*

Federation of Small Business in the UK: *www.fsb.org.uk*

India's Chamber of Commerce: *www.indianchamber.org/*

Institute of Directors: *www.iod.com*

Institute of Chartered Accountants Business Advisory Service: *www.businessadvice serviceblog.com/about-bas/*

School for Social Entrepreneurs: *www.the-sse.org/*

Technology sector and creative industry routes to funding: the UK's Technology Strategy and funding options are outlined at: *www.computerweekly.com/news/2240205646/ Technology-Strategy-Board-announces-30m-funding-for-SMEs-in-creative-industries*

Figure 3: Business funding – Further information portals

1.8 Reviewing operations management

Any corresponding set of organisational tasks and corporate interoperability requires proficiency in operations management (OM). By the end of this sub-chapter we will be able to:

- define operations management
- explain the role of operations managers and their importance in delivering profit margins
- be familiar with some baseline guidance and tools used by OM.

This section therefore follows a logical approach to developing baseline knowledge and competency in this topic, necessary for starting an enterprise and piecing together various business components as that enterprise scales up. What, in essence, is operations management?

All companies employ a range of people, processes, equipment and technology in order to successfully manufacture end-products or provide services (outputs). All organisations are unique, because they deploy different people, processes and technologies to achieve such outputs. According to management expert, Professor Harvey Millar, OM can therefore be thought of as, "the set of activities that create value in the form of goods and services by transforming inputs into outputs (67)". The US Department of Education defines operations management as, "the field concerned with managing and directing the physical and/or technical functions of a company or organisation, particularly those related to development, production and manufacturing" (68).

One of the principal industry guides for operations managers is the *Body of Knowledge Framework* (OMBOK) developed by APICS, a pre-eminent industry body for operations managers. I provide a little more detail about this pre-eminent body and guidance document towards the end of this chapter. OMBOK states that: "Operations management focuses on the systematic direction of the processes involved in the sourcing, production and delivery of products and services. It calls for a holistic or systems view of the processes with major impact on the costs required to operate a company ... Operations management concepts apply to the complete chain of activities in the production and delivery of products and services, including those that cross commercial and geographical boundaries" (69).

Thus, operations directors and managers are responsible for operations strategy. This relates to policies and plans governing the use of the organisation's productive resources, with the aim of delivering profits and, therefore, supporting long-term competitive strategy. In summary, delivering maximum efficiencies within the production cycle. OM is destined to grip and influence the following internal business activity, reflects strategic management academic, Hill (70):

- Price: set mainly by purchase price, use costs, maintenance costs, upgrade costs, disposal costs
- Quality: specification and compliance
- Time: productive lead time, information lead time, punctuality
- Flexibility: mix, volume, gamma
- Stock availability.

OMs are extensively responsible for understanding how goods and services in their organisation are produced. To gain the most elementary view of production, some operations managers may therefore seek to look *backwards* along the production process, starting from the time that the end-product reaches the customer (and possibly beyond), then moving retrospectively towards the time when it was just a product concept. They will want the best possible 'helicopter view' of the production chain; their remits will often oversee various business functions, such as marketing (to generate demand), production (including stockholding and preservation), human resources (HR), and perhaps, also, financial control responsibilities. For example, the operations manager may well have responsibility for how well the company performs at revenue collection, and/or settling accounts with key suppliers, and prioritising those over lower priority creditors. Moreover, they may also manage customer relations teams in order to bring together the acquisition of customer feedback (gathered at the end of the product cycle), with actions at the beginning of any product cycle, such as research, development, commissioning and recruitment.

Cost control

In many large organisations – including some US-based commercial banks – asset protection and security practitioner roles have often been organised within the remit of operations management. OM roles do attract academic and management school interest because analysts are keen to understand how people can best organise themselves for 'productive enterprise', says Millar (71). Businesses ultimately seek 'profitability'. Therefore, a core priority of an OM will be to reduce production costs and drive up efficiencies, particularly in more mature markets where competition may be saturated, and margins precariously thin. 'Operations based activities', the processes of bringing a product to market, will usually swallow up at least a large portion of initial revenues earned from a customer-base. Mass production does not always lead to mass profits; in fact, it can lead to the opposite if OM functions underperform. In this sense, weak operations management at any point during the production cycle, including poorly managed cost controls, credit controls and external customer service issues, will, ultimately, lead to longer-term resiliency challenges for companies.

Case study: Cost controls: the relationship between production and price

Following public concern at rising consumer energy prices, a UK Parliamentary Select Committee convened to examine the issue. Why was it that customer fees surged each year, well beyond inflation and wholesale market prices? At a key point in the hearing a Member of Parliament asked:

MP: "How can these profits be fair when the people cannot afford to pay for their energy?"

William Morris (Chief Executive SSE): "The reason it's fair is, if I don't make a five per cent profit on my business, I can't afford to continue employing my 20,000 people ... which are equally members of our society in Britain ... and I can't actually afford to operate the company ... it's less than supermarkets make, it's a fraction of what mobile phone companies make, although. .. I do accept the point ... it's still a big number". (72)

	2011	2012	2013
Sales	£100,000	£200,000	£150,000
Cost of goods	£80,000 (80%)	£160,000 (80%)	£105,000 (70%)
Gross margin	£20,000	£40,000	£45,000
Finance costs	£6,000	£12,000	£9,000
Subtotal	£14,000	£28,000	£36,000
Taxes at 25%	£3,500	£7,000	£9,000
OM contribution (net profit)	£10,500	£21,000	£27,000

Figure 4: Notional role of OM in delivering improved profits

The table above illustrates an imaginary start-up company. It demonstrates the importance, to the business, of controlling operational costs. If we look at the 'cost of goods' row, then we can see that a more effective control of business costs will lead to a greater profit margin.

For example, although sales revenues dipped from £200,000 in 2012 to £150,000 in 2013, profits were significantly greater overall in 2013 because operational management functions had reduced the costs of production from 80% of revenues in 2012, to just 70% in 2013.

If we now extrapolate the impact of improved cost controls further, to, say, a company 100 times the size, profits could either be £2.7m (with production costs at 70%) or £2.1m (80%). This £600,000 profit margin is a sizeable difference. It could enable a growing company to invest in new employees, recruitment, or indeed provide some return for investors and shareholders.

OM decision-making areas

At a strategic level, OMs therefore ensure that resources across the organisation are used as effectively as possible. The basic management functions of many OMs will include oversight of:

- planning
- staffing
- project direction
- organising
- leading, supervising, accountability/control.

According to Millar, there are ten critical 'decision areas' that he describes as 'dimensions' to operations management roles. With some explanatory examples, these include:

1. Design of goods and services: who are our customers and what do they need?
2. Managing quality: what level of performance are we trying to achieve and what are our customers' expectations? Who is responsible for quality control?
3. Process and capacity design: processes and demand curves have different capacity requirements.
4. Location strategy: where should we be based?
5. Layout strategy: how should we lay out the facility? How large should it be to meet our short or longer term plans?
6. Human resources and job design: how do we provide a reasonable working environment? How much product can we expect our employees to produce?
7. Supply-chain management: how safe and resilient are our suppliers? How much should we diversify the supply chain?
8. Inventory: retaining the right balance of stock; asset protection.
9. Scheduling: coordinating different projects/productions within available processes and capacity; managing scale-up and scale-down.
10. Maintenance: how do we build reliability? Who is responsible? (73)

OM management tools

Below are two overarching management tools – *Just in Time* and *Gantt* – that are often deployed by some operations and project managers.

Just In Time: JIT strategy aims to reduce in-process inventory costs and carrying costs of stock and assets. This strategy of reducing all unnecessary overheads will increase return on investment, so the argument goes. Most famously pioneered by Toyota, production processes are designed with 'signals' (Kanban) that issue an alert as to when the next stage of a manufacturing process will begin. JIT practitioners view storage of unused inventory as a waste of resources. Business management analyst, Shinego Shingo, is perhaps the most pre-eminent JIT disciple and he advised Toyota on business structures during the 1970s and 80s. Shingo famously stated: "In the Toyota production system, overproduction is generally considered undesirable and many people regard it as an evil and make efforts to minimise it" (74).

Such practices nowadays might be frowned upon. Some fear that JIT methods generate added risk exposure, as businesses with low inventories and microscopic storage are more vulnerable to major disruptions. This is because their internal contingencies will be limited and dependence on others for supplies and stock during a crisis may be fatal. Yet JIT adherents point to the importance for low-inventory companies to develop close relations with suppliers, and to train all employees across all business functions, to save resources on hosting dormant and ossifying stock. In recent years, as the economic pendulum has swung back towards austerity, management towards quantification, and ICT technology provides us with extra contingencies, perhaps it is no coincidence that JIT theorists are back in fashion.

Gantt charts: Project management was strengthened from around 1910 by management consultant, Henry Gantt, who developed a tool to give an overarching view of multiple operational activities. Nowadays we might call this a 'helicopter' view. Described succinctly, the Gantt chart will list the following in a spreadsheet, or by way of a visual map:

- What are all the tasks of this project?
- Who is responsible for each task?
- How long will each task take?
- What hurdles might your team encounter?
- What is the overall deadline?

The excellent business advice website, *mindtools*, sums up the strengths of Gantt charts well: "This detailed thinking helps you ensure that the schedule is workable, that the right people are assigned to each task, and that you have workarounds for potential problems before you start" (75). There are hundreds (if not thousands) of real-world examples of Gantt charts when one conducts a 'Google images' search. If entrepreneurs are not already familiar with Gantt, then it is well worth spending a little time researching some appropriate examples, and considering how those might best be adapted to your work environment. Being an entrepreneur or a manager in a fast-moving sector, such as the security industry, does often overwhelm us; and it is easy to begin to feel a loss of control over projects or enterprises. Both Gantt and JIT methods provide strategic controls and the tactical management mechanisms to rein in the worst excesses of fast-paced, multifaceted business environments.

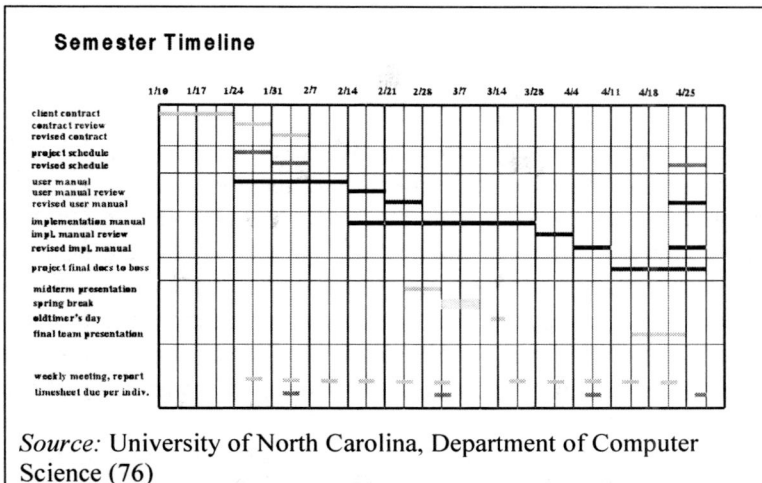

Source: University of North Carolina, Department of Computer Science (76)

Figure 5: Gantt chart in action

Operations management: Further information and guidance

APICS is the leading professional association for supply chain and operations management. It regularly produces a *Body of Knowledge Framework for Operations Managers*, known within the sector by its acronym: OMBOK.

This is designed to be an overarching publication, generic in nature, which provides structured, consistent and revised guidance and pan-industry approaches to operations management. Some editions are available to freely download (77).

The website *mindtools* provides hundreds of useful business information briefings and video clips, including a video presentation on making your own organisational Gantt chart (78).

1.9 Business networking

"Sometimes, idealistic people are put off the whole business of networking as something tainted by flattery and the pursuit of selfish advantage. But virtue in obscurity is rewarded only in Heaven. To succeed in this world you have to be known to people." – Associate Justice of the US Supreme Court, Sonia Sotomayor (79)

For some in business, 'networking' instils the common sense of dread usually reserved for delayed housework, dog walks on a freezing weekday evening, or a twice-postponed journey to the dentist. While others seem to positively relish the opportunity to meet new folks or exchange pleasantries with their existing contacts at, say, the upcoming Chamber of Commerce dinner.

With business networking being, potentially, the single most lucrative source of sales generation for a start-up or unknown brand, why is it that some entrepreneurs and managers choose to avoid networking?

Consider, for a moment, what the word 'networking' means. The word can be split. **Net-working** suggests a proactive connection between a pool of people that can be 'netted' within the same environment! There is also an implication that this activity is very much about 'work'; there can be little guilt as to politely disengage from a conversation to pursue an important business lead that may have arrived into the room. This part of the book will seek to draw some of the sting away from some fears that managers and entrepreneurs might have as to the value of networking. What is business networking? How can managers and entrepreneurs' benefit from it? To be clear, a suitable definition is proposed by the website *businessballs.com*: "Business networking is an effective low-cost marketing method for developing sales opportunities and contacts, based on referrals and introductions – either face-to-face at meetings and gatherings, or by other contact methods, such as phone, email, and increasingly, social and business networking websites" (80).

Top tips for business networking

Recommended by the author and others cited below:

- Plan beforehand: who might be there, how might you properly engage them and win their interest? Develop and rehearse your 'elevator pitch' (see Figure 6 below).

- Ask good opening questions: ones that connect you to the other attendee including: What is your connection to this event/sector? What attracted you to this event? Where are you from?

- Set your emotion disposition to 'curious': don't clock-watch, engage with the event, relax and generate genuine interest in each individual and company there, to identify possible connections with your own.

- Focus on relationships rather than numbers: don't set a numerical target of people to meet. Instead, develop qualitative conversations and establish relationship foundations.

- Develop your 'story'; ensure that you have an engaging narrative to describe who you are, what you do, and why your organisation does it. Communicate in a manner free of complicated insider terminology.

- Have a nice business card; according to Michael Margolis in his excellent article '5 storytelling tips to make networking feel good again', published on Linkedin (81): "There's no better way to make a bad impression than when exchanging business cards. Avoid the following: (a) not having a business card, or (b) having a cheap looking business card."

- Be positive on everything and everyone that you come into contact with (82). Do not express negative thoughts or question the integrity of others … these are public forums! According to psychology author, Donald A Laird, "Abilities wither under faultfinding, blossom under encouragement" (83).

- Develop and host your own business networking event and invite your target audience. Perhaps host these with strategic partners and product collaborators to share the pressures and costs of organisation.

1. Your name	Confident, sincere, direct
2. Your business name	Loud and proud
3. Based and covering where?	Make it relevant and realistic to the situation
4. Your personal specialism?	Express what positive outcomes you achieve; the types of needs that you can address
Source: Business Balls.com and adapted in parts by author (84)	

Figure 6: Developing your elevator pitch

Case study: Interview with JKW Law

London-based lawyer, John Walmsley, established his company of legal consultants, JKW Law LLP, some years ago, and soon began to expand his 'net' into commercial waters by establishing some well-received topical network briefings. Each month, clients and useful contacts are extended an invite to hear John's team address and examine emerging, and very pertinent, legal and commercial issues. My interview below hears John summarise some important lessons for those who seek to make the most from either attending or running their own 'networking' events:

> Me: What do you feel are the two or three main skills required for any business consultant in their approach to networking?

> JW: The ability to listen and ask relevant questions, and then tailor your elevator pitch or presentation to your audience. Be flexible. Don't waffle. Be honest and straightforward. Try to assist them in their networking as an ideal follow up. An introduction, or offer to share your network, or invite to useful networking event. Try to be memorable.

> Me: What are one or two challenges/frustrations to networking?

> JW: That you see too many people doing the same thing as you! Don't be put off. Exchange professional courtesies and then move on quickly. That you do not feel you can be a good networker because you are not a good talker. Start by listening and the rest will follow ... People ditch a relationship too soon. Play the long ball game and plant your seeds. Nurture the relationship and it could be three or four years later – you get the recommendation or the contract. (85)

Security networking opportunities

The following is a summary of some pre-eminent security groups for education and networking purposes:

> **ADS:** the pre-eminent Aerospace, Defence and Security trade association based in the UK which runs, or partners, more than 150 networking events around the world every year. According to its website: "ADS has offices in England, Scotland, Northern Ireland, France and India, with new offices planned in China and the Middle East. ADS was formed from the merger of the Association of Police and Public Security Suppliers (APPSS), the Defence Manufacturers Association (DMA) and the Society of British Aerospace Companies (SBAC) in October 2009. ADS also encompasses the British Aviation Group (BAG)". Further information: *www.adsgroup.org.uk/*.

> **Association of Certified Fraud Examiners (ACFE):** The ACFE is very much a global organisation but also usefully runs many national chapters. According to a dedicated UK section on the ACFE's central website, "the UK Chapter holds

regular events throughout the year in London, Birmingham, Manchester, Edinburgh and Glasgow". Further information: *www.acfeuk.co.uk/*.

ASIS UK: Formerly the American Society for Industrial Security, but now with a global footprint and national/regional chapter meetings. In its own words: "The UK Chapter runs dynamic seminars and training days throughout the year, publishes a quarterly newsletter containing articles from some of the country's leading security practitioners and acts as a voice for the security profession, representing members' views at the highest levels". Further information: *www.asis.org.uk/*.

British Retail Consortium (BRC): The BRC runs an annual retail crime prevention conference, consults and forms policy to prevent retail crime, and engages its members through events and policy formulation and lobbying campaigns. Further information: *www.brc.org.uk/brc_home.asp*.

British Security Industry Association (BSIA): The BSIA is a large trade association in the UK for private sector security services and contractors. In November 2013, the BSIA launched its 'Specialist Services Section' that offers, "specialist services including Close Protection, Technical Surveillance Counter Measures, Surveillance, IT Forensics, Cyber Security and Security Consulting including Critical National Infrastructure". Further information: *www.bsia.co.uk/*.

British Standards Institute (BSI): The BSI is based in Chiswick, south west London, and runs a plethora of security and business continuity-related committees which develop standards and publicly available specifications across an expansive range of resiliency issues. The Group's mission is to 'make excellence a habit'. The central Societal Security Committee (SSM-1) and its offshoots provide ample opportunities for 'principal' subject matter experts to contribute to, and peer review, emerging national and international standards in their domain. Further information: *www.bsigroup.co.uk/*.

The Business Continuity Awards: Run by *CIR Magazine*, each year the great-and-the-good of the security and resilience professions gather to be lambasted by a guest host, usually a high-profile comedian. The recent roll of comedic honour includes Glasgow's Kevin Bridges, Stephen K Amos, and *Mock the Week's* garrulous host, Dara O'Briain. Those foolish enough to attempt to 'out-joke' the host are suitably humiliated and shot down to size. But with around 500 guests at each gala dinner, and amid an atmosphere of relaxed revelry, the Awards provide an excellent and fun networking environment. Further information: *www.cirmagazine.com/businesscontinuityawards/*.

Business Continuity Forums (BC): Such BC forums are located on a random basis across UK local authority areas, and are usually facilitated by the local emergency planning office. Some forums run active educational and network briefings including (at the time of writing) in Belfast, Bristol, Cardiff, Liverpool, Manchester and Milton Keynes. Moreover, some BC forums run 'buddy schemes', whereby larger companies support and mentor smaller companies in BC practices, such as in the UK city of Manchester.

Business Continuity Institute (BCI): The BCI is the leading BC standards and guidance membership forum and is intensively engaged in writing and refining its published works. The BCI runs membership events, an online library, develops and accredits courses (including the BCI Diploma, Level 5 with Bucks New University) and published the pre-eminent 'Good Practice Guidelines' for Business Continuity: a must-read for security and resilience professionals. Further information: *www.thebci.org/*.

Communications Electronic Security Group (CESG): CESG is the UK Government's 'National Technical Authority' for information assurance (information security), based in Cheltenham. CESG helps run an annual cyber security challenge for aspiring information security professionals and accredits 'providers' and 'consultants' as certified services in information assurance that can be accessed via their website. Further information: *www.cesg.gov.uk/Finda/Pages/FindA.aspx*.

Chambers of Commerce: Branches run network meetings on a whole variety of sector-by-sector topics (including business networking and other business development skills). London's own Chamber of Commerce and industry runs its own dedicated defence and security committee and network for members. Further information: *www.londonchamber.co.uk/lcc_public/home.asp*.

City of London Crime Prevention Association (CoLCPA): According to the CoLCPA: "The Crime and Disorder Act of 1998 placed unprecedented emphasis on both the role and the importance of crime prevention partnerships between the police and communities (CoLCPA website: 2013)". This impressive networking and briefing organisation for businesses and stakeholders in London's 'Square Mile' boasts more than 700 members and runs regular crime prevention and business resilience briefings. CoLCPA also operates a 'Women's Network Group'. Further information: *www.cityoflondoncpa.org.uk/about/*.

Continuity Forum – Building business continuity and resilience: The Continuity Forum is a member organisation pulling together a vast array of networking, training and published products, to support and expand knowledge of business continuity and resilience. It provides a bridge between business continuity disciplines and security professionals via its 'Security and Counter Terrorism Information Portal'. Further information: *www.continuityforum.org/ content/page/security-and-ct-portal*.

Council of International Investigators (CII): The CII is an international body with a 'code of ethics' but with national contacts and membership resources. Its calendar of education and networking events is very much global and its website can be accessed at: *www.cii2.org/*.

Counter-Terror Expo: One of the largest security industry calendar events, if not the UK's largest, Counter Terror Expo's website explains that it "is the premier international event delivering over 9,500 buyers and specifiers from the entire security sector within Government, Military, Law Enforcement, Emergency Services, Private Sector and the Security Services". Further information: *www.counterterrorexpo.com/*.

CSARN: City Security and Resilience Networks is a UK-based (but not UK-centric) not-for-profit membership organisation whose goal is to provide education and commercial networking briefings for senior security managers and resilience directors. The format offers dynamic, agile presentations with advice and guidance rooted in real-world scenarios. CSARN recently opened a network chapter in Australia. The organisation provides business intelligence feeds to its members via its fortnightly *Security Risk Monitor* which covers the following chapters: terrorism and political violence; cyber security; domestic extremism and disorder; protest and disruption. Further information: *www.csarn.org* and for Australia/NZ: *http://csarn.org.au/*.

Federation of Small Business: The Federation is a huge regional and local based business network that campaigns on behalf of members. It provides a range of infrastructure for entrepreneurs and small businesses including economic briefings, newsletters, network events, discounts on office hire and member helplines to troubleshoot problems from understanding tax systems to government policy impacting their area. Further information: *www.fsb.org.uk/*.

HEBCON: the Higher Education Business Continuity Network is a group of BC and security practitioners within scholarly environments that meet and host conferences to share good practice. The website's functionality and utility is (at the time of writing) mainly focused around registered members and is therefore relatively unexciting for others who may be job or course hunting. Further information: *www.hebcon.ac.uk/*.

Institute of Civil Protection and Emergency Managers (ICPEM): ICPEM is a long established networking and educational forum that links academics, security and business continuity practitioners; many of whom are based in public sector emergency management roles. ICPEM's website lists academic courses in emergency planning, resilience and disaster management, available around the world. Further information: *www.icpem.net/*.

INFOSEC: Annual exhibition and information event for information security professions featuring hundreds of exhibitors, education seminars, and a networking pool of more than 10,000 guests. Further information: *www.infosec.co.uk/*.

Institute of Directors (IoD): With plush offices at 116 Pall Mall, London, and elsewhere around the UK, which buzz with entrepreneurs and senior managers within fast-growing SMEs, the IoD is always a hugely useful networking hub. The organisation also provides a fantastic array of inspirational public speakers. Further information: *www.iod.com/*.

Information Security Forum: According to its informative website, the Information Security Forum is … "dedicated to investigating, clarifying and resolving key issues in information security and risk management, by developing best practice methodologies, processes and solutions that meet the business needs of our members". The Forum is a large global organisation but with a UK network that can be contacted via a central website: Further information: *www.securityforum.org/*.

London First: London First represents several hundred large, London-based multinational companies and lobbies vociferously on behalf of its members in areas of skills, transport, security and policing. It runs regular network information briefings on business security and resilience with high-profile speakers. Further information: *www.londonfirst.co.uk*.

National Security Inspectorate (NSI): The NSI aims to "be the ultimate reassurance in fire, security and related facilities management approval". The NSI evolved from a number of trade quality organisations that were concerned about poor standards within the security and fire alarm industry that had potentially caused major lapses in health, safety and security functions, and undermined consumer confidence in industry solutions around crime and fire prevention. The NSO carries out what it describes as: "robust, high quality audits of home security, business security and fire safety service providers". Companies apply to be audited and quality checked by the NSI in order to provide customers, and their own internal stakeholders, with assurance and confidence. Further information: *www.nsi.org.uk/*.

Register of Chartered Security Professionals: According to the institution's website: "Chartered Security Professionals (CSyP) must be of undisputed integrity and have a good awareness of general security principles and a high level of expertise, operating at a strategic level, or the senior end of the operational level, of security practice. Admittance to the Register demonstrates to clients, employers, peers and the public an ability to deliver quality results and a commitment to Continual Professional Development". Further information: *www.csyp-register.org/*.

The Security Institute: In its own words, "The Security Institute's aims are to provide objective standards for, and an independent assessment of, the professional competence and experience of those practising the art and science of security both nationally and internationally, and to raise awareness of professional security practices for the benefit of the public and industry". It does this by hosting networking and educational events, advising and publishing guidance, and delivering its Diploma in Security Management. Further information: *www.security-institute.org/home_page*.

Security Excellence Awards: Organised by United Business Media, these pre-eminent awards are rightly dubbed the "Oscars of the security business sector" by its proud convenors. Around 1,000 guests pile each year into the Hilton Hotel, Park Lane to applaud and reflect on good practice and also excellent academic achievement, since the introduction of the Wilf Knight Award. Further information: *www.securityexcellenceawards.co.uk/*.

Security Industry Authority (SIA): Apart from its licensing and enforcement responsibilities, the SIA runs an 'approved contractor scheme'. The SIA also runs various conferences including its annual stakeholder gathering and forums allied to areas of licensing responsibilities, including a Close Protection Forum. Further information: *www.sia.homeoffice.gov.uk/Pages/about-stakeholder-conference.aspx*.

The Association of British Investigators (ABI): Formed more than 100 years ago, the ABI is the most pre-eminent UK organisation to lobby and promote standards and networking among private investigators, including private detective agencies. An academy, with links to publications and training, is accessible online. Further information: *www.theabi.org.uk/*.

TINYg: Terrorist Information New York Group is an influential networking and educational forum run between the large financial institutions of New York and London, involving the likes of the Bank of America, Nomura Bank (London), JP Morgan and other significant contributors. Membership is free (at the time of writing). Audiences tend to be senior directors and managers responsible for security functions at Transatlantic, or global-facing organisations. The group was formed by former London and New York law-enforcement officers, respectively, David Evans and Kevin Cassidy. Further information: *www.tinyg.info/*.

Women's Security Society: Significantly underrepresented in the security sector, this network group is growing in numbers and influence. It lists among its objectives: "To share knowledge, provide support and encourage the empowerment and success of women in the security industry", and also, "To reach out to women in the security industry through networking events and a web based forum". For further details: *www.womenssecuritysociety.co.uk/about-us/*.

2.0 Social media marketing

"Instead of telling the world what you're eating for breakfast, you can use social networking to do something that's meaningful." – Business guru Edward Norton (86)

A huge amount of data exists around social media in terms of activity, but far less around behavioural influence. Notwithstanding, by the time of the London 2012 Olympics, it was apparent that the most prominent social media platforms had become larger than some of the world's most populated nation states, and the companies which owned them were worth more in cash terms than some of the poorest countries on earth.

Twitter – There are more than 800 million accounts worldwide, with an estimated 232 million monthly active users, reported *Business Insider* in 2013 (87).

Facebook – There are more than 845 million accounts. 27.5% of Europe is registered on Facebook. In January 2009 more than 175 million active users were recorded; slightly less than Brazil's population (190m) and twice the population of Germany (88). 1 in 7 people in the world has a Facebook profile.

Linkedin – There are over 135 million members, with six million of these in the UK, showed CSARN research at the beginning of the London 2012 Olympics (89).

YouTube – Is the third most visited website in the US. 78% of all traffic is outside the US. It accounts for 10% of internet traffic (90).

Other key social media platforms frequently used by businesses are: Foursquare, Google+, Instagram and company website interactive blogs.

Social media marketing: Increased exposure = increased risk

Although exposure has increased, a company's ability to control the narrative around its products or performance has clearly weakened. Academics, Kaplan and Haenlein, spent the past decade analysing the impact of social media on business practices, and recently reported:

"... businesses have increasingly less control over the information available about them in cyberspace. Today, if an internet user types the name of any leading brand into the Google search, what comes up among the top five results typically includes not only the corporate webpage, but also the corresponding entry in the online encyclopaedia Wikipedia. Here, for example, customers can read that the 2007 model of Hasbro's Easy-Bake Oven may lead to serious burns on children's hands and fingers due to a poorly-designed oven door, and that the Firestone Tire and

> *Rubber Company has been accused of using child labour in its Liberian rubber factory."* (91)

For some fun data sets comparisons about social media use, an expert, Daniel Brian, produced a video called *A Day in the Life of Social Media* (92). Brian reports that some 65 million Facebook users now access their accounts via smartphones. He reports that pop icon, Lady GaGa, has more Twitter 'followers' than twice-elected President, Barack Obama, and also that the pop star will 'reach' more people in a single Tweet than combined printed editions of popular newspaper titles, the *Wall Street Journal*, *USA Today* and *New York Times*.

There is an incredible and diverse array of splendid advice in relation to using social media to your advantage. Like much security management work, the challenge for aspiring entrepreneurs is really to separate the 'wheat' from the 'chaff'. With various permissions we bring forward some of the most practical and pertinent for security practitioners and start-ups who are keen to develop their brand with the assistance of social media.

Ryan Moore's excellent presentation posted at *maturesocialmedia.com* is titled *22 Tips for Social Media*. His quarter-hour film clip is expressed with crystal clear clarity (93). Moore provides a realistic menu for business executives who may not be naturally gifted technologists! To summarise, Moore recommends:

1. Write blog content for your target audience.
2. Use social media for customer service.
3. Measure social media return on investment by analysing how it performs compared to more channels or advertising methods.
4. Mobile check-in deals aren't just for restaurants and bars.
5. How frequently you blog *does* count.
6. Twitter: if you follow more people than who follow you, you could harm your search engine credit score.
7. Show your users that you really appreciate their contributions.
8. Blog about the problems your service or product solves – not about the product or services: 'talk about things people want' … 'provide tips and advice'.
9. Think of marketing as storytelling, and think of your customers as the characters; '… learn how to tell a great story about your brand'.
10. Depressing tweets, vague tweets, these are all tweets that are better kept to yourself.

11. What does your social media strategy really need? It needs to answer simple questions. According to Moore: "Give people what they really want, which is simple answers". You are here to 'help people', not give complicated biographies of your company.

12. The medium isn't the message. 'Find out where your people are.' What social media are they likely to use/need?

13. Use geo-location Twitter searches to identify local prospects to connect with.

14. Use social media data to find your key influencers, outline your media plan and develop your message. Identify 'key influencers' and 'cross-promote with them'.

15. Create a Facebook group to stay connected with those you meet at conferences months after the last panel. Particularly if there is something that everybody is advocating or lobbying for.

16. Consider the timing of your social media posts – time of day, time of week and time of year. Think about what is latest news, and, equally, what might be insensitive timing.

17. If you're going to tell people to 'Like' your company on Facebook, have something of value waiting there for them.

18. If your company makes a mistake on social media – step out and own up to the mistake.

19. Use social media contests as an opportunity to learn more about your customers.

20. Leverage social search and boost your rankings for target key words by offering content (eBooks, webinars, etc.) and having community members pay with a Tweet.

21. Include social sharing and follow buttons on your site, your emails, and your blogs.

22. Summary: 'Do it!' (94).

To develop your profile for Facebook, the YouTube videos that show interviews with Amy Porterfield, a social media analyst, offer good value for entrepreneurs. In a 2012 interview, Porterfield outlined four key steps to building a professional Facebook profile:

1. Optimise your Facebook contacts

2. Quickly grow a lucrative fan base of quality leads

3. Create ongoing, massive engagement

4. Turn your fans into profitable super fans.

The above is a headline summary, but Porterfield's detailed menu of suggestions to gain traction and credibility over social media platforms, including Facebook, are listed in the references section at the end of the Chapter (95). Likewise, social media academics, Kaplan and Haenlein, produced a paper *Ten pieces of advice for companies deciding to use social media.* This important paper – entitled *Users of the world unite!* – discusses multidimensional questions that will be pertinent for businesses, such as around tone and attitudinal approach. For example, how can companies appear *social* rather than exploitative? How can companies ensure that they are not perceived as invasive, as they reach out across online communities (96)? The tone and pitch of specific social networks is an important domain to understand for entrepreneurs and professionals looking to increase their profile and market footprint. With the advent of 2.0 online communities, an ICT-driven communications democracy whereby we can all interact and become published content producers, means that we have the greatest ever opportunity to reach new markets. Yet potential customer attention spans are possibly dwindling due to information overload. Several experts attest to the reduction of attention spans, caused by information saturation. Apparently, in 1998, the estimated human attention span was 12 minutes. A decade later it was five minutes. Moreover, we humans receive five times more information than we did back in 1986 (97). This may well be the case, but perhaps as living proof, the author did not have time to corroborate the data! What must be true, though, is that the entrepreneur has a very limited window of opportunity over social media platforms in order to capture the heart and minds of potential new customers.

When establishing our business advisory company, CSARN, several years ago, our marketing director, Tom Hough, took the lead in developing a social media footprint which soon seemed to gather a degree of prominence within the UK and allied security sectors. "Keep it simple", Hough reports. "Lots of relevant free and topical content, decent headlines, good collaborative networks, and the release of information to a disciplined schedule, appear to be the ingredients that work well for commercial security companies over social media platforms", says Hough (98). The Hough family company, *Cava Media*, successfully set up the popular publication, the *Crisis Response Journal,* before his company turned its hand to co-founding CSARN in 2009.

The jigsaw pieces of inspiration and ideas for your social media footprint can be given a sense of coherence and order by drawing up a social media strategy. According to business writer, Kim Lachance Shandrow, there are ten questions to ask when creating a social media marketing plan.

Kim Lachance Shandrow – Ten questions to ask when creating a social media marketing plan

1. **What should my company aim to achieve with social media?** Brand exposure, products, promotions, etc.
2. **Who should set up and maintain my company's social media accounts?** The right people, access controls, authority.
3. **Should my company have a presence on all popular social media sites?** Advice is to start with one or two, then grow correspondingly with audience interest.
4. **What are the best social networks for small businesses?** Twitter, Google+, Slideshare, Facebook, Pinterest.
5. **How often should we post content?**
6. **What types of content should we post?** Short videos, useful links, helpful tips.
7. **Should we use social media to provide customer feedback?**
8. **How can we convert social media followers into customers?**
9. **How can we measure the success of our social media marketing efforts?** Metrics and analytics are often free and available for each medium.
10. **What is the biggest mistake to avoid?** Not having a plan!

Source: Kim Lachance Shandrow, Entrepreneur journal online, 2013 (99)

2.1 Negotiation

"... to get concessions, they [ambassadors] have to make concessions." –
UN Secretary General Kofi Annan, 2006 (100)

Poor negotiation skills can cost your company a lot of money. Conversely, good negotiation skills can earn your company pots of cash. Weak negotiation skills can turn a conversation into a disaster. Strong negotiation skills can avert a crisis and maximise future opportunities. This part of the book asks:

- are there case studies that can help our learning?
- what seem to be the core ingredients to effective negotiation?

Lessons from the political domain in the sphere of negotiations can be instructive. President George W Bush's former Under-Secretary of State for Arms Control, later Ambassador to the United Nations, John Bolton, stated the following: "Negotiation is not a policy. It's a technique. It's something you use when it's to your advantage, and something that you don't use when it's not to your advantage". However, as Bolton was to find out, displaying such naked self-interest saw him hit numerous brick walls at political negotiating tables (101). (Bolton was hardly heartbroken by this.) The late Richard Holbrooke adopted a more subtle approach. He was a skilled, long-serving US Government negotiator, who famously led the brokering of a fragile yet relatively enduring peace process amid Bosnia's civil war. Holbrooke observed the following: "World War I was not inevitable, as many historians say. It could have been avoided, and it was a diplomatically botched negotiation" (102). Policy negotiation achievements are a little like a prolonged commercial sales strategy: positive results can only ever be created and realised due to the involvement of a range of people and fully functioning teamwork. Negotiation is an area of essential corporate leadership which can pose difficulties for those who dislike negotiating, or those who fear losing control of a self-imposed agenda. But as US President Bill Clinton warned the people of Northern Ireland after the 1998 Good Friday peace deal: "keep your eyes on the prize" (103).

Case study 1: The 12-month ambassador – John Bolton

He may well have provoked amusing anecdotes in some US media circles, but fiery UN Ambassador, John Bolton, was described as "rude" by Iran's foreign ministry in 2004 and a "human scum and bloodsucker" by North Korean diplomats a year earlier, in response to several insensitive comments (104) (105). Both countries were thought to be emerging nuclear powers with unstable leaderships at the time. But by the end of his prematurely revoked term of office, Bolton's political achievements can be counted in debits rather than credits. For instance, he actively scuppered multilateral arms control initiatives proposed at the UN, which included provisions to restrict and improve monitoring around small arms sales and biological weapons transfer controls. Bolton described his finest moment in political life as 'unsigning' the Rome Statute, which sought to establish the International Criminal Court. Although Bolton did have some influential republican party supporters who backed his 'hard ball' negotiation tactics (including vice-president Cheney), when it came to his own confirmation in the US ambassador role to the UN he was rejected, including from some senators within his own party. After just one year, Bolton was forced to resign as ambassador. Moreover, and most unusually, he failed to elicit any immediate commendation from secretary general, Kofi Annan. Bolton's belligerence may well have been toasted by a minority of influential political supporters back in the US and his no-nonsense straight-talking did help to propel him into a prominent government position within the administration of President George W Bush (2001-09). But the precincts of New York's UN buildings were different audiences with vastly different perspectives and agendas. Bolton's inability to change his tone (not necessarily his objectives), and empathise with other national leaders, who also had anxious domestic audiences, meant that he soon lost his precious job. But worse. Perhaps tarnished by his intransigent approach, his beloved uncompromising agenda has been buried far deeper than was thought possible before he began in post.

Case study 2: The seasoned negotiator – Richard Holbrooke

Richard Holbrooke also served as the US Ambassador to the United Nations (1999-2001); leaving office because of a change in Presidency, from Bill Clinton to George W Bush. During his brief tenure, Holbrooke was credited with resetting and repaying a troublesome membership fee dispute between the UN and US Government. Holbrooke received applause from both republicans and democrats in the US House of Senate. Holbrooke secured official consultative status for a Jewish woman's group in the face of some Arab-state opposition. Moreover, Holbrooke held six consecutive debates on African conflicts that were receiving little international diplomatic attention beforehand. Holbrooke initiated and led UN delegations into Congo, Rwanda, Uganda, Zambia and Zimbabwe. As an assistant secretary of state in Bill Clinton's first administration, Holbrooke was tasked by his government to attempt to bring peace to warring factions in former Yugoslavia. As the US's 'lead negotiator', Holbrooke was quickly viewed on all sides as chief architect for ending Bosnia's bloody three-year civil war. He cajoled and led warring political leaders to accept the 1995 Dayton Peace Accords; many of the provisions he personally devised. His memoir *To end a war* is a widely respected isomorphic lesson plan for successful negotiation and diplomacy in warring environments (106). Holbrooke's tactics did include moving national leaders and delegations to remote locations in order to prevent damaging pre-negotiation posturing by negotiation teams in the media. He forged first name and friendly business relationships with all delegation leaders including ex-Yugoslav president, Slobodan Milosevic. Milosevic was later indicted, but not successfully prosecuted, for war crime at The Hague International Criminal Court. Holbrooke said that he … "had no moral qualms negotiating with people who do immoral things". Holbrooke was reported by the BBC in 1999 as saying: "If you can prevent the deaths of people still alive, you're not doing a disservice to those already killed trying to do so", (107). Holbrooke was nominated for the Nobel Peace Prize in the mid-1990s. Holbrooke was appointed by President Barack Obama as Special Envoy to Afghanistan in 2009. However, the path of negotiation seldom runs smoothly. He was reported as falling out with US military leaders and Afghanistan's incumbent President when he suggested running a second round of elections in response to voter fraud allegations. Despite his clear pragmatism in dealing with any tyrant who crossed his desk, Holbrooke hinted at the importance of 'negotiating anchors': "I make no apologies for negotiating with Milosevic and even worse people, provided one doesn't lose one's point of view" (108).

Commercial negotiations

According to the National Audit Office, the UK Government wasted £31bn during financial year 2010-11 due to "poor negotiation skills" (109). Negotiation specialist, James Stuart, reports that UK companies lost approximately £75bn "in revenue or extra cost due to poor negotiation" (110). Negotiations can begin to go wrong right from the outset, argues management strategist, Adam Galinsky. Galinsky writes about the "dramatic effect of anchors" and finds a case against those who advocate a guarded approach where numerical or positional goals might be held back.

Case study: Galinsky's research into negotiating 'anchors'

Galinsky writes: "Because of the inherent ambiguity of most negotiations, some experts suggest that you should wait for the other side to speak first. By receiving the opening offer, the argument goes you'll gain valuable information about your opponent's bargaining position and clues about acceptable agreements. This advice makes intuitive sense, but it fails to account for the powerful effect that first offers have on the way people think about the negotiation process. Substantial psychological research suggests that, more often than not, negotiators who make first offers come out ahead".

Galinsky adds:

> "Because they [people] pull judgments toward themselves, these numerical values are known as anchors. In situations of great ambiguity and uncertainty, first offers have a strong anchoring effect – they exert a strong pull throughout the rest of the negotiation. Even when people know that a particular anchor should not influence their judgments, they are often incapable of resisting its influence. As a result, they insufficiently adjust their valuations away from the anchor" (111).

---

*1. **Go first.** Many people hate to be first to toss out a figure because they think they might miss out on an opportunity. ("If I offer $10k and he would have been happy with $5k I'll spend a lot more than I have to.") Occasionally that might happen, but it makes more sense to go into a negotiation assuming the other party is smart and has a reasonable sense of the value of whatever they want to buy or sell. Making the first offer lets you set the 'anchor' for negotiations to follow. Studies ... show that when a seller makes the first offer, the final price is typically higher than if the buyer made the first offer. Why? The buyer's first offer will always be low, which sets a lower anchor. In negotiations, anchors matter.*

*2. **Be quiet.** When we're nervous we tend to talk a lot and therefore miss a lot. Let silence be your friend. If you make an offer and the seller says, "No way", don't respond immediately. To fill the silence the seller will give reasons why your offer is too low ... and in the process may give you information you wouldn't have received otherwise. Stay relatively quiet, listen, and when you do speak, ask open-ended questions. You can't meet in the middle (or, hopefully well to your side of the middle) unless you know what the other party really needs. Give them time to tell you.*

*3. **Know what you want.** You should always know what you need – and what you're willing to spend or pay. If you don't have a clue about the cost of a particular service, don't expect the other party to educate you; that puts even the most ethical person in an awkward position. At the least have a sense of the market price for the product or service you want to purchase. Then you can adjust your offer based on the quality and quantity you will actually receive.*

*4. **Assume the best case.** High expectations typically lead to high outcomes. Ask for what you want, and go into the negotiation assuming you'll get it. Why not? You can't receive if you don't ask. My wife is the eternal negotiation optimist; she always assumes she can make a deal on her terms. And she almost always does – because she confidently asks for what she wants.*

5. Avoid setting ranges. *Service buyers often ask for estimates in ranges: "I know you don't have all the information you need, but based on what I've told you, what's a ballpark figure?" Ranges create anchors too. If you don't have enough information to provide a solid estimate, don't. And never say, "Well, somewhere between $10k and $20k ... " because the buyer will naturally want the final cost to be as close to $10k as possible, even if what you're asked to provide should cost well over $20k.*

6. Only make concessions for a reason. *Say a buyer asks you to cut your price, saying, "All I can afford is $500". Make sure you get something in return. Say, "For $500 I can do X and Y", and take Z off the table. Every concession should involve a trade-off of some kind; otherwise your price was simply too high to begin with. Use the same logic if you're buying; the classic home negotiation move is to ask for, say, all the appliances and fixtures when you counter at a higher number. Always ask for something in return, and don't be afraid to ask for things you don't really want early on so you have items you'll be happy to take back off the table later.*

7. Never be Harry Truman. *Truman kept a sign that said "The buck stops here" on his desk to remind him that his was usually the final decision. In negotiations it's tempting to say you have the final word and ultimate authority (especially if that's true.) Don't. To avoid getting cornered or pressured, always have a reason to step away and get the okay from another person, even if that other person is you.*

8. Make time your friend. *Never, ever, rush. Never see a negotiation as something to wrap up as soon as possible. A negotiation is an investment in time, and most people don't want to lose their investments, so the more time the other person has in a deal, the more they'll want to close the deal -- and the more they will voluntarily give up in order to get you to say yes.*

9. Ignore face value. *Negotiating is a little like being on* Survivor *[a TV programme]; in the spirit of the 'game', many people feel it's okay to be less than forthcoming or honest. Don't assume everything you hear is true. Statements like, "I can't go a penny lower", are more likely to be negotiating tactics than truths. Listen, but toss a few grains of salt onto what you hear. Look closely for what lies under the posturing and positioning.*

10. Give the other person room. *People get defensive or attack when they feel trapped, and neither helps a negotiation move forward. Push too hard and take away every option and the other party may have no choice but to walk away. You don't want that, because you should ...*

11. Forget about winning and losing. *Negotiating can feel like a game but it's not. No one should win or lose. The best negotiations leave both parties feeling they received something of value. That's how you want a negotiation to end up, because a negotiation should ...*

12. Create a relationship. *Take, but don't take too much. Give. But don't give too much. Establishing a long-term business relationship should always be your goal. And when you've finalised the deal, say thanks – and mean it.*

Source: Jeff Haden, CBS Money (112)

Figure 7: Jeff Haden's 12 negotiation tips

2.2 Company structures, corporate returns and regulation

Part of being an effective entrepreneur is being aware of various company structures and how liabilities can work to your advantage or otherwise. In this section we look briefly at the structure of Private Limited Companies, Public Limited Companies, Limited Liability Partnerships and Community Interest Companies. Moreover, only by understanding how another company is incorporated, can we actually understand some key commercial or operational drivers that underpin the ethos and methods of its business. By *incorporated* we mean the registration of that company with the authorised national or regional bodies responsible for holding information and registering companies as legal entities in any geographic domain, such as Companies House in the UK.

Many countries follow similar legal approaches to the UK Companies Act (2006) or its predecessors. In the UK there are four types of company as defined by the commerce registration body, Companies House:

Private company limited by shares: This company has a share capital and the liability of each member is limited to the amount, if any, unpaid on their shares. A private company cannot offer its shares for sale to the general public.

Private company limited by guarantee: This company does not have a share capital and its members are guarantors rather than shareholders. The members' liability is limited to the amount they agree to contribute to the company's assets if it is wound up.

Private unlimited company: An unlimited company may or may not have a share capital but there is no limit to the members' liability.

Public limited company (PLCs): A public company has a share capital and limits the liability of each member to the amount unpaid on their shares. It may offer its shares for sale to the general public and may be quoted on the stock exchange (113).

Some companies are established as **Limited Liability Partnerships (LLPs)**, and this can be quite popular among some sectors including legal and accountancy domains. LLPs are usually a logical way of bringing together a large critical mass of existing equity partners from, perhaps, smaller companies looking to merge into a larger corporation. The benefit is that at the same time 'partners' do not theoretically lose decision-making power within the new company structure. Many accountants and lawyers are 'equity partners' within the company. This means that they own shares in the company. Partners are often empowered to elect the chief executive officer (CEO) and company chairman roles within the LLP (114).

Employee ownership schemes are not confined to law and accountancy and can be a smart way to incentivise growth. Perhaps one of the more familiar examples of an employee-owned business is the upmarket retailer, the John Lewis Partnership: "People who work in our business are not just employees, they're actually the owners of our business. And they have a constitutional right to ownership", CEO Charlie Mayfield proudly recounts in a company promotional video (115).

Such non-hierarchical structures are anathema to many security environments, but are becoming popular, particularly in technology and creative arts environments. Benefits of employee owned companies include:

- working horizontally across projects and locations, and not causing friction by upsetting established hierarchies or silos
- engaging employees into a security and emergency planning culture of mutual aid and assistance, because, ultimately, they are all business owners.

Disadvantages might be:

- an inability to properly take steps to mitigate against internal business security threats (including collective rights to health and safety) due to individual employee over-empowerment that may even impede sensible preventative or disciplinary action
- critical and priority business decision making is slowed down, or becomes slower than competitors.

Company returns

Once companies are registered by national authorities, they will receive a certificate of incorporation, or similar. Various demands for company returns are then issued by the regulatory body, in order for companies to remain legally compliant. Returns can be driven by events within the company, requiring records to be changed and updated with the regulator. Some examples might be: an update being required for senior personnel alterations; adjustments to share capital allocations; or a change of registered office location. For further information on updates, companies should consult their own regulator for any alterations that need to be altered. These are described as 'event driven filings' by UK Companies House (116).

Moreover, Companies House, and other similar national bodies, require companies to return a snapshot of their activity, usually on an annual basis. This is popularly known as filing company 'returns' (117). Please note, that this process is distinctly different to filing taxation returns, and other mandatory information that might be required by relevant government departments and regulatory bodies.

Case Study: UK Companies House – what information needs to be in a company return?

- List of company officers.
- Trading dates and registering dormant activity.
- Registering and/or confirming your Standard Industrial Classification code and the nature of your company business. You can add or amend your business activity.
- Information on share capital and shareholder details. (This is not required for LLPs or non-shareholder companies.)

Source: UK Companies House website, 2013

After submission by the company secretary, annual returns will either be accepted or rejected by Companies House. Different organisational structures are required to appoint certain roles in order to guarantee clear organisational responsibility for financial reporting. In the UK, public companies must meet the following Companies House criteria:

- it must have at least two directors (who may also be members of the company)
- it must have at least one director who is an individual
- all individual directors must be aged 16 or over
- it must have at least one secretary
- the secretary must be qualified to act as a secretary.

A qualified secretary is someone who:

- has held the office of secretary of a public company for at least three of the five years before their appointment
- is a barrister, advocate or solicitor, called or admitted, in any part of the United Kingdom
- is a person who, by virtue of his or her previous experience or membership of another body, appears to the directors to be capable of discharging the functions of secretary
- is a member of one of the following professional bodies:
  o Institute of Chartered Accountants in England and Wales
  o Institute of Chartered Accountants of Scotland
  o Institute of Chartered Accountants in Ireland
  o Institute of Chartered Secretaries and Administrators

o Association of Chartered Certified Accountants
o Chartered Institute of Management Accountants
o Chartered Institute of Public Finance and Accountancy (118).

UK Companies Act 2006

The UK Companies Act (2006) was established by the then government to tighten shareholder engagement within companies. It also had the stated intent to make it easier to establish companies within the UK. The Act replaced the 1985 Companies Act. Conversely, as reporting data was increased, some business organisations countered that the Act had added more 'red tape' to business reporting. Nevertheless, the Act tightened some areas of concern. One change required that company directors must be at least 16 years of age. Directors no longer had to report (and effectively publicise) a home address. In addition, PLCs became mandated to hold their Annual General Meetings (AGMs) within six months of the financial year-end.

The Act was, however, welcomed by some other small business owners, because a couple of perceptibly cumbersome procedures were diluted:

- *Company secretaries* – a private company no longer needs to appoint a company secretary, but may do so if it wishes.

- *Shareholders' written resolutions* – the requirement for unanimity in shareholders' written resolutions was abolished, and the required majority is similar to that for shareholder meetings – a simple majority of the eligible shares for ordinary resolutions, or 75% for special resolutions (119).

Chapter 1: Wrap-up

In closing this chapter on **entrepreneurship**, we reflect on some of the approaches and attributes that will help your company gain the competitive edge. These include:

- Don't cut corners, or get a reputation for doing so. Longer-term relationships enable the client and vendor to develop a trusted synergy based upon an intuitive understanding of one another, says Jason Towse, Managing Director at Mitie Total Security.

- Competitive intelligence (CI) is a process which identifies and researches various important market information sets. When brought together, CI provides a company with insightful and actionable information which will help it to gain a 'competitive advantage' over others in the field.

- Companies that know their operating environments really well, and also uphold professional practices around individual and organisational resilience, will ultimately gain competitive advantage over their commercial peers.

- Entrepreneurs should familiarise themselves with some widely familiar business-environment analysis models, such as PESTLE, SWOT and Porter's Five Forces analysis. If deployed correctly, these management tools can hugely assist enterprises to harness control of resources and target operations to optimum effect.

- Developing advanced capability and expertise in the important sphere of IP protection, may well help you to win new clients, and also expand revenue streams from existing buyers.

- Perception is reality. Entrepreneurs sometimes start out in teams or alliances of individuals coming together to fill a market gap. You may all be juggling a variety of commercial interests. Therefore, if you have a perceived *conflict of interest* in the eyes of your team members (remember, you might not think so, but we are talking about *perception*), be really clear from the outset about your commercial aims and interests. Full disclosure is always better than falling out.

- According to the University of Connecticut Business School, "The 21st century may well be the time when the balance of power shifts to Brazil, Russia, India and China, nations collectively referred to as BRICs. These nations constitute the shape of the future, giving rise to a new world economy". Therefore, think as laterally as possible about where to scope out next for new business.

- Do not 'put all your eggs in one basket'. Ongoing power struggles and regular changes of influential personnel are hardly uncommon in emerging markets.

- A neutral and open-minded application of sensible business intelligence analysis techniques – such as PESTLE and SWOT – is strongly advised before the establishment of security functions and consultancies in emerging markets.

- It is worth accepting from the outset that – as in a job interview – applying for funding, and then accepting a potential investor, is a two-way process. A poor investor match, based on poor information sharing, or divergent business philosophies, can sink an enterprise faster than an unexpected torpedo attack.

References

1) Author interview with Jason Towse, Managing Director of Mitie Total Security Management (2014)

2) Off-record contextual conversation with two EMEA Corporate Security Managers at CSARN and UK Foreign Office business briefing (London, 29/11/2012)

3) CNN Wire Staff. (17th August 2010) 'Karzai issues decree disbanding private security firms', accessed and downloaded on 16/01/2015 at: *http://edition.cnn.com/2010/WORLD/asiapcf/08/17/afghanistan.security.firms/index.html*

4) New York Times (08/08/2008) 'No such thing as set back', accessed and downloaded on 23/01/2015 at: *www.nytimes.com/2010/08/08/fashion/08With.html*

5) Fuld, L., (2013) 'What is Competitive Intelligence?', downloaded on 10/09/2013 from: *www.fuld.com/company/what-is-competitive-intelligence/*

6) Porter, M., E., (1980) 'Competitive Strategy: Techniques for Analyzing Industries and Competitors' (p.6), accessed and downloaded on 09/09/2013 from: *www.iseg.utl.pt/aula/cad1505/Textos_Apoio/Techniques_Analyzing_Industries_a.pdf*

7) Brody, R., (2008) 'Issues in Defining Competitive Intelligence: An Exploration', in Journal of Competitive Intelligence and Management, Volume 4, Number 3, 2008, (p.4) accessed and downloaded on 09/09/13 from: *www.scip.org/files/JCIM/02.%20JCIM%204.3%20Brody%20%28WEB%29.pdf*

8) Society of Strategic and Competitive Intelligence Professionals: accessed at: *www.scip.org*

9) Fuld and Company (2013) 'Boiling the Frog: A Global Survey and Report about Potential Industry Shocks That Concern Life Sciences Executives', White Paper, accessed and downloaded on 10/09/2013 from: *www.fuld.com/Portals/17073/resource-center/white-papers/pdf/fuld-and-company-white-paper-boilingthefrog2013.pdf?utm_content=9079503&_hsenc=p2ANqtz-8HCrRetkxK-M81owaLEQoJrLJhLuPh_2uG0vdyw5x3WRsrgwruC7d1q2A5lMEFaDkD2JrJgeFWMwN47VVF2bDzmb607a7ZPc39Cdg7wdo8wa_GY4&_hsmi=9079503*

10) Academy of Competitive Intelligence (2006) 'The First Competitive Intelligence Certification Programme Celebrates Fifth Anniversary; Reduces Chances of "HP Fiasco'; Downloaded on 10/09/13 from: *www.marketwire.com/press-release/first-competitive-intelligence-certification-program-celebrates-fifth-anniversary-reduces-699754.htm*

11) SCIP's website can be found at: *www.scip.org/*

12) Porter, M., E., (1979), 'How Competitive Forces Shape Strategy', Harvard Business Review, March/April 1979

13) Intellectual Property Office website can be accessed at: *www.ipo.gov.uk*

14) World Intellectual Property Organisation website can be accessed at: *www.wipo.org*

15) Reports on the work of G8 and Intellectual Property were accessed and downloaded on 02/02/2015 at: *www.g20civil.com/documents/200/548/*

16) Among several definitions of 'patent' the author accessed and downloaded the Hothouse business advice website on 02/02/2015 at: *www.dit.ie/hothouse/researchcommercialisation/understandingintellectualproperty/*

17) Clarification of copyright principles provided by University of California and accessed and downloaded on 02/02/2015 at: *http://copyright.universityofcalifornia.edu/ownership/joint-works.html*

18) 'Industrial design rights' accessed and downloaded on 02/02/2015 at: *http://laws-lois.justice.gc.ca/eng/acts/I-9/index.html*

19) United States Trademarks and Patents Office, accessed and downloaded on 16/01/2014 at: *www.uspto.gov*

20) Princeton University website, 'Trade Dress', accessed and downloaded on 02/02/2015 at: *www.princeton.edu/~achaney/tmve/wiki100k/docs/Trade_dress.html*

21) United States Patent and Trademark Office (2013) 'Trademark, patent or copyright?' Downloaded on 10/09/2013 from: *www.uspto.gov/trademarks/basics/definitions.jsp*

22) WIPO guide for Small and Medium sized companies, accessed and downloaded on 02/02/2015 at: *www.wipo.int/sme/en/*

23) WIPO toolkits for specific countries, accessed and downloaded on 02/02/2015 at: *www.uspto.gov/ip/iprtoolkits.jsp*

24) Interview conducted with Rob Scott, Managing Director of SSG Security, on 02/02/2015

25) OECD, 'The Economic Effect of Counterfeiting and Piracy, Executive Summary' OECD, Paris. 2007. Retrieved 2007.

26) WTO: 'Trade related aspects of intellectual property rights', accessed and downloaded on 02/02/2015 at: *www.wto.org/english/tratop_e/trips_e/t_agm0_e.htm*

27) FBI presentation, (16/09/2015) Terrorist Information New York Group, New York: U.S.

28) Action Fraud was accessed and downloaded on 02/04/2014 at: *www.actionfraud.police.uk/about-us/who-we-are*

29) International Chamber of Commerce: 'Business Action to stop counterfeiting and piracy', accessed and downloaded on 02/04/2014 at: *www.iccwbo.org/advocacy-codes-and-rules/bascap/* and: International Chamber of Commerce (ICC), (2013), 'Controlling the Zone: Balancing facilitation and control to combat illicit trade in the world's free trade zone': accessed and downloaded on 16/09/2013 from: *www.iccwbo.org/*

Advocacy-Codes-and-Rules/BASCAP/International-engagement-and-Advocacy/Free-Trade-Zones/

30) Op. Cit., OECD 'The Economic Effect of Counterfeiting and Piracy, Executive Summary'
31) Jain, S., et al (2006), 'New Horizons in International Business: Emerging Economies and the Transformation of International Business', Cheltenham: Edward Elgar Publishing
32) Manktelow, A. et al (2014), 'Guide to Emerging Markets: The business outlook, opportunities and obstacles', London: The Economist
33) Internet World Stats: accessed and downloaded on 04/02/2015 at: *www.internetworldstats.com/asia/in.htm*
34) Op., Cit., Manktelow et al
35) Ibid.
36) Heakal, R., (2014) 'What is an emerging market economy?' Accessed and downloaded on 07/10/2014 at: *www.investopedia.com/articles/03/073003.asp*
37) Bloomberg: 'The top twenty emerging markets': accessed and downloaded on 06/10/2014 at: *www.bloomberg.com/slideshow/2013-01-30/the-top-20-emerging-markets.html#slide10*
38) Global Issues website: 'Rich Nations Agreed At UN to 0.7% of GNP To Aid': accessed and downloaded on 07/10/2014 at: *www.globalissues.org/article/35/foreign-aid-development-assistance*
39) European Interagency Security Forum website: accessed on 07/10/2014 at: *www.eisf.eu/*
40) Interview with Lisa Reilly, EISF, conducted on: 11/11/2014
41) Stiglitz, J., (2014) 'The world needs a sovereign debt restructuring mechanism', accessed and downloaded on 12/10/2014 at: *www.emergingmarkets.org/Article/3389531/JOSEPH-STIGLITZ-The-world-needs-a-sovereign-debt-restructuring-mechanism.html*
42) Forbes (2014), 'What makes emerging economies markets great investments?' Accessed and downloaded on 12/10/2014 at: *www.forbes.com/pictures/eglg45gdjd/why-invest-in-emerging-markets-2/*
43) Ibid.
44) Goldman Sachs (2001), 'Building Better Global Economic 'BRICS', Global Economic Paper No. 66: accessed and downloaded on 06/02/2015 at: *www.goldmansachs.com/our-thinking/archive/archive-pdfs/build-better-brics.pdf*
45) Morgan Stanley's 'Emerging Market Index', accessed and downloaded on 06/11/2014 from: *www.msci.com/products/indexes/country_and_regional/em/*
46) ASIS International and IOMF (2012), 'The United States Security Industry', accessed and downloaded on 06/02/2015 at:

www.asisonline.org/Documents/ASIS%20IOFM%20Executive%20Summary%208.23.13.%20final.pdf

47) Whitney, R., D., (15/08/2013) 'SSN Study: $350bn US Security Market Expected to Grow': accessed and downloaded on 13/09/2014 at: *www.securitysystemsnews.com/article/study-350-billion-us-security-market-expected-grow*

48) Business Case Studies (2013), 'Marketing theory', accessed and downloaded on 13/09/2013 at: *http://businesscasestudies.co.uk/business-theory/marketing/marketing-mix-price-place-promotion-product.html#axzz3RRsvGyoi*

49) JE website (2015), 'Marketing Mix Four Ps', accessed and downloaded on 11/02/2015 at: *http://sportmbond.weebly.com/5/post/2013/10/markting-mix-four-ps.html*

50) Op. Cit., 'Business Case Studies' (2013)

51) Fitton., L., quote was accessed and downloaded on 11/02/2015 at: *www.businessinsider.com/fantastic-marketing-quotes-2011-9?op=1&IR=T*

52) BBC Online (13/05/2004) 'Trouble at the Top', accessed and downloaded on 13/09/2015 at: *http://news.bbc.co.uk/1/hi/business/3704669.stm*

53) Statoil (2013), 'The In Amenas Attack', accessed and downloaded on 13/06/2014 at: *www.statoil.com/en/NewsAndMedia/News/2013/Downloads/In%20Amenas%20report.pdf*

54) Yourbusinessmatters.com (2013), accessed and downloaded on 10/07/2013 at: *www.yourbusinessmatters.net/*

55) BDRC Continental (2013), 'SME Finance Monitor, The Uncertainty of Demand', accessed and downloaded on 16/02/2015 at: *http://doc.ukdataservice.ac.uk/doc/6888/mrdoc/pdf/6888_sme_finance_monitor_report_q1_2013.pdf*

56) Funding Circle website (2015), accessed and downloaded on 16/02/2015 at: *www.fundingcircle.com/*

57) Yourbusinessmatters.net (2013), 'Credit where credit's due', accessed and downloaded on 16/02/2015 at: *www.yourbusinessmatters.net/credit-credits-due-finance-dilemma/*

58) HMG website (2015), 'Business finance explained', accessed and downloaded on 16/02/2015 at: *www.gov.uk/business-finance-explained/invoice-financing*

59) Department for Business, Innovation & Skills (April 2013), 'Access to Finance Schemes', was accessed and downloaded on 17/02/2015 at: *www.gov.uk/government/uploads/system/uploads/attachment_data/file/192618/bis-13-p176b-sme-access-to-finance-measures.pdf*

60) Department for Business, Innovation & Skills, 'Government Information and Advice' was accessed on 16/02/2015 at: *www.gov.uk/government/publications/helping-small-business-government-information-and-advice*

61) HMG 'Business is Great' website (2015), was accessed on 16/02/2015 at: *www.greatbusiness.gov.uk/*
62) BusinessUSA website (2015), was accessed on 16/02/2015 at: *www.state.gov/business/*
63) Prince's Trust website (2015), accessed on 16/02/2015 at: *www.princes-trust.org.uk/*
64) PRIME website (2015), accessed and downloaded on 16/02/2015 at: *www.prime.org.uk/*
65) Greenwise business website (04/09/2013), 'Consider 'Green' routes: £5m Green energy fund to target SMEs', accessed and downloaded on 23/09/2013 from: *www.greenwisebusiness.co.uk/news/5m-green-energy-fund-to-target-smes-4071.aspx*
66) Daily Telegraph (05/08/2015), 'SOAPBOX, SMEs are missing out on funding because alternative funders are no good at marketing themselves, says Will King', accessed and downloaded on 5/08/2015 at: *www.telegraph.co.uk/finance/festival-of-business/10220565/SOAPBOX-SMEs-are-missing-out-on-funding-because-alternative-funders-are-no-good-at-marketing-themselves-says-Will-King.html*
67) Millar, H., (2013), Operations Management video, Pearson Education, accessed and downloaded on 22/10/2013 at: *www.youtube.com/watch?v=3F33ZantQdI*
68) U.S. Department of Education Institute of Education Sciences: Classification of Instructional Programs (CIP). Retrieved on October 26, 2009 from CIP 2000 - CIP Lookup to Occupational Crosswalks
69) APICS (n.d) 'Operations Management Body of Knowledge Framework' (3rd. Ed.) downloaded on 21 10 2013 from: *www.apics.org/industry-content-research/publications/ombok/apics-ombok-framework-table-of-contents/apics-ombok-framework-1.1*
70) Hill, T., Manufacturing Strategy-Text and Cases, 3rd ed. Mc-Graw Hill 2000
71) Op.Cit. Millar, H.,
72) Transcript from the Energy Select Committee, House of Commons, 29th October 2013, provided by the BBC and accessed at: *www.bbc.co.uk/news/business-24705280*
73) Op. Cit., Millar, H.,
74) Shingo, S., (1989) 'A Study of the Toyota Production System', Productivity Press: New York. Extracts downloaded on 21 10 2013 from: *http://books.google.co.uk/books?hl=en&lr=&id=RKWU7WElJ7oC&oi=fnd&pg=PR11&dq=A+study+of+the+Toyota+Production+System,+Shigeo+Shingo,+Productivity+Press,+1989,+p+187&ots=ni9Q5zuzdK&sig=IkSpldTISIcoOBRDoXuiu3wyqzY#v=onepage&q=A%20study%20of%20the%20Toyota%20Production%20System%2C%20Shigeo%20Shingo%2C%20Productivity%20Press%2C%201989%2C%20p%20187&f=false*

75) Mindtools (2013), 'Gantt Charts: planning and scheduling team projects', downloaded on 21 10 2013 from: *www.mindtools.com/pages/article/newPPM_03.htm*

76) University of North Carolina, Department of Computer Science: downloaded on 21 10 2013 from: *www.cs.unc.edu/~stotts/145/pix/gantt.gif*

77) APICS, OMBOK (3rd. ed.) was accessed and downloaded on 20/10/2013 at: *www.apics.org/industry-content-research/publications/ombok/apics-ombok-framework-table-of-contents/apics-ombok-framework-1.1*

78) Mindtools (2013), Gantt charts with James Manktelow and Amy Carlson was accessed and downloaded on 12/11/2013 at: *www.mindtools.com/pages/article/newPPM_03.htm*

79) Brainyquotes.com (2013), accessed and downloaded on 17/02/2015 at: *www.brainyquote.com/quotes/authors/s/sonia_sotomayor.html*

80) BusinessBalls.com (2013), Business Networking, downloaded on 12 11 2013 from: *www.businessballs.com/business-networking.htm*

81) Margolis., M., '5 storytelling tips to make networking feel good again', downloaded on 12 11 2013 from: *www.getstoried.com/5-storytelling-tips-to-make-networking-feel-good-again/*

82) Op., Cit., Businessballs.com

83) Laird., D., et al., (2010), 'Poise and Self Confidence in Dealing with Others', Whitefish, Montana: Kessinger Publishing

84) Businessballs.com (2013)

85) Author interview with John Walmsley, JKW Law LLP, on 22/01/2015

86) Brainy Quote website: accessed on 20/03.2015 at: *www.brainyquote.com/quotes/quotes/e/edwardnort449658.html*

87) Business Insider (06/11/2015), 'Twitter's Dark Pool' was accessed and downloaded on 31/03/2015 at: *www.businessinsider.com/twitter-total-registered-users-v-monthly-active-users-2013-11*

88) Kaplan, A., and Haenlein, M. (2009), 'Users of the world unite! The challenges and opportunities of Social Media', Kelley School of Business, Indiana University: downloaded on 27/11/2013 from: michaelhaenlein.com/Publications/Kaplan,%20Andreas%20-%20Users%20of%20the%20world,%20unite.pdf

89) CSARN (2012), Security Viewpoint: 1, 'The role of social media in emergencies', downloaded from the CSARN.org website on 02/12/2013 from: *http://news.csarn.org/2012/07/csarn-security-viewpoint-1-the-role-of-social-media-in-emergencies.html*

90) Ibid.

91) Op. Cit., Kaplan and Haenlein

92) Brian., D., (2010), 'A Day in the Life of Social Media': was accessed on 20/02/2014 at: *www.youtube.com/watch?v=iReY3W9ZkLU*

93) Moore., R., (2012), '22 Brilliant Social Media Tips': (14.49), was accessed on 20/02/2014 at: *www.youtube.com/watch?v=6kaMmKAYHs0*

94) Ibid.

95) Porterfield, A., (2012) webinar was accessed on 20/02/2015 at: *www.youtube.com/watch?v=9VfXljgensI*

96) Op. Cit., Kaplan and Haenlein

97) Trackvia Blog (2015), 'Your shrinking attention span: the truth', was accessed and downloaded on 31/03/2015 at: *www.trackvia.com/blog /productivity/truth-shrinking-attention-span*

98) Author interview with Tom Hough, carried out on 31/03/2015

99) Shandrow, K., L., (16/09/2013), 'Ten questions to ask when creating a Social Media Marketing Plan', was accessed and downloaded on 31/03/2015 at: *www.entrepreneur.com/article/228324*

100) Annan, K., cited in the New York Times (04/12/2006), at: *www.nytimes.com/2006/12/04/world/05nationscnd.html*

101) Bolton, J. US Ambassador to the United Nations, cited by brainyquotes.com and accessed and downloaded on 12/10/2013 at: *www.nytimes.com/2006/12/04/world/05nationscnd.html*

102) Holbrooke, R., Under Secretary of State in the U.S. Government, cited by brainyquotes.com

103) Guardian (3/10/02), 'Clinton tells Ulster don't turn back' accessed and downloaded on 31/03/2015 at: *www.theguardian.com/politics/2002/ oct/03/uk.labourconference6*

104) Kaplan, Lawrence F. (March 29, 2004), 'THE SECRETS OF JOHN BOLTON'S SUCCESS' The New Republic.

105) Soo-Jeong. Lee (August 4, 2003). 'North Korea bans Bolton from talks", The Washington Times

106) Holbrooke., R., (1998), To end a war, New York, New York: Random House. – ISBN 978-0-375-50057-2

107) BBC website (2010), Obituary: Richard Holbrooke, downloaded on 03/12/2013 from: *www.bbc.co.uk/news/world-us-canada-11977155*

108) Ibid.

109) Gap Partnership (2013), 'This is more than just Negotiation Training', downloaded on 29/11/2013 from: *www.thegappartnership.com/p/ negotiation-training b.aspx?gclid=CL2s762firsCFa-WtAodQksAiA*

110) Stuart (2011), The Essence of Negotiation, accessed and downloaded on 29/11/13 from: *www.managementexchange.com/hack/essence-negotiation*

111) Galinsky., A., (2004), 'When to Make the First Offer in Negotiations', Harvard Business School, downloaded on 02/12/2013 from: *http://hbswk. hbs.edu/archive/4302.html*

112) Haden., J., (2011), '12 Negotiation Tips for People who Hate Negotiating', downloaded on 02/12/13 from: *www.cbsnews.com/news/12-negotiation-tips-for-people-who-hate-negotiating/*

113) Companies House (2013), FAQs downloaded on 03/12/13 from: *www.companieshouse.gov.uk/infoAndGuide/faq/companiesAct2006.shtml* and also: Companies House (2013), Incorporation and Names, downloaded on 03/12/13 from: *www.companieshouse.gov.uk/about/pdf/gp1.pdf*

114) UK PLC website (2013), LLPs Frequently Asked Questions: downloaded on 03/12/13 from: *www.ukplc.com/company-types/specialist-uk-company/limited-liability-partnership/llp-faqs.html*

115) John Lewis Partnership 'Employee Ownership, A Shared Passion' video, accessed and downloaded on 13/10/2013 at: *www.johnlewispartnership.co.uk/media/webcasts-and-videos/employee-ownership-a-shared-passion.html*

116) Companies House (2013), Life of a Company Part 2 - Event driven filings, downloaded on 03/12/13 from: *www.companieshouse.gov.uk/about/gbhtml/gp3.shtml*

117) Companies House: Annual Return Demo (2012) – a brief and useful guide to filing your company return. What data do you need to submit, when and how? Accessed and downloaded on 02/10/2014 at: *www.youtube.com/watch?v=2bd55GxkhaE*

118) Companies House website (2013), role of a company secretary, accessed and downloaded on 18/02/2015 at:

119) UK Companies Act 2006: Part 20 Private and public companies, ss 755–767

CHAPTER 2: BECOMING A DEVELOPED
SECURITY MANAGER

2.1 Context

"Management is doing things right. Leadership is doing the right things."
– Peter Drucker, management consultant, academic and author.

The actual size of the global security market is difficult to estimate. The British Security Industry Authority recently estimated that the world market for security and fire protection was worth £178.6bn (1). With so many security practitioners bidding for such a variety and volume of work, it is vital that security consultants can genuinely understand and project reassurance that they can deliver an all-encompassing security capability. After all, clients are entrusting them with the safety of their most prized assets: their people.

In order to survive and prosper in dynamic and complex modern operating environments, businesses increasingly seek strategic partnerships. Such synergy will reach deep into their sales channels and supply chains. Moreover, C-suite executives and senior managers often operate under tightening regulatory burdens and extended, strict, legal, economic and reputational parameters. Brand integrity is sacrosanct. In emerging markets, where standards and norms may be under-developed and inconsistent, the strategic and tactical competence of the security function gains enormous significance to the overall corporate health and well-being of an organisation. In many respects, medium-to-high risk security operations draw out the best from security enterprises, as non-security staff look to them for professionalism, reassurance and leadership in an emergency or crisis.

Reassurance and the projection of continuity and unalarmed contingency planning, seems to be a recurring success factor among enterprises that I have seen fair well amid uncertain times of economic crashes, sprawling conflicts, political disorders and natural disasters. The US military came to view the post-Cold War era as a Volatile, Uncertain, Complex and Ambiguous (VUCA) worldwide operating environment (2). Principal sources of threat have moved from being established national alliances and blocs, to rather random, fluid sub-state terror groups (sometimes operating within the haven of a failed state). Security risk uncertainty has been compounded by malfunctions in the economic sphere. By the late 2000s, a deeply wounding worldwide economic crash, precipitated by a wholesale write-down of toxic debt, caused bank crashes and government-led (tax-funded) 'bail-outs'. Moreover, the risk of uncontrolled sovereign debt and its impact on future social order is still ranked highly by the World Economic Forum

Global Risks Report, most principally in Europe and America (3). Yet these same economic factors have prompted the security industry to innovate around technologies and provide more 'intelligence led' working in response to client risk. Risk assessment and prioritisation of risk treatment is now a fundamental, core business management activity.

For clients, a credible security consultant will be required to understand, plan and also skilfully communicate a strategic view of risk. They should have researched the client company to such a point of expertise that they can think laterally about the array of risks and vulnerabilities that challenge their client's overall organisational resilience. Security entrepreneurs will therefore be requested to convey a high degree of reassurance that they are not just subject matter experts in their own field of security risk management, but are corporate business coaches and enablers. It's a lot to prove for somebody who is also a full-time entrepreneur!

2.2 Role of security director

The professionalisation of private sector security services is a phenomenon much commented on in modern times. As a long-serving manager and prominent security author, Charles 'Chuck' Sennewald observed wryly:

"In the past five decades the security function has climbed up from the depths of organisational existence, from dank and smelly basement offices, to the heights of executive offices and a place in the sun. Despite some major downsizing, corporate mergers, and the growing emergence of facilities management and technology replacing some security personnel, security is now viewed as a critical part of most organisations today, with security professionals reporting directly to senior management, if not the chief executive officer" (4). The requirement to meet and surpass an array of proliferating professional standards, protocols and codes of conduct, insurer demands and nascent legislation, has driven up the service level quality of security companies, it has been widely argued.

In addition, there is also a prerequisite for organisations to protect their corporate reputations in challenging media environments, where a negative news story can reach influential audiences – such as potential customers or key stakeholders, including government ministers – within seconds. The performance of any security team, its incumbent professionalism, integrity and utility, therefore does play a significant role in shaping perceptions of entire organisations or sectors. For example, scandals involving private security functions have engulfed most UK oil and defence corporations at some point. This has led to all manner of longer-term resiliency issues, such as frequent site protests, political inquiries and an enduring aura of brand toxicity, in the eyes of important local/regional stakeholders.

Thus, it is fair to say, that few executives sit in a more risky role upon an organisation's central dashboard than the modern day security director. Depending on the organisational structure and grand title, security directors can be relatively low-ranking, on many occasions not a C-suite executive director. Whilst others might report directly into the CEO or sit within the executive board. During a period of perceived 'peacetime', many colleagues will fail to see security functions as anything other than an irritating overhead. Business development, telesales, marketing and invoicing are all visible financial engines that drive businesses forward. On quiet days and weeks, when (ironically) the often-invisible but busy hand of security has actually delivered on its pledge to create a secure workplace, many outside executives will inevitably view security functions as a drag upon the business.

Nevertheless, during major threats and incidents, the security team will gain prominence. Utilisation and professionalism by the wider business will be demanded from every quarter. The *observable* skill of a security function's response will be assessed and hopefully well received. There will be clearer exposure of the sheer scale of prior planning involved in crisis management to non-security employees. Staff will be seeking reassurance and many will become professionally and emotionally dependent on the security function.

Thus, the security director operates under twin pressures. They need to put in place a security strategy that prevents loss to the business and much of this hard work is invisible, because successful security measures often remain unseen. Yet a security director will also position themselves to become a master of value-added services, nudging their company to an overall state of improved organisational resilience. In effect, an effective security director becomes the ambassador for overall security-related resilience issues across the whole business. That's quite an imposing level of personal and departmental responsibility.

Whatever an organisation's shape or structure, the security director "should not be viewed narrowly as a unique security specialist but rather as an effective executive (first) in the security field (second)", says Sennewald (5). As a senior manager, they are effectively a company leader, a strategic planner and departmental/management goal setter (6).

Security entrepreneurs will often be bidding for business along a dotted procurement line into an organisation's security director. An external security consultant should carefully research and map-out the client's organisational structure, culture, key players and stakeholders. After all, they are entrusting contractors with their own colleagues' welfare and their own immediate career reputation.

There will be an expectation of a security director that potential consultants and contractors have done this necessary groundwork. However, decent online researchers beware! Organisational structure maps (sometimes called 'organograms') are often static, one-dimensional and outdated. They rarely give the necessary context or colour in order to help external contractors confidently approach security directors for new business. Further research around the ethos and interests of leading executives and target markets is well advised, before compiling a business proposal. Harvard Business Review management analyst, Bob Frisch, points to the importance of understanding that in each larger enterprise a de facto 'kitchen cabinet' exists; a small coterie of people who work closely with the CEO or executive chairman who take the lead in most major decision making within the target company (7). Before any presentational pitch, or meeting with company executives, an advanced security consultant will diligently conduct market research and specific analysis around an organisation's security risks, but also try to establish the main motivations or goals of its executive leadership. This enables the external consultant to step into the shoes of potential buyers and understand how they might be able to assist their clients to achieve their objectives. Even if business is not won on the day, this intelligence-led business development approach will bring in longer-term results in terms of reputation and corporate muscle memory.

Case studies in business management

Two cases below illustrate that major corporations can be as different as night and day in terms of purpose, vision, operation and aspiration. Spend some time reading each case study and consider how you might organise the role of security director should you be offered the role:

Case study 1: Royal Dutch Shell Group (RDSG)
A hybrid of two mergers at the 20th century's beginning, gave birth to RDSG, one of the world's foremost oil 'super majors'. In part due to its corporate heritage and evolution, RDSG implements a decentralised, confederated organisational structure, based upon autonomy for independent operating companies. The Committee of Managing Directors forms the Group's top executive team drawn from the chairman and vice-chairman of two original parent companies: Royal Dutch Petroleum Co and Shell Transport and Trading Co plc. The overall group is truly international, comprising of more than 200 operating companies, regional headquarters and service companies. During the 1970s, due to falling crude oil prices and depressed margins, RDSG diversified beyond petroleum.

RDSG is organisationally complex and fragmented due to its structural heritage. Its ethos and decentralised autonomy granted to operating companies, does enable the

---

group to legitimately claim its place at the elite of forward-looking strategic planning. RDSG achieves this by nurturing and adopting 20 year planning horizons. This is in stark contrast to the more usual four to five year business plans at other major companies. RDSG also expresses pride in cultivating cross-organisational learning. RDSG's governance, executive and service functions were taken through a major restructure in 1996 by the then group chairman, Cor Herkstroter, President of Royal Dutch. This change was actioned in order to reduce waste and replication, and also to improve overall group coordination across more than 100,000 employees. Nevertheless, because executive power "was vested in a committee rather than a single chief executive", the company "lacked the strong individual leadership that characterised other majors" (8). This somewhat remote and opaque structure is credited with a 'flat-footed and inept' response to the Brent Spar publicity debacle, when Shell UK planned to dump an empty, disused oil storage facility in deep Atlantic waters, west of Scotland, in 1995. Moreover, the execution of writer and environmentalist campaigner, Ken Saro-Wiwa, by the Nigerian state military, also in 1995, led to violent protests against Shell worldwide. Saro-Wiwa had fought against oil waste dumps and environmental degradation by the multinational petroleum industry including RDSG. Nearly two decades on, both crises cast a shadow over RDSGs international reputation and fuel particular sensitivities in west Africa (9).

Case study 2: Walmart Stores Inc
Walmart was founded by Sam Walton of Arkansas, US, who espoused a folksy and homespun business ethos with the advent of his discount stores in the 1960s. His central leadership philosophies still underpin Walmart, the world's largest retail colossus, several years after his passing. Walton's stated vision includes demonstrating 'respect of the individual' and staff are termed business 'associates' and allocated stockholdings. Customers are entitled to friendly, accessible shops with the 'lowest prices' and 'best possible service'. Walton insisted that his stores should "strive for excellence" with new ideas (10). Early on, Walmart challenged American retail orthodoxy by building its stores near towns with lower population clusters and also constructing its own storage and distribution centres that could serve several stores within one day. It had previously been thought that 'supermarkets' could only survive near clusters of 100,000 residents or more. Walton also took supply chain resilience seriously. He ordered that no supplier should be responsible for more than 2.5% of Walmart's customer offering. Customer service and decentralisation of store management was paramount. Because of this, Walton insisted that all senior executives spent the working week at their frontline business operation. They were rotated frequently to build-up knowledge capital and maintain motivation.

By 2003, Walmart topped the *Fortune Global 500* list as the world's largest company and biggest private sector employer at 1.4 million employees (11). Sales from *Walmart stores*, *Sam's Clubs* (warehouse stores), international operations and *McLane Company Inc* (distribution company), reached $260bn in 2004. Because it modelled its strategy and management style on Walmart, UK retailer, Asda, was successfully acquired by Walmart several years ago. Not all of Walmart's international operations have been embedded without glitches. "We built large parking lots at some of our Mexican stores only to realise that many of our customers there rode the bus to the store, then trudged across these large parking lots carrying bags of merchandise ..." reported John Menzer, head of Walmart's international division (12). The company claims to work smarter after these teething lessons to avoid mistakes induced by cultural and geographic misunderstandings.

Despite being the world's largest retailer, the company footprint is only substantial in a handful of countries (US, Canada, Mexico, UK, Germany (with supercentres only)) and is making headway into emerging markets elsewhere including China. The size and scale of Walmart's purchasing power is vast, therefore its buying price negotiating ability is 'both desired and feared' by suppliers. According to business analyst, Robert M Grant, "Wal-Mart buyers are well aware of their ability to take full advantage of economies of scale available to their suppliers and to squeeze their margins to [a] razor-thin level" (13). Indeed, product purchasing is the one core business area of Walmart that appears highly centralised, with all stock-buying decisions made by gruelling interview processes with procurement experts at the company's Bentonville headquarters.

Shrinkage (theft) is reportedly low at Walmart's stores; this is mainly credited to a store bonus scheme where all store associates (staff) receive extra pay for tackling and preventing store crime. Although Walmart's company ethos appears superficially traditionalist and folksy, its integrated marketing and IT strategies are exceptionally efficient in order to maximise the customer experience and exploit new markets. The company was a pioneer in the 1970s of electronic data interchange (EDI) with its vendors, and bought its own two-way, interactive private satellite network in 1984, with voice and video transmission and credit card authorisation. Since 1990 the company has efficiently used ICT for 'data mining', to ensure that "the right item [is] in the right store at the right price" (14). In comparison to any competition that Walmart may have, the company spends a fraction of its revenues on media advertising. In the past, under Walton's leadership, the company promoted patriotic causes and launched a 'Buy American' programme during President Reagan's term at the White House. Although Walmart is a strong international buyer, it sources supplies from low-cost economies, including around \$15bn of imports per year from China (15). During recent times, Walmart has attracted the ire of 'Occupy' protest campaign activists, mainly in the US. Meanwhile, the resonance of Sam Walton's 'lowest possible price, highest possible quality' mantra – synchronised with the proficiency of its supply chain management and data analysis capabilities – all serve Walmart's strategic ambitions well, even after a sustained period of economic austerity.

2.4 Fitting security into a wider context of resilience

"... we live in a brittle society where threats and natural hazards are more frequent and intense than a decade ago." – Charlie Edwards, *Resilient Nation* (16)

So far, in this chapter, we have taken a closer look at two multinational companies, considered the complex role of security director, and broadly established that security management is an unpredictable and expansive responsibility that moves fluidly like an ink spillage, into many outlying domains of organisational resilience. Most notably, security has much synergy with functions that are also responsible for emergency planning, business continuity, risk management and information assurance.

The security function can act as an organisational shock absorber which can prevent a negative incident morphing into wider crisis or contagion. Therefore, much professional focus nowadays centres around how well the modern security professional can understand, and proficiently plan for wider issues that have a strong likelihood of impacting wider organisational resilience issues. Security staff at every level should see themselves as the company's eyes and ears, attuned to the overall welfare and progress of the organisation.

What is resilience? Before we progress further, it is worth spending a little time considering this sector buzzword. This is because understanding the emerging discipline of organisational resilience is so intrinsically important, in order to attain respect and sustain a solid reputation, particularly after the 9/11 terrorist atrocities in New York.

Several years ago, the think-tank DEMOS established an advisory group of corporate and public sector emergency planners to consider what was meant by *resilience*. DEMOS then produced an influential pamphlet, *Resilient Nation*. The publication identified various international case studies of good practice and generated much interest from policy-makers and practitioners. The project advisory group defined resilience as: "The capacity of an individual, community or system to adapt in order to sustain an acceptable level of function, structure, and identity" (17). The sector is now drenched in competing definitions. Sutcliffe and Vogus describe resilience as, "the maintenance of positive adjustment under challenging conditions" (18). While academic, Alastair McAslan, offers that resilience is the "ability of something or someone to cope in the face of adversity – to recover and return to normaility after confronting an abnormal, alarming, and often unexpected threat" (19).

The DEMOS report confirmed thinking among many security and emergency planning professionals that it was impossible to, "expect the emergency services to arrive in an instant during the event of a major disaster". The report stated on its cover page that ... "next generation resilience relies on citizens and communities, not the institutions of state ..." (20). This grassroots thinking chimed more with the US Federal Government model, which emphasises local empowerment and resourcing. In the US, emergency planning is rooted in county and state-level agencies and power is passed upwards towards Federal Government. Although this procedure has rapidly altered with the creation of the Department for Homeland Security (DHS) and the Federal Emergency Management Agency (FEMA) after the 9/11 terrorist atrocities. The National Infrastructure Advisory Council (NIAC), which reports into the DHS, issued a *Critical Infrastructure Resilience* report in 2009 which stated:

"… the challenge facing government is to maintain its role in protecting critical infrastructures, while determining how best to encourage market forces to improve the resilience of companies, provide appropriate incentives and tools (including national standards) to help entire sectors become resilient, and step in when market forces alone cannot produce the level of security needed to protect citizens, communities and essential economic systems" (21).

The thrust of government and official thinking is that private organisations should take the lead on emergency preparedness and start 'expecting the unexpected' as business group London First recommended in their well-received business continuity pamphlet, by the same name, issued to corporations in partnership with the UK National Counter Terrorism Security Office (NaCTSO) and BCI several years ago (22). Moreover, with cutbacks to government budgets impacting heavily on fire and rescue, policing and defence departments across most major economies since the global financial crash, the sphere of organisational resilience has become, potentially, a greater and wider source of income for security consultancies than was envisaged a couple of decades ago.

So how can we plan for resilience? Decent team organisation by way of clear lines of authority, clear tasking, mutual trust, accessible hierarchies (to report problems), and transparent goals, all continue to be successful management values that underpin flourishing security enterprises. For most organisations, a potential slip-up by a security-tasked employee is a significant key point of failure, both in terms of asset and reputational loss. Thus, specific training, instruction and a consistent goal of *surpassing* compliance – rather than merely achieving it – are all vital ingredients to a successful organisational security function. Some of the job and task roles will be as follows: *security manager; assistant security manager; building security; investigators; asset protection; fraud prevention; asset tracking; security guarding; close protection officers and team leaders; loss prevention and inspection; control room operators; undercover agents; CCTV and surveillance officers.* But the modern reality is that most security operatives could conceivably carry out other security functions; they are not mono-trained or solely interested in a single business area. Substantial security professionalism is more a mindset, than a trade. All security professionals are expected in the modern era to actively absorb, understand and ultimately translate an array of corporate security risks, which may well start out as harmless intangibles, but if left ignored or mishandled, can cause severe organisational damage in the longer run.

2.5 Sub-disciplines of organisational resilience: Security, emergency planning and business continuity

Much has been written about the convergence or closer integration of security-related functions within enterprise organisations during the past two decades. Some of this has been driven by ICT and the importance of addressing cyber/information security because all such risks interrelate and interact. The industry trend has been towards a closer synthesising of, or even indeed, the formal integration of security with emergency planning (EP) and business continuity management (BCM). These three speheres have become accepted in many quarters as the core-subdisciplines of *organisational resilience* (23). Business continuity is a diverse and widely debated concept. Helpfully, the *Business Continuity Institute* website describes BC as: "taking reponsibility for your business and enabling it to stay on course whatever storms it is forced to weather" (24). For most academics and practitioners, BC is more about keeping an organisation at maximised levels of resilience. BCM professionals do this by addressing the impacts of major disruptions in a planned manner (hopefully beforehand), rather than forensically analysing future threats or causes of risk. The integration of these three disciplines in the workplace has been addressed in some companies by creating broader resilience or risk management portfolios. In many companies, during recent times, such resiliency job roles have been pushed upwards in the organisational structure, into the echelons of upper middle management, or even to executive director levels. Security company, G4S, kindly hosted a high-level roundtable discussion on the topic of *Organisational Resilience,* shortly before the London 2012 Olympics and Paralympics. Out of 15 major companies in attendance, more than half of those represented held job titles that indicated responsibility for organisational resilience, in contrast to traditional functions of security (25).

On the downside, the integration of EP, BCM and security remains a hotly contested, and unresolvable marriage of convenience in many larger companies. Duplication and territorial tensions can be commonplace, even if an overarching director of resilience, or equivalent, is in place. Integration of enteprise risk management functions has also invariably led to efficiencies and a sense that some executive leadership teams have used the integration of security, BC and EP functions to cut overall risk management resources which could stretch the finite bandwith of security management to breaking point. To do *more with less* may well be a modern workplace mantra. Moreover, sometimes it is actually poor work practices or ambivalent business cultures, rather than a lack of resources that can undermine organisational resilience, or a company's ability to adapt quickly enough to unfolding threats.

Some major organisational failures during contemporary times do powerfully demonstrate that large organisations which have experienced significant crises have often deployed substantial resources into so-called risk management strategies. Yet they were either unable to realise the scale of hazard occuring before them, or were institutionally incapable of adapting to avoid or mitigate it. For example, academic, Geary Sikich, points to oil-major BP being stuck in an 'activity trap', where the company was unable to free itself from traditional patterns of process and behaviour, both prior to, and after, the 2010 Deepwater Horizon disaster. The company suffered huge reputational damage, and fines totalling several billion dollars, after a dozen oil platform workers were killed on a subsidiary platform in the Gulf of Mexico and billions of gallons of oil were poured into the marine environment. Moreover, in the cash-rich telecommunications sector, following a fire at a components factory in Alburquerce, US, the manufacturer, Philips, notified its main customers, Nokia and Ericsson. Nokia immediately sourced alternative components and effectively tied up the contingency market. Confidently believing that its own organisation was resilient, and that the problem at Philips would soon be fixed, Ericsson's leadership failed to respond and sourced no alternatives in the first week. When the Swedish company finally attempted to locate back-up alternatives, few were to be found. Ericsson were unable to carry out new product launches and the company made 16bn Krona ($1.5bn) of losses later that year. It has, to date, struggled to recapture its dominant market share. Indeed, when we reflected on the Royal Dutch Shell Group's troubles in the 1990s, several pages ago, official reports do not indicate that the company experienced the Brent Spar and Ken Saro-Wiwa crises because it was starved of cash and resources. Financial resources were aplenty. Common sense less so, perhaps.

As McAslan contends: "Resilience also suggests an ability and willingness to adapt over time to a changing and potentially threatening environment" (26).

In essence, measures to embed and strengthen resilience do clearly include market and threat analysis, prior crisis planning (including life-like rehearsals), regular monitoring and auditing of risk management systems, legal compliance and competent crisis response. These are rather obvious ingredients that most of us know and delight in practising and talking about. But there is so much more meaning to the term *organisational resilience*. It is a mindset, a company culture and a team awareness dynamic within any company ... from the receptionist, to the top floor C-suite executive.

2.6 Management and balancing important priorities

There is sometimes frustration with management theories and 'number crunchers' in any setting, and the security management sphere is hardly any different. But regardless of our own personal leadership traits and workplace approaches, the setting and organisation of strategies, department priorities, policies and crisis management plans, will usually require the approval and buy-in of colleagues and stakeholders who are not strongly related or connected to security management approaches and concepts.

There is no single panacea for security management. No dominant rule book. Shelves of books, toolkits, formal guidance and articles from practitioners and researchers have been produced; each with different nuances and emphases. Just a fraction of these appear in this book's reference sections at the end of each chapter. Nevertheless, these documents do have at least one common denominator. They are all produced from the worldview of their author. Indeed, the recipients and clients of your security strategies are equally as diverse. They may well have a knowledge gap at a technical level about security management, but they will have their own perceptions, life experiences and career skills that may well inform some strong counter-views to what your department hopes to achieve. With many security products and services often invisible to busy end-users, security practitioners might want to be extra alert to the fact that data sets (such as service level agreements being surpassed) really can evidence success. Credible and favourable statistics carry great importance when convincing clients of the benefits of hiring or retaining your services.

From the client's perspective, they will be seeking a measurable return on investment (ROI) from their security functions. It's worth security consultants' bearing in mind that there may also be some additional pressure on their own client, who may themselves have had to argue persuasively with other work colleagues in order to reach outside the organisation to bring in extra layers of security. "ROI must be communicated clearly at all times by all security contractors", says Jon Hill, managing director of close protection solutions company, Polaris. "My client is not just the security director at a given organisation, but his boss, his executive team and his CEO, who come into contact with my staff day in and day out (27). If things go quiet, they need to know that they are not pouring money down a drain by retaining us", Hill concluded.

There are several ideas by security contractors to provide reassurance to customers that they are sustaining value for money. Interim feedback reports can be submitted to clients with auditable and transparently presented customer feedback data. For longer-term contracts, the client will often stipulate service level agreements (SLAs), and if this isn't the case, security contractors shouldn't be shy to ask for such parameters. Far from being a 'rod for their own back', SLAs can provide a structured framework to actively demonstrate achievements and competence by the contractor or entrepreneur. Measurables, including key performance indicators (KPIs), can also assist individual consultants; a 360 degree appraisal of performance areas, success criteria and a restatement of the client's goals, are likely to assist both sides in the longer-run. Too many security contracts still fall foul of (often unwritten) agreements and ad hoc relationships which can then offer no defence against service termination by the client. This is because the contractor never bothered to establish what the client's goals and success criteria were in the first place.

For the security manager or consultant, service delivery data can be measured in a number of ways. For example, by visibly reducing the loss of quantifiable assets across specific business areas, or the entire business itself. In addition, security managers and function heads might also be able to reduce annual expenditure on related expenditure, such as reducing legal costs, the downtime of IT systems, or perceptible increases in customer satisfaction or site visitor reassurance.

Calculating loss and showing value

Perhaps the best way to illustrate the financial value of a security function is to tabularise the loss (shrinkage) to the business from criminal activity. Deal in hard data, build on trend analysis, establish patterns and set realistic targets. If no such data exists, carry out comparative analysis at similar venues or other company branches, but be crystal clear with so-called comparative analysis that you are – to all intents and purposes – performing a very useful baseline illusion. After all, you don't want the company leadership getting carried away by setting unrealistic goals and holding over-inflated expectations!

For example, in Figure 8 below, we are going to take the average retail shrinkage in the UK (of 1.37% recorded in 2011, according to the BRC) and apply it to some imagined profit and loss (P&L) figures for an invented company we've named *Buckinghamshire Food Malls Inc*. We can actually calculate loss by researching any type of quantifiable loss metrics that would be comparable to performance measurements being gathered in any other business department or enterprise. Some examples being: trading days lost, unit jobs lost, cash loss, and so on.

Trading year	SALES (£)	Shrinkage	P/L Loss £m	Trading days lost	Unit staff loss (50K)
2012/13	1bn	1%	10	3	200
2013/14	1bn	1.37%	13.7	4	274

Figure 8: Imagined shrinkage of Buckinghamshire Food Malls Inc.

To explain; if Buckinghamshire Food Malls Inc had reduced its shrinkage by 0.5% in 2012/13, it would have made another £5m in gross profit. If, at first, to achieve this extra profit the company had to invest in four full-time security staff, and some upgraded CCTV and motion detection equipment (the whole package costing some £2m), then the company would have made an additional £3m profit *because* of investment into the security function. Moreover, further security personnel and systems could have reduced shrinkage even further during the next financial year (2013/14). If the security management function within a business can evidence, calculate and communicate clear data sets in terms of loss prevention, then they can begin to earn acceptance across a wider organisational culture that they do offer a tangible and potentially significant corporate return on investment (ROI). Could a sales or marketing department generate £3m in profits each year? It's a moot point but the mathematics described above does provide a tangible basis for many security management functions to demonstrate clear value to the bottom line of many companies.

Case study: UK Foreign Office number crunchers: I'm not a number, I'm a free man!

The business guru, Adam Gordon, wrote in his book *Future Savvy* (2009): "For better or worse, quantitative analysis has become the authoritative form of knowledge ... economics, once an area of social analysis, has become a field of turbo-maths, while management academics produce papers that more closely resemble particle physics than anything real managers actually do" (28).

In his book *Getting Our Way,* seasoned diplomat, Sir Christopher Meyer, ex-UK Ambassador to the US, provides a different perspective. Meyer turned his attention to a final despatch of Sir Ivor Roberts, an outgoing ambassador to Italy, who sent the following gripe to Britain's Foreign Secretary:

"The culture of change has reached Cultural Revolution proportions ... Can it be that in wading through the plethora of business plans, capability reviews, skills audits, zero-based reviews ... we have forgotten what diplomacy is all about? ... Why have we failed so significantly to explain to the likes of the Cabinet Secretary that well-conducted diplomacy cannot properly be measured ... ? We manage or contain disputes; very rarely do we deliver a quantifiable solution" (29).

In summary, accepting and deploying the utility of explicit key measurables (data sets) by embracing business quantification methods, will undoubtedly give any security company the competitive edge. But each success story does require further communication to the client; because spreadsheets and algorithms hardly sell themselves! Security contractors that engage with data, yet can also translate it as an engaging narrative, will notice that others begin to receive the correct message: namely, that their company think from the client's standpoint and make their return on investment the number one priority.

Security leadership and management

Charles A Sennewald's popular book, *Effective Security Management*, provides an excellent list of security management tasks. These include

- talks to employees
- giving direction to lower level supervisors
- establishing loss prevention goals
- planning new loss prevention programmes
- hiring new security officers
- reading reports
- attending meetings (logical ways to coordinate and set activity)
- making decisions about new equipment (30).

Sennewald then describes five managerial functions:

1. *Planning:* "Determining future activities necessarily involves a conceptual ... look ahead and a recognition of needed future actions – whether they be tomorrow or next year. It involves looking forward, conceptualising future events, and making decisions today that will affect tomorrow ... The higher the level of management, the more time is spent planning."
2. *Organising*: "Determining what activities need to be done; grouping and assigning those activities; delegating the necessary authority to subordinates to carry out the activities in a co-ordinated manner."
3. *Directing:* "The managerial function deals directly with influencing, guiding or supervising subordinates in their jobs."
4. *Coordinating:* It is the manager's job to ensure that the various tasks are scheduled and implemented in an efficient and economical manner."
5. *Controlling:* "... consists of forcing the tasks that have been undertaken to confirm to prearranged plans. Thus planning is necessary control" (31).

For Sennewald, the potential achievement of leadership, from senior managers through to supervisors, is contingent on an individual's realistic 'span of control'. This is a human resource management concept which translates the amount of employees that a supervisor can effectively manage at any given time. With ICT advances, and a corporate shift to cross-functional teams, traditional spans of control have shifted from an ideal low ratio (1:4 supervisor to employee, or less), to higher (read busier) ratios. It follows that managers with larger empires will be less able to successfully perform in other management functions. Sennewald believes that the most obvious ingredient of a successful manager is that they "should be able to think clearly and purposefully about a problem" (32). Other factors impact upon an ability to exercise supervision over a challenging span of control including the types of job roles under supervision (including the attendant risk levels), the level of administrative support, the experience and competence of subordinates, and the location of subordinates or the supervising manager. The following spans of control are recommended as either good or survivable by Sennewald:

- ideal: 1:3
- good: 1:6
- acceptable: 1:12.

Summary of security management leadership

Perhaps then, the key to being an advanced security consultant revolves a lot around decent research, performance recording and active lines of accurate feedback to customers. Research, ask, and be confident to ask for clarification again from customers: what are their longer-term goals? What, in the best case scenario, do they want from their chosen security provider? From your research, are there realistic cost savings that you could make, on their behalf, by implementing your innovations and solutions?

Moreover, manage expectations and be realistic from the outset. A cold call for security from an unknown quantity often comes at a time of organisational crisis. It could be a knee-jerk response to an incident, or a perceived serious security breach.

Security procurement can be an emotionally-driven, volatile buying environment, whereby potential customers run hot and then turn cold; especially when a crisis cools down. At all times, be careful to offer a proportionate response, based on what is best for the client organisation. Consider how your suggested solutions will be viewed a little further down the timeline. (Defence Secretary, Bob McNamara, called this form of pragmatic, cool-headed response the 'daylight test'.) Don't let the heat of the moment determine your company's future fate. This will reinforce your company's reputation as objective, rational, and a potential long-term counsel to the client.

For me, the advanced security professional, or aspirant security director, could do worse than to aim to satisfy the following conditions summarised by my bleak, but memorable, mnemonic: **RAIN**:

Resilient; personally resilient; strong team player, coordinator and trusting delegator; succession planner; good communicator and contingency planner; keen to test, rehearse and review.

Adaptive; flexible and innovative but has agility based on wisdom; lateral thinking around risk and threat; respectful orthodoxy challenger yet a student of traditional activity; unafraid to articulate unprecedented actions and innovations; yet strongly educated in existing good practice and context.

Informed; well briefed and ahead of events; builds credible and robust information sources and feedback loops; core member of the wider business; rooted in a knowledge of good practice and laws; a keen reviewer; an avaricious listener at all staff and customer levels.

Networked; can access and appreciate 'outside' advice; confident and popular networker; turns contacts into meaningful mutual aid and information sources; ambassador for the business within the sector; confident to share key contacts; not an aggressive pursuer of *quid pro quo*.

2.7 Adding value: Developing the business that clients require

"If you want to be a millionaire, start with a billion dollars and launch a new airline." – Sir Richard Branson, entrepreneur and chairman of Virgin group of companies

If entrepreneurs don't always know what their potential customers really want, then it may be true to say that on many occasions customers also don't know what they require either! That is why it is so important to understand as much as possible about what they do require and why. The diverse range of security services and products can often appear quite intimidating or off-putting to outside buyers. Solutions to combat crime and treat risks are sometimes complicated and built upon compromise; to adjust to civilian working environments and fluctuating market conditions. Moreover, when security planning is at its weakest – perhaps when we are implementing things on the back-foot, in a reactive sense – a proper, reflective, cost benefit analysis process might only occur well after a major incident has occurred. Therefore, it is not untypical for buyer motivation to quickly evaporate. Security solutions are increasingly complex and integrated – they fuse together human, physical and technological ingredients – and impact upon most, if not all, corporate departments. The development and integration of major security activities and systems, such as the rolling out of access controls across a multi-sited corporation, can be large-scale and project-based. They are also likely to cause disruption. After some time, key influencers within the client organisation may have significantly cooled towards the project. Progress and client-value should be demonstrated at all times during implementation of a security project. Moreover, leadership and management are increasingly mobile in modern corporate environments, so beware: it may be that your initial buyers and sponsors have already left the building!

At this point, let's try to step into your customer's shoes. For a moment we will consider individual human cognitive responses to major emergencies. Psychological analysis tends to demonstrate more impulsive and/or accelerated decision making, and survivalist family groupthink, as the first phase of psychological response. Leading psychologist, Daniel Kahneman, and others, have dubbed 'instinctive' decision making as a 'system one' response (34). Then a gradual slow-down in decision making occurs as the mind begins to relax, reflect and analyse the recent experience. This is described by Kahneman as 'system two' of cognitive decision making. Psychologists refer to this phenomenon of binary decision making as dual process theory. In colloquial terms, this equates to the mind responding and activating instinctively in a survivalist mode of urgency. Then we humans experience a 'cooling down period'. We begin to consider some isomorphic lessons in relation to our experience, in order to make clear sense of what we have been through, and why. Therefore, the remainder of this section will address how entrepreneurs can better understand, motivate and retain present customers. We also offer various suggestions as to how one may become the next Sir Richard Branson or Bill Gates! Paul Schoemaker, a research director at the world-renowned Wharton Business School, contends that business development professionals really need to get into the 'head' of their customers (35).

Stand in your customer's shoes – look beyond your core business and understand your customer's full range of choices.

Staple yourself to a customer order – carry out 'secret shopper' type exercises or role-play scenarios, to fully respect your customer's experience of your services.

Learn together with customers – run seminars and knowledge share on issues of common interest, such as leadership and management (as GE did in China).

Lean forward and anticipate – try to envision what the future looks like, perhaps through tools, such as 'scenario planning'.

Figure 9: Schoemaker's top tips: Think as your customers would

Communications with any customer base require several types of approach based around principles of: visibility, partnership, ethics and empathy. Long-term market considerations should be firmly rooted in your short-term behaviour. These are sometimes difficult strategies to achieve. As business coach J Haselmaier emphasises, some customers are not always clear in their own minds as to precisely what solution it is that they require. By asking the key question, 'what is it, precisely, that you feel you need?', the power of the purchaser can substantially shift to the entrepreneur; who is ultimately a little like a family doctor that needs to treat an anxious patient with a remedy. According to Haselmaier: "Unfortunately, determining the real needs of a potential customer is not as simple as asking them what they want. Many people are unable to clearly articulate their most pressing and compelling product or service requirements …". Hasselmaier adds: "To learn what your customer really needs, you must watch them and talk with them. You must be sure you understand their concerns and overall business issues. Only by thoroughly understanding the broad environment your customer lives in on a day-to-day basis, as well as their specific and detailed issues and concerns, can you apply the creative efforts necessary to design a compelling solution that will be successful".

To be clear: customers often don't know what they want. Indeed, there are copious amounts of excellent online guidance for entrepreneurs and consultants seeking a little help to understand customer relations. Nevertheless, to some consultants, there is possibly a perception of weakness given by way of asking questions from their customers. Moreover, some potential customers choose to be neutral and stand-offish from suppliers nowadays; such are the levels of compliance and probity enforced by many procurement environments. In addition, how often can we realistically ask for customer advice and feedback? Won't we look foolish or lose our sense of authority? Could we waste valuable time and resources unpicking popular solutions that work well with other similar customers? These are all sensible questions to which there can be no instructive answers from this author, other than to say that is down to the entrepreneur to know (research) their specific market, customer and range of product options well enough in order to answer these questions. It is, of course, far better to ask all the right questions from the outset, rather than provide a cupboard-full of wrong answers further down the line.

Earlier in this book, we spent a little time looking at business analysis of the operating environment. We looked at gathering competitive intelligence and market intelligence. We used popular business analysis research tools, including PESTLE and SWOT modelling. Such tools are critical in enabling us to understand market trends and common themes that are driving, or reducing, customer demand. It is fair to say that some of the best researchers I know are also – not by coincidence – some of the best entrepreneurs that I know. These are the people that have taken regular time to investigate and monitor their own operating environment, as a good doctor might fully appraise a wheezing patient. Those who travel by autopilot will only be able to fly so fast and so high for a limited amount of time. As Sir Richard Branson recently told *Forbes Magazine*: "Researching the competition has never been the Virgin way. Many of our products and services come about because we pay attention to what the market is missing or what's not being done well" (37).

Case study: The product lifecycle explained

Accepted by many business management analysts are the very important notions of *industry* and *product lifecycles*. Several decades ago, Harvard Business School analyst, RP Rumelt, measured and reported on increased diversification practices by Fortune 500 companies (38). Some further prominent work on diversification followed. Drawing together studies from the US corporate sector during the 1970s and early 1980s, Galbraith and Kazanjian reported:

> *"Present competitive conditions coupled with the restructuring of several major industries has forced firms to reassess their current product-market position. In some instances, firms have been pushed toward a strategy of diversification. This is typically the case with single-business or dominant business-firms that find themselves at the mature stage of the industry lifecycle".* (39)

According to Harvard professor, Michael Porter: "The hypothesis is that an industry passes through a number of phases or stages – introduction, growth, maturity and decline". (40)

With the expansion of trade liberalisation and e-commerce, industry and product lifecycles may be shortening. Corporate success is certainly more dependent on innovation, adaptability and information security/assurance, coupled with demonstrable capacities of continuity and contingency, in order to deal with latent global risks; man-made or otherwise.

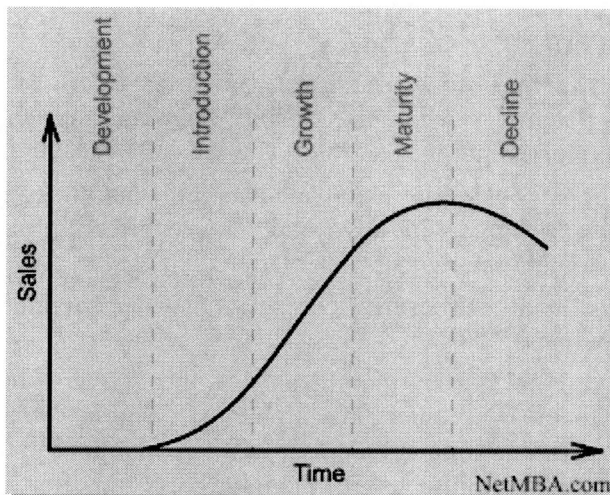

Figure 10: Industry/product lifecycle explained

Sourced from website: ideaelevator.co

How can we Identify client requirements?

To summarise, how might we identify precisely what our existing or potential customers require? Here are some actionable ideas that may help your enterprise to harness its competitive edge:

Focus groups: a facilitator, or two, conducts a small focused audience through a list of quantitative, semi-structured and qualitative questions. This method is particularly useful for organisations with a high public profile which often attracts large volumes of multi-themed feedback. Groups are also effective for assessing emotions and initial responses.

Surveys and data mining: effective for gaining trend analysis or even gap analysis, where you suspect operations are going awry, or perhaps higher potential demand is not being met. Analysts, Symphony IRI, run 100,000-strong 'customer networks' for Walmart, whereby the conglomerate's suppliers, and aspirant suppliers, can view and purchase consumer analysis (42).

'Secret Shopper' and 'Undercover Boss': experience your own service in the 'first hand' by attending the front-line customer experience anonymously and passively. For further information, watch an episode of *Undercover Boss* – there are popular editions in the UK and US. There are many to choose from but one of my favourites is a Securitas CEO returning to the shop-floor and a university Chancellor in California stepping into the shoes of campus staff and employees. Both episodes are provided in our references section at the end of this chapter (43).

Knowledge sharing and leadership: by running briefings and seminars for clients and potential customers; absorb learning and capture data from interactive exercises into the sessions.

Feedback loops: operating social media platforms and website forums, or closed feedback forums with key stakeholders, to feed in innovative ideas or feedback customer experiences/observations.

Competitions: run purposeful competitions to generate new ideas and customer pipelines.

Marketing partnerships: running any of the above – including industry events – in tandem with others in your supply chain or channel sales partners to the wider market. Trade associations are often looking to badge themselves with partner events because it saves them the costs and effort of delivering their own event. By doing this, your enterprise will get a guaranteed larger audience and extra credibility of working with an established trade association.

Unique sales proposition

Now that we know a) our market environment and b) our potential customers better, entrepreneurs may wish to now consider what it is about our people and our services that make *us* essential to *them*? How can we convince them of the benefits of accepting our proposals? How can we help them to achieve their goals and make their commercial journey easier?

Amid so much good online and published guidance for entrepreneurs and business development executives, the UK Business Link and the Canadian Business Network is clear and purposeful. Companies are advised to develop and continuously remind their employees about their unique approaches and products. Their guidance states: "Every business needs a reason for their customers to buy from them and not their competitors. This is called a *Unique Sales Proposition* (USP). Your USP can be identified by completing the phrase 'Customers will buy from me because my business is the only'" ... (43).

An example might be that you are the only company to only employ former Special Forces personnel, or that you were the first company to insist that all your maritime security operatives possessed an International Certificate of Competence for skippering a vessel. Nevertheless, it is important to appraise the uniqueness and value of your USP regularly because security industry markets do move exceedingly fast. What began as a USP not so long ago, may have subsequently morphed into standard, expected, industry practice and appear somewhat stale.

Please note, your USP should change as your business or your market changes. And you can have different USPs for different types of customer. "However good your product or service is, the simple truth is that no-one will buy it if they don't want it or believe they don't need it. And you won't persuade anyone that they want or need to buy what you're offering, unless you clearly understand what it is your customers really want", observes the Canada Business Network (45).

2.8 Why do businesses fail?

Many business start-ups fail within the first 12 months. According to the US *Small Business Administration,* more than 50% of small businesses fail within five years (46). Corporate analyst, Michael Ames, gives the following reasons for small business failure in his important book *Small Business Management*:

- Lack of experience
- Insufficient capital (money)
- Poor location
- Poor inventory management

- Over-investment in fixed assets
- Poor credit arrangements
- Personal use of business funds
- Unexpected growth (47).

Professor Edward Deming, one of the world's most eminent management consultants, famously identified 'five diseases of management'. Deming was credited with helping to substantially rebuild Japan's broken economy after World War Two, contributing with management thought that enabled the country to become the world's second most powerful economy within a decade. Deming urged that manufacturers cooperate over wider market and economy-related issues; that marketing is the science of understanding what repeat customers think; and that initial stages of services and design must include research. Deming's five diseases of management are described below, courtesy of the excellent business website *Mindtools.com*:

1. No consistent purpose: strategy and goals continuously change. Prior strategies and initiatives are not given time to succeed. Staff morale declines as employees feel that they can't achieve objectives.
2. Focus on short-term profits: companies focus on short-term growth and sales at the expense of longer-term projects and therefore fail to anticipate future growth and see the end of market and product cycles.
3. Managing by fear: whereby employees focus only on short-term goals and avoiding sanctions; rather than having managers that approach appraisals by coaching, empathy and identifying opportunities for employee development.
4. High senior management turnover: it takes time for managers to develop and embed into their role and to develop the relationships and authority that will be necessary for them, and their department, to succeed. High turnover permeates down into the mindset of all employees, impacting retention across the organisation. It can also seriously risk the transfer and leakage of critical knowledge capital to competitors, or motivate existing managers to establish competitor start-ups.
5. Focus only on visible figures/statistics; rather than subjective human factors such as 'happy customers, high product quality' and a 'positive work environment'(48).

Avoiding business failure by addressing hazards and risks

One glaring omission from the above list of reasons for business failure is a poor or unprepared response to a major incident or crisis. Major incidents, such as fires or natural disasters, may threaten business survival in its entirety. But tragic events also present opportunities for security enterprises and consultancies to demonstrate their expertise, and also their intrinsic organisational skills in emergency and contingency planning. Ames' omission represents a much wider knowledge and competency gap manifest among many business managers, strategists, entrepreneurs and investors: namely, crisis leadership. The fact remains; skills in contingency and crisis planning could actually become critical success factors for new and emerging enterprises, as companies become more engaged with organisational resilience as a core executive business strategy.

Addressing reasons for failure: The balanced scorecard

Addressing the last of Deming's points (see above), the *balanced scorecard*, developed by Robert Kaplan and David Norton, is a strategic management tool that serves to recognise that non-financial data – such as customer satisfaction or staff knowledge capital – may be just as significant to longer-term organisational prosperity as, say, quantitative sales figures and balance sheets.

Kaplan and Norton refined and elaborated upon a 'dashboard' of organisational performance measures that had originated from French engineers. According to the *Balanced Scorecard Institute*, "the balanced scorecard approach provides a clear prescription as to what companies should measure in order to 'balance' the financial perspective" (49). The following four perspectives should be taken into account in the overall measurement of company performance, the Institute recommend:

> **The learning and growth perspective:** staff training and company cultural approaches; company approaches to self-improvement; knowledge of employees ... the only repository of a company's knowledge.

> **The business process perspective:** internal business processes, such as metrics to monitor management knowledge of how well the company is running, and whether services conform to customer requirements and expectations.

> **The customer perspective:** customer retention data; present revenues may indicate a healthy business but if customers are dropping away from the business this fact may be missed before it is too late to respond and repair.

> **The financial perspective:** Existing financial data is crucial but perhaps additional financial data is required on the dashboard, such as expanding costs, risk assessments and any cost benefit analysis undertaken (50).

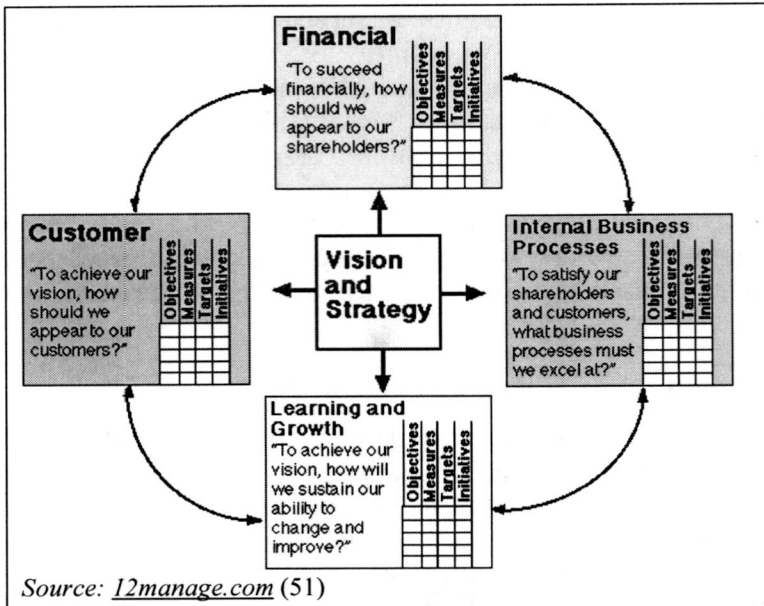

Source: *12manage.com* (51)

Figure 11: The balanced scorecard in action

Critical success factors

Entrepreneurs are advised to develop critical success factors (CSFs), alternatively known as key results areas (KRAs), that are defined organisational goals, established to help one measure the direction and success of their company. According to the business advice website, *Mindtools*, CSFs serve as a reference point for senior management (at least) to revert back to, in order to check progress and also raise some CSFs as permanent agenda items at senior management team meetings, boards and shareholder meetings (52). CSFs can be a wide set of principles; they can include, designing products that are attractive to customers, monitoring market requirements, delivering staff satisfaction and retaining valued employees. Nevertheless, it is expected that several CSFs will be client focused. I present two examples:

1. Imagined company, H & A Security Services, will carry out an annual client survey and receive at least 95% 'good' or 'excellent' feedback from customers across the Middle East and North Africa (MENA) region.

2. H & A will introduce a new free business intelligence bulletin covering MENA region every week for our key clients (£50,000 per year or above value contracts).

2.9 The requirement for professional proficiency

"No plan of operations extends with certainty beyond the first encounter with the enemy's main strength." – (Prussian military strategist, Field Marshall Helmuth von Moltke)

Security, as a profession, perhaps has a collective 'chip on its shoulder'. Many security professionals perceive themselves to be part of a relatively embryonic and underdeveloped profession. But this isn't necessarily the case. Many student essays and sector presentations that this author bears witness to, tend to bemoan the indisputable fact that the security and risk management sector needs to be more advanced and professional. (We're hardly alone in this.) References are commonplace to 'security' as a discipline being in some way substantially younger and inferior in comparison to the more established professions of law and medicine. Maybe it's fair comment. Medicine and science are sometimes rightly enshrined with a 'halo effect'. Yet the legal profession has conjured up a myriad of howlers. Grossly unfair and unprofessional results include, in the UK, the notorious false conviction of the so-called *Guilford Four* and *Birmingham Six* group terrorism suspects. This was caused, in part, by very well educated judges who inexplicably failed to deliver a fair trial by keeping key witnesses away from a courtroom. Moreover, many centuries ago, other scientists conspired to create the professional and religious excommunication of their colleague, Galileo, who bravely maintained his inconvenient but accurate hypothesis that the world was indeed round.

In medicine, a large number of pharmaceutical practitioners and doctors – colluded and collaborated in the sale of the *Thalidomide* drug during the 1950s and 60s. Dozens of senior medical practitioners – who had signed the Hippocratic Oath at the outset of their illustrious careers – maintained that the drug was safe for pregnant mothers, despite much emerging evidence to the contrary. This professional disaster led to tens of thousands of infant deaths and severe, irreversible, abnormalities for survivors and their families. Harold Evans, at *The Guardian* newspaper, described the case as "the greatest man-made global disaster" apart from war. The perpetrators at a German pharmaceutical company evaded prosecution (53).

Security management's roots clearly go back to the earliest eras of homo sapien survivalist strategy. Risk awareness and mitigation go back at least as equally as far as the grand old established professions. Security was practiced by individual hunter-gatherers and by tribal group collectives; internal rivalries and insider threats, addressed by various counter-measures, have been manifest from the outset of human activity. Security is not a new profession. In fact, from time immemorial, most human beings (a far higher proportion throughout history compared to the human race today) practiced individual and collective security management techniques, for reasons of personal and group survival. Private soldiery and alliances of vigilantes has been traced back over several millennia. Organised state armies and public authority law-enforcement roles that can – only to some extent – offer human protection, have existed for just a fraction of humanity's time on the planet! The terminology that we know today, which offers us phrases such as *protective security*, *asset protection* and *intelligence*, all summarise the basic defensive or offensive functions that ancient communities or territories were used to practising as second nature up to the latter part of the Middle Ages. Moreover, these behaviours and defensive functions did occur alongside exacting academic rigour and critical examination that was applied by academics and students of warfare who looked closely at the domains of: body-guarding, spying, military strategy, target hardening, border controls, asset protection, and so on. Some famous historical examples of security management include:

- Samurai warriors in Japan forging an alliance and network among themselves to successfully repulse the 1281 Mongol invasion.

- Swiss guards units that served as palace and bodyguards to the Vatican and the Pope, and also – from the 15th century – to protect European royal families.

- Public ostracism and shaming for those who committed antisocial behaviour among Inuit Eskimo societies, to deter crime and subversion (54).

- The development of omnipotent intelligence and counter-intelligence structures, which included running spy networks, post service infiltration and decoding experts, implemented by Queen Elizabeth I's loyal secretary, Sir Francis Walsingham (55).

- Production of highly esoteric military, protective security doctrine across various centuries and territories, including by Sun Tzu (*The Art of War*: circa 4th-6th Century BC), military theorist Carl von Clausewitz (1780-1831), and Prussian military strategist Helmuth von Moltke the elder (1800-91), who was credited with pioneering colour-coded war gaming.

- Policing by volunteers, groups and networks of so-described 'vigilants' ('vigilantes) before professionalised police forces were formed and became publicly owned by expanding governments and taxpaying bases.

- The building design of fortresses and castles – secured by moats, watch towers, several-metre-thick walls and security guards – and also manorial homes (with priest 'hiding' holes, safe rooms and secret passages to help evacuation).

- Protective walls, such as Hadrian's (AD122 onwards) and the Great Wall of China that marked out territory and also added protective security for communities vulnerable to pillaging. The *Anti-Fascist Protection Rampart,* more commonly identified as the *Berlin Wall* (1961 to 1989), was an ultra-modern variation.

Organisational cultures and proficiency

Most business environments are different. This section will examine different cultural attitudes to security-related training and exercising. Progress has clearly been made in a general sense, whereby the extant security industry in many geographical domains has become more professionalised, with individual practitioners becoming more proficient, and overall sector accountability becoming far more transparent. Moreover, the mass emergence of *participative* business cultures, whereby companies will emphasise a greater importance on individual employee empowerment, can often pose a key attitudinal and philosophical challenge for security and contingency practitioners. This is possibly because the majority of practitioners still emanate from a professional background in law enforcement or military spheres, where hierarchies and management orders are far less likely to be challenged or visibly critiqued.

Military and law-enforcement cultures

In such structured work domains as military and law enforcement, chains of command and orders are usually crystal clear, during peace time at least. The kinetic and grave nature of problem-solving – and also the underpinning authority of hierarchical decision makers – means that members of law-enforcement and military communities are usually socialised more effectively to follow orders within any workplace environment. Moreover, armed forces and law enforcement agencies still retain (and have a realistic prospect of continuing to do so) certain legal and moral covenants which give them the authority to encroach into the private sphere of their employees; whether it is through background vetting, arranging overseas housing and travel, preventing or monitoring political affiliations, or signing up employees to various, and probably quite important, codes of conduct.

Engaging and effective examples of organisational cultural socialisation can be found within many military domains, which can invoke history and a sense of purpose to their organisational mission. A case in point is the *British Army Doctrine Publication* produced by the aptly-named Development, Concepts and Doctrine Centre at Shrivenham's UK Defence Academy. With razor-sharp clarity, this document expresses the importance of a coherent workplace philosophy (56). Its' mission statement is as follows:

"This Army Doctrine Publication (ADP) builds on foundations laid by the highest Defence doctrine to provide the philosophy and principles for the British Army's approach to operations. The philosophy and principles guide the practices and procedures that are found in tactical field manuals and other subordinate doctrine" (57).

The entire doctrine is focused, arguably, to provide a coherent and disciplined body of national security with an action-oriented team structure whose central goal is, ultimately, to provide peace through strength. Although some security plans within the private sector may indeed share some rhetorical flourishes that would suit Army doctrine – such as offering a Lawrence of Arabia quote to inspire *espirit de corps* – a rather bracing reality of civilian industrial life is that no major company would permit its security function to define its overarching philosophy and principles. Or, for that matter, subordinate or compel other business functions into a protective security culture, unless it was an extreme, high-risk environment. Moreover, it is likely that any attempt to establish an overarching organisational *doctrine* would be emphatically squashed!

In any environment, moral and emotional leadership is an accepted vehicle to spur on employee motivation and achievement. Self-esteem, love and a sense of belonging are quite high up on Maslow's famous triangle that illustrates our 'hierarchy of needs' as human beings (58). This is why the Army Doctrine Publication emphasises values of patriotism and duty. The ADP then underpins such cultural values by invoking historical parallels:

"Duty is the devotion to a cause, mission and the team that transcends an individual's personal interests or desires. In times of real adversity, when it appears that there is nothing left to give, duty requires soldiers to lead and strive even more" (59). "I hold my duty as I hold my soul", from British playwright William Shakespeare's play, *Hamlet* (60).

Culture in private companies

Inspiring words from Shakespeare indeed! But how can security managers in the private sector possibly hope to replicate such a rhetorical call to arms, without sounding slightly absurd? One of the repeated mantras within the security industry and policing circles is that all security measures have to be 'proportionate'. In fact, the more we consider, any serious drive to embed security and resilience proficiency within lower-risk civilian organisations is significantly hampered by the relatively lax, and slightly anodyne, operating environments where companies know that they should indeed 'expect the unexpected' but don't quite believe that any of the world's ills will directly impact them.

The ability to practically influence executive decision making, and to be perceived as an authority figure – is often down to the personality traits and leadership techniques of various security managers. Because, after all, the vast majority of compliance within civilian life is *voluntary* and judged against the famous saying; 'What's in it for me?' McAslan's thoughtful 2010 *Straw-man paper* titled *Organisational Resilience* takes into consideration such a complex dynamic in corporate business and suggests: "In reality, few organisations will experience major disruptions and therefore experience can best be achieved through exercises and rehearsed drills. IBM (2007) and others stress that exercises should be conducted regularly, following changes to the organisation's mission and/or structure, or following significant changes to the operating environment" (61).

KPMG's impressive paper *Living on the Frontline: the Resilient Organisation* recommends that following a traumatic incident, employee counselling could be required. "This is borne out by studies of individuals who were directly affected by 9/11. These revealed that in the medium term after the attack, three quarters of those surveyed experienced depression, nearly half had impaired concentration and a third developed insomnia. Significantly, (resilience planning) must be flexible enough to cope if a significant number of staff are either unable or unwilling to work in the aftermath of a disaster (62)."

Importance of doctrines and mission statements

Despite clear advantage gained from establishing strong mission statements and inspiring employees by spectacular corporate goals, individual compliance to corporate decision making is based predominantly upon *voluntary* adherence and acquiescence. In cases where criminal law has *not* been breached, real power within civilian workplace domains barely exists. This fact applies as equally to security management operatives as it does any other corporate sector officer or executive. Moreover, human rights-related laws, and the rise in litigious claims against protective security functions, in some countries, does mean that security managers would be ill-advised to carry out any physical or access-controlled counter-measures against perceived adversaries in most civilian settings. (*See Chapter 3 on Legislation and Regulations.*)

The word 'doctrine' would certainly not be acceptable for most private sector organisations utilising English language. Doctrine is defined by *FreeDictionary.com* as: "A principle or body of principles presented for acceptance or belief, as by a religious, political, scientific, or philosophic group; dogma". In government parlance doctrine can be understood as: "A statement of official government policy, especially in foreign affairs and military strategy" (63).

Many private sector employees may agree with the Lebanese journalist, Amin Maalouf, when he said: "Doctrines are meant to serve man, not the other way around" (64). Indeed, a significant portion may well have consciously opted to not join the armed forces or law enforcement roles because their organisation's activities are perceived to be too rigid, intrusive or hierarchical.

Case study: Mission statement of global investment bank Morgan Stanley

Widely praised for its preparation for several years before, and its response to, the 9/11 attacks on the World Trade Center in New York (where it had its HQ), Morgan Stanley offers an encouraging and inspiring mission statement of intent on its website:

Mission statement: Morgan Stanley's mission is to deliver the finest financial thinking, products and execution in the world. We strive to lead with integrity, put clients first, win in the marketplace, think like an owner and keep our balance.

Company culture: Each and every individual in our franchise has his or her own distinct identity forged from a unique set of abilities, life experiences, interests, talents and backgrounds.

Diversity strategy: In all aspects of our franchise, our commitment to diversity begins with our most valuable resource – our people (65).

Like millions of enterprises around the world, although employee safety and security is paramount, for Morgan Stanley, these topic disciplines are not their reason-for-being: shareholder profit is.

Moreover, if we think back to the army doctrine in many private organisations, security *operations* are rarely permitted in the civilian sphere, unless led by a law-enforcement agency. Indeed, recommendations around protective security arrangements in private companies – especially if they are blunt and non-consultative – may be perceived by managers outside the security function as a direct threat to organisational resilience. This is because some people fairly perceive that some security measures create more threats than they solve. Here are some questionable examples of security improvements: access controls that would block a quick evacuation; introducing CCTV at access points where coincidentally staff smokers congregate; this may be perceived as overly aggressive. Alternatively, random bag searches carried out upon employees in low or moderate-risk environments could be viewed as totally draconian. Such intrusive measures could establish the view that staff are mistrusted, increase staff turnover and dissatisfaction, or even lead to allegations of bullying and discrimination. As Briggs and Edwards point out: "the foundation of effective security is trust, and there is a danger that an over-formalised and rigid approach to security undermines rather than reinforce trust" (66). Such cultural obstacles can be bridged by providing a sensible explanation of security improvements via induction sessions, feedback forums and other 'ice-breaking' methods (67).

Thus, achieving the right cultural fit in terms of recommending a suitable security strategy that gels well with wider organisational culture, is a critical business skill. A security manager who is deficient in understanding the organisational context and culture of their employer or client, could also be absolutely proficient in all other necessary technical security areas. But they cannot possibly claim to be 'proficient' until they improve their organisational cultural antennae.

Proficiency and training

> *"The safety policy and procedures were in place: the practice was deficient."* – Lord Cullen's report into the Piper Alpha disaster, 1990 (68)

London-based fitness instructor, Roger Green, is an ex Royal Marines Commando. He adeptly summarises an ethos of training that might appear anathema to some civilian sector workplace environments:

> *"If you run the same route or conduct the same weights programme every day, your body will get used to this, and you will not improve performance. Circuits and boot camps are excellent as they employ a principle called 'dislocation of expectation' meaning you do not know what is going to come next, so your body is shocked, but this leads to increased performance and progression, and ultimately a change in body shape"* (69).

The British Marines' training mantra of 'dislocated expectations' has an underpinning philosophy and purpose. It is to acknowledge that we find out more about individual and team potential by being tested in unfamiliar domains and analysing reactions to negative or unpredictable events. Such a method does highlight, in comparison, the risks of rehearsing and training for crises in sterile and familiar environments. How can we maximise the benefits of training if activities are designed not to tip delegates out of their comfort zone and course feedback is issued on the proviso that it does not dent self-confidence or upset existing organisational equilibrium?

Case study: Ohio, US emergency services training

The following extract is from a report by psychiatrists into police training in Akron, Ohio, that was designed to deal with mental health issues that officers may interface with as incident first responders:

"The first week long training occurred in late May 2000 with 20 Akron police officers and three paramedic lieutenants from the Akron Fire Department. All officers were volunteers and were screened by the training director to determine their appropriateness for this team of officers who were most likely to encounter individuals experiencing mental illness crises. Communication skills and being self-motivated to improve skills and knowledge about mental illness were the prime selection criteria for the program. Officers received a 40-hour introduction to mental health and mental illness with an intensive overview of the local mental health system and its points of access. Officers visited psychiatric emergency services, went into the community with case managers, and visited a consumer-directed social center. They received extensive training in verbal de-escalation skills and engaged in realistic role playing to practice these skills in simulated crises at the NEOUCOM Center for the Study of Clinical Performance. Officers were encouraged to consider, when appropriate, linkage and referral for care to the mental health system as a preferable alternative to arrest (70)."

Intended to assist emergency planners in civilian domains, many UK local authority emergency planning teams provide valuable advice and templates for employers and businesses seeking to enhance business continuity management (BCM) capabilities. Sometimes local authorities will also facilitate 'buddy' initiatives, whereby larger companies mentor and assist smaller neighbouring businesses. Many security and BCM guidance documents and templates are also published online by UK local authorities. For example, a write-up of crisis training by Humber emergency planning service:

"During the exercise, you might want to think about blowing the objectives up and taping them around the room so people are constantly reminded of them."

Then later:

"Testing smaller parts of the plan has some real benefits. It allows you to involve experts whose role in a bigger exercise might be so small that you couldn't justify bringing them along. We recently ran a media specific exercise where we were able to involve media officers and spent two hours talking about details we would have brushed over in ten minutes in previous exercises (71)."

Here is some further advice from international IT services provider, Capgemini: "As the goal of testing is to discover defects in the plan, a successful test is the test that does not successfully execute all aspects of a continuity or disaster recovery plan" (72). Both documents summarise a training environment that is hardly lifelike in comparison to a fast-moving and often emotionally-impacted crisis situation. But by considering some of the granular parts of wider contingency planning, this type of important detail (such as up-to-date individual contact telephone numbers) may well get missed in a fully-fledged kinetic dress rehearsal. Such detailed planning, often tackling a critical emergency planning phase at a time, can provide the overall scaffolding to achieving maximised individual and team proficiency, so long as the overall strategy is upheld, and component parts are integrated into a functioning contingency strategy. Such documents also reveal the real-world limitations of testing for security and emergency incidents in most civilian environments. The reality is that, in corporate and civilian environments, security management is not the central purpose of everyday working life for the vast majority of busy employees. It is merely viewed as an important background function. Thus legal, cultural and emotional considerations do have to be treated seriously; particularly by outside consultants who may well not have built up enough internal goodwill within the client organisation to offset any subsequent insensitivities or glitches.

Proficiency: Learning and education

Proficiency can be taken to mean a high degree of skill and expertise, incorporating capabilities of excellence, adroitness, professionalism and aptitude within a role or subject discipline. At the time of writing, a search on Google of 'proficient security' conjures around 15.5 million results, including a company based in Essex that goes by that very name, *Proficient Security*. Undoubtedly, millions of examples of proficiency in the kaleidoscopic range of security activities practiced by millions of security sector employees, do actually exist. But in this book, for the purposes of clarity and brevity, we are going to have to be a little bit discriminating! Flagship award ceremonies, including the annual UK-based *Security Excellence Awards* and the US-based *ASIS Accolades Awards* do provide some security management good practice examples (73).

Human beings can build individual proficiency by embracing a range of techniques. These include: active learning (experiential and observational), training, role-playing and war-gaming but also the accumulative expertise generated by reading and a sense of inquiry. Successful security entrepreneurship is founded upon aggressive and relevant knowledge acquisition – such as access to business intelligence and regional risk reports – in order to provide us with *insight* and higher levels of knowledge than that achieved by our competitors or adversaries.

Nevertheless, as a concept, *proficiency* also suggests an extra dimension of capability; awareness. As we will see, awareness is inextricably related to experience. If Malcolm Gladwell's notion that it takes 10,000 hours of practice to 'master' a discipline is a little daunting, then perhaps help is at hand (74). The famous *four-phase learning matrix* also known as the *conscious competence ladder* does help us to understand at what levels of proficiency we may realistically be said to have achieved.

In essence, humans move up a four-phase competence ladder as they acquire more knowledge and experiential learning. In all domains of learning and competence measuring, individual awareness of knowledge gaps, or unconscious expertise, can be quite unrealistic. (Most of us sadly convince ourselves that we are great car drivers, especially on an empty road.) But I'm sure those who have tried to master a new language, or learn a new musical instrument, will recognise the following four stages (see Figure 12 below), even if they haven't necessarily reached all of them yet.

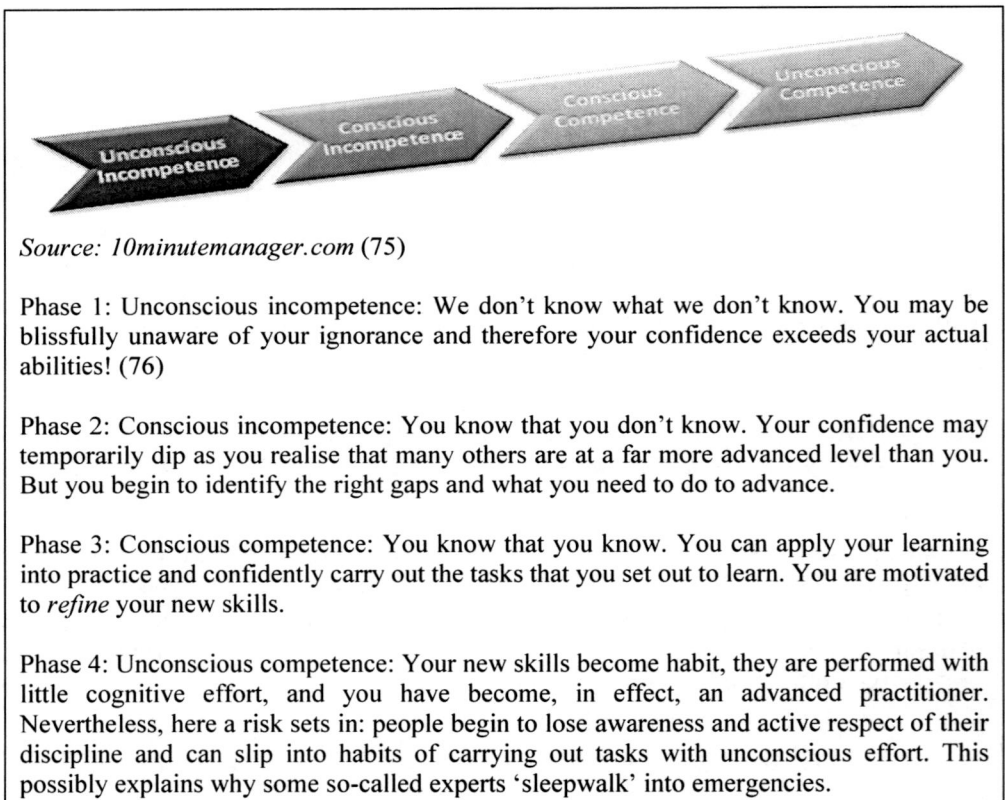

Source: 10minutemanager.com (75)

Phase 1: Unconscious incompetence: We don't know what we don't know. You may be blissfully unaware of your ignorance and therefore your confidence exceeds your actual abilities! (76)

Phase 2: Conscious incompetence: You know that you don't know. Your confidence may temporarily dip as you realise that many others are at a far more advanced level than you. But you begin to identify the right gaps and what you need to do to advance.

Phase 3: Conscious competence: You know that you know. You can apply your learning into practice and confidently carry out the tasks that you set out to learn. You are motivated to *refine* your new skills.

Phase 4: Unconscious competence: Your new skills become habit, they are performed with little cognitive effort, and you have become, in effect, an advanced practitioner. Nevertheless, here a risk sets in: people begin to lose awareness and active respect of their discipline and can slip into habits of carrying out tasks with unconscious effort. This possibly explains why some so-called experts 'sleepwalk' into emergencies.

Figure 12: The conscious competence learning matrix explained

How human beings learn

It is worth familiarising ourselves with the work of some of the most influential educationalists of modern times. Eminent among them is Benjamin Bloom (77). Bloom chaired a committee of US-based educational psychologists to identify methods of most effective learning in order to promote higher forms of thinking. His work culminated in a diagrammatic 'taxonomy of learning' (see below). Bloom and his educationalist supports advocated methods of learning based around evaluation, analysis and creation, and stepping upwards beyond rote learning and the retention of supposed *facts*.

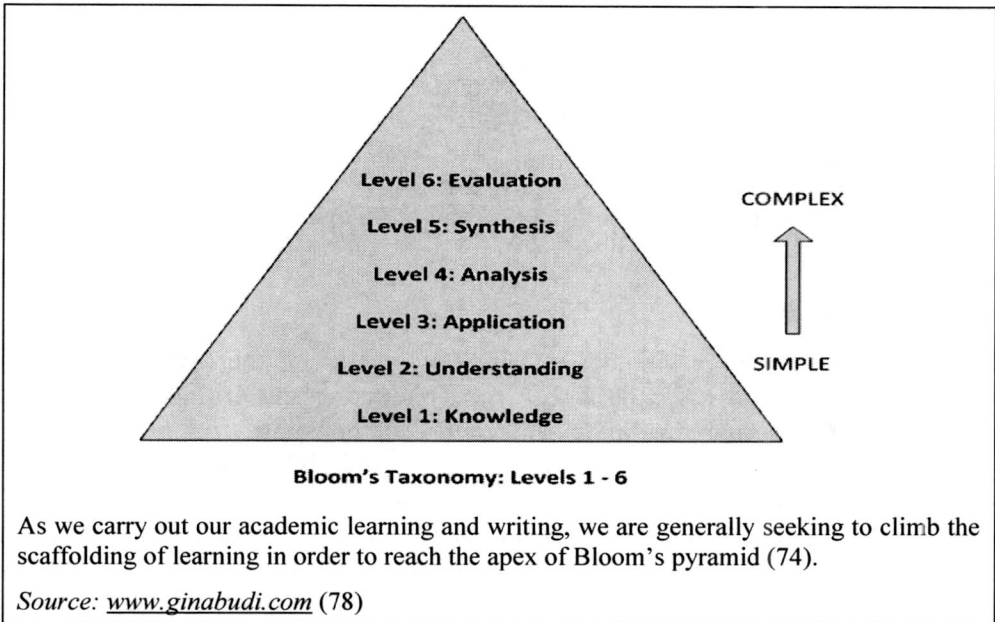

Level 6: Evaluation

Level 5: Synthesis

Level 4: Analysis

Level 3: Application

Level 2: Understanding

Level 1: Knowledge

COMPLEX

SIMPLE

Bloom's Taxonomy: Levels 1 - 6

As we carry out our academic learning and writing, we are generally seeking to climb the scaffolding of learning in order to reach the apex of Bloom's pyramid (74).

Source: www.ginabudi.com (78)

Figure 13: Bloom's taxonomy of learning

Experiential learning

In many ways, David Kolb consolidated Bloom's findings around the cognitive domain when he demonstrated that human beings learn through processes of discovery and experience, and then experimentation. Experience plays the primary role in our learning processes Kolb asserts. Kolb illustrates this through his *Experiential learning cycle model*; now adopted and understood by educationalists around the world (79).

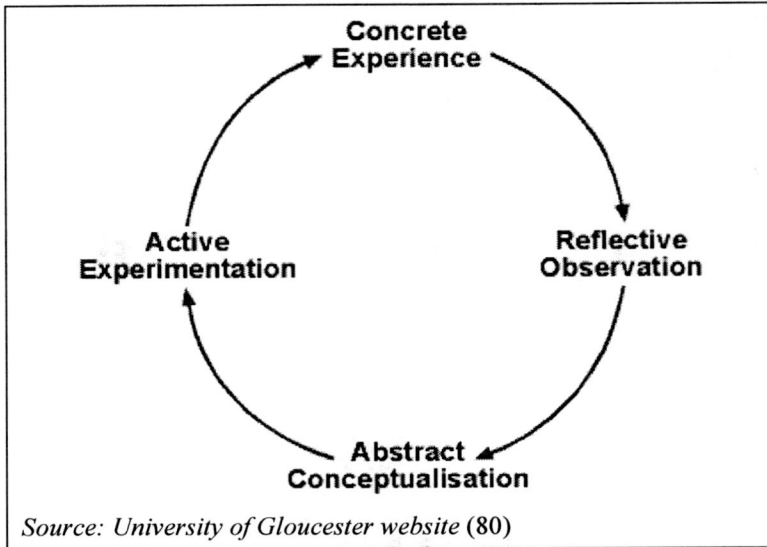

Source: *University of Gloucester website* (80)

Figure 14: Kolb's Experiential learning cycle

Dual process theory

Nobel Prize-winning psychologist, Daniel Kahneman, neither contradicts Bloom or Kolb but he uses his experience from conducting and critiquing decades of exercises in cognitive psychology in order to demonstrate *dual process theory*. This well-established cognitive learning concept is by no means Kahneman's invention. But his book *Thinking fast and slow* is a collection of remarkable observations which clearly demonstrate the strengths of reflective thinking, and show up the pitfalls of relying on gut instinct, immediate decision making (81). Kahneman's book shows us that the celebrated notion of an accurate 'policeman's hunch' might be a little more harmful than traditionalists might like to accept!

Kahneman provides several humorous and compelling exercise scenarios for readers to demonstrate that the human brain functions as two complementary systems: *System 1* is effortless, instinctive, intuitive and unconscious. However, this can be overridden by a *System 2* which is more effortful, analytical, intentional and reflective. Such decision making often 'corrects' System 1, asserts Kahneman (82).

PERCEPTION	INTUITION SYSTEM 1	REASONING SYSTEM 2
PROCESS	Fast Parallel Automatic Effortless Associative Slow-learning Emotional	Slow Serial Controlled Effortful Rule-governed Flexible Neutral
CONTENT	Percepts Current stimulation Stimulus-bound	Conceptual representations Past, Present and Future Can be evoked by language

Source: *Dave Insbury files online* (83)

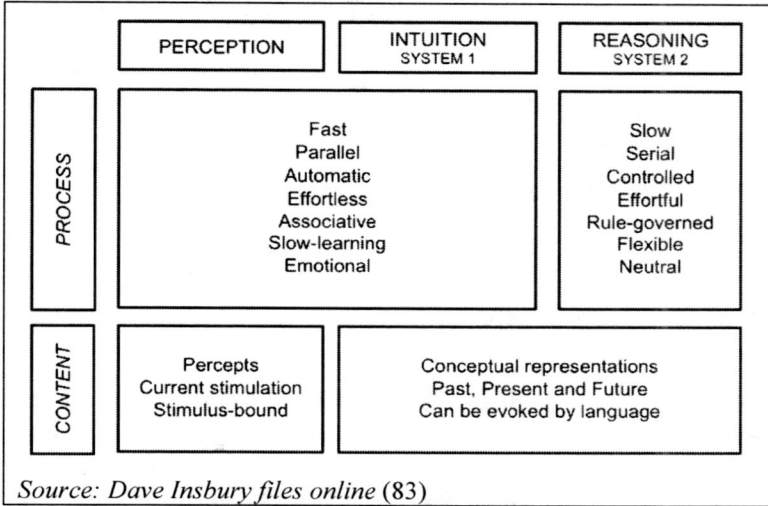

Figure 15: Dual process theory in action

E-learning and personal development

Increasingly, students and tutors are almost fully dependent on virtual learning environment (VLE) teaching approaches. As a tutor, my own students are located in the many medium-to-high risk environments; some face curbs to internet access. Some learners are based on vessels conducting anti-piracy and other maritime security operations. Others are located within states experiencing chronic social, political and military disorder, or inside disaster recovery zones. Such operating environments present major challenges around access to e-learning and support technologies. Nevertheless, security staff based in such locations still require professional development; indeed, perhaps it becomes even more vital to instil training and educational cultures.

As such, the well-researched findings of e-learning pedagogic specialists, such as Karen Barnstable, Pam Moule and Gilly Salmon, have added real value to the distance learning field.

In her blog *Stable Transitions: A Journey of Learning,* Karen Barnstable produced three top tips for online tutoring instructors. The *Three Ps of Online Instruction* include being 'proactive'. Barnstable states: "know your course, know your students", by way of "regular announcements and interventions". Second, be 'professional' by issuing "timely responses, established office hours, the use of professional language *inter alia*" (84). Third, be 'personable' and consider how to "add inspiration or suggestions to responses". Barnstable seems to recommend a much heightened level of personal communications with distant learners and also a more direct, instructive, approach compared to traditional classroom delivery methods.

Salmon produced a five-stage model for e-moderating by identifying five core stages for course moderators:

1. Access and motivation
2. Online socialisation
3. Information exchange
4. Knowledge construction
5. Development (85).

Fellow e-learning specialist, Pam Moule, found that some e-learning programmes were "too dependent on group networking and brainstorming and therefore could hinder students' progress through stages of the [Salmon] model, and potentially up the e-learning ladder" (86). Moule further recommends that there is significant "potential available to use e-learning as part of an integrated approach that includes face-to-face delivery" (87). In the security management sphere, this has indeed been achieved by various higher education establishments in the UK – including Buckinghamshire New University, Cranfield and Portsmouth University – that blend e-learning with classroom delivery and tutorials held over VOIP and/or digital media platforms, such as Skype and Blackboard.

Higher education: UK professional standards framework

Educationalist John Dewey, from the famous Chicago school, reflected in his book *How We Think* that: "We do not learn from experience ... we learn from reflecting on experience" (88). A century later, consolidating Dewey's findings, a *UK professional standards framework* was produced by the *Higher Education Academy*. The HEA's framework sought to better prepare students for a knowledge-based economy, whereby the vast majority of national university education was more strongly aligned to providing a mix of practical and academic learning techniques. The aim was to help lever graduate and post-graduate students into a stronger employment market position; to improve prospects for graduate employability. The 2011 Framework comprises of 16 overall areas of activity, existing across 'three dimensions', these being: *areas of activity, core knowledge* and *professional values* (89).

Originally intended for university and college lecturers, the framework actually provides a very decent professional overview of some key ingredients required in order to develop thought-leadership and high-end market respectability. It's a truly useful document for security practitioners interested in continued professional development for themselves, or for conceptual implementation across a larger organisation, including corporate environments. What better way can there be, either by becoming a subject matter expert or developing a campus of expertise within your company, in order to attract clients and wow stakeholders?

Awareness and proficiency

> *"We are sometimes blind to what we see. And we are also blind to what we are blind to."* – Nobel literature award winner and psychologist, Daniel Kahneman (90)

The key to achieving proficiency is, of course, a great exertion and sense of inquiry around one's chosen specialism. Possessing a demonstrable body of relevant knowledge, inevitably does lead to respect by peers and fellow professionals. But, does such an encyclopaedic knowledge-base of our discipline invariably mean that we are proficient? Not at all! Security management is a role whereby colleagues and clients look to us to have continuous *situational awareness*. The following two video clips may provide some surprises as to how deficient most of us human beings are at recognising situational changes:

Case study: How good is your 'situational awareness'?

Please download these two video clips from YouTube that will test your awareness: For the first, how many passes does the team in white make? **(1.09)**
www.youtube.com/watch?v=Ahg6qcgoay4

If that was too easy, move on to the second video exercise: What changes in this scene? **(1.56)**
www.youtube.com/watch?v=ubNF9QNEQLA

Further information: Proficiency and standards bodies

It would take a whole book to capture the entire educational and standards architecture within the security industry. Below I describe several notable organisations:

British Standards Institute

> *"Standards are a tried and tested way to work more efficiently and effectively. They help organisations to improve their performance, reduce their risk and help them be more sustainable (91)."* – BSI online

The BSI facilitates several committees of subject matter experts (SMEs) to produce and agree basic guidance for a plethora of security management, information security management, emergency management and business continuity-related challenges. The principal forum – yet not the only board – overseeing security and business continuity-related matter is the societal security management (SSM) committee, at present working on standards and/or publicly available specifications in crisis management, private security contracting and overall organisational resilience. Key guidance so far produced by SSM and more technical committees, include:

BS 8418 – 2010 CCTV

BS 8243 – 2010 Alarms

BS 7858 – 2009 Security screening of employees

BS 8484 – 2009 Lone worker devices

BS 7984 – 2008 Key-holding and response services

PAS97 – 2009 Mail screening

BS 8507-1 2008 Close protection services

ISO/IEC 27001 – Information security

ISO27031 – ICT continuity and best practice

BS 25999-2 Business continuity (now ISO22301).

Much of the guidance produced by the world's most prominent standards organisations, including Australia, Canada, France, Germany, the United States and Japan, can end up being promoted, debated and accepted as international standards by the International Standards Organisation.

The emergence, and growth, in security and related disciplines has had a profound impact on supply chains and, indeed, all entrepreneurs. Many buyers, particularly public authorities, seek reassurance from within their supply chain that contractors and service providers are fully compliant and accredited to certain national and international standards. For example:

"The UK government, in a strategic effort to make Cloud services available to UK public sector organisations, has set up the Cloud Store, through which Cloud services can be procured. In order to be listed, a Cloud Service Provider has to go through a formal accreditation process. This builds on a fully-scoped ISO27001 certification and is usually to provide services rated at either IL2 or IL3 (92)."

National occupational standards (NOS)

NOS are baseline standards written by industry practitioners to ensure that workplace qualification courses cover key areas within a stipulated job area. For example, in the security domain, several NOSs exist to assist training providers and course validation authorities (such as the influential not-for-profit organisation *Skills for Security*) design, develop and monitor the standard of training courses (academic levels 1-3). They can also be vital in helping organisations develop their own training initiatives, appraisals, policies, operating procedures and guidance. NOS publications include:

- security search operations (2013)
- eEvent security operations (2013)
- electronic security systems (2013)
- security management (2012)
- mechanical fire protection (2012)
- port security operations (2011)
- CCTV operations (2011)
- providing close protection (2011)
- enforcement agents (2011)
- security and loss prevention
- private investigators (2010)
- security dog handling (2009)
- physical security (2009)
- human identity and biometrics (2009)
- information destruction operations (2009).

Source: Skills for Security website: 2013 (93)

National security inspectorate (UK) (NSI)

The NSI aims to "be the ultimate reassurance in fire, security and related facilities management approval". The NSI evolved from a number of trade quality organisations which were concerned about poor standards within the security and fire alarm industry which potentially caused major lapses in health, safety and security functions and undermined consumer confidence in industry solutions around crime and fire prevention. The NSO carries out what it describes as: "robust, high-quality audits of home security, business security and fire safety service providers". Companies apply to be audited and quality checked by the NSI, in order to provide customers, and their own internal stakeholders, with assurance and confidence (94).

UK security industry authority

Following a number of high-profile lapses in standards of private sector security practice, the UK government passed the Private Security Act 2001, and established a security industry authority (SIA). The SIA issues licenses for a variety of security functions and also runs an approved contractor scheme, a bill which included the formation of a formal security authority, which was accountable to the Home Office and its lead government minister. According to the organisation's website: "SIA licensing covers manned guarding (including security guarding, door supervision, close protection, cash and valuables in transit, and public space surveillance using CCTV), key holding and vehicle immobilising. Licensing ensures that private security operatives are 'fit and proper' persons who are properly trained and qualified to do their job" (95). Nicely put.

Chapter 2: Wrap-up

In closing this chapter on **Management**, we reflect on some of the approaches and attributes that will help your company gain the competitive edge. These include:

- According to veteran security management guru, Charles (Chuck) Sennewald: "Despite some major downsizing, corporate mergers, and the growing emergence of facilities management and technology replacing some security personnel, security is now viewed as a critical part of most organisations today, with security professionals reporting directly to senior management, if not the chief executive officer".

- During major threats and incidents, the security team will gain prominence. Utilisation and professionalism by the wider business will be demanded from every quarter. The *observable* skill of a security function's response will be assessed and hopefully well received.

- Before any presentational pitch, or meeting with company executives, an advanced security consultant will diligently conduct market research and specific analysis around an organisation's security risks, but also try to establish the main motivations or goals of its executive leadership.

- The security function can act as an organisational shock absorber which can prevent a negative incident morphing into wider crisis or contagion. Therefore, much professional focus nowadays centres on how well the modern security professional can understand and proficiently plan for wider issues that have a strong likelihood of impacting organisational resilience issues.

- Substantial security professionalism is more a mindset, than a trade. All security professionals are expected in the modern era to actively absorb, understand and ultimately translate an array of corporate security risks, which may well start out as harmless intangibles, but if left ignored or mishandled, can cause severe organisational damage in the longer run.

- ROI must be communicated clearly at all times, by all security contractors. As one CP company boss put it: "My client is not just the security director at a given organisation, but his boss, his executive team and his CEO, who come into contact with my staff day in and day out".

- Accepting and deploying the utility of explicit key measurables (data sets), by embracing business quantification methods, will undoubtedly give any security company the competitive edge. But each success story does require further communication to the client; because spreadsheets and algorithms hardly sell themselves!

- Security procurement can be an emotionally-driven, volatile buying environment, whereby potential customers run hot and then turn cold; especially when a crisis cools down. At all times, be careful to offer a proportionate response, based on what is best for the client organisation. Consider how your suggested solutions will be viewed a little further down the timeline. US Defense Secretary, Bob McNamara, called this form of cool-headed, pragmatic response the 'daylight test'.

- Progress and client-value should be demonstrated at all times during implementation of a security project. Moreover, leadership and management are increasingly mobile in modern corporate environments, so beware: it may be that your initial buyers and sponsors have already left the building!

- Those entrepreneurs and managers who travel by autopilot will only be able to fly so fast, and so high, for a limited amount of time. As Sir Richard Branson recently told *Forbes Magazine*: "Researching the competition has never been the Virgin way. Many of our products and services come about because we pay attention to what the market is missing or what's not being done well".

References

1) BSIA (2012)
2) McAslan, A. (2010), *'Organisational Resilience Understanding the Concept and its Application'*. Torrens Resilience Institute. Available from: *http://torrensresilience.org/images/pdfs/organisational%20resilience.pdf*

3) World Economic Forum (2013), 'Global Risks Report'
4) Sennewald, C. (2003) 'Effective Security Management', New York: Butterworth-Heinemann
5) Ibid p.44
6) Ibid. p.43
7) Frisch, B., (2011), 'Who really makes the decisions in your company?' HBR, accessed and downloaded on 19/02/2015 at: *https://hbr.org/2011/12/who-really-makes-the-big-decisions-in-your-company*
8) Grant, R., (n.d.) 'Contemporary Strategy Analysis' p. 121
9) Ibid. p.129
10) Ibid. p.89
11) Ibid. p.67
12) Ibid. p.74
13) Ibid. p.75
14) Ibid
15) Ibid. p.82
16) Edwards. C., (2009), 'Resilient Nation'
17) Ibid.
18) Sutcliffe, K.M. and Vogus, T.J. (2003), 'Organizing for Resilience', University of Pennsylvania. Available from: *http://cpor.org/ro/sutcliffevogus(2003).pdf*
19) McAslan, A. (2010), *'Organisational Resilience Understanding the Concept and its Application'*. Torrens Resilience Institute. Available from: *http://torrensresilience.org/images/pdfs/organisational%20resilience.pdf*
20) Op. Cit., Edwards: 2009: 16
21) (NIAC: 2009: 10)
22) London First, NaCTSO and BCI (2006), Expecting the unexpected: Business continuity in an uncertain world
23) A number of academic courses refer to Business Continuity, Security and Emergency Planning being core sub-disciplines of 'organisational resilience' including the Bucks New University MSc programme
24) BCI website (2015), 'What is BC?' accessed and downloaded on 20/02/2015 at:
25) G4S Organisational Resilience Roundtable, hosted by Robert Hall, at London Headquarters, July 2012
26) McAslan: 2011: 7
27) Interview with Jon Hill, MD of Polaris, in London on 25/02/2015
28) Gordon., A., (2009) Future Savvy
29) C., Meyer 2009:17
30) C., Sennewald
31) C., Sennewald 2003: 4

32) C., Sennewald (2003: 59)
33) Branson., R, (n.d.) quoted online and downloaded on 21 10 2013 from: *www.brainyquote.com/quotes/authors/r/richard_branson.html#3Qr25uycsi bMjv4x.99*
34) Kahneman., D., (2012), 'Thinking fast and slow', London: Penguin
35) Schoemaker (2013), 'Five ways to know what your customers want before they do' downloaded on 21 10 2013 from: *www.inc.com/paul-schoemaker/5-ways-to-know-what-your-customer-wants.html*
36) Haselmaier., J, (2013) 'Think You Know How To Meet Customer Needs?', downloaded on 21 10 2013 from: *www.pragmaticmarketing.com/resources/think-you-know-how-to-meet-customer-needs*
37) Shawbel, D., (23/09/2014), 'Richard Branson's Three Most Important Leadership Principles', accessed and downloaded on 22/02/2015 at: *www.forbes.com/sites/ danschawbel/2014/09/23/richard-branson-his-3-most-important-leadership-principles/*
38) Rumelt (1982), 'Diversification Strategy and Profitability.' Strategic Management Journal 3., pp. 359-69
39) Galbraith., J., and Kazanjian, R., (1986) 'Strategy Implementation: Structure, Systems and Processes (2nd ed.): West Publishing, St Paul, MN
40) Porter., M., (1980) 'Competitive Strategy'. New York: Free Press
41) Ideaelevator.co.uk was accessed and downloaded on 22/02/2015 at: *http://ideaelevator.co/tag/product-life-cycle/*
42) SymphonyIRI., (2013) 'Data Sheet: Walmart Customer Advantage', downloaded from: *www.iriworldwide.com/Portals/0/ArticlePdfs/ Customer-Advantage-DS.pdf*
43) (2013) Undercover Boss UK: Securitas's Chief Executive Geoff Zeidler steps out of the boardroom *www.youtube.com/watch?v=CQX8UMaf60g* (47.39) and (2013) Undercover Boss USA: University of California Riverside Chancellor sees his campus through the eyes of visitors and staff (English narration, Spanish subtitles):
44) InfoEntrepreneurs (2013) 'Know Your Customer's Needs', downloaded on 21 10 2013 from: *www.infoentrepreneurs.org/en/guides/know-your-customers--needs/*
45) Canada Business Network online, 'Infoentrepreneurs' accessed and downloaded on 22/02/2015 at: *www.infoentrepreneurs.org/en/guides/know-your-customers--needs/*
46) Longley., R, (2013) 'Why small businesses fail', accessed and downloaded on 22/10/2013 at: *http://usgovinfo.about.com/od/smallbusiness/ a/whybusfail.htm*

47) Ames., M., (1983) 'Small Business Management', West Publishing, St Paul MN

48) Mindtools (2013), 'Five diseases of management, downloaded on 21 10 2013 from: *www.mindtools.com/pages/Newsletters/22Oct13.htm*

49) Balanced Score Card Institute: accessed and downloaded on 08/11/2013 at: *http://balancedscorecard.org/Resources/AbouttheBalancedScorecard/tabid/55/Default.aspx*

50) Ibid.

51) 12manage.com, (2013), Balanced Scorecard, downloaded on 08/11/2013 from: *www.12manage.com/images/figure_bsc.jpg*

52) Mindtools (2013), 'Critical Success Factors: Identifying the Things That Really Matter for Success', accessed and downloaded on 21/10/ 2013 from: *www.mindtools.com/pages/article/newLDR_80.htm*

53) Evans, H. (14/11/2014), 'Thalidomide: how men who blighted the lives of thousands evaded justice', accessed and downloaded on 22/02/2015 at: *www.theguardian.com/society/2014/nov/14/-sp-thalidomide-pill-how-evaded-justice*

54) Robinson, P., (2013), Natural Law & Lawlessness: Modern Lessons from Pirates, Lepers, Eskimos, and Survivors, University of Pennsylvania, accessed and downloaded on 08/11/2013 at: *http://scholarship.law.upenn.edu/cgi/viewcontent.cgi?article=1388&context=faculty_scholarship*

55) Budiansky, S., (2006), Her Majesty's Spymaster: Elizabeth I, Sir Francis Walsingham, and the Birth of Modern Espionage: UK: Plume Books

56) Army Doctrine Publication Operations, (2010) Shrivenham: Development, Concepts and Doctrine Centre. Downloaded on 21 10 2013 from: *www.gov.uk/government/uploads/system/uploads/attachment_data/file/33695/ADPOperationsDec10.pdf*

57) Ibid

58) Simply Psychology online (2015), 'Maslow's Hierarchy of Needs', accessed and downloaded on 22/02/2015 at: *www.simplypsychology.org/maslow.html*

59) Op., Cit., ADP: 2010: pp.2-23

60) Shakespeare, W., (1603), 'Hamlet', Act 2, Scene 2, published in London between 1603 and 1605

61) McAslan, A: 2010: 11

62) McAslan and KPMG, 2007, p.12

63) Freedictionary.com, definition of "doctrine" accessed and downloaded on 22/02/2015 at: *www.thefreedictionary.com/doctrine*

64) Maalouf, A., (n.d.) cited on goodreads.com website, accessed and downloaded on 25/02/2015 at: *www.goodreads.com/quotes/463454-doctrines-are-meant-to-serve-man-not-the-other-way*

65) Morgan Stanley, (2013) Mission Statement, Company Culture and Diversity Strategy, downloaded on 21 10 2013 from: *http://bankingisback. toigofoundation.org/firmProfile_MS.html*

66) Briggs, R. and Edwards C, (2006) 'The Business of Resilience', London:Demos. p.37

67) Ibid

68) Cullen Report. In Oil & Gas UK, (1990), 'Piper Alpha Disaster Lessons Learned': accessed and downloaded on 21/10/2013 at: *www.oilandgasuk.co.uk/ cmsfiles/modules/publications/pdfs/HS048.pdf*

69) Green, R., (2013) Personal Fitness Training philosophy downloaded from website on 21 10 2013 from: *www.rogergreenpersonaltraining.com/*

70) Teller et al (2006), Crisis Intervention Team Training For Police Officers Responding To Mental Disturbance Calls, Psychiatric Services, February 2006, Vol. 57, No. 2

71) Humber Emergency Planning Service (2009), Business Continuity step-by-step guide Part 3 Testing and exercising your business continuity plan, downloaded on the 06 11 2013 from: *www2.eastriding.gov.uk/ EasySiteWeb/GatewayLink.aspx?alId=103463*.

72) Cap Gemeni (2013), 'End to end business continuity testing', accessed and downloaded on 06/11/2013 from: *www.capgemini.com/sites/default/ files/resource/pdf/bc_continuity_whitepaper.pdf*

73) ASIS (2013), ASIS International Selects 2013 Accolade Winners, downloaded on 21 10 2013 from: *www.asisonline.org/News/Press-Room/Press-Releases/2013/Pages/ASIS-International-Selects-2013-Accolades-Winners.aspx#1383821488653l&false* and: United Business Media (UBM), Security Excellence Awards, accessed and downloaded on 06/11/2013 at: *www.securityexcellenceawards.co.uk/*

74) Gladwell., M., (2008) Outliers, New York: Little, Brown and Company

75) 10minutemanager.com, 'Competence Ladder', accessed and downloaded on 07/11/2013 from: *http://10minutemanager.com/wp-content/uploads/2013/10/ Competence-ladder.jpg*

76) Mindtools (2013), 'Conscious Competence Model', accessed and downloaded on 07/11/2013 at: *www.mindtools.com/pages/article/ newISS_96.htm*

77) Bloom, B., (1956), 'Taxonomy of Educational Objectives', Handbook I, The Cognitive Domain 1, New York: David McKay Co Inc.

78) *www.ginabudi.com*

79) Kolb, D., (1984), 'Experiential Learning: experience as the source of learning and development', Englewood Cliffs: Prentice Hall

80) University of Gloucestershire. (2015), accessed and downloaded on 23/02/2015 at: *www2.glos.ac.uk/gdn/gibbs/ch2.htm*

81) Op., Cit., (Kahneman: 2012)

82) Ibid

83) Insbury, D., files downloaded on 21 10 2013 from: *http://davesainsbury.files.wordpress.com/2013/02/untitled.png*

84) Barnstable, K., (2012), 'Three P's of Online Instruction, in Stable Transitions: A Journey of Learning': accessed and downloaded on 23/11/12 from: *http://kbarnstable.wordpress.com/2012/09/05/three-ps-of-online-instruction/*

85) Salmon, G., (2000) 'E-Moderating, the key to teaching and learning online': London and New York: Taylor and Francis

86) Moule, P., (2007), 'Challenging the five-stage model for e-learning: a new approach', ALT-J, Research in Learning Technology, Vol.15, No.1, March 2007

87) Ibid

88) Dewey, J., (1910), 'How We Think', New York: Heath & Co.

89) Higher Education Academy, (2012), 'Framework Guidance Note 3: What are the Dimensions?' March 2012. Accessed and downloaded on 23/11/2012 from: *www.heacademy.ac.uk/ukpsf#dimensions*

90) Op., Cit., (Kahneman: 2012)

91) British Standards Institute, pages for security related activity, accessed and downloaded on 08/11/2013 from: *www.bsigroup.co.uk/en-GB/standards/#standards*

92) IT Governance (2013), 'Cloud Security Governance', downloaded on 08/11/2013 from: *www.itgovernance.co.uk/cloud-governance.aspx*

93) Skills for Security (2013), National Occupational Standards, access website at: *www.skillsforsecurity.org.uk/index.php/help/35/2*

94) National Security Inspectorate in the UK can be accessed at: *www.nsi.org.uk/about-us/*

95) Security Industry Authority UK website can be accessed at: *www.sia.homeoffice.gov.uk/Pages/home.aspx*

CHAPTER 3: SECURITY LEGISLATION AND REGULATION

3.1 Context

"Compromise is the best and cheapest lawyer." – Robert Louis Stevenson, Scottish novelist, poet and travel writer.

This chapter will give readers an understanding of some of the ranges of laws, regulations, codes of practice, guidelines and procedures, which impact on the role of a security practitioner. Much of the following material is focused upon the UK legal system, which is a foundation to many legal systems around the world. Readers beyond UK legal domains are advised at all times to reflect upon what they are learning, and conduct further research, in order to fully understand legal compliance in their country or theatre of operation. Towards the end of this chapter we will take a closer look at aspects of international law; a legal domain comprising of many dilemmas and potential pitfalls.

At the end of this chapter, readers will be able to:

- know the background to common law, civil law and statute law
- understand important human rights laws
- appreciate other key legislation in relation to security activities
- ahow knowledge of health and safety at work principles
- understand what is meant by international law
- show familiarity with other pre-eminent laws from other jurisdictions that impact corporate activity and compliance policy.

3.2 Types of law in UK

Common law

- Dictionary – *"The ancient customary law of the land."*
- Common law has existed from time immemorial, or for a sufficiently long time that it has been held by judges to have always been the law.
- It was the ancient system of laws based on previous court decisions (*precedents*) which have been recorded, and define what the common law relating to a particular matter has always been.
- Common law remains in place until replaced by an Act of Parliament (statute law).

Civil law

- Definition – *"The law of a State relating to private and civilian affairs. It is concerned with disputes about the duties and the rights between individuals and organisations."*
- Property – Ownership/boundary disputes/trespass.
- Contract law – Phone contracts/tickets for a service.
- Consumer law – Faulty goods.
- Work related disputes – Unfair dismissal/gender discrimination/ negligence/duty of care.
- Libel (written) slander (verbal) – Offensive/untrue newspaper article or untrue public statement.
- Copyright disputes/intellectual property rights.

Statute law

- Dictionary – *"A law expressly enacted by the legislature (a law making body)."*
- In England it is written law that has passed through the Houses of Parliament as a '*Bill*' and becomes an '*Act*' when it receives royal assent.
- Royal assent is when the sovereign physically signs a '*Bill*' to create an '*Act*'.
- A statute is more commonly known as an '*Act of Parliament*'.
- '*Criminal law*' is 'common and statute' crime law.

3.3 UK human rights laws

We will now spend the next few sections looking at prominent UK-based human rights laws. Although UK law is a popular foundation for many other national legal systems, when reading this section, it is worth applying further research to thoroughly understand the legal environment in your country of operation. There is, rightly, much public scrutiny and political focus upon human rights issues. Security practitioners need to understand the underpinning motivations behind human rights legislation. Why were they brought in? Moreover, how might they impact your employees and operations? Laws are not just rigid, abstract rules of behaviour. But laws and protocols in this domain can be written codifications that enshrine individual, inalienable rights, such as the right to life, a fair trial, dignity and freedom of expression. Upholding such legal and moral values does lie at the heart of delivering security management initiatives that transmit authority to all those impacted. International human rights law, including in relation to conflict management and individual human rights, is covered a little later in this chapter (at 3.6).

The Human Rights Act 1998

The Human Rights Act 1998 came into effect on 2 October 2000. It is an extremely significant piece of legislation, which incorporates the European Convention on Human Rights (ECHR) into the law of the United Kingdom. More is explained in relation to ECHR in our later firearms sub-chapter (at 6.6).

Introducing convention rights into UK law

- Before the introduction of the act, people in the UK could only enforce their convention rights by making an application to the European Court of Human Rights.
- This is a lengthy and complex process. Since 2 October 2000, individuals have had a right of redress in the UK courts. In broad terms, the act gives effect to convention rights in three ways:
  1. All legislation must be interpreted wherever possible, in a way that will uphold and protect convention rights.
  2. Public authority (including the courts) must act in compliance with convention rights, unless they are prevented from doing so by legislation.
  3. Any new legislation must be drawn up with regard to the convention to ensure it respects convention rights, and any current legislation which is not compatible with the convention, can be amended under a 'fast track' procedure.

Absolute rights and qualified rights

Certain rights, such as the prohibition on torture, are absolute rights, and cannot be restricted, even in times of war or other public emergencies.

Other rights, such as the right to privacy, are qualified rights which can be interfered with in certain circumstances.

Any interference must be lawful, necessary in a democratic society and proportionate to the aim it seeks to achieve.

Article 2: Right to life

Everyone's right to life shall be protected by law. Nobody shall be deprived of their life intentionally, save in the execution of a sentence of a court following their conviction of a crime for which this penalty is provided by law.

Article 4: Prohibition of slavery and forced labour

This article prohibits slavery and forced or compulsory labour. It does not apply to prisoners, military service and civil obligations, or in emergencies.

Article 8: Right to respect for private and family life

- Everyone has the right to a private and family life, home and correspondence.
- There shall be no interference by a public authority with the exercise of this right, except such as is in accordance with the law and is necessary in a democratic society in the interests of national security, public safety, or the economic well-being of the country, for the prevention of disorders or crime, for the protection of health or morals, or for the protection of the rights and freedoms of others.

Article 9: Freedom of thought, conscience and religion

- Everyone has the right to freedom of thought, conscience and religion; this right includes freedom to change religion or belief, and freedom, either alone or in community with others, and in public or private, to manifest one's religion or belief, in worship, teaching, practice and observance.
- Freedom to manifest one's religion or beliefs shall be subject only to such limitations as are prescribed by law and are necessary in a democratic society in the interests of public safety, for the protection of public order, health or morals, or for the protection of the rights and freedoms of others.

Article 11: Freedom of association and assembly

Everyone has the right to freedom of peaceful assembly and to freedom of association with others, including the right to form, and to join, trade unions for the protection of their interests.

Article 14: Prohibition of discrimination

The enjoyment of the rights and freedoms set forth in this convention shall be secured without discrimination on any ground, such as sex, race, colour, language, religion, political or other opinion, national or social origin, association with a national minority, property, birth or other status.

3.4 Other UK laws relating to security management

Private Security Industry Act 2001

- Section 1 – Established the security industry authority (SIA) as the government regulatory body for England and Wales. Scotland and Northern Ireland joined soon after.
- Section 3 – Offence for a self-employed (sub-contracted) person to work in the private security industry without being the holder of an SIA licence.
- Section 5 – Offence for a person or company to use, or supply, any unlicensed security operator (contracted staff – any licensable sector).
- Section 5 is an 'indictable offence'.
- Enforcement – SIA investigators and whistle-blowers.

Citizen's powers of arrest

In the UK, a citizen can lawfully arrest a person (1). The power comes from Section 24A(2) of the 1984 Police and Criminal Evidence Act – widely known as 'PACE'. Similar powers do exist in many other countries. You may be entitled to carry out a citizen's arrest on anybody:

- Who is committing an indictable offence, or if the citizen has reasonable grounds to suspect that they are committing an indictable offence. (These include theft and most types of assault.)
- Who has committed an indictable offence, or who the citizen reasonably suspects to have committed an indictable offence
- Who is causing a 'breach of the peace'.

When you arrest someone, if you can, you must tell them:

- who you are
- that they are under arrest
- what they have been arrested for
- that the police will be called
- that they will be detained until police arrive
- if necessary – hold the person but
- only use reasonable and justifiable force and exercise restraint.

Strong advice:

- if possible – obtain a witness

- make immediate notes of the arrest
- be prepared to be sued!

Indictable offences

- Indictable offences are those which can be tried in a crown court, or higher court, by a jury. For private security industry operatives, indictable offences include the more serious crimes for which a security officer may make an arrest:
  o Theft, fraud, serious assault, robbery, burglary, rape, criminal damage, arson, firearms offences, kidnap and ransom, blackmail, manslaughter, murder etc.

Common law – Use of force

Common law has always recognised the right of a person to protect him/herself from attack, to act in defence of others and, if necessary, to inflict violence on another in so doing. If no more force is used than is reasonable to repel the attack, such force is not unlawful. In relation to firearms use, we look further at use of force laws in Chapter 6, Protective Security.

It is lawful to use reasonable force on another as long as it is in the execution of the following:

- self defence
- to effect a lawful citizen's arrest
- to save a life
- to prevent a crime being committed
- in stopping a breach of the peace.

Statute law – Use of force

Individual responsibility: The responsibility for any use of force will rest upon the person who uses it, and is likely to have to be justified in a court of law.

Section 3 Criminal Law Act 1967: "A person may use such force as is reasonable in the circumstances in the prevention of a crime or in effecting or assisting in the lawful arrest of offenders or suspected offenders or of persons unlawfully at large".

The law relating to assaults

Definition of an 'assault': "An assault is the intentional application of force to the person of another without their consent, or the threat of such force by act or gesture if the person threatening has or causes the person threatened to believe that he/she has the present ability to affect his/her purpose".

Assault may also be called 'common assault', assault is the least serious of the three similar offences, which are, actual bodily harm and grievous bodily harm. An assault can range from verbal abuse and physically threatening behaviour, to unwanted physical contact and actual physical assault.

Making someone fear that there is a potential threat of being hurt by an offender may also be classed as an assault; however, this is dependent on all circumstances.

The law relating to assaults

Criminal Justice Act 1988: Section 39 – common assault

Offences Against The Person Act 1861:

> Section 18 – Grievous bodily harm (GBH) with intent
>
> Section 20 – GBH and unlawful wounding
>
> Section 47– Actual bodily harm (ABH)

Conspiracy

Under the Criminal Law Act 1977, amended by the Criminal Attempts Act 1981, conspiracy is the discussion among two or more people in which they agree that one or all of them will commit an offence. Conspiracy is applicable whether or not the offence is actually carried out.

Trials for conspiracy take place in the crown court and sentences are the same as for the offence that was the subject of the conspiracy.

Criminal damage

Under the Criminal Law Act 1971, criminal damage is the unlawful destruction or damage of property, or the threatened destruction or damage of property.

Criminal damage can include disfiguring property with graffiti.

Lawful damage of property may take place if the damage takes place in order to protect neighbouring property in an emergency, e.g. a fire that threatens to spread.

Theft

Under the Theft Act 1968, theft is an act of taking another person's property dishonestly and without the intentions of returning it.

Robbery

Robbery is defined as taking property from a person, accompanied with threats of violence, or actual violence to the victim.

Going equipped

This offence under the Theft Act 1968 refers to offenders who are found carrying tools that they may intend to use to commit an act of theft.

The tools would need to have been adapted for the purpose, and if they were not adapted, the prosecution would have to show that, in all probability, there is an intention to commit the offence.

Racially aggravated offences

It is a criminal offence to attack or abuse a person because of their race or religious beliefs, or to incite racial hatred.

Such attacks and abuse include:

- attacking or damaging their property
- attacking a person or their family
- threatening or abusing them verbally
- publishing abusive material.

Harassment

Under the protection from Harassment Act 1997, harassment is defined as a set of behaviours that threaten or harass an individual.

There are two offences here:

1. One is simply behaviour that amounts to harassment.
2. The second, more serious offence includes behaviour that causes another person to become fearful that there may be a violent outcome.

Incitement

Incitement is essentially persuading or encouraging another person to commit an offence, whether or not that offence is in the event committed.

Incitement cases are tried in court, in which the offence itself would be tried. In a magistrate's court, the maximum sentence is the same as for the offence itself.

In the crown court, the sentence is at the court's discretion.

Manslaughter

Killing another person either with or without intending to.

There are several types of manslaughter, grouped as 'voluntary manslaughter' and 'involuntary manslaughter'.

For either, the maximum sentence is life imprisonment.

In a murder trial, a person may be found not guilty of murder but manslaughter, for one of three reasons;-

1. The killing came about because the offender was provoked to the point where he suddenly and temporarily lost control of him/herself, and provocation was enough to make any reasonable person lose control.
2. The killing was part of a suicide pact and was acted out with the full intention that the killer would also die in the process.
3. The killer could not be held responsible for his act because of an abnormality of mind; this is not the same as being found not guilty of murder because of insanity.

Involuntary manslaughter

Three types:

1. **Constructive manslaughter** is causing the death of a person by an unlawful act. The act need not be against the person, but could, for example, be against a building; and the risk of injury needs to be one that would be apparent to any reasonable person, whether it was apparent to the defendant or not.
2. **Gross negligence manslaughter** is causing the death of a person for whom the accused has duty of care, e.g. by a doctor to their patient by a negligent act or failure to act.

3. **Reckless manslaughter** is causing the death of a person by an act of recklessness; the offender sees the risk associated with what they are doing and carries on regardless.

Murder

- Killing another person, with, in that immortal and well-known phrase, 'aforethought'.
- For a killing to be considered murder, the killer must intend either to cause the victim's death or to commit GBH (which then brought about the victim's death).
- Murder may be committed either through a positive act of killing, or through an act of omission.
- British citizens who commit murder in foreign countries are guilty of an offence under UK law, and may be tried in this country.

Terrorism

The Terrorism Act 2000 has got 131 sections. To summarise some key points:

Section 1 Terrorism: interpretation

- In this Act 'terrorism' means the use or threat of action where –
  o the action falls within subsection (2)
  o the use or threat is designed to influence the government [or an international governmental organisation] or to intimidate the public or a section of the public
  o the use or threat is made for the purpose of advancing a political, religious, racial, or ideological cause.
- Action falls within this subsection if it –
  o involves serious violence against a person
  o involves serious damage to property
  o endangers a person's life, other than that of the person committing the action
  o creates a serious risk to the health or safety of the public or a section of the public
  o is designed seriously to interfere with or to disrupt an electronic system.
- The use or threat of action falling within subsection (2) which involves the use of firearms or explosives is terrorism whether or not subsection (1) (b) is satisfied.

- In this section –
  - o 'action' includes action outside the United Kingdom
  - o a reference to any person or to property is a reference to any person, or to property, wherever situated
  - o a reference to the public includes a reference to the public of a country other than the United Kingdom
  - o 'the government' means the government of the United Kingdom, of a part of the United Kingdom, or of a country other than the United Kingdom.
- In this Act a reference to action taken for the purposes of terrorism includes a reference to action taken for the benefit of a proscribed organisation.

Section 43: Search of persons

- A constable may stop and search a person whom he reasonably suspects to be a terrorist, to discover whether he has in his possession anything which may constitute evidence that he is a terrorist.
- A constable may search a person arrested under section 41 to discover whether he has in his possession anything which may constitute evidence that he is a terrorist.
- (3) A search of a person under this section must be carried out by someone of the same sex.
- A constable may seize and retain anything which he discovers in the course of a search of a person under subsection (1) or (2) and which he reasonably suspects may constitute evidence that the person is a terrorist.
- A person who has the powers of a constable in one part of the United Kingdom may exercise a power under this section in any part of the United Kingdom.

Trespass

What is the definition of 'trespass'? Put simply, a dictionary definition is: *"The entering of (or remaining on) property without permission of the occupier"*.

'Simple trespass':

- Which statute covers the law relating to *simple trespass*?
- None – It's a civil matter!
- Exceptions?

- Owner must formally ask trespassers to leave his/her home/property or land – Refusal – The owner may use a reasonable and justifiable amount of force to eject.
- Police will attend a trespass incident and assist but will generally only act to prevent a 'breach of the peace'.
- Can trespassers really be prosecuted? Trespass is <u>not</u> a crime – but is still a wrongful act.

Aggravated trespass

Under the Criminal Justice and Public Order Act 1994, there is a related offence of 'aggravated trespass', in which the offender enters private land (in the open air) with the intention of threatening people who are going about their lawful business on that land, or trying to prevent them doing so.

3.5 Other UK laws relating to corporate management and workplaces

Health and Safety Act Work Acts

- Individuals are vulnerable to the operations of organisations – accidents happen!
- Deaths and/or injuries not only impact on the individual but also on the organisation/business.
- Individuals and organisations are legally obliged.
- You may be held responsible. There are lots of legal precedents where careless bosses (or those proven to be) have been sent to prison.

Consider – Who is at risk?

- Employees
- Contractors and subcontractors
- Clients and customers
- Suppliers
- Visitors
- Anyone else?

What hazards/threats may individuals be exposed to?

- Slips, trips and falls
- Falling objects/structures

- Hazardous materials
- Fire
- Explosions
- Water hazards/drowning.

What hazards/threats may individuals be exposed to?

- Machinery
- Traffic
- Travel
- Overloading/overcrowding
- Poor planning
- Actions/omissions of personnel
- Negligence.

Hazards and threats should be prevented and mitigated by carrying out risk management. For real detail about conducting such a process, turn to Chapter 6. It is the responsibility of management to prevent, as far as practicable, risks from hazards and threats, or any combination thereof from materialising.

Sources of main UK health and safety legislation:

- Health and Safety at Work etc. Act 1974.
- Workplace (Health, Safety and Welfare) Regulations 1992.
- HM Government has the responsibility for enacting laws and regulations within the UK.
- EU: Legislation and directives impact UK workplace practices.
- Regulations of Health and Safety in the UK are led by the Health and Safety Commission (HSC). The executive department of the HSC is the Health and Safety Executive (HSE).

HASAW Acts, statutory instruments and regulations

The HSE owns a significant amount of primary and secondary legislation. The primary legislation comprises the Acts of Parliament, including the Health and Safety at Work Act 1974. The secondary legislation is made up of statutory instruments (SIs), often referred to as 'regulations'. It is enforced by the HSE and local authorities.

What does health and safety regulation really mean? Health and safety laws and regulations require a response from employers:

- Employers have a duty to protect people.
- If found guilty of non-compliance or negligence, employers face legal penalties.
- Employers must ensure that a thorough *risk assessment* of all aspects of the organisation's operations has been conducted with regard to the potential effect on personnel.

However, responsibility does not solely rest with the employer. It is also the responsibility of every employee and individual on the organisation's property (including those travelling offsite) to ensure that they do not cause hazards to themselves or other personnel by:

- their own actions
- their own negligence
- their own omissions.

Responsibilities of the employer and employee:

- Management must therefore inform employees and any/all other individuals what must/must not be done by raising awareness, instilling a sense of responsibility and ultimately by ensuring compliance.
  Consider:
  o How might management best go about this?
  o What problems are likely to be encountered?
  o How might these be overcome?

Employers must:

- ensure as far as possible that health, safety and welfare are maintained in the workplace.
- appoint a 'competent person'.
- "A competent person is someone who has sufficient training and experience or knowledge and other qualities that allow them to assist you properly. The level of competence required will depend on the complexity of the situation and the particular help you need" (HSE).

Businesses with more than five employees must:

- hold an official record of risk assessments
- have a formal health and safety policy.

All businesses must:

- ensure that staff understand and comply with the health and safety policy.

Responsibilities of the employee:

Employees have a responsibility to ensure they:

- take reasonable care of their own health and safety
- take reasonable care that they don't put other people at risk by what they do – or don't do in the course of their work
- cooperate with the employer regarding health and safety
- do not misuse or interfere with anything provided for health, safety or welfare
- by law, a risk assessment is required. Basic risk assessment approaches outlined by the HSE are outlined below. However, for other examples of risk assessment techniques please go to Chapter 6, Protective Security.

Risk assessments – definitions

- A hazard is anything that may cause harm, such as chemicals, electricity, working from ladders, an open drawer, etc.
- "The risk is the chance, high or low, that somebody could be harmed by these and other hazards, together with an indication of how serious the harm could be", writes the HSE.

Risk assessments – Five steps to success

1. Identify the hazards
2. Identify who may be harmed and how
3. Evaluate the risks and decide on precautions
4. Record your findings and implement them
5. Review your assessment and update as necessary.

(Source: UK Health and Safety Executive)

Step 1 – Identify the hazards

- How?
    - o visual inspection
    - o questioning of personnel

    o questionnaires
- Who can provide information?
  - o staff, suppliers ...
- Attention to detail essential
- Think outside own operations/premises.

Step 2 – Identify who may be harmed and how

A range of people may be harmed and their vulnerability will be influenced by a variety of factors including:

- work performed
- work location
- knowledge/awareness of hazards and risks
- actual harm that may be caused – death, injury
- others including age, etc.

Step 3 – Evaluate the risks and decide on precautions:

- Prioritise. Some risks will be more serious than others
- In health and safety it is rare that a risk is regarded as acceptable, so doing nothing is not normally an option
- The HSE indicates that what is done should correspond with best practice and regulation.

Decide on precautions:

- Can work be conducted in a less risky way? Not always
- Can access to the hazard be prevented? Not always
- Can work be organised to reduce exposure to the hazard?
- Can PPE be issued? Problems?

Step 4 – Record and implement findings

Record

- How?
- Where?
- Why?

Implement: Now having assessed the risks, decide on precautions that must be implemented.

Step 5 – Review and reassess

- Over time operations may change, therefore new risks may appear, or old ones change in priorit.
- Changes require a reassessment of the risk
- All changes to the risk, and ways to deal with it, must be communicated.

Requirements for health and safety protection

- Within the working environment there are a number of general requirements for health and safety measures to be implemented. These do, however, vary according to the specific industry or environmental requirements necessary. Additional considerations could include:
  o **Maintenance** – Facilities, machinery, equipment and vehicles, etc.
  o **Ventilation** – adequate provision of uncontaminated air
  o **Temperatures** – laid down by regulation
  o **Lighting** – adequate for work and movement
  o **Cleanliness** – workplaces should be clean, with waste removed
  o **Floors and traffic routes** – sufficient routes to allow for safe movement. Consider height/width, speed limits, condition of surfaces, etc.
  o **Falls** – Consider use of fences, rails, harnesses and dangers of falling objects – stacking of material, etc.
  o **Transparent/translucent** – these type of surfaces must be clear of materials and marked so that they can be seen
  o **Sanitary/wash facilities** – accessible, clean, well lit, provided with hot/cold water, soap and means of drying
  o **Drinking water** – provided by upward jet or suitable cups
  o **Clothing and changing** – appropriate facilities where there is a need to change
  o **Rest and meals** – suitable and sufficient facilities

Health and safety – security's contribution

- The primary role of a security department is maintaining security.
- However, with health and safety there is the opportunity to maximise the value of security staff.

- Security staff should be trained to understand the hazards inherent in an operational site and be encouraged to be alert to recognise problems.
- Do assignment instructions include health and safety?
- Are there procedures for reporting and recording?

The activities of security

During the course of their duties, security staff can assist in monitoring and enforcing health and safety regulations. They should be looking for:

- Hazards and obstructions
  - o At ground level
  - o On stairs/elevated walkways
- Vehicle movements – speed/routes
- Wearing of personal protective equipment (PPE)
- Any others?

How security might best assist health and safety

It may be useful for security staff to be provided with a tour of the facility by a representative of the health and safety department, to identify hazards and risks that should be reported, etc.

In summary, the health and safety function is:

- a legal requirement
- essential for the well-being of all employees, visitors and customers
- the responsibility of all
- a sensible and responsible business function
- time consuming
- an ongoing process.

Remember: If things go wrong, ignorance is not acceptable as an excuse!

Other workplace laws: Vicarious liability

According to the Advisory and Conciliation Service (ACAS) an independent employment arbitration organisation, vicarious liability refers to:

"Vicarious liability refers to a situation where someone is held responsible for the actions or omissions of another person. In a workplace context, an employer can be liable for the acts or omissions of its employees, provided it can be shown that they took place in the course of their employment (3)."

- Vicarious liability is liability of one person for the acts or omissions of another
- The most frequent form of vicarious liability is that of an employer for the acts and omissions of an employee
- Must be in the *'course of employment'*
- Question of law to decide.

How to avoid vicarious liability?

- Introduce a policy in relation to employee conduct
- Provide clear guidelines to independent contractors for acceptable behaviour
- Provide practical training to help employees deal with incidents safely
- Ensure managers are vigilant in relation to your staff's health. Stress may affect an employee's judgement
- Incidents are more likely to happen at high-risk events, such as concerts and parties, during the busy seasonal period, so ensure staff have extra support

Reporting of Injuries, Diseases and Dangerous Occurrences Regulations 2013 (RIDDOR), is the law that requires employers to report and keep records of incidents and accidents that cause harm and near misses (4). The relevance of this type of information is critical in that it can provide real substance when conducting risk assessments. For example, information collated around prior incidents and trends can help enormously when grading risks within a facility. Many organisations beyond UK shores do use the RIDDOR system in order to provide reassurance, accurate organisational risk analysis and also as a quality performance benchmark.

Corporate Manslaughter and Corporate Homicide Act 2007

The offence

An organisation to which this section applies is guilty of an offence if the way in which its activities are managed or organised:

- causes a person's death

- amounts to a gross breach of a relevant duty of care owed by the organisation to the deceased (Subsection 1).

A breach of a duty of care by an organisation is a gross breach if the alleged conduct amounts to a breach of that duty that falls far below what can reasonably be expected of an organisation in the circumstances. The organisations to which this section applies are:

- a corporation
- a department or other body listed in Schedule 1
- a police force
- a partnership, or a trade union or employers' association that is an employer.

An organisation is guilty of an offence under this section only if the way in which its activities are managed or organised by its senior management is a substantial element in the breach referred to in Subsection 1. Senior management means the persons who play significant roles in:

- the making of decisions about how the whole, or a substantial part, of its activities are to be managed or organised
- the actual managing or organising of the whole, or a substantial part of those activities.

Relevant duty of care

A 'relevant duty of care', in relation to an organisation, means any of the following duties owed by it under the law of negligence:

- A duty owed to its employees, or to other persons working for the organisation, or performing services for it;
- A duty owed as occupier of premises;
- A duty owed in connection with:
  - o the supply by the organisation of goods or services (whether for consideration or not),
  - o the carrying on by the organisation of any construction or maintenance operations,
  - o the carrying on by the organisation of any other activity on a commercial basis, or
  - o the use or keeping by the organisation of any plant, vehicle or other thing;

- A duty owed to a person who, by reason of being a person within subsection (2), is someone for whose safety the organisation is responsible.

A person is within this subsection if:

- they are detained at a custodial institution, or in a custody area at a court or police station
- they are detained at a removal centre or short-term holding facility
- they are being transported in a vehicle, or being held in any premises, in pursuance of prison escort arrangements or immigration escort arrangements
- they are living in secure accommodation in which they have been placed
- they are a detained patient.

No individual liability

An individual cannot be guilty of aiding, abetting, counselling or procuring the commission of an offence of corporate manslaughter.

An individual cannot be guilty of aiding, abetting, counselling or procuring, or being art and part in, the commission of an offence of corporate homicide.

Penalties

On conviction, a corporation may be ordered to remedy any breach, or to publicise its failures, or be given an unlimited fine.

Summary

- State the offence
- State the organisations to which it applies
- Describe relevant duty of care
- Explain what is meant by senior management
- Know the penalties.

Bribery Act 2010

Came into force April 2011. The act:

- introduced a corporate offence of failure to prevent bribery by persons working on behalf of a business. A business can avoid conviction if it can show that it has adequate procedures in place to prevent bribery
- made it a criminal offence to give, promise, or offer a bribe, and to request, agree to receive, or accept a bribe, either at home or abroad. The measures cover bribery of a foreign public official
- increased the maximum penalty for bribery from seven to ten years imprisonment, with an unlimited fine.

Case study examples of offences of bribing another person

A person ('P') is guilty of an offence if either of the following cases applies.

Case 1 is where:
(a) P offers, promises, or gives a financial or other advantage to another person, and
(b) P intends the advantage:
    (i) To induce a person to perform improperly a relevant function or activity, *or*
    (ii) To reward a person for the improper performance of such a function or activity.

Case 2 is where:
(a) P offers, promises, or gives a financial or other advantage to another person, *and*
(b) P knows, or believes, that the acceptance of the advantage would itself constitute the improper performance of a relevant function or activity.

Offences relating to being bribed:
A person ('R') is guilty of an offence if any of the following cases applies.

Case 3 is where:
R requests, agrees to receive, or accepts a financial or other advantage intending that, in consequence, a relevant function or activity should be performed improperly (whether by R or another person).

Case 4 is where:
(a) R requests, agrees to receive, or accepts a financial or other advantage, and
(b) The request, agreement or acceptance itself constitutes the improper performance by R of a relevant function or activity.

Case 5 is where:
R requests, agrees to receive, or accepts a financial or other advantage as a reward for the improper performance (whether by R or another person) of a relevant function or activity.

Case 6 is where:
In anticipation of, or in consequence of R requesting, agreeing to receive, or accepting a financial or other advantage, a relevant function or activity is performed improperly-
(a) By R, or
(b) By another person at R's request or with R's assent or acquiescence.

Function or activity to which bribe relates

For the purposes of this act a function or activity is a relevant function or activity if:

- it falls within subsection (2)
- meets one or more of conditions A to C.

The following functions and activities fall within this subsection (2):

- any function of a public nature
- any activity connected with a business
- any activity performed in the course of a person's employment
- any activity performed by, or on behalf of, a body of persons (whether corporate or unincorporated).

Conditions

- Condition **A** is that a person performing the function or activity is expected to perform it in good faith.
- Condition **B** is that a person performing the function or activity is expected to perform it impartially.
- Condition **C** is that a person performing the function or activity is in a position of trust by virtue of performing it.

A function or activity:

A function or activity is a relevant function or activity even if it:

- has no connection with the United Kingdom
- is performed in a country or territory outside the United Kingdom.

In this section 'business' includes trade or profession.

Improper performance to which bribe relates

For the purposes of this act, a relevant function or activity:

- is performed improperly if it is performed in breach of a relevant expectation
- is to be treated as being performed improperly if there is a failure to perform the function or activity and that failure is itself a breach of a relevant expectation.

'relevant expectation' –

- In relation to a function or activity which meets condition A or B, means the expectation mentioned in the condition concerned
- In relation to a function or activity which meets condition C, means any expectation as to the manner in which, or the reasons for which, the function or activity will be performed that arises from the position of trust mentioned in that condition.

Anything that a person does (or omits to do) arising from, or in connection with that person's past performance of a relevant function or activity, is to be treated for the purposes of this act as being done (or omitted) by that person in the performance of that function or activity.

Bribery of foreign public officials:

- A person ('P') who bribes a foreign public official ('F') is guilty of an offence if P's intention is to influence F in F's capacity as a foreign public official.
- P must also intend to obtain or retain –
  o business
  o an advantage in the conduct of business.
- P bribes F if, and only if:
  o directly or through a third party, P offers, promises, or gives any financial or other advantage –
    ■ to F
    ■ to another person at F's request or with F's assent or acquiescence
  o F is neither permitted nor required by the written law applicable to F to be influenced in F's capacity as a foreign public official by the offer, promise or gift.

Failure of commercial organisations to prevent bribery:

Section 7 created the 'broad and innovatory offence' of the failure of commercial organisations to prevent bribery on their behalf. This applies to all commercial organisations which have business in the UK.

As well as the organisation, individuals and employees may also be guilty.

The offence is one of strict liability, with no need to prove any kind of intention or positive action.

Prosecution and penalties:

- If an individual is found guilty of a bribery offence, tried as a summary offence, they may be imprisoned for up to 12 months and fined up to £5,000.

- An indictment however, faces up to ten years' imprisonment and an unlimited fine.

- The crime of a commercial organisation failing to prevent bribery is punishable by an unlimited fine. In addition, a convicted individual or organisation may be subject to a confiscation order under the Proceeds of Crime Act 2002, while a company director who is convicted may be disqualified under the Company Directors Disqualification Act 1986.

Data Protection Act 1998

The 1998 Data Protection Act came into force early in 1999 and covers how information about living identifiable persons is used.

The act covers eight 'data protection principles':

- The Data Protection Act requires that appropriate security measures are in place to safeguard against unauthorised or unlawful access/processing of personal data.

- The act also states that personal data cannot be held unless it is registered with the data protection registrar.

- The Data Protection Act gives the right to compensation when personal data that is held is inaccurate, and the right to have inaccurate data corrected or erased.

What is personal data?

Personal data means data which relates to a living individual who can be identified –

- from those data

- from those data and other information which is in the possession of, or is likely to come into the possession of, the data controller

- includes any expression of opinion about the individual and any indication of the intentions of the data controller, or any other person in respect of the individual.

Sensitive personal data means personal data consisting of information as to:

- the racial or ethnic origin of the data subject

- their political opinions

- their religious beliefs or other beliefs of a similar nature

- whether they are a member of a trade union (within the meaning of the Trade Union and Labour Relations (Consolidation) Act 1992)
- their physical or mental health or condition
- their sexual life
- the commission, or alleged commission by themselves of any offence, or any proceedings for any offence committed, or alleged to have been committed by, the disposal of such proceedings, or the sentence of any court in such proceedings.

The eight data protection principles:

1. Personal data shall be processed fairly and lawfully and, in particular, shall not be processed unless:
   (a) At least one of the conditions in Schedule 2 is met, and:
   (b) In the face of sensitive personal data, at least one of the conditions in Schedule 3 is also met
2. Personal data shall be obtained only for one or more specified and lawful purposes, and shall not be further processed in any manner incompatible with that purpose or those purposes.
3. Personal data shall be adequate, relevant and not excessive in relation to the purpose or purposes for which they are processed.
4. Personal data shall be accurate and, where necessary, kept up to date.
5. Personal data processed for any purpose or purposes shall not be kept for longer than is necessary for that purpose or those purposes.
6. Personal data shall be processed in accordance with the rights of data subjects under this act.
7. Appropriate technical and organisational measures shall be taken against unauthorised or unlawful processing of personal data and against accidental loss or destruction of, or damage to, personal data.
8. Personal data shall not be transferred to a country or territory outside the European Economic Area unless that country or territory ensures an adequate level of protection for the rights and freedoms of data subjects, in relation to the processing of personal data.

Data subject access:

- Is the right of an individual to access personal data relating to him or her that is held by a data controller

- An individual shall be entitled at reasonable intervals and without undue delay or expense
- To be informed by any data user whether they hold personal data of which that individual is the subject
- To access any such data held by a data user
- Where appropriate, to have such data corrected or, in some cases, destroyed.

Offences and punishment:

You may commit an offence under the Data Protection Act 1998 if you 'knowingly or recklessly':

- obtain or disclose personal information, or the information contained in personal data
- procure the disclosure to another person of the information contained in personal data without any consent.

This does not apply if you can show that the obtaining, disclosing or procuring:

- was necessary for the purpose of preventing or detecting crime
- was required or authorised by, or under, any attachment, by any rule, or by the order of a court
- that you acted in the reasonable belief that you had, in law, the right to obtain or disclose the data, or to procure the disclosure to the other person
- that you acted in the reasonable belief that the person concerned would have consented if he/she had known of the obtaining, disclosing or procuring and circumstances of it
- that in particular circumstances the obtaining; disclosing or procuring was justified as being in the public interest.

The penalties for these offences are that on summary conviction there can be a fine up to £5,000, or on conviction on indictment, an unlimited fine.

Regulation of Investigatory Powers Act 2000

This act is sometimes known as 'RIPA' in UK police and media spheres. The main purpose of the act is to ensure that the relevant investigatory powers are used in accordance with human rights. These powers are:

- the interception of communications
- the acquisition of communications data (e.g. billing data)
- intrusive surveillance (on residential premises/in private vehicles);
- covert surveillance in the course of specific operations
- the use of covert human intelligence sources (agents, informants, undercover officers)
- access to encrypted data.

For each of these powers, the act ensures that the law clearly covers:

- the purpose for which they may be used
- which authorities can use the powers
- who should authorise each use of the power
- the use that can be made of the material gained
- independent judicial oversight
- a means of redress for the individual.

3.6 International law, conflict and human rights

"Nothing in the present Charter shall impair the inherent right of individual or collective self-defence if an armed attack occurs against a Member of the United Nations, until the Security Council has taken measures necessary to maintain international peace and security. Measures taken by Members in the exercise of this right of self-defence shall be immediately reported to the Security Council and shall not in any way affect the authority and responsibility of the Security Council under the present Charter to take at any time such action as it deems necessary in order to maintain or restore international peace and security." – Article 51, Chapter 7, UN Charter, which provides for 'Actions with respect to threats to the peace' (5)

Context

International laws and regulations can often appear clear and concise on the surface. But there can be a great variety in interpretation, just as there may be with any domestic legislation. This section will aim to provide you with a grounding in some legal protocols and key perspectives at international and supranational levels of legal interpretation and decision making. We will introduce you to some key influencers and thinkers that inhabit legal and academic space in the security and resilience fields.

Perhaps the first and only rule of thumb with international law is that sometimes it is *not* a de facto legal obligation (with implied sanctions for breach) within individual nation states. In fact, on further analysis, there may not be a strictly legal obligation on many military and political leaders to follow some so-called 'international laws' at all. This is because nation states and national parliaments/assemblies may well sign up to various international treaties and protocols, such as various Geneva Conventions. But unless the principles are subsequently passed by parliaments or heads of government in a sovereign state, then that international law may not have any national rules of enforcement to underpin it. To break international law may be a moral failure by a government or set of individuals, and even cause revulsion at times but some legal analysts contend that much of 'international law' is unenforceable; indeed that the phrase is misused.

For example, the United States has been criticised by many human rights campaigners and academics for breaking various Geneva Conventions protocols during its self-proclaimed 'War on Terrorism' which began with military campaigns in Afghanistan (2001) and Iraq (2003). Influential academic, Noam Chomsky, wrote:

> *"The idea that all states are 'equal and parties to the agreements that bind them' has long been codified in international norms, such as the Geneva Conventions—first enacted in 1864 to protect the wounded in terms of war and since expanded through a number of additional protocols, most notably in 1949 and 1977—and the principles of the Nuremberg Tribunal, established to prosecute Nazi war crimes during World War II and adopted by the International Law Commission of the United States in 1950 (6)."*

Chomsky articulates many perceived breaches of international law by the US in a chapter headed 'outlaw states', in a methodically researched and passionate expose of poor compliance to international law. However, the fact remains, that the United States had never ratified the two additional protocols of the 1977 Geneva Convention into domestic law by the time that he wrote his powerful and unswervingly significant narrative (7).

International humanitarian law

Earlier in this chapter we looked in a little detail at the 1998 UK Human Rights Act (sub-chapter 3.3). According to Pictet, *International humanitarian law* (law of war) is a set of codes, protocols and legislation that attempts to regulate armed conflict or hostilities between states, and more recently, between states and informal insurgent groups.

International humanitarian law governs both the legality of justifications for war and the legality of wartime conduct. Key legal terminology includes: *jus ad bellum*: when states can resort to war, and *jus in bello*: how states must behave themselves during war.

Core principles of international humanitarian law can be found in major international treaties, such as the Geneva Conventions of 1949, and the first Geneva Convention of 1864. The lesser-known *Hague Conventions* that are produced intermittently by the Hague Conference on Private International Law, can also provide legal frameworks around international conflict resolution and private laws; more details below (9).

Case study: What are the Geneva Conventions?

The Geneva Conventions are a series of treaties on the treatment of civilians, prisoners of war (POWs) and soldiers who are otherwise rendered hors de combat, or incapable of fighting. The first Convention was initiated by the International Committee for Relief to the Wounded (which became the International Committee for the Red Cross and Red Crescent). This convention produced a treaty designed to protect wounded and sick soldiers during wartime. The Swiss Government agreed to hold the Conventions in Geneva, and a few years later, a similar agreement to protect shipwrecked soldiers was produced. In 1949, after World War II, two new Conventions were added to the original two, and all four were ratified by a number of countries. The 1949 versions of the Conventions, along with two additional Protocols, are in force today.

Convention I: This Convention protects wounded and infirm soldiers and medical personnel against attack, execution without judgment, torture, and assaults upon personal dignity (Article 3). It also grants them the right to proper medical treatment and care.

Convention II: This agreement extended the protections mentioned in the first Convention to shipwrecked soldiers and other naval forces, including special protections afforded to hospital ships.

Convention III: One of the treaties created during the 1949 Convention, this defined what a prisoner of war was, and accorded them proper and humane treatment as specified by the first Convention. Specifically, it required POWs to give only their name, rank, and serial number to their captors. Nations party to the Convention may not use torture to extract information from POWs.

Convention IV: Under this Convention, civilians are afforded the protections from inhumane treatment and attack afforded in the first Convention to sick and wounded soldiers. Furthermore, additional regulations regarding the treatment of civilians were introduced. Specifically, it prohibits attacks on civilian hospitals, medical transports, etc. It also specifies the right of internees, and those who commit acts of sabotage. Finally, it discusses how occupiers are to treat an occupied populace.

Protocol I: In this additional Protocol to the Geneva Conventions, the signing nations agreed to further restrictions on the treatment of 'protected persons' according to the

---

original Conventions. Furthermore, clarification of the terms used in the Conventions was introduced. Finally, new rules regarding the treatment of the deceased, cultural artefacts, and dangerous targets (such as dams and nuclear installations) were produced.

Protocol II: In this Protocol, the fundamentals of 'humane treatment' were further clarified. Additionally, the rights of interned persons were specifically enumerated, providing protections for those charged with crimes during wartime. It also identified new protections and rights of civilian populations.

- The United States has ratified the four Conventions of 1949, but has not ratified the two additional Protocols of 1977.

- Disputes arising under the Conventions, or the Protocols additional to them, are settled by courts of the member nations (Article 49 of Convention I), or by international tribunals.

- The International Committee of the Red Cross and Red Crescent has a special role given by the Geneva Conventions, whereby it handles, and is granted access to, the wounded, sick, and POWs.

The following information was supplied courtesy of the Legal Information Institute, based at Cornell University Law School, New York (10)

The Hague Conventions

The Hague Conference on Private International Law is a global inter-governmental organisation with 75 member states at the time of writing, including the European Union. It seeks to bring together a number of seemingly quite random legal spheres and domains in order to help "unify private international law at the regional level, for example within the Organisation of American States or the European Union".

The most widely ratified conventions deal with:

- the abolition of legalisation (Apostille)
- service of process
- taking of evidence abroad
- access to justice
- international child abduction
- intercountry adoption
- conflicts of laws relating to the form of testamentary dispositions
- maintenance obligations
- recognition of divorces.

Cross-border mediation in family matters, choice of law in international contracts, and the "possible need for the development of a global instrument in these areas" are also on the agenda of the Hague Conventions body.

(Source: Hague Conventions website)

The United Nations

With 193 national members, the United Nations Secretariat began operations in 1946. "It was staffed with a mere 300 people working primarily for the Preparatory Commission and engaged in providing conference services for a fledgling world body that was beginning to chart a course to positively change the world", explains the organisation's encyclopaedic website. By 1949, the UN had established headquarters in New York and employed several thousand staff. The organisation has shifted emphasis from conferences and the facilitation of dialogue, into becoming a global secretariat that seeks solutions into its three main thematic areas established by the 1945 UN Charter: peace and security; the protection and promotion of human rights; and human development. Today the UN still has very limited resources. For context, it directly employs just 44,000 people, some 10,000 less than just one city council in the UK.

In practical terms, it is worth understanding the United Nations as to be both the engine room and 'Guardian Angel' of *most* international law. It is via this relatively small international body, and its sibling bodies dotted around the world, that most international law is quietly proposed, drafted, sometimes sabotaged, and monitored (11). Moreover, a plethora of disputes are raised to the International Court of Justice (ICJ) in The Hague, Netherlands, and adjudications and solutions are found.

Case study: Saving the whale: UN court opens hearings on whaling dispute between Australia and Japan

The United Nations' highest court has opened hearings in a case concerning charges by Australia that Japan is using a scientific research programme to mask a commercial whaling venture.

In a news release, the Hague-based International Court of Justice (ICJ) announced that hearings began yesterday in the case concerning *Whaling in the Antarctic* (Australia v Japan; New Zealand intervening).

The court says that in May 2010, Australia instituted proceedings alleging that "Japan's continued pursuit of a large-scale programme of whaling under the Second Phase of its Japanese Whale Research Programme under Special Permit in the Antarctic ('JARPA II'), is in breach of obligations assumed by Japan under the International Convention for the

---

Regulation of Whaling ('ICRW'), as well as its other international obligations for the preservation of marine mammals and the marine environment".

At the end of its application, Australia requested the ICJ to order that Japan: end the research programme, revoke any authorisations, permits or licences allowing the programme's activities; and provide assurances and guarantees that it will not take any further action under the JARPA II or "any similar programme until such programme has been brought into conformity with its obligations under international law".

Source: UN website: June 2013 (12)

International courts

The International Criminal Court (ICC) and International Court of Justice (ICJ) are two distinctly separate bodies. In addition, the UN Security Council will sometimes directly mandate the establishment of special tribunals to prosecute military and political leaders for war crimes, including genocide. UN mandated tribunals include:

- International Criminal Tribunal for the Former Yugoslavia
- International Criminal Tribunal for Rwanda
- Special Court for Sierra Leone.

The International Court of Justice is the principal judicial body of the UN and is based in The Hague, Netherlands. The court was established by the 1945 UN Charter and began work, from Hague's Peace Palace, in 1946. The ICJ settles formal disputes between member states and also provides 'advisory opinions' on legal matters referred to it by UN-authorised bodies and agencies (13). According to the ICJ: The court itself does not have a mandate to investigate complaints from non-member bodies, such as NGOs, even when it may be clear that gross violations of international law have been carried out. It is different from the International Criminal Court, in that the ICJ is not a criminal court and does not have jurisdiction to prosecute individuals accused of war crimes against humanity (14).

International Criminal Court

"The history of the establishment of the International Criminal Court spans over more than a century. The 'road to Rome' was a long and often contentious one", reports campaign group, *Coalition for the International Criminal Court* (15). It roots are traced back from Gustave Moynier, one of the founders of the International Committee of the Red Cross, who proposed a permanent international criminal court in response to the crimes of the 1870s Franco-Prussian War. The drafters of the 1919

Treaty of Versailles wished to create an ad hoc international court to try the Kaiser and alleged German war criminals for their World War I actions. Following World War II, the Allies set up the Nuremberg and Tokyo tribunals to try Nazi Axis war criminals. Although the UN General Assembly adopted the Convention on the Prevention and Punishment of the Crime of Genocide in 1948, the Cold War stopped efforts for an international war crimes court; there was unsurprisingly an inability to agree upon a definition. Wars in Bosnia-Herzegovina and Croatia, as well as in Rwanda in the early 1990s, and the mass commission of crimes against humanity and genocide, spurred the UN Security Council to establish two temporary tribunals to hold individuals to account for the atrocities. In July 1998, at the Rome Conference, 120 nations voted in favour of establishing the ICC, with seven nations voting against the Treaty: the United States, Israel, the People's Republic of China, Iraq, Libya, Qatar and Yemen opposed. 21 states abstained. The Treaty entered into force in 2002 when the 60th UN member state ratified it (16).

3.7 Prominent business laws related to international business

For security practitioners with a roving or global footprint, the following laws and provisions are well worth developing a degree of competence and awareness around.

Sarbanes-Oxley (SOX) was an act passed in 2002 in the US, in response to several corporation accounting scandals. Its colloquial name in the business community Sarbanes-Oxley or Sarbox – is taken from the principal legislators who drove the 11 provisions through the US Congress. Its full name is the *Public Company Accounting Reform and Investor Protection Act,* and the notion that stricter financial governance controls were needed in large, often internationalised corporations, drove forward similar legislation in Canada, India, South Africa, Japan and Europe. Various provisions tighten laws and enforcement in spheres of: auditing and accounting, conflicts of interest, corporate and criminal fraud accountability and white collar crime penalty enhancements. Protections for whistle-blowers are increased, while penalties for those carrying out frauds, such as destroying financial records, are ratcheted up as a deterrent. The FBI and US Attorney's Office now place global resources to tackling corporate crime as evidence by several news releases from the Agency attesting to detections and prosecutions set against the act and its provisions (17).

Foreign Corrupt Practices Act: Also commonly known by its acronym, FCPA, this act was originally passed in 1977 in the US to prohibit the bribery of public officials, particularly by corporate entities. In 1998 the anti-bribery provisions of the act were amended to "now also apply to foreign companies and persons who cause, directly or through agents, an act in furtherance of such a corrupt payment to take place within the territory of the United States" (18).

Encryption laws: Inspired and fuelled by a relentless conveyor-belt of data breach horror stories, many national governments and the European Union have taken it upon themselves to begin to develop protocols, directives and laws around the encryption of data and 'demanding new obligations for data security', reports London law company, Field Fisher Waterhouse. Their informative yet succinct report, *The Legal Obligations for Encryption of personal data in Europe and Asia*, outlines the work of the EU Data Protection Working Party, which has developed a formal 'opinion' around Cloud computing practices. At the time of writing, advised data management processes have only been alchemised into the formal EU Data Protection Directive (1995) and a Privacy and Electronic Communications Directive of 2002. But do expect forward movement with this in light of recent Cloud breach and surveillance scandals. In order to anticipate future compliance, security contractors are advised to keep abreast of all national and international data security directives and laws as they travel on business trips, and also plan a strategy around information security. "We are witnessing a global harmonisation of the legal need for encryption", reports Field Fisher Waterhouse (19). Nevertheless, in many popular emerging markets, data encryption may be treated by authorities as a threat, or an unlawful act which could therefore attract suspicion and investigation.

Chapter 3: Wrap-up

In closing this chapter on **Legislation and Regulations**, we reflect on some of the approaches and attributes that will help your company gain the competitive edge. These include:

- There is, rightly, much public scrutiny and political focus upon human rights issues. Security practitioners need to understand the underpinning motivations of human rights legislation. Why were they brought in? Moreover, how might they impact your employees and operations?

- Be aware of international laws and protocols that may impact your business, including regulations and protocols that may emanate from bodies well beyond your day-to-day purview, such as international bodies including the EU, WIPO and WTO, or 'catch-all' laws passed by powerful trading nations, including the US and China.

- Develop a proficient knowledge of laws within your own operating environment that impact upon security management and organisational resilience-related tasks. Allegations or official findings that your company, or a client organisation, breached legal compliance, can lead to severe reputational damage for all companies involved – even if innocence is proved later down the line. Keep your competitive edge by being proactive and overtly-vigilant around compliance.

- Don't forget about data and information security laws. These can vary quite widely between jurisdictions. Security contractors are advised to keep abreast of all national and international data security directives and laws as they travel on business trips, and also plan a strategy around information security risks.

- Demonstrate to your clients and commercial peers that you are proactively assessing the legal environment and watching out for the welfare of the wider sector, not just your company. Be confident to raise issues within the industry, lobby government for changes, write articles, carry out social media, and host business briefings for concerned clients and stakeholders in relation to matters of laws and compliance.

References

1) Myers., R., (2011) Guardian: 'A legal guide to making a citizen's arrest', accessed and downloaded on 19/01/2014 from: *www.theguardian.com/law/2011/aug/09/guide-to-citizens-arrest*
2) The HSC and HSE websites are excellent sources of information. For reporting incidents at work: HSE (2013) Another excellent source of information is the Workplace Law Network, link: *www.workplacelaw.net/*
3) ACAS (2014) Understanding what Vicarious Liability can mean for employers, accessed and downloaded from: *www.acas.org.uk/index.aspx?articleid=3715*
4) Reporting accidents and incidents at work. HSE. Accessed and downloaded on: 12/12/2014 at: *www.hse.gov.uk/pubns/indg453.pdf*. A checklist for compliance to the Health and Safety Acts was accessed and downloaded on 22/02/2015 at: *www.direct.gov.uk/en/Employment/HealthAndSafetyAtWork/DG_4016686*
5) UN Charter Chapter 7 can be accessed at: *www.un.org/en/documents/charter/chapter7.shtml*
6) Chomsky., N., (2006), 'Failed States', London: Hamish Hamilton
7) Legal Information Institute (2013)
8) Jean Pictet (1985), 'Development and Principles of International Humanitarian Law',
9) Hague Conventions Conference website can be accessed at: *www.hcch.net/index_en.php*

10) Legal Information Institute, based at Cornell University Law School, New York

11) BBC News (2010), 'Birmingham City Council to make £230m of savings', can be accessed and downloaded at: *www.bbc.co.uk/news/uk-england-birmingham-10636616*

12) UN News media (27/06/2013), 'UN Court opens hearings on whaling dispute between Australia and Japan'

13) International Court of Justice website can be accessed at: *www.icj-cij.org/information/index.php?p1=7&p2=2#1*

14) Ibid

15) Coalition for the International Criminal Court website (2014) can be accessed at: *www.iccnow.org/?mod=home*

16) Ibid

17) FBI news release (20/04/2015), 'Former Corporate Executives Charged with Securities Fraud and Tax Offenses for Wide-Ranging Commercial Bribery Scheme', accessed and downloaded on 30/03/2015 at: *www.fbi.gov/newyork/press-releases/2014/former-corporate-executives-charged-with-securities-fraud-and-tax-offenses-for-wide-ranging-commercial-bribery-scheme*

18) Department of Justice online, was accessed on 30/03/2015 at: *www.justice.gov/criminal/fraud/fcpa/*

19) Fresh Field Waterhouse (February 2013), 'The Legal Obligations for Encryption of personal data in Europe and Asia'

VIDEOS

A number of videos were consulted in writing this chapter that illuminate some of the complexities and controversies in relation to understanding domestic and international law. These are most useful in reflecting upon this chapter's content and could be important additional learning tools for developing your own knowledge of Legislation and Regulations. The videos are listed below:

(2012) Law Firm Bond Pearce analyses the impact of the Corporate Manslaughter Act on UK business (5.15):

www.youtube.com/watch?v=IETQ6zfxyBk

(1988) 'Death on the Rock, SAS Executions in Gibraltar', Thames Television: A video that was hugely controversial in the 1980s where the tension between law and security management can sometimes become severe (43.40):

www.youtube.com/watch?v=x7MBqTw2vl0

(2012) Should the Human Rights Act be replaced by a Bill of Rights', an LSE 'British Government' panel discussion (1.26:06):

www.youtube.com/watch?v=l_HDmD-JxZk

(2011) BBC Question Time, 'Was Iraq War Legal' – different perspectives on law (17.51):

www.youtube.com/watch?v=xxOU7yt8-44

(2012) Big Think, International Law Explained (4.37):

www.youtube.com/watch?v=8Zeein83DdU

(2013) Lauterpacht Centre for International Law, Cambridge University Lecture – The True Nature of International Law (1.01.51):

www.youtube.com/watch?v=wb6N7YWDUgg

(2013) Pentagon Papers Case: Supreme Court Decision (1.38.43):

www.youtube.com/watch?v=WPBIae8HVNc

(2013) William Spaniel, of Game Theory, What is the United Nations Security Council? (8.54):

www.youtube.com/watch?v=aQN-ZraOjts

CHAPTER 4: PRIVATE INVESTIGATIONS

4.1 Context

"Whether its corporate investigations or comedy, there are certain inherent truths to trying to get what you want while trying to be a decent person doing it." – Nick Kroll, comedian and actor.

This chapter will reflect on the private investigations' operating environment that has emerged after the 2012 Lord Leveson inquiry into mobile phone message intercepts by newspapers and hired private investigators in the UK. We will look briefly at any relevant isomorphic lessons for security practitioners. This chapter is also designed to provide an insight into the demands, role and expectations of a private investigator and investigation caseload. It will enable readers to formalise existing knowledge and provide a framework for conducting investigations in business environments or in private client casework. This section will provide readers with knowledge, skills and the procedural context to conduct investigation work in a legal and ethical manner.

Not all investigations need be conducted by a law enforcement agency. Indeed, as a security consultant, or as part of an in-house security team, the need to conduct a robust and auditable investigation post a breach of security, may be a critical process for an organisation when people, finances and reputations are involved. Our content will include direct and/or indirect coverage of:

- the role of the private investigator in commercial, industrial and private client cases
- affidavits and process serving
- tracing missing people (MISPERS)
- surveillance techniques (on foot and by vehicle; concealment)
- electronic surveillance, the law and ethics
- witness statements, interviews and accident reports
- repossession
- criminal investigations (criminal damage; criminal defence; counterfeiting; false accounting; forgery, fraud; theft)
- crime scene analysis
- forensic investigation and evidence
- legal issues and the court process

- data protection issues.

Government involvement in investigations and criminal detection was virtually non-existent until the nineteenth century. Modern policing (the 'new' police) was introduced in the UK from 1829 and professionalised publicly-owned police authorities became embedded across many American, European and colonised territories from the late 1800s onwards. According to Johnston, central government: "… made little or no attempt at criminal detection. Crime was brought to the courts when victims prosecuted offenders. Officials did not go out to find it. Justices dealt with the evidence, but detection and apprehension of suspects was left to victims, who often went to great lengths to regain stolen property" (1).

No matter how peaceful or well organised a society becomes, many potential crimes, misdemeanours, suspect prosecutions and civil law disputes, do continue to require investigation. The "vacuum of government provision created a market for private investigators" before the twentieth century (2). This remains the case today. In the nineteenth and early twentieth centuries, companies formed in-house security services – or company 'police'. Governments and some subversive groups recruited private companies with investigators to gather and disseminate intelligence on competitors, including the use of *Pinkerton National Detective Agency* to carry out espionage upon confederate force activity during the American Civil War. Moreover, Gill and Hart point to industrial intelligence gaining traction whereby PI companies began "infiltrating labour unions during the Great Depression" (3). Another vast private security company was named *Brinks*.

Private investigators (PIs) have been given certain descriptions throughout history; old literary and screen references to leathery, cynical old 'gumshoes' became quite popular in American movies well before, and after, the Second World War. A PI's work can also overlap with the role of an *enquiry agent* who is often tasked with identifying the location of, and subsequently issuing, legal notices. This could be to recover property and debts. Other terms describing allied work in this sector include *bailiff, process servers* or *commercial agents*.

In the UK, *felon associations* and *thief taker* organisations formed to help victims seize and recover stolen items from alleged perpetrators, and to perhaps mete out some summary justice. *Bounty hunters* or variations, including vigilantes who carried out neighbourhood self-defence among other tasks, existed within some communities and areas of common banditry. The supposedly ultra-maverick lifestyle of private detectives and their cases became popular to depict and embellish by a plethora of fiction authors. Perhaps some of the most famous characters being Conan Doyle's creation of Sherlock Holmes, Agatha Christie's Hercule Poirot and Miss Marple in Britain and Raymond Chandler's sluggish but resilient gumshoe, Philip Marlowe, from *Big Sleep* fame in 1930s America (4).

4.2 Role of private investigators

Some tasks and requests to PIs will overlap with other security management functions. This will therefore raise various issues around integration with other projects and employees. Do bear in mind that in many domains, activities carried out by PIs may require a state or government licence. If a security enterprise extends its operations into running what might be considered traditional PI activity, it is advisable to be clear on the structure and processes of managing and accounting for these types of security functions. It is therefore crucial to be quite clear and task/team accountability must be permanently prioritised and successfully managed. If something goes wrong with a lack of oversight, or legal compliance, ignorance is not a mitigating factor with many prosecutors. Roles and responsibilities of PIs can be very diverse and include the following activity:

- process serving and affidavits
- finding missing persons
- identifying, monitoring and recording potential corruption or system abuse
- gathering business intelligence
- finding or retrieving stolen assets
- identifying and investigating criminal activity, with a view to supporting the police and prosecutors in making a successful case before the judiciary
- 'spotting' and recording/reporting suspicious behaviour
- carrying out business intelligence, including due diligence checks.

A core publication for many aspirant private investigators is The Security Institute's well-received *Good Practice Guide*, 2010 (5). Another good source of information is the *Association of British Investigators* (ABI), now more than a century old. According to the organisation's informative website: "The ABI campaigns tirelessly for regulation in our profession and promotes excellence, integrity and professionalism within its membership". The association believes that it has, "become the kite mark of the investigation industry" (6). Such information is vital in order to help enterprises remain legally compliant. In 2013, the UK Home Office announced plans for PI activity to require a Security Industry Authority (SIA) licence, yet this provision had not been introduced at the time of writing. International NGOs have also been formed to share knowledge and improve working practices within the sphere of private investigations. The *Institute of Professional Investigators* and also the *World Association of Professional Investigators* are two of the most prominent support networks in a field of expertise that involves several hundred thousand operators around the world (7 & 8). The ABI produce an excellent toolkit *An Introduction to Private Investigation*, deliver professional investigation training (Level 3), and suggest that future licensing will perhaps synchronise to standards set out by the corresponding BSI publication *BS 102000 Code of Practice for the provision of investigative practices* (9). Compliance can only be guaranteed though by the reader consistently monitoring governmental and legislative initiatives in this sphere, within their country of operation.

4.3 Affidavits and process serving

"Process servers have never been busier than during these challenging economic times dealing with a rising number of collections, foreclosures and other legal matters." – National Association of Professional Process Servers (NAPPS) (10)

Case study: Don't shoot the messenger

When a husband and wife team of 'process servers' parked up outside a judge's house in Nashville, US, during 2012, to serve a civil court warrant, the male member of this duet of private investigators received more than he had bargained for.

A judge, Michael Rowan, was being chased by legal research company LexisNexis for $8,600. But Mr Rowan was also running for elected office. He was coincidentally distressed at the amount of cars parked opposite his neighbour's house where there was a party.

Mr Rowan is a military veteran and 'successful boxer' according to his campaign website. He admitted punching the process server, Jeremy Frank, who knocked alone at his door, while his wife and business partner remained in the car:

> "I thought he was trying to get permission to park in my driveway", Rowan said of the visitor. "He never told me who he was."

Mrs Kasey Frank – wife and business partner of Jeremy – confirmed later to her local newspaper in Nashville that her husband had a bump on the back of his head and required a CT scan at the local hospital.

Source: Joey Garrison, The City Newspaper: 03/06/2012 (11)

This type of violent incident around process serving is unusual but not unique. In September 2011, a process server was shot in the abdomen as he exited some domestic premises in Prescott, Arizona, US. Bob Palmer from *Palmer Investigations* told local police that his colleague had, for the fifth time, attempted to serve the alleged assailant with a civil summons (12). During 2012, Meldenhall Mayor, Steve Womack More, was found guilty of 'simple assault' upon a process server. While the very same process server was charged with 'trespass' but later cleared (13). The service of process has been defined as the ... "Delivery of a writ, summons, or other legal papers to the person required to respond to them" (14). The NAPPS newsroom provides a cacophony of tragic stories of investigators being attacked, summoned to court, or even being shot at (15). Process servers thus work in a dynamic and volatile work environment. There are more than 2,000 members of NAPPS and most PIs are sole traders or work in small companies. The widely regarded Hallcrest Report found that there were around 70,000 private investigator employees in the US working for some 15,000 companies (16). It is not uncommon for small companies to be evolving networks of close-knit family members, or ex-military and police colleagues; a tight network with trust and intuitive partnership at its core. Process serving is viewed as a critical, impartial, third party public service by its membership body NAPPS. "Very few people really know what we do, and the few who do often are misinformed and have an inaccurate perception of what a professional process server actually does", reports NAPPS Board President Jeff Bannister (17). The delivery of legal notices to parties and witnesses in legal actions can include the distribution of *Affidavits of Service* which have been defined as: "a written or printed declaration or statement of facts made voluntarily, confirmed by the oath or affirmation of the party making it, and taken before an officer having the authority to administer such oath. An affidavit of service is intended to certify the service of a writ, notice or other legal document", explains NAPPS (18).

The domain of private investigations has tightened in modern times. Such an appetite for regulation is likely to grow, due to substantial scandals involving some PIs, and the roll-out of surveillance-facilitating technology down to street level. Moreover, the true implications of the 2012 Leveson inquiry and report into unlawful communications interceptions by journalists and PIs, mainly in the UK, are yet to be fully absorbed (19). To promote professionalism and public reassurance, NAPPS and other PI-related professional associations have produced standards and best practice guides. NAPPS recently published its much heralded *Policy Manual* which provides rules and guidance in relation to conflicts of interest, grievances and unprofessional conduct (20). Such clear guidance should not be viewed as a hindrance to aspiring entrepreneurs and managers in the PI field. Moreover, it serves to drive up professional competence and reinforce parameters for a workplace sphere that can be highly discretionary and emotionally draining. By its very nature this type of work does create, "strong pressures for misconduct", says Prenzler (21).

Local idiosyncrasies

In summary, every country has a different legal and commercial environment. Many advanced industrial economies will operate licensing regimes for some or all PI-related work, either at state or national government level. Local laws can be rooted in cultural or local business practice, and can scupper investigations by some unique and seemingly idiosyncratic restrictions. In the US, for instance, process servers are widely prohibited from serving notices on Sundays and official public holidays. Rules around the delivery and execution of warrants are often clear cut and understandable after basic research. Yet aspiring PIs should exercise caution and further research around compliance: for example, what are the rules around contact hours? How does one mitigate counter-claims of harassment? Moreover, what constitutes trespass and self-defence? You may well locate the right individual, but will the courts take the view that you adhered to due process while executing your role as investigator and/or process server?

Case study: Dad, football and family photos

Several years ago a PI scenario was outlined by the eminent security analyst, Dr Martin Gill:

> "We've been going out on surveillance operations since the age of ten … Dad would be taking the family out to the seaside for the day, then he'd stop the car for a while and ask us to play football in front of someone's garden. He would then take a picture of whoever came out to complain, probably to check who lived at that address …"

Sourced from Gill and Hart, 1997 (22)

4.4 Tracing missing people

> *"Over 6.6 billion people, across 57,268,900 square miles, speaking 6,500 different languages ... Where do you start looking?"* – Source: Missing Abroad website, a branch of the Lucie Blackman Trust (23)

This part of the book will seek to provide contextual commentary and routes into attempting to confront and answer some of the following:

- What constitutes being 'missing'?
- Who goes missing and why?
- How can we trace them, and hurdles?

According to London-based LBC radio station, 110 children go 'missing' in Britain's capital city each day (24). Most are found safe and well. But many missing person's cases – often known as 'Mispers' within police and detective environments – remain sadly unsolved.

The charity *Missing People* estimate that "an estimated 250,000 people go missing" in the UK (25). The National Policing Improvement Agency (NPIA) report that "an estimated 216,000 individuals were reported missing to UK police forces in the year 2010-11" (26). There appears to be an even gender split among victims (27). An estimated two-thirds of all missing persons reports to police forces do concern children and young people under 18 years of age (28). Among adults, those aged 24-30 years were the most likely to be reported missing, followed by 18-23 year olds (29). Moreover, researchers Tarling and Burrows found that some 99% of all reported missing person's cases were 'solved' within one year (30).

Unsurprisingly, given the vast range of incidents and scenarios within the 'mispers' field of analysis, a single or pre-eminent definition of a 'missing person' has been difficult to establish. It is worth reminding ourselves, that under most (if not all) legal systems, individual adult citizens do possess an inviolable *human right* to go missing and disappear from known or unknown human contacts. That is almost universally the case in liberal democratic societies, unless an individual is restricted by some form of legal custody or sanction – such as a parole order, a control order, or, indeed, a detention order under mental health legislation.

Work carried out by the charity *Missing People,* and other likeminded organisations, is very useful in enabling those new to this topic area to begin to grapple with a complex and often upsetting topic area in which private investigators are often called to participate. *Missing People* explain that: "One problem with providing a definition is that a person who is considered to have gone missing by friends or family members may not see their situation in the same way. An individual may simply consider themselves to have started a new life elsewhere, or to have left a situation which they may have seen as negative or dangerous. This raises difficult questions about who decides if an individual has gone missing or not" (31). Nevertheless, the charity has usefully pulled together several definitions from a range of law enforcement and academic sources:

- *"A break in contact which either the missing person or someone else defines as going missing, and which may be either intentional or unintentional."* (32)

- *"... a social situation in which a person is absent from their accustomed network of social and personal relationships to the extent that people within that network define the absence as interfering with the performance by that person of expected social responsibilities, leading to a situation in which members of the network feel obliged to search for the missing person and may institute official procedures to identify the person as missing."* (33)

- *"Anyone whose whereabouts is unknown whatever the circumstances of disappearance. They will be considered missing until located and their well-being or otherwise established."* (34)

The final definition above is significant as it was set by the Association of Chief Police Officers (ACPO) in the UK and underpins police investigative practice.

Working closely with ACPO, the UK *Missing Persons Bureau* is a government-funded agency that keeps a national database of "missing persons and unidentified cases" (35). The agency assists police forces and works with authorities to cross-match the identification of individuals, bodies and remains. Its website does provide some downloadable guidance for friends and families to establish whether, and why, a person has become missing. It enables lay people and police to ask some relevant questions in order to establish clues and information which may help to locate a loved one, or alternatively provide reassurance that they are *not* missing. The Bureau's *What you need to know* factsheet provides examples of information types that police or investigators might require to establish risk levels and future search procedures (36). This website also provides links to other overseas national bodies committed to locating missing persons, such as the Brazil-based *Missing Kids* organisation, and the US charity, *Let's Bring Them Home*, who focus their support towards locating missing adults (37). UK Foreign and Commonwealth Office consular sections and Consular Directorate will also be significantly involved in supporting families of UK nationals reported as missing overseas. Practical and emotional support includes the provision of isomorphic experiences in overseas investigations, prosecutions, right through to financial aid in some cases. Necessary supporting and counselling in psychological resilience for affected families and friends will sometimes be best provided from charities and NGOs. Such organisations will often have individuals and families who have suffered similar experiences. Moreover, they are often crucial, independent, information gatherers in that they can support missing persons cases. For example, The *Lucie Blackman Trust* (a charity formed by the family of a young English woman murdered in Japan), has now established *Missing Abroad*, a group network which provides emotional and practical support for families faced with missing persons cases. The *Missing Abroad* website provides guidance, toolkits and supportive contacts for those planning travel overseas, and focuses its support on families dealing with overseas Mispers cases (38).

Originally designed for police investigators, Grampian Police produced the now-widely-used *Missing Persons: Understanding, Planning and Responding* guide which focuses on many causes and also tracing historical patterns that can often unlock further clues and evidence in order to solve a missing persons case (39). The report makes clear some useful 'rules of thumb' in terms of linking possible causes of disappearance with logical follow-up search locations. Moreover, the document provides estimated search radiuses that correspond to a timeline traced back to the suspected or known time of disappearance. Other key organisations that will assist for child Mispers cases in the UK include the police-run *Child Exploitation and Online Protection Centre* (CEOP) and the campaign network

Parents and Abducted Children Together (PACT) which now partners the UK Home Office around international parental child abductions (40).

How can we trace Mispers?

We have heard that some 99% of missing persons cases brought to the police receive some form of closure. Moreover, missing child cases will often be deemed 'high-risk' cases by police forces and quickly generate an allocation of police detectives and back-up. Private investigators may be commissioned to find children who have been either kidnapped overseas, or taken to foreign climes by separated parents. But some 34% of missing persons are adults in the UK (41). Some of these cases are highlighted on Missing People and Missing Abroad's informative websites. Only a small minority of adult cases can generate significant public interest. Many cases have become deemed 'cold'. Police services have been unable to resource, for various reasons (including an individual's right to privacy), cold cases and therefore families, friends and employers turn to private investigators. Approaching a case may be overwhelming and for a layperson; where should they start? The metaphor of searching 'for a needle in a haystack' is apt, particularly if one is directly impacted by the trauma and uncertainty of a case. But to reverse the metaphor, private investigators should be adept at removing and reducing much of the haystack and closing in on the needle by systematic (possibly intelligence-led) detection techniques. Some tactics may require extremely resilient levels of versatility, spontaneity, self-discipline and granular attention to detail. Amateur and professional investigators are often up against careful, scared or manipulative people who do not share the same interests; for their own motives, or by their own reasoning, they may want the case unsolved. Case workers should expect the unexpected: to come up against hurdles that include cheating spouses, bogus insurance or welfare claimants, disappearing bail breakers, frightened witnesses, professional, organised criminals, worried co-conspirators, protective and blinkered family members, and so on. Indeed, the supposed missing person may have started a new life, accompanied by a blissfully creative new alias, official identity cards and an equally reinvented new wife to boot. A casual slip up by visiting a family tombstone at Christmas, or an indiscreet new family photo in an expat brochure, may be the only needle that some missing people throw back into the investigator's haystack. A most entertaining read which helps the reader to step easily into a *voluntary* missing person's shoes, was published by American investigator, Edmund Pankau. I'm not sure whether *How to Hide Your Assets and Disappear* gives more ideas to the investigator or the escapee, but it certainly is a favourite sunshine holiday read of mine! (42)

Building a missing person's profile

Building a missing person's personal profile is critically important in order to establish a plausible search strategy that is well organised, realistic and methodical. This will enable investigators to establish the routine and vapour trail of contacts, which might well lead to the person's discovery. But 'profiling' will also facilitate an ability to 'step into the shoes of the subject'; to begin to think and act as they might. To better anticipate their behaviour and decision making. Where might they go to? Who might they talk to? Who, or what, might they turn to in times of perceived vulnerability and adversity? What are they escaping from? (Including boredom.) What locations might be attractive options for them to move into, either for sanctuary or excitement?

Qualitative analysis will also include detailed physical profiling. A National Crime Information Center (NCIC) 'Missing Person File', at the FBI, will document many physical manifestations including medical conditions, personal descriptors, jewellery, body characteristics, internal characteristics, dental characteristics and other miscellaneous data (43).

Profiling processes will include, and map-out, the daily, monthly and, if appropriate, the annual routine of an individual. Social and professional networks will be examined. Family, extended family and genealogy (family trees) might provide clues. Travel routines, workplace journeys, transport mode preferences and radiuses will be looked into. Contextual behaviour and psychology in relation to the individual will be addressed. Strong likes and dislikes should be recorded. The following information based upon background questions to a personal risk assessment may be useful for profiling (44):

Personal history: who in their family is influential to/over them? Who are/have been business partners?

People: who do they come into contact with, such as close friends, colleagues and teachers/trainers/instructors? Or perhaps those who dislike, or are fixated, or jealous of them? What type of things do they buy?

Places: locations they visit or hang-out? Favourite places and routines, such as gym or secret friend, and location/routine timings?

Personality: what sort of personality do they have and how does it impact upon others?

Prejudices: Are they *perceived* to have any strong prejudices, or do they possess any strong prejudices that may get them into difficulty?

Politics/religion: Are they perceived to have associations or strong beliefs? Are they a member of a religion or group commonly targeted by adversaries?

Private life: What complications, background history, leisure pursuits, affiliations and associations are there?

Records that may help you locate a missing person

Based in picturesque Kew, London, the UK National Archives provides a good starting point for official documents that may help us trace a missing person. A visit to its expansive and meticulously organised premises may not however be necessary. National Archives online provide for birth, marriage and death indexes, and electoral registers and records. Contemporary election address records are also offered by the private company: *192.com*. This company's approach to disclosing UK citizens' names and addresses as a paid-for service (unless one opts out, and by then it's often too late), is, admittedly, of potential use for investigators. As we have seen in prior chapters, records are kept of all registered private company directors by UK Companies House, or parallel organisations outside the UK. Although an obligation to publish a director's home address was removed by UK Companies House several years ago. People hoping to find out about a person who may have changed their name will "often find that it [proof] does not exist", states National Archives guidance (46). This is because changing one's name via *deed poll* is a private contract with just one other party. A name change can be recorded between a private citizen and a solicitor, who may choose to retain a copy for several years afterwards. But there is no obligation to record this data elsewhere. To provide a sense of formalisation, the party may pay to register their deed poll with the Enrolment Books of the Supreme Court of Judicature (formerly the Close Rolls of Chancery). If this optional process occurs, researchers can check the *London Gazette* (or *Belfast Gazette,* in Northern Ireland) where all enrolled deed polls must be advertised (47). But the *London Gazette* is not a publicly available newspaper. Alternatively, the Royal Courts of Justice carry details of cases registered at the Supreme Court from 2004. The National Archives contain the indexes of deed polls prior to 2004 but do not offer an online database to research, by the time of writing.

The DVLA also host a wide range of vehicular data. But do bear in mind that conformity with data protection laws are the fundamental modus operandi for any reputable PI. (Although, noticeably, the DVLA has gotten into difficulties by selling drivers' details to car park management companies who have themselves been fined for malpractice (48).) In some countries, tax returns and welfare benefit accounts are being used to locate missing children; possibly caused by parental or family abductions. Family members can drop their guard and declare obligations around supporting previously undisclosed children, or in some cases family members have used a missing child's social security number within tax returns or benefit claims (49). Dental and medical records can also be key tools for checking against any profiles of unidentified individuals carried across thousands of web and social media sites. Current or outdated passports could indicate preferred locations, routes and reveal past travel patterns that were undisclosed or perhaps hidden from families and friends. Those who had formal relationships with missing persons or suspects, such as parole and police officers, GPs, nurses, and former employers, can all be considered for use in Misper enquiries. Often knowledgeable people, beyond the sphere of family or friendship influences and conspiracies, can be very useful in helping to join the dots of clues together. This was evidenced in the eventual success of locating Californian kidnap victim, Jaycee Dugard. Ms Dugard was missing for 18 years and the case ran cold until a vigilant campus security officer became suspicious about the activity of one Phillip Garrido around a young lady. After checking with Garrido's parole officer and discovering that the Garridos were biologically childless, the barriers to investigation unravelled and Dugard was set free (50).

Search tactics for Mispers cases

Internet search engines: Go to Google and other search engines and enter various name combinations, phone numbers, possible favoured work and residency locations, favourite trade and hobby publications, local newspapers, sports clubs and video links, dating and social meeting websites.

ICT: Try to access the internet search history on equipment used by the missing person. Don't forget that pertinent information may be stored in the Cloud, or in a variety of known or unknown email accounts. Ask authorities to do this, if appropriate. Search diaries, workbags, trouser and jacket pockets for passwords, if you can't guess them.

Social media: platforms such as Twitter, Facebook, MySpace and other sources of OSINT, have been continuously useful in attempting to identify the location of missing people and the self-declared dead, some of whom aim to gorge themselves on 'winnings' from insurance pay-outs and unpaid loans.

192.com: Online 'information directory' but also offers 'background reports' on property ownership, addresses, directorships, alive or dead status, county court judgments, among other nuggets of nosiness. The website also offers a 'see who's looking service' for people to find out who may be checking them out; a 'watching the watcher' service so-to-speak (51).

Media and professional databases: such as Lexis Nexis which are regularly accessed by journalists, lawyers and professional investigators (52).

Magazine subscriptions: people can change their official identities but it is far harder to change hobbies and interests. For example, if somebody lives and breathes their subscription to *Motor Boat Monthly*, then chances are that they will continue to pine for hardcopy images of super-yachts, fly-decks and tropical harbour locations. They may even have moved to one, or redirected the subscription to a new address.

Surveillance: dates such as anniversaries, birthdays, St Valentine's Day and the Christmas festive period are schedules when missing persons are prone to expose themselves to past emotion anchors. Places of sentimental value, including family tombstones or sites of major family incidents (such as honeymoons, deaths and suicides), can also be fruitful locations to monitor.

Documents and communications: wallet contents, CVs, receipts, bank cards, bills (including itemised phone accounts), credit card and bank statements, diaries and address books, medical and pharmaceutical correspondence, old phones, SIM cards, and PCs and old desktop computers, all provide clues and pointers. Bank and phone records are only accessible by police and official government agencies in most circumstances.

Saved files and cuttings: what types of documents, either on a computer or in hardcopy newspapers/magazines, have been saved or consciously recorded by the missing person, or suspected witnesses and perpetrators? Check generic sounding files as benign file titles are often used to hide or forage away secret vices; such as sexual predilections, debts, feuds or travel planning.

What hurdles may investigators face?

What issues may impede successfully finding a missing person? The following barriers will require resolution and prior planning by security management professionals:

Trauma management: The charity Missing People produced a report into *Families and Missing* that gives us some insight into the impact on family and friends of the Mispers. Manifestations of family and friends' trauma can be memory loss, fatigue, impatience and anger management issues, insomnia and physical illness.

Misinformation: Transferred by friends and witnesses either deliberately or unintentionally, sometimes acting out of a sense of misdirected duty towards the missing person (for example, covering up a sexual or embarrassing encounter). Moreover, there may be heightened suspicion among family members and friends that another family member or friend is to blame. In this scenario, information may not be forthcoming. Be aware of who else is in the room if it appears key information is explicitly being held back, appears vague, or is in conflict with prior accounts.

Law and regulations: Each domain is different but UK investigators should pay particular attention to the RIPA Act 2000; Data Protection Act 1998; the Children Acts of 1989 and 2004; the Human Rights Act 1998; the Bribery Act (2010); the Health and Safety at Work Act (1974). You may need to look back at Chapter 3, *Security Regulations* and also pay careful attention to the upcoming surveillance sub-chapter (4.5).

The charity *Missing People* have published several guidance documents to support those families, friends and organisations that are impacted by missing person's cases. The following guides are excellent comprehensive toolkits and security companies with work in this area are advised to peruse the following *Missing People* reports:

- Missing: key numbers
- Who goes missing?
- Missing children and young people
- Missing adults
- What is missing?
- Families and missing
- Mental health and missing
- Missing children Europe
- Missing children and the European Union
- The UN Convention on the Rights of the Child
- The English Coalition for Runaway Children
- Missing 16 and 17 year olds
- Forced marriage, 'honour' based violence and missing
- Trafficked children and missing
- Homelessness and missing

(Source: Missing People website) (53)

Figure 16: Further information and guidance on Mispers

4.5 Surveillance techniques

In the previous section, the subject of missing persons was introduced. One possible technique that may be needed to trace a missing person would be the use of surveillance. This sub-chapter will examine techniques used by investigators to conduct surveillance operations. Much of the open source literature, whether training courses or manuals, has been developed from police, military and security service techniques. An excellent example of this is P Jenkins' book, *Surveillance Tradecraft* (54).

Surveillance has long been regarded as a 'dark art'. However, with much information and commercial training available, there is a lot more awareness of the topic, by not only those wishing to avoid surveillance but also by the general public. In this section we shall examine the reasons for surveillance, the various elements of a surveillance operation, and look at methods used to defeat surveillance and the legal and ethical aspects of conducting surveillance.

At the end of this section we should understand the process and techniques required during a surveillance operation. This will not, nor is it intended to, replace practical experience.

According to the Regulation of Investigatory Powers Act 2000:

Surveillance includes:
- *[Continuous] Monitoring, observing or listening to persons, their movements, their conversations or their other activities or communications*
- *Recording anything monitored, observed or listened to in the course of surveillance*
  And
- *Surveillance by or with the assistance of a surveillance device* (55).

Surveillance can be either overt or covert. If surveillance is overt then the subject of the surveillance will be aware this is taking place. If the aim of the operation is to deter undesirable or criminal activity then this may be a suitable option. Covert surveillance should ensure that the subject and third parties are unaware that surveillance is being conducted.

It must be remembered that provisions within the UK RIPA law only apply to official bodies. However, commercial surveillance should bear in mind the structures of RIPA when planning to conduct covert surveillance activities. Covert surveillance, whether directed or intrusive (RIPA, 2000) should only be undertaken when all other methods of gathering the required information have been exhausted, or would have been deemed unlikely to succeed. To ensure that resources are not wasted, the method and tactics adopted for the surveillance have to be tailored with reference to:

- the intelligence already available about the subject of the task
- the objectives of the task
- the limiting factors.

Once the decision has been made to conduct surveillance on a subject, the techniques to be used must also be chosen. Note: throughout this sub-chapter, *subject* is used to describe the focus of the surveillance. The other term that may be encountered is *target*. This is another example of how an operator's background can influence their terminology. In military circles *target* has been used, however civilian organisations prefer *subject* as it removes the implication that the *target* will be fired at.

Surveillance methods – foot, mobile, technical

Surveillance has been likened to surrounding the subject with a net, to keep a subject under constant observation directly, or using technical aids; this net therefore needs to change shape to allow the surveillance operators to remain unnoticed. 'Unnoticed' is used as opposed to unseen, as it is impossible to conduct surveillance without being seen, if not by the subject then by the third parties in the area. Very often it is these third parties who will spot, and potentially compromise, the surveillance operator rather than the subject.

This leads to another aspect of surveillance; the need for the surveillance operator to blend into the background. This is achieved through careful choice of clothes, appearance and vehicles, not only as an individual but also as a team. The operator needs to be the 'Grey Man', a 'Mr Everybody' who looks like Mr Average or Mr Nobody. This equally applies to Ms Everybody too (56).

Case study

A surveillance operator was approached by two young adult males while driving past a taxi company's offices. The car being driven was a large saloon and resembled the taxis used in the area. The situation was such that it would have been unwise to offer them a lift, the operator therefore mimed that they weren't a taxi and continued on their way. Here the third party was not only the two males but also the locals who by the nature of the underlying threat took notice of what went on in their locality. The surveillance task was in a 'rough' estate and the local 'neighbourhood watch' was very effective at monitoring unusual activity too.

The case study illustrates an aspect of surveillance, that of third party awareness. Should the subject become aware of surveillance, the team (and it is unusual for a surveillance task to be conducted solely by an individual) may notice another aspect of surveillance – anti surveillance. Here it is necessary to distinguish the difference between two similar terms, *counter surveillance* and *anti surveillance*.

Although they would appear to mean the same, in surveillance terminology they have different applications.

Anti surveillance: is an action, or series of actions, carried out by the *subject* in order to detect or defeat surveillance being carried out against the subject. An aware subject (cognisant of surveillance and its methods) will carry out routine anti surveillance (AS) as a matter of course. An alert team will become aware of this and adapt their behaviour accordingly.

Counter surveillance: is the act of imposing surveillance, on behalf of the subject by a third party, against a person or persons suspected of monitoring the subject. In brief they are '*watching the watchers*'. Counter surveillance (CS) is an aspect of tradecraft that takes ability and skill, as the CS team will be working against 'aware' targets.

Covert surveillance: The subjects of a surveillance task are usually people. However, vehicles, places and objects can also be monitored. In the trade, the reason for surveillance can be boiled down to the following pattern of questions, known as the '5Ws and How'.

1. Where   *they go*
2. What   *they do*
3. Who   *they meet*
4. When   *they do it*
5. Why   do *they do it*
6. How   *they do it*

Surveillance may be imposed in order to:

- obtain evidence of illegal or unauthorised activity
- obtain a detailed pattern of life
- develop or confirm information from other sources
- locate missing people
- confirm the whereabouts of an individual at all times
- obtain evidence for use in a court of law.

In order to achieve continuous monitoring of the subject, the following methods of surveillance are needed, often in combination. **Foot,** in this case the team will deploy to monitor the subject when the subject moves on foot. Should the subject use a vehicle then the team will need to use similar means to be **mobile.** Very often locations used by the subject can be observed from a **static** location and these three methods can employ **technical** aids to assist in gathering information, which when analysed may produce intelligence.

When engaged in foot or mobile surveillance, the progressive or 'leap frog' method can be used. It involves the observation of the subject as they progress along a certain route, with the operators stationing themselves at fixed points, until the subject disappears from view. Use of this method is not too common because of the time involved and the poor chances of obtaining good results.

If subjects follow the same route each day, their destination can be determined without following them, if the operator stations himself each day at the point where the subject disappeared from view the previous day. This is an option for an operator working without a team. To further assist in understanding trade methods, the anatomy of a surveillance task will be dissected:

Planning and briefing

Before any surveillance takes place, careful planning will have been undertaken. It is likely that the legal aspects of the task will have been examined. This is especially true in commercial tasks. It is at this stage when the need for surveillance is confirmed and the decision is taken to use a surveillance team.

Be aware that while criminal enterprises or terrorist groups will still do the planning, they will not scrupulously obey the law. It is likely, however, that they will deploy similar tactics. Following the planning, all members of the team will be thoroughly briefed. Documents pertaining to the planning and briefings should be retained for future use and to demonstrate duty of care, in the event of any incidents during the task.

Following the planning and briefing, a surveillance operation comprises of four phases. Once begun, the four phases form a continuous cycle that may continue for hours, days, weeks or months.

1. The 'stake out' or the 'plot'

(Terminology varies depending on the backgrounds of the operators. Some agencies will use 'stake out' others will use the expression 'the plot'.)

A stake out comprises of a *trigger* and other operators covering the ground options that the subject may take. These possible 'stand-off' (start) locations are sometimes referred to as *the box*. The trigger may be at a static location, a person on foot, in a vehicle, in a building or a rural observation post (OP). It may also be a technical trigger, a remotely viewed camera, a movement sensor or an audio device. Alternatively, the trigger may be an insider, or an informant, however these can be unreliable due to delays in passing information. Should it not be possible to position a trigger, then the operators forming the box will need to be continuously aware and ever-vigilant to enable the correct subject to be picked up as they pass out of the box.

The trigger needs to able to observe the start point. The start point may be a residential or business premises, an associate's address, or any known location the subject habitually visits. This may be provided by a client or result from investigations carried out as part of the planning process. The trigger should be close enough to be able to identify the subject when they appear but not in an obvious position. The trigger should have adequate communications; a covert radio 'fit' is preferable, although mobile phones can be used by the team forming the box. The trigger location should be capable of remaining in place for as long as necessary, although the trigger's duties can be rotated through team members, should the situation demand. The entire team will need to be consciously aware of any suspected third party interest.

The team forming the box should provide cover to all the potential routes, or options, that a subject may take. This will be dictated by the ground. They should remain relaxed, yet alert, in communications with the trigger and out of sight of the start point.

Case study

A subject was due to visit a certain address that could be observed from a café opposite on a given date. The team was able to put a trigger into the café and by rotating the team cover, the expected time of arrival of the subject. As often happens the subject did not show and the team lifted off to return the next day, which also led to a fruitless observation.

2. The pick up

This is probably the most crucial phase, as failure to pick up the subject will result in there being no *follow*. A poor pick up can be caused by information not being passed on in a timely manner by the trigger. A failure of the trigger to identify movement by the subject will result in a poor follow and possibly a 'lost' subject.

To avoid this, a good pick up should consist of:

- clear indication of movement by the subject. 'Standby-standby'
- mode and direction of travel. 'On foot, right – right – right towards ...'
- acknowledgement from team when possible
- continuous commentary by the trigger of the subject's actions, until the trigger is 'unsighted'
- 'control' taken of the subject by an operator in the box – 'Golf has the eyeball'.

It is imperative that the trigger does NOT move until the subject is out of sight and has broken the box. This is an occasion when a subject, or those acting on behalf of the subject, may become aware of the surveillance, as they spot people or vehicles moving at the same time as the subject.

3. The follow

The *follow* phase of the operation starts when the subject leaves the box. Once this has occurred, the whole of the team will move into position in order to follow the subject to the next location. An aware subject may, as part of their AS procedures, leave their location, break the box and return to test for movement by a team. The team 'on plot' should have been made aware of this possibility during their briefing.

A successful follow will depend upon:

- no movement until the box has been broken
- good communications
- clear continuous commentary from the 'eyeball' [the operator in control of the subject]
- good navigation and the forward thinking of the team
- teamwork
- competent and regular handovers
- competent foot and mobile skills – competent driving
- effective lost subject drills
- determination and initiative.

4. The housing

At some point the subject will have to come to a stop. This initiates the *housing* phase. The 'stop' could be a residence or business address, a shop, or all manner of locations. When the subject stops for any amount of time, other than for a temporary halt in traffic, etc., then the subject should be classed as *housed*.

A successful *housing* will be achieved if:

- control is maintained at all times. An initial 'stop-stop-stop' from the eye-ball
- followed by a continuous commentary
- a trigger is established as the priority

- consider whether to move in or remain outside a premises – operational objectives and intelligence will dictate this
- multiple entry and exit points. Can these options all be covered by the team?
- the 'stake out' plotting up phase begins again as the team readjust their locations to 'box' the subject by covering as many options as possible.

It is a rare surveillance task that consists of a single stake out, pick up, follow and housing. The subject may visit many locations, meet many people, use different modes of transport, etc. They may leave their home on foot, walk to a bus stop, catch a bus to the railway station, meet a colleague [co-conspirator?], take a train to an airport, transfer to a taxi or hire a car. A surveillance team will gradually build up a picture of their subject and be aware of these options and thus prepare for them. Therefore a capability to change from foot to mobile, to foot surveillance, is essential. Fortunately the principles are the same for both of these methods.

4.6 Technical surveillance

The team may not have the assets to continue surveillance of a subject. Consider how many operators that a national agency might be able to deploy in comparison to a commercial organisation. Often commercial operations will work to sub optimal levels, perhaps a two person team. A Mispers case may only have a single operator. National agencies will have greater resources and be able to muster helicopters, drones, motorcycles, covert observation vans and cars, all equipped with state of the art technical aides.

The four phases of an operation apply to both foot and mobile surveillance. They can be assisted by the use of technical devices. Technical surveillance is constantly evolving as the technology available changes. The devices available to provide technical surveillance include: video cameras (in various configurations, both overt and covert); audio recording and transmitting devices; tracking equipment and computer monitoring. All these are available to commercial companies and individual operators (57).

Cameras in many guises can be used to gather evidence of the subject's activities. They can be carried by the surveillance team, mounted in cars, vans and motorcycles, or body worn. Static cameras can be deployed to provide a trigger, or to capture activity at a location. They can be set to record at a pre-set time, or to be motion activated. This will allow operators to leave the vehicle unoccupied, thereby reducing suspicion.

Another technical aid often used is a tracking device. These are now cheaply available. They rely on a combination of GPS and mobile phone technology.

These devices can be monitored remotely on a laptop or smartphone to allow the surveillance team to give the vehicle or package they are attached to greater separation, thus reducing the possibility of compromise. However, be aware that it is only the tracker which is traced not the subject (58).

Lift off, stand down and debrief

At the end of a surveillance serial, the building block of a surveillance operation, the team will, on instruction from the team leader, 'lift-off' the subject. This is when surveillance is temporally removed from the subject. This is usually after the subject has been housed and is unlikely to move again, or when the task has achieved its goal. A *debrief* will take place when all the information about the subject's movement, meetings and other activity is collated, referenced to the log books, kept by the operators or a dedicated *loggist,* and to any photography or other evidence gathered. The team leader may then decide, in consultation with the client, that sufficient information has been collected and the team will then be told to 'stand down'. This is the end of the surveillance task.

Surveillance and the law

Although we have already covered law and regulations (Chapter 3), this section outlines UK-based legislation that affects surveillance operations carried out within the UK.

The Human Rights Act 1998

This act applies to public authorities but individuals and companies engaged in surveillance activities should bear it in mind when planning and conducting an operation, as they may be sued in a civil court for an infringement. (60)

Article 8: Right to respect for private and family life

Everyone has the right to respect for his private and family life, his home and his correspondence.

There shall be no interference by a public authority with the exercise of this right, except such as is in accordance with the law and is necessary in a democratic society in the interests of national security, public safety, or the economic well-being of the country, for the prevention of disorder or crime, for the protection of health or morals, or for the protection of the rights and freedoms of others.

The Regulation of Investigatory Powers Act 2000 (RIPA)

It should be noted that while RIPA applies to official bodies, the police, military and local authorities for example, a commercial organisation or individual carrying out surveillance is not bound by RIPA. Following the principles of the act should ensure their actions are within the law, especially with regard to Article 8 of the HRA.

Covert surveillance

Section 26(9)(a) of RIPA states that: surveillance is covert if, and only if, carried out in a manner calculated to ensure that persons subject to the surveillance are unaware it is taking place.

Surveillance

As previously mentioned in Part 1, Section 48(2), RIPA defines surveillance as:

- monitoring, observing, listening to persons, their movements, conversations, other activities or communications
- recording anything monitored, observed or listened to in the course of surveillance
- surveillance by, or with the assistance of, a surveillance device.

Surveillance can be directed or intrusive, these are defined as:

Directed surveillance

Section 26(2) of RIPA:

This is covert but not intrusive (and not an immediate response to events) but undertaken for a specific investigation or operation in a way likely to obtain private information about a person. It must be necessary and proportionate to what it seeks to achieve and may be used by the wide range of authorities identified in the legislation.

Intrusive surveillance

Section 26(3) of RIPA:

This is covert and carried out in relation to anything taking place on any residential premises or in any private vehicle. It involves a person on the premises or in the vehicle, or is carried out by a surveillance device. Except in cases of urgency, it requires a commissioner's approval to be notified to the authorising officer before it can take effect. The power is available to the same law enforcement agencies as under the 1997 Act.

Private information

Section 26(10) of RIPA: In relation to a person, includes any information relating to his private or family life.

Collateral intrusion

This is when third parties are in the area being observed but are not the subject of surveillance.

Sensitive collateral intrusion

When a subject meets with a person for which it is expected there is a professional code of confidence. For example, this would include a doctor or solicitor (60).

The official government body dealing with suspected surveillance breaches is the Office of the Surveillance Commissioners. The chief surveillance commissioner, commissioners and assistant commissioners are appointed by the Prime Minister. Commissioners hold, or have held, high judicial office. One of their chief responsibilities is to scrutinise all notifications, renewals and cancellations of authorisations of property interference and intrusive surveillance (61).

Data Protection Act 1998

One of the main functions of the Information Commissioner and his staff is to ensure that organisations that are processing data are doing so in line with the obligations that are placed upon them by the various pieces of legislation, such as: the Data Protection Act, Freedom of Information Act, and the Privacy and Electronic Communications Regulations. This means that information gathered through surveillance should be protected correctly under the terms of the act (62).

Trespass

A person who strays from a right of way, or uses it other than for passing and re-passing, commits trespass against the landowner.

In most cases, trespass is a civil rather than a criminal matter. A landowner may use 'reasonable force' to compel a trespasser to leave, but not more than is reasonably necessary (63). Unless injury to the property can be proven, a landowner could probably only recover nominal damages by suing for trespass. But of course you might have to meet the landowner's legal costs. Thus a notice saying 'Trespassers will be Prosecuted', aimed for instance at keeping you off a private drive, is usually meaningless. Criminal prosecution could only arise if you trespass and damage property. However, under public order law, trespassing with an intention to reside may be a criminal offence under some circumstances. It is also a criminal offence to trespass on railway land and sometimes on military training land.

It may be necessary, from an operational point of view, to access private land to place a tracking device. Considering trespass it may be better to seek an opportunity when the vehicle is on public land.

Criminal Procedure and Investigations Act (CPIA) 1996

This allows surveillance to take place in any public place with the proviso that trespass has not been committed (64).

Protection from Harassment Act 1997

A person must not pursue a course of conduct which amounts to harassment of another, and which he knows, or ought to know, amounts to harassment of the other. This legislation has been used by subjects who detect surveillance and identify those conducting it. However, chapter 40 of the act states that there is a defence of preventing or detecting crime, or that the conduct was reasonable (65).

Protection of Freedoms Act 2012

This act concerns various aspects of RIPA. This mainly applies to government organisations (66).

4.7 Witness statements

"Witnesses are not 100% accurate. They are giving you an idea of what they think they saw." – Professor Kesser, CompTIA Security (67)

Witnesses can be incredibly useful sources for assisting investigations and piecing together unexplained cases. However, the flip-side is that witnesses can be notoriously unreliable or inconsistent with other perspectives at the scene. People often think that they have witnessed something, but an entirely different set of circumstances may well have occurred. Thus, corroboration and verification, by the use of other witnesses, or gathering physical evidence, will hopefully build an evidential picture and/or provide new lines of inquiry.

Witnesses or complainants can be notoriously unreliable. Some may be vexatious, by having 'an axe to grind'. Others could be over-keen and embellish facts to assist investigative procedures. Some could be hesitant and cautious, unsure that they have seen anything of significance, so that they hold back on coming forward and then the memory fades. A British celebrity recently had allegations of sexual assault dropped against him that formed part of the UK police's overall investigation coined *Operation Yewtree*. One complainant reported after several decades that she had been assaulted by the defendant upstairs in a seaside theatre. Following a site-visit by the defendant's own private investigator, and the examination of architectural planning documents, diaries and local newspaper records, facts revealed that the comedian had not performed at that theatre on the cited evening. Moreover, the theatre, and alleged crime scene, had no upstairs. Indeed, a whole host of allegations cited by police officers had to be systematically researched and were successfully rejected by the entertainer's own private investigation team. This defence was achieved principally by site visits, the interviewing of friends and former partners, and cross-matching diaries and local newspaper records (68).

Timing in witness statements is crucial. "The more time goes by, the more we tend to forget", explains Professor Messer of CompTIA Security (69). For Messer, three basic rules to taking witness statements apply:

- Identify who might have seen the incident. You won't know until you ask.
- Interview and document ASAP. People may not be around later.
- Not all witness statements are 100% accurate. Humans are fallible (70).

Interviews, witness statements and accident reports

The Police and Criminal Evidence Act (1984) is perhaps the most significant law in relation to gathering witness statements and was introduced to strengthen the integrity of interviewing techniques. Previously, high-profile cases of over-zealous police interviewing techniques that led to miscarriages of justice, had led to rising and alarming levels of social discontent. Moreover, a creeping realisation materialised within criminal justice and policing communities that several high-profile criminal convictions were, in all likelihood, 'miscarriages of justice'. Two famous cases where police interviewing intimidation was documented became known as the *Guildford Four* and *Birmingham Six* miscarriages. Both groups subsequently had convictions quashed in 1989 and 1991 but only after serving more than a dozen years each in prison for terrorism offences that they did not commit and were entirely uninvolved with.

The Police and Criminal Evidence Act (PACE) tightened rules around taking witness statements by ensuring that interviews were formalised and audio-recorded. Otherwise, so-called *evidence* would potentially become inadmissible, if it was suspected to be extracted under duress, or conditions that broke any of the new seven codes of practice for rules of evidence.

PACE: Code C: of particular importance to those taking witness statements is Code C for the detention, treatment and questioning of persons by police officers, and Code E on the audio recording of interviews with suspects. A new Code of Practice was introduced in the UK in 2010 and this is outlined in its entirety by the most useful Health and Safety Executive website (71).

Case study: What is a witness statement?

A witness statement is a document recording the evidence of a person, which is signed by that person to confirm that the contents of the statement are true.

A statement should record what the witness saw, heard or felt. However, it is also important to record anything that may open up a new line of enquiry, or help in corroborating other information.

Types of witness statements:

Statements provided voluntarily in compliance with section 9 of the Criminal Justice Act 1967 (LP70s) – 's9 statements'.

An s9 statement is taken from a person who has voluntarily given the statement. It does not rely on s20 (2) HSWA powers. s9 statements are recorded on form LP70.

Under s9 CJA the contents of a written statement will be admissible, without the witness attending court to give oral evidence, if the following conditions are satisfied:

- The statement purports to be signed by the maker;
- The statement contains a declaration by the maker that it is true to the best of his/her knowledge and belief, and that it was made knowing that, if it were tendered in evidence, the maker would be liable to prosecution if s/he wilfully stated in it anything which he knew to be false or did not believe to be true (known as a 'perjury declaration');
- A copy of the statement is served on the other parties before the hearing where the statement is tendered in evidence; and
- No other party object to the statement being tendered in evidence.
- Rule 27 of the Criminal Procedure Rules should also be complied with.

You also need to be aware of the following other provisions of section 9 CJA:

- If the statement is made by a person under 18, you must ensure that the age of the witness is included on the statement.
- If the witness cannot read the statement, you should read the statement to them before they sign it and sign a declaration that you have done so.
- If the witness statement refers to any document as an exhibit, a copy of the document should be served at the same time as the statement.

Source: UK Health and Safety Executive website: 2014 (72)

Police services are not the only organisations that ask people to produce witness statements. Other executive agencies, tribunals and many private companies may wish to carry out investigations and produce legally valid witness statements.

Guidance for conducting a witness statement

For your own purposes, Figure 17 provides a witness statement template based upon some good practice found in UK police services:

(Please follow this structure in your statement; leave a line between sections)

1 Single sentence summarising what this statement refers to;
2 Who you are (name, date of birth, company, job) and details of anyone else who you will mention in the statement who you already know;
3 Time and location of incident – be specific if possible;
4 What happened – start from before the incident and include everything until the incident finished;
5 Detailed descriptions of people you mention in the statement, including clothing.

Source: Metropolitan Police Service (73)

Figure 17: 5 part statement

Don't forget:

(Make sure you include the following information somewhere in your statement)

A Amount of time under observation
D Distance from suspect
V Visibility
O Obstructions to the view of the witness
K Known or seen before (where and when)

A	Any special reason for remembering suspect
T	Time lapse; how long has elapsed since the witness saw the suspect
E	Error or material discrepancy between the description given in the first and subsequent accounts by the witness

Source: Metropolitan Police Service (74)

Figure 18: ADVOKATE

Date of birth:
First Names: Surname:
Age:
Sex:
Height:
Time:
Addresses:

Source: Metropolitan Police Service (75)

Figure 19: Data standards

The critical importance of producing a highly professional and legally compliant statement from suspects and witnesses is absolutely paramount. If corners are cut, cases will collapse. Moreover, if allegations can be substantiated that due process was not followed, it is likely that the end result will be dissatisfaction for all parties concerned.

Case study: Wiltshire Police: The detective's dilemma

A breach of arrest rules saw convicted murderer, Chris Halliwell, a taxi driver from Wiltshire, escape justice for the alleged killing of Becky Godden-Edwards. Following surveillance, Halliwell had been arrested for the murder of Sian O'Callaghan from Swindon on Thursday 24 March 2011. The lead suspect had dumped a car seat cover and head rest in an industrial bin and bought an "overdose quantity of pills" (76). Miss Callaghan had been reported missing at the weekend after a night out with friends and her body had not been found. But on route to a police interview, Detective Superintendent, Steve Fulcher, called colleagues to ask that chief suspect Halliwell be diverted to Barbury Castle, on Swindon's periphery. The investigator said he had wanted to "look him in the eye" and ask Halliwell to take him to O'Callaghan who may still be alive. Fulcher said: "On the one hand, I was cognisant of Mr Halliwell's rights. But my primary duty was to save Sian's life. My view was, there was an equation to balance between Mr Halliwell's right to silence and Sian O'Callaghan's right to life. My view was that Sian's right to life took a prior claim (77)". Without being cautioned, Halliwell relented after a non-aggressive conversation, and they drove to a location where Sian O'Callaghan's body was recovered. Halliwell then told Fulcher that "you and I need a chat". Without knowing what he was about to be told, Fulcher offered Halliwell another cigarette and proceeded to listen. He believed that he had developed a rapport with the murderer and did not want to disrupt his flow of information by interrupting his dialogue to read his arrest rights. Halliwell told Fulcher that he had killed another young lady in 2004. They then drove together to a Gloucestershire location. In a remote countryside field, the body of one Becky Godden-Edwards was recovered. Halliwell pleaded guilty to the murder of Sian O'Callaghan. Other evidence, such as CCTV images showing the young lady entering his taxi and her blood on the recovered car seats covers, confirmed Halliwell's guilt. Yet, in an extraordinary turn of events, Halliwell ceased cooperation with the police and hired a criminal defence barrister, Richard Latham QC. Latham accused Fulcher of returning to a 1970s style of policing. British judge, Mrs Justice Cox, threw out Wiltshire Police's emerging case against Chris Halliwell for the murder of Becky Godden-Edwards. The evidence was inadmissible because police had not followed 1984 PACE Act guidelines. Detective Superintendent Fulcher was later found guilty of gross misconduct by the Independent Police Complaints Commission and resigned (78). The mother of Becky Godden-Edwards told news reporters: "No-one would have found Sian in a million years where they found her, where he dumped her body … It was Steve Fulcher's experience. OK, he bent rules – but he bent them for good reason" (79).

Victim personal statements

Victim personal statements (VPS) have been introduced in the UK in order to provide the justice system – including the police, legal representatives, magistrates and judges – the opportunity to see the impact of a crime upon a victim's life. Making a VPS is voluntary and the initiative is offered to all individual victims of crime, as well as small and medium sized enterprises in the UK.

According to the UK Ministry of Justice, a VPS is an important document to record for official purposes because it is can:

- explain the effect that the crime is having (or has had) on the victim's life physically, emotionally, financially, or in any other way
- express concerns about intimidation from the suspect
- express concerns about the suspect being granted bail
- ask for support from victim support
- request compensation.

Police officers will also need to complete a support form – MG19 (80). The VPS scheme also applies to UK Health and Safety at Work cases and prosecutions. According to the Health and Safety Executive: "A 'victim', in relation to HSE's work, is an individual, injured as a result of another person (including a corporate body) committing an offence under the relevant statutory provisions or, where there has been a fatality, the bereaved relatives or partners" (81).

4.8 Crime scene analysis

"Crime scene investigation is the meeting point of science, logic and law." –
Julia Layton (82)

Establishing borders of a crime scene, recording its contents, and deploying a
systematic approach to identifying and collecting evidence, are just some of the
highly skilled requirements necessary for successful crime scene analysis.

The science of crime scene analysis was strengthened by one Edmond Locard,
who developed what was thought to be the world's first forensic crime laboratory
in Lyon, France, in the early twentieth century. Locard began to introduce forensic
science into criminal investigations work and was pivotal in shifting the
circumstantial and unscientific elements of crime investigations, into more
scientific, dispassionate, evidence gathering. Locard's celebrated work underpins
many crime scene investigation approaches today.

Locard famously said that: "It is impossible for a criminal to act, especially
considering the intensity of a crime, without leaving traces of this presence" (83).
This idea subsequently became popularly known among investigators and teachers
as *Locard's Exchange Principle*.

Case Study: Crime scene analysis: FBI model

The FBI's crime scene analysis involves six steps that collectively make up their profiling
process:

Profiling inputs: This involves the collection and assessment of all of the materials relating
to the specific case. This would typically involve any photographs taken of the crime scene
and victim, a comprehensive background check of the victim, autopsy protocols, other
forensic examinations relating to the crime, and any relevant information that is necessary
to establish an accurate picture about what occurred before, during, or after the crime. This
stage serves as the basis for all others, and should incorrect or poor information be provided,
the subsequent analysis will be affected.

Decision process models: This stage simply involves arranging all of the information
gathered in the previous stage (profiling inputs) into a logical and coherent pattern. This
might also include establishing how many victims were involved, for example, with the
purpose of establishing whether the crime was the result of a serial offender.

Crime assessment: This stage would typically involve the reconstruction of the sequence
of events and the specific behaviours of both the victim and perpetrator. This will aid the
analyst in understanding the 'role' each individual has in the crime and should assist in
developing the subsequent profile of the criminal.

The criminal profile: This is the process of providing a list of background, physical, and
behavioural characteristics of the perpetrator. In the FBI model, this stage may also

---

involve providing the requesting agency with directions on how to most appropriately interview the individual. This stage would also inform investigators how to identify and apprehend the perpetrator.

The investigation: Here, the actual profile is provided to requesting agencies and incorporated into their investigation. If no suspects are generated, or if new evidence comes to light, the profile is reassessed.

The apprehension: It is stated that the purpose of this stage is to cross check the profile produced with the characteristics of the offender once they are apprehended. This would occasionally be extremely difficult as the offender may never be apprehended, apprehended in another jurisdiction and not available for cross checking, arrested on some other charge, or simply cease criminal activity.

Source: University of Vancouver (84)

The FBI's six-step investigations model is one of the most widely taught methods practiced around the world today. It is common practice for various police forces dotted around the world to send employees to take part in the Bureau's Fellowship Programme. Another important source of information for investigators is ACPO's *Murder Investigation Manual* (2006 and 2012 editions). The guide is open source and helps to teach, support and provide operating procedures for investigators. The comprehensive ACPO document is an engaging and vital read for investigators. Sections relating specifically to crime scene management tend to be in the document's second chapter (85). Credible guides on crime scene analysis can be found online and these include Griggans' MS PowerPoint slides (86).

4.9 Evidence: What is it? Why is evidence so flawed?

"An individual's perception of events and memory of what happened can be incomplete or inaccurate." – National Forensic Science Technology Centre (87)

What is evidence? How is it that, on so many occasions, we read about dead certain prosecutions collapsing into a pyre of recrimination and regret? At a recent murder trial, a famous defendant claimed that he had mistakenly shot his girlfriend, several times. He discharged gun rounds through an opaque bathroom door, at around 3am, believing his partner to be an unknown intruder. The forensic evidence showed that the first bullet hit the young lady's hip; the fourth round fatally entered her head. The young victim was likely to have omitted sounds during the incident that would have specifically identified her to her partner, so the prosecution argued. Their case was rejected as a South African judge accepted that athlete Oscar Pistorius had *mistakenly* identified his girlfriend as an intruder.

Recently, this author sat hoping for a quiet, solitary lunch in a Hampstead café. A group of four young people soon sat at the next table at 1pm. In strong American accents they spoke raucously and very loudly to one another. They took turns to refer to a young female group member as 'Duchess'. Some customers at surrounding tables raised their eyebrows in bemused frustration; others simply got up and left after a while. The last thing that those diners will remember, in all likelihood, is a loud group of American students in that damned Hampstead café!

Another male in this boisterous group remained noticeably quiet and took notes. After 20 minutes of near-deafening noise, this author resolved to interrupt this awful group of *perceived* hooligans. But before he made his move, quite suddenly, silence fell across their table. "Guys, that was really good", said the quiet young man in a crisp, tangible London accent, "but Christopher you do keep coming in late with that second question. It threw Katie". This group of British drama students then set about quietly discussing, correcting and perfecting a scene from a famous American play. For those who left the café earlier, before 1.15pm, an impression of boisterous behaviour by a group of uncontrolled young Americans had probably been firmly established. But for the rest of us, we had the privilege to watch some quite brilliant synchronised group acting. Perhaps by tomorrow's stars of theatre and cinema.

To be clear, evidence "is the information that helps in the formation of a conclusion or judgement" (88). Evidence can fall into two categories – *circumstantial* and *direct*. Circumstantial evidence depends on inferences to connect together which may corroborate an emerging, irrefutable conclusion of fact. Direct evidence supports the validity of the conclusion without further need of examination or deliberation. Testimonies, including witness and expert witness statements (verbal and written), are usually treated as circumstantial forms of evidence.

For example, several witnesses saw Heidi enter the house she shared with her partner. A passing couple of witnesses then heard a pop of three or four gunshot rounds. Three minutes later, several witnesses saw Heidi exit the house quickly and run towards her motorbike. The forensic scientist, an expert witness, then attested to the court that Heidi's boyfriend's blood and DNA samples had been found on the motorbike handlebars. Moreover, a 9mm semi-automatic pistol, later confirmed to be the murder weapon, was hidden behind a mouse hole in Heidi's father's back garden shed. Several circumstantial witness testimonies corroborate some key observations. Now there is a strong inference that Heidi is guilty of the manslaughter, or murder, of her boyfriend.

However, direct evidence from the upstairs flat has been retrieved by way of a covert mini-CCTV camera. Footage shows that her boyfriend was violently threatening Heidi for approximately 90 seconds with a pistol. After stamping up and down, possibly in anger, he turns the gun upon himself. During the coroner's proceedings, no known reason is given for the covert surveillance. There is evidence from detectives that Heidi's boyfriend was the purchaser and regularly viewed private footage of Heidi in his lounge. The weaknesses of circumstantial evidence and the strengths of direct evidence are an enduring dilemma for investigators and prosecutors alike.

Types of evidence

Testimony: a solemn declaration (oral or written) as to the truth of something made by a witness or an 'expert witness'. 'Hearsay' evidence (an out-of-court statement provided by somebody who won't be cross examined) is often not permissible in criminal court proceedings in many countries unless specifically permitted by the judge or both legal teams.

Documentary: invoices, contracts, wills, photographs, tape recordings, films, printed emails, phone bills, delivery receipts.

Real: physical evidence that plays a role in proving the case (or in some countries, or of possible use to the defence team as 'exculpatory evidence' – see below). This could be a suspected murder weapon, hidden documents, prior editions of documents before they were tampered with, biological evidence including DNA, significant crime scene parts, such as blood and saliva samples, vehicle tyre prints, crushed garden foliage, direction of ingress and egress (entry and escape route).

Digital/electronic: Emails, digital photos, ATM transaction receipts/logs, instant message histories, word processing and print histories, computer backups, GPS histories, Wi-Fi tracks, hotel electronic door locks, digital, video and audio histories, electronic travel cards (including the Oyster, in London).

Exculpatory: information that could materially benefit the defendant. In some countries, if prosecutors come across such data, it must be made available to the defence team. An example may be a witness statement or previously unknown alibi that either exonerates the accused, or reduces likelihood of their guilt or involvement.

Scientific: this is usually forensic and genetic evidence usually generated by subject matter experts. Due to the fallibility of scientific research, some court jurisdictions ask for findings to be peer reviewed and corroborated by other expert witnesses.

Science serving justice

The National Forensic Science Technology Centre (NFSTC) online provides some excellent descriptions as to how physical evidence can help to initiate and corroborate evidence provided by testimony. Detectives are taught to accept that physical evidence is left behind at every scene because "every contact leaves a trace", as per *Locard's exchange principle*. Examples of physical evidence cited by the NFSTC include:

- biological material – blood, semen or saliva
- fibres
- paint chips
- glass
- soil and vegetation
- accelerants
- fingerprints
- hair
- impression evidence – shoe prints, tyre tracks or tool marks
- fracture patterns – glass fragments or adhesive tape pieces
- narcotics.

According to the NFSTC:

> *"... evidence tells a story and helps an investigator recreate the crime scene and establish the sequence of events. Physical evidence can corroborate statements from the victim(s), witness(es) and/or suspect(s). If analysed and interpreted properly, physical evidence is more reliable than testimonial evidence; testimonial evidence is more subjective in nature. An individual's perception of events, and memory of what happened, can be incomplete or inaccurate. Physical evidence is objective and when documented, collected and preserved properly, may be the only way to reliably place or link someone with a crime scene. Physical evidence is therefore often referred to as the 'silent witness'."* (89)

In fact, understanding the nature of *evidence* as a stand-alone concept, and its psychological and attitudinal impact upon any given audience, can be a powerful skill for all security practitioners. Whether one wishes to prove a business case to investors or colleagues, or is actually going through the process of running a workplace investigation, we might wish to be mindful that there are four dominant types of evidence:

1. Statistical evidence: the use of numbers or data to emphasise a certain point; often deployed by TV advertisers to prove the credibility of their products, or airlines and rail networks to demonstrate punctuality.

2. Testimonial evidence: the use of spokespeople, witnesses and authoritative endorsers to support an assertion or organisation. For example, this may be the use of independent 'third party endorsers' by political parties on literature, or in news reports prior to elections.

3. Anecdotal evidence: sometimes dismissed as untrustworthy or merely 'hearsay', but such snippets and background information can be very useful sources to build a more complete evidential picture. Anecdotal evidence has a very obvious negative; a person or group of persons may conspire maliciously to create a chain of evidence in order to damage a person or organisation. Thus, it is important, for reasons of ethics and fairness, to seek to corroborate anecdotal evidence with other types of evidence, such as physical evidence.

4. Analogical evidence: rarely (if ever) are two scenarios exactly the same. Therefore, analogical evidence is required to prove cases whereby existing research and understanding might be undeveloped or inapplicable. An example might be that a security consultant has been tasked to provide a regional risk analysis report on a newly established nation state. This new state will have different political, law enforcement and military structures. It may have previously been part of a wider Federation and/or have been occupied by foreign troops. Scenarios in recent history could be territories in former Yugoslavia, the 1993 split of Czechoslovakia, the creation of sovereign Southern Sudan or Aceh, formerly annexed by Indonesia. Estate agents (realtors) use powerful analogical data when valuing a home (90). Analogical evidence might be described as 'comparative analysis' in academic spheres.

False evidence

The term *false evidence* can be said to include:

- forged evidence: an item of evidence manufactured or doctored to support a courtroom outcome

- planted evidence: an item which has been deliberately left, or moved, at a crime or evidence scene, to imply or influence a courtroom outcome. For example, in the case of two policeman, Hutton and Johnston, who planted shell cases to secure two false convictions for the so-called 'Crewe murders' in New Zealand in 1970 (91)

- tainted evidence: evidence incorrectly or unlawfully gathered, perhaps by an illegal search, robbery, intimidation/coercion, or incitement

- suppressed evidence: evidence that is either lawfully or unlawfully prevented from being brought into the trial. (This omission could arguably distort any result or perceptions of guilt, so the defence could claim.)

Case study: False evidence and miscarriages of justice

An inaccurate application of the now-discredited *Griess test*, in order to 'prove' that a young Irish lady, Judith Ward, did indeed handle the M62 bomb which killed a dozen coach-bound British soldiers and family members, was carried out by then-eminent Home Office laboratory scientist, Dr Frank Skuse. Incorrectly deemed to have come into contact with nitrite ions, Miss Ward was cleared at the Court of Appeal but only after serving 18 years in jail. Similar forensic findings by Dr Skuse were vehemently criticised behind the scenes by other forensic scientists during the late 1970s and 80s. This revelation, that science had been applied incorrectly, led to the eventual identification of other 'miscarriages of justice', including as new evidence for the successful Birmingham Six appeal in 1991. Testimony by a former Home Office Inspector of Explosives, claimed that Ward could not be found guilty based on the scientific data presented. (There was no other physical evidence.) In several incidents, Skuse's flawed findings supported other false evidence types including testimonies and witness statements. Yet confessions were extracted under duress and alibi evidence, which clearly supported the defendants and a 'not guilty' verdict, was held back. Such poor professional practice by the police and judiciary, and weak checks and balances around the evidence process, had profound long-term consequences: severely impacting the victims, those falsely accused, investigators and police force reputations, and the wider British judicial system. Indeed, some might argue, that such miscarriages destabilised the entire British political and security environment. The British Court of Appeal stated: "… there is … impressive … expert opinion … that Dr Skuse's tests … were of no value in establishing contact between the appellant and … explosives …" (92).

Chapter 4: Wrap-up

In closing this chapter on **Private Investigations**, we reflect on some of the approaches and attributes that will help your company gain the competitive edge. These include:

- Do bear in mind that activities carried out by private investigators may require a state or government licence. If a security enterprise extends its operations into running what might be considered traditional PI activity, it is advisable to be clear on the structure and processes of managing and accounting for these types of security functions. Relaxed or no oversight is not an option.

- Formal guidance and standards should not be viewed as a hindrance to aspiring entrepreneurs and managers in the PI field. Moreover, it serves to drive up professional competence and reinforce parameters for a workplace domain that can be highly discretionary and emotionally draining.

- Commercial surveillance operatives should bear in mind the strictures of domestic laws, such as RIPA in the UK, or the Espionage Act in the US, when planning to conduct covert surveillance activities. Covert surveillance, whether directed or intrusive (RIPA, 2000), should only be undertaken when all other methods of gathering the required information have been exhausted or would have been deemed unlikely to succeed.

References

1) Johnston, L. (1992), 'The Rebirth of Private Policing', London: Routledge, p.9
2) Prenzler, T. 'Private Investigators', in, Gill, M. et al (2006), 'The Handbook of Security', New York: Palgrave Macmillan, pp. 423-437
3) Gill, M. and Hart, J. (1996), 'Historical Perspectives on Private Investigation in Britain and the US', Security Journal, Vo.l 7, pp. 273-80
4) A useful synoptic reminder has been produced and published at the ListVerse website: ListVerse (2013), 'Top Ten Fictional Detectives' accessed on 17/12/2013 and downloaded from: *http://listverse.com/2011/01/18/top-10-fictional-detectives/*
5) Darrock-Warren A., and Gill D., (2010) 'Good Practice Guide For Workplace Investigations', Warwickshire: The Security Institute
6) Association of British Investigators (ABI) website was accessed on 17/10/2013 at: *www.theabi.org.uk/*
7) The Institute of Professional Investigators website can be accessed at: *www.ipi.org.uk*
8) World Association of Professional Investigators: website accessed on 17/12/2013 at: *www.wapi.com*
9) ABI toolkit for PIs available at ABI website (see above). BS 102000 can be accessed at: shop.bsigroup.com/ProductDetail/?pid=000000000030271051
10) NAPPS Newsroom was accessed on 17/12/2013 at: *www.napps.org/newsroom.aspx*
11) Garrison, J., (2012) 'Judge candidate accused of assaulting person serving him with summons', The City Paper (03/06/2012), accessed and downloaded on 17/12/2013 from: *http://nashvillecitypaper.com/content/city-news/judge-candidate-accused-assaulting-person-serving-him-summons*

12) Irish, L., (2011), 'Process Server shot by Prescott man after serving papers', The Daily Courier (26/09/2011), accessed and downloaded on 17/12/2013 at: *www.napps.org/pdf/newsreleases/TheDailyCourier_PrescottAZ.pdf*

13) WAPT.com (15/03/2012), 'Meldenhall Mayor guilty of simple assault', accessed and downloaded on 17/12/2013 at: *www.napps.org/pdf/newsreleases/ Mendenhall%20Mayor%20Fined%20for%20Assault.pdf*

14) LegalDictionary (2013), 'Service of Process' downloaded on 17/12/2013 from: *http://legal-dictionary.thefreedictionary.com/Service+of+Process*

15) NAPPS, (27/01/2011), news release, NATIONAL PROCESS SERVERS ASSOCIATION UNVEILS NATIONAL EDUCATION CAMPAIGN, accessed and downloaded on 17/12/2013 at: *www.napps.org/pdf/newsreleases/ NAPPS%20Campaign%20Launch%20Release_01%2027_2011_FNL.pdf*

16) Op. Cit., Prenzler, T.

17) Op. Cit., NAPPS news release

18) NAPPS: Process Serving Best Practices: 2013: downloaded on 17/12/2013 from: *www.napps.org/best_practices.asp*

19) Leveson Inquiry: (2012), 'Culture, Practices and Ethics of the Press', the full report can be accessed and downloaded at: *www.levesoninquiry.org.uk/*

20) NAPPS online (2015), Policy Manual, accessed and downloaded on 03/03/2015 at: *http://napps.org/members_policy.asp*

21) Op., Cit, Prenzler, p.429

22) Gill, M. and Hart, J. (1997) 'Policing as a business; the organisation and structure of private investigation', Policing and Society, Vol.7, pp.117-41 (p.131.)

23) Missing Abroad, a group formed by the Lucie Blackman Trust, can be accessed at: *www.missingabroad.org/*

24) LBC Radio: 'Help a London Child: Christmas Appeal' media notice was accessed and downloaded on 07/01/2013 from: *www.lbc.co.uk/help-a-london-child-christmas-appeal-2013-82667*

25) Missing People charity online can be accessed and downloaded at: *www.missingpeople.org.uk/missing-people/about-the-issue/about-the-issue*

26) NPIA (2011), 'Missing Persons: Data Analysis 2010/11, National Policing Improvement Agency', Bramshill: NPIA, p.6

27) Ibid. p.15

28) Ibid. p.16

29) Biehal, N., Mitchell F., and Wade J. (2003) 'Lost from View', Bristol: The Policy Press, p.8

30) Tarling, R. and Burrows, J. (2004) 'The nature and outcome of going missing: the challenge of developing effective risk assessment procedures', International Journal of Police Science and Management, Vol. 6, No. 1, 16-26, p.20

31) Missing Persons Bureau (n.d.), 'Has someone you know gone missing: what you need to know?', accessed and downloaded from the MPB website on 07/01/14 at: *http://missingpersons.police.uk/en/resources/report-a-missing-person*

32) Op. Cit. Biehal, Mitchell and Wade

33) Payne, M. (1995) 'Understanding 'Going Missing': issues for social work and social services', British Journal of Social Work, 25, 333-348. p.333

34) ACPO (2005), 'Guidance on the Management, Recording and Investigation of Missing Persons', (Bramshill: National Centre for Policing Excellence on behalf of the Association of Chief Police Officers), p.8

35) UK Missing Persons Bureau can be accessed at: *http://missingpersons.police.uk/*

36) MPB online (2015), 'What you need to know' factsheet and others were accessed and downloaded on 03/03/2015 at: *http://missingpersons.police.uk/en/resources/factsheets-for-families*

37) Missing Kids (Brasil) website: *http://br.missingkids.com/missingkids/servlet/PublicHomeServlet* and Let's Bring Them Home website: *http://lbth.org/ncma/*

38) Op. Cit., Missing Abroad website

39) Grampian Police (2007), 'Missing Persons: Understanding, Planning, Responding'

40) PACT online was accessed on 03/03/2015 at: *www.pact-online.org/* and the Child Exploitation and Online Protection (CEOP) website can be accessed at: *http://ceop.police.uk/*

41) Op. Cit., Missing People online

42) Pankau, E., (2000), 'How to Hide Your Assets and Disappear', New York: Harper Collins

43) FBI National Crime Information Center (NCIC) 'Missing Person File' was accessed and downloaded on 08/01/2014 from: *www.oregon.gov/osp/CJIS/docs/missing_person_data_guide.pdf*

44) BSI (2008), BS 8507-1 2008 Close Protection Operations guidance

45) National Archives: change of name guide can be accessed at: *www.nationalarchives.gov.uk/records/research-guides/change-of-name.htm*

46) Ibid

47) London Gazette can be accessed at: *www.thegazette.co.uk* The Belfast Gazette can be accessed at the same web address.

48) Daily Mirror online (2012), 'DVLA cashing in by selling drivers data to firms including illegal parking racket', accessed and downloaded on 08/01/2014 from: *www.mirror.co.uk/news/world-news/dvla-cashing-in-by-selling-drivers-data-1676004*

49) The Examiner: 'Tax Returns could help find missing kids': downloaded and accessed on 08/01/2014.

50) Biography.com (2013), Jaycee Dugard Biography, accessed and downloaded on 08/01/2014 from: *www.biography.com/people/jaycee-dugard-20993627*

51) 192.com can be accessed online at: *http://192.com*

52) LexisNexis can be accessed and downloaded at:

53) Op. Cit., Missing People website

54) Jenkins, P., (2010), 'Surveillance Tradecraft, the professional's guide to covert surveillance training', Third Edition. Harrogate: Intel Publishing

55) Harfield, C and Harfield, K., (2005), 'Covert Investigations'. First Edition. Oxford: Oxford University Press

56) Op. Cit., Jenkins

57) Examples of technical surveillance platforms were accessed and downloaded on 02/02/2014 at: *www.dogcamsport.co.uk/covert-camera-packages.html*

58) Examples of tracking devices were accessed on 02/02/2014 at: *http://trackershop-uk.com*

59) Liberty80, (n.d). 'Article 8 Right to a private and family life' [online]: accessed 22/01/2015 at: *www.liberty-human-rights.org.uk/human-rights/ human-rights/the-human-rights-act/what-the-rights-mean/article-8-right-to-a-private-and-family-life.php*

60) RIPA 2000 accessed on 02/02/2014 at: *www.legislation.gov.uk/ ukpga/2000/23/contents*

61) Office of Surveillance Commissioners online can be accessed at: *https://osc.independent.gov.uk/*

62) Data Protection Act was accessed on 02/02/2014 at: *www.legislation.gov. uk/ukpga/1998/29/contents*

63) Tresspass law was accessed on 02/02/2014 at: *www.cps.gov.uk/legal/ s_to_u/trespass_and_nuisance_on_land/*

64) Criminal Procedure and Investigations Act (CPIA) 1996, accessed on 02/02/2014 at: *www.legislation.gov.uk/ukpga/1996/25/contents*

65) Protection from Harassment Act 1997, accessed on 02/02/2014 at: *www.legislation.gov.uk/ukpga/1997/40/contents*

66) Protection of Freedoms Act 2012, accessed on 02/02/2014 at: *www.legislation.gov.uk/ukpga/2012/9/section/29/enacted*

67) Professor Kesser (2011), Video: 'Screenshots and Witnesses', CompTia (3.05): *www.youtube.com/watch?v=pZVxzFaZJ_8*

68) Lasserri, A., with Davidson. J., (2014) 'My sex arrest agony', was accessed on 14/10/2014 at: *www.thesun.co.uk/sol/homepage/news/5357950/jim-davidson-reveals-agony-of-sex-arrest.html*

69) Op. Cit., Kesser

70) Ibid.

71) Health and Safety Executive (2013), 'Witness Statements', and 'Questioning of Suspects', accessed and downloaded on 08/01/2014 from: *www.hse.gov.uk/ enforce/enforcementguide/investigation/witness-witness.htm*

72) Ibid

73) MPS (2014) Conducting a witness statement

74) Ibid

75) Ibid

76) The Guardian, (19/10/2012), 'Sian O'Callaghan murder: the Detective's Dilemma', accessed and downloaded on 04/03/2015 at: *www.theguardian. com/uk/2012/oct/19/sian-ocallaghan-murder-detective*

77) Ibid

78) The Times (31/01/2014): 'Detective guilty of misconduct over killer's confession': accessed at: *www.thetimes.co.uk/tto/news/uk/crime/ article3983432.ece*

79) BBC News (15/05/2014), Becky Godden Misconduct Detective Steve Fulcher Resigns', accessed and downloaded on 05/03/2015 at: *www.bbc.co.uk/news/uk-england-wiltshire-27431025*

80) Criminal Justice System (2009), 'Victim Personal Statements: A guide for police officers, investigators and criminal justice practitioners', accessed and downloaded on 08/01/2014 from: *www.justice.gov.uk/downloads/ victims-and-witnesses/working-with-witnesses/vps-guide-cjs-practitioners.pdf*

81) Op. Cit., Health and Safety Executive, 2013

82) Layton. J. (N.D.), 'How Crime Scene Investigations work', accessed and downloaded on 18/03/2014 from: *http://science.howstuffworks.com/csi.htm*

83) Edmund Locard quote, circa 1912

84) FBI CSA model: accessed and downloaded on 18/03/2014 from: *http://web.viu.ca/.../CASE_STUDY_REPORT_FORMAT_GUIDELINE.doc*

85) ACPO (2006), Murder Investigation Manual: accessed and downloaded on 18/03/2014 from: *www.acpo.police.uk/documents/crime/2006/ 2006CBAMIM.pdf*

86) Griggans (2014), 'Investigating a Crime Scene': accessed and downloaded on 18/03/2014 from: *www.slideshare.net/griggans/investigating-a-crime-scene*

87) NFSTC website (2014), 'Types of Evidence', accessed and downloaded on 02/04/2014 from: *www.nfstc.org/pdi/Subject01/pdi_s01_m01_01.htm*

88) Writing Simplified (2014), 'Four types of evidence', accessed and downloaded on 02/04/2014 from: *www.writingsimplified.com/2009/10/4-types-of-evidence.html*

89) Op. Cit., NFSTC online

90) Op., Cit., Writing simplified (2014)

91) NZ Herald (26/09/2010), 'Book claims dead cop killed Crewes', accessed and downloaded on 06/03/2015 at: *www.nzherald.co.nz/nz/news/article.cfm?c_id=1&objectid=10676159*

92) R v Ward (1993) 96 Cr. App. R 1

CHAPTER 5: INFORMATION SECURITY

5.1 Context

"I think computer viruses should count as life. I think it says something about human nature that the only form of life we have created so far is purely destructive. We've created life in our own image." – Professor Stephen Hawking, theoretical physicist and author.

Information is precious and we should guard it well. For example, while writing this chapter I knocked on an elderly neighbour's door only to discover a post-it note stuck to the porch window: "Dear Postman, I am not at home today. Please leave the parcel I'm expecting at the depot".

This chapter will therefore examine threats to one of our most critical types of asset: information. An employee's ability to readily access any necessary company information is a vital ingredient to the running of a fast-moving, inspirational enterprise. Yet, on the contrary, security and IT departments will need to ensure that some, or most information held by the company, is kept as safe and secure as possible. This is not just for reasons of legal compliance that have been broadly covered in Chapter 3: Legislation and Regulations. But, it is also due to the fact that an unguarded release of important information – either caused accidentally or deliberately – can lead to such knowledge being lethally exploited by our adversaries. It was the US War Office that famously produced some stark propaganda posters during World War Two which warned: "Loose Lips Might Sink Ships". This was mainly a warning to civilians and resting soldiers against idle chat and the disclosure of sensitive information in public places. Nevertheless, in the digital media era, many companies are waking up to a stark corporate reality: idle security planning around information assets will, equally, threaten individual and corporate survival.

When most of us depend on ICT to make a living, how can we begin to mitigate against critical information loss? This chapter will also outline some core procedures and concepts that are designed to protect our business critical information and provide ICT systems with continuity. Concepts, such as *intelligence*, *espionage* and *insider threat* will be examined in this chapter. What do they mean? Are they realistic? How can we adapt to diverse, multilateral threat vectors in order to achieve the right balance between corporate defence (security and IT) and market-facing business functions, such as, sales, business development and marketing? Finally, this chapter offers some recommendations in order to allow readers to plan for a proportionate and integrated set of countermeasures. This chapter is broken down into several sub-sections including:

5.1 Context

5.2 Why target our information?

5.3 Intelligence and espionage

5.4 Insider threats

5.5 Counterfeiting and IP

5.6 Technical security countermeasures

5.7 Cyber security

5.8 Mitigation: developing a security policy and standards

5.9 Wrap-up: why consultants appear to be succeeding or failing in the emerging cyber security market

5.2 Why target our information?

Philosopher, Friedrich Nietzsche, perhaps came up with one of history's most unforgettable quotes when he pontificated that "all knowledge is power". Another lesser known truism was reported by accountancy company Deloitte: "Many companies lack a clear understanding of exactly what their intellectual property is …" (1). This conclusion is unsurprising but it also serves as a stark warning to security managers. Consider in the widest possible terms where your company's most important corporate information is located. Only then can we prioritise protections across certain domains of people, property and assets.

Case study: Who might target our information?

The following five real-world scenarios demonstrate just how diverse threats and risks to personal and company information can be:

- Under-pressure, company researchers in the Pakistan defence sector downloaded counterfeit anti-virus software, produced by a neighbouring Chinese company. They were under severe time restraints when trying to fix a pre-contract delivery design fault but they failed to carry out due diligence or pre-plan continuity issues that could have prevented sensitive research data being sent abroad.

- A government special adviser from a NATO member-state lost their Blackberry in a suspected 'honey trap' incident while visiting China. The unencrypted phone included sensitive diplomatic, professional and personal data. Many emails and texts related to senior government ministers and other NATO member-state political leaders (2).

- A tracking device reportedly became attached to the car of an England football captain. The player believed that family and friends were leaking his whereabouts to the media (3).

- A leading television comedian and script writer had his main laptop stolen. Script drafts and vital editorial comments for the latest hit television series were not backed-up (4).

- A cyber-attack group, known as *Anunak* or *Carbanak,* reportedly sent malicious software (malware) to hundreds of US-based banking staff. This enabled them to steal more than £300m from customer bank accounts. The same group had previously attacked major US retailer companies. The malware installed a variety of network reconnaissance tools, including key loggers and other 'bespoke attack software kits'. Video footage was used to establish bank employee work patterns. Further 'painstaking research conducted by the attackers places it on a comparable level with cyber attack campaigns attributed to nation states', reported business security group, CSARN (5).

In its popular annual *Data Loss Barometer* publication, accountancy company KPMG point to information loss now being a way of life for anybody with an online profile: "Over the past five years, more than one billion people globally have been affected by data loss incidents" (6), researchers found. Securing our valuable information has perhaps become the most kaleidoscopic of all tasks. Because whichever way we tilt the lens when we look at risk, a host of other interconnected risks fall into play. For example, handwritten scripts by a treasured TV producer could easily burn in a house-fire or fall into the hands of competitors or burglars. Moreover, they would still need typing up and emailing to all of the production team, including the actors!

Two common challenges occur for security practitioners as they interface with information and cyber security issues. Like any *hazard identification* stage of risk assessment, it remains extremely difficult to identify threats and vulnerabilities. The naked dependency of most organisations upon ICT, and the sheer speed and agility of organised cyber attackers, means that – at the time of writing – initiative very much rests with the aggressors, who are often mercurial in structure and motivated in purpose. Companies and security contractors are increasingly turning to the information security management system (ISMS) Standard *ISO27001* in order to introduce proportionate and sensible controls across ICT platforms and the work domains that any high-tech machinery is supposedly there to serve (7). Compliance with the international Standard is also becoming a prominent benchmark for customers in order to assess the suitability and credibility of contractors within their supply chain. Because information security risks are so overarching, familiarity with ISO27001 is therefore strongly recommended for any security practitioner.

What assets need protection?

According to expert Alan Calder, information security can be defined as the "preservation of confidentiality, integrity and availability of information". Calder also recommends that information security "cannot be achieved through technology alone" (8). Intellectual property assets that typically require some level of planned protection include: customer data (including bank card and personal contact details); contracts, deals and negotiations; passwords; staff information; research and development findings; business/market intelligence; designs and processes, including the organisation's own business continuity and crisis management plans; IT systems and infrastructure. We may also need to take into account plans for further protections around certain key people or sites within an organisation. In turn, property and assets held by key persons, or at core facilities, such as vehicles, mobile phones and computers, are particularly attractive targets for adversaries. The knowledge and information chain extends well into family networks, friends, suppliers, and even routine locations used by those holding precious information, or who are targets for prying eyes. For example, several newspapers reported that a hidden listening device had been found at a favoured restaurant, and preferred table, used by Premier League football manager, José Mourinho (9).

In sum, the *entire* success of a security management function is very much dependent upon its contribution to data protection issues and cultures within any project or organisation. This can only be done by evaluating and anticipating weaknesses and then closing the gaps. Details matter. The loss of a principal's smartphone, or failure to recover an unencrypted memory stick which contains sensitive data, can nowadays be just as embarrassing for a security function as a serious physical security breach might well be.

Nevertheless, if ICT security procedures are too constrictive, the enterprise might also stall, customer response times may lengthen and investigations and prosecutions may grind to a halt. Disproportionate access restrictions therefore can play to the law of unintended consequences, where compliance actually *deteriorates* because exhausted and frustrated employees seek to 'cut corners'. They may even parachute themselves out of the gridlocked office window into friendlier and more relaxed corporate climes. According to accountancy company Deloitte: "Employees without access to flexible IT policies are less satisfied with their job. Only 62% of employees without access to flexible IT policies report feeling satisfied at work. Up to 83% of employees with access to flexible IT policies (such as social media access) report feeling satisfied at work" (10).

Calculating the value of information

Understanding the value of information to an organisation is by no means an easy task. Indeed, some critics say that it can't sensibly be done. The Information Assurance Advisory Council (IAAC) however provide a huge array of useful advice in this sphere to help companies and contractors manage risk and provide 'assurance' in delivering governance, security and process integrity to information and data systems (11).

Great efforts and convoluted process are laid on by some companies to protect sensitive data. Moreover, many clients won't realistically want to share critical information with incoming security contractors, at least in the first instance. Despite a client's reluctance to share the type of information that can positively help to inform risk assessment and security planning, security contractors must crack on with their job and be content to make some informed assumptions. For instance, pharmaceutical or drinks recipes, foreign bank account numbers, embarrassing complaints against senior employees, luxury assets and company heirlooms, are often stowed away for safe keeping by company owners and chief executives. Even if the client keeps a security contractor ignorant of such important details, the disappearance of such assets will hardly endear a security function to the executive team afterwards!

The discipline of valuing company information is sometimes referred to as *infonomics*. Information analyst, Doug Laney, has developed several models that calculate the value of information which can be of particular help to chief information officers (CIO). Data can be separated into two categories argues Laney. The first, non-financial, or economic data, may not have an actual price tag but can be prioritised and ranked relative to what its 'intrinsic value is' (12). The second category is tangible financial data which can be modelled along the lines of established accounting practices, in order to arrive at a numerical cost and/or quantity of loss. Finding the cost value of information was applied by many companies after the 9/11 terrorist atrocities in New York. A value is given to the data "by measuring lost revenue and how much it would cost to acquire the data", reports Laney (13). If you're struggling to do this, then adopt the approach of any decent private investigator. Step into the shoes of a potential adversary. Look at the scenario from their mind's eye. *What are they seeking to take from your organisation? What are they seeking to achieve? What do they believe they will gain?* Loss or 'shrinkage', an American retail idiom, can be calculated in financial denominations. But other denominations can include loss of market share, profit or revenue, customer life value (CLV). Moreover, reputational loss could even be equated to a percentile loss of support, perhaps for an NGO or political party. (This may, in turn, cause a future revenue loss due to a reduction of subscribers.) A variety of predictive analysis techniques – such as financial modelling, data mining and decision trees – may already be in use by the client, in order to establish information assurance. One would hope that this is the case with any medium or larger size corporation. Security contractors should consider making themselves aware of any information assurance scoping work and policies that are undertaken by any client; a company's approach to information assurance is often reflective of its wider culture and management approaches.

Predicting loss calculations can be a straightforward exercise in some cases. For example, the cost of research and developing a new medical drug for the global market can be around $5bn (14). There is some information out there that can be described as 'perfect information' for businesses because there is a large degree of certainty around costs and reasonable benchmarks for comparisons (15). For instance, the theft of assets or property destruction can be calculated by insurers and accountants with brutal efficiency. Yet with any of these scenarios, the loss of information and intellectual property can cause incalculable further damage, perhaps unseen in the aftermath, and only more visible with the passage of time. We therefore cannot always reasonably anticipate every business loss or count the cost beforehand because there are often additional human and operating environmental impacts that can reverberate in a very unpredictable manner for many years afterwards. For example, can we ever really know how many government contracts a large company lost *solely* because its employees had an inconvenient habit of leaving unencrypted memory sticks and company laptops with client details in restaurant bars and commuter trains? There may have been many other reasons for losing potential future contracts, such as the rise of competitors, or a change in procurement policy. Prolonging the search for perfect, quantifiable information – in contrast to accepting imperfect data – may well delay strategy, or direct us down a path of inquiry that is not central to our task: holistic information security. Don't get buried by maths and algorithms. Elevating the overall principle of information security to a consistent priority action among security practitioner teams is, perhaps, the safest overall calculation to make from the outset.

5.3 Intelligence and espionage

In a security context, the words *intelligence* and *espionage* are often used interchangeably; although to do so is not always accurate.

For many, both terms conjure up images of clandestine operations, or a murky undercover world of mutual assured deception. When intelligence and espionage activities become publicised they can attract a high degree of profile, alarm, apprehension and incredulity, or, admiration and amazement, such as revelations in the 1950s that British and American spies had tunnelled under Soviet-controlled East Berlin and were reading diplomatic telegrams to and from Moscow.

Critics have seized on the many obvious ethical and operational pitfalls to gathering intelligence and also the practice of the tradecraft known as *espionage*. Yet many security practitioners, business organisations and policy-makers see significant value in supporting and deploying intelligence work and operations. This willingness is, in part, because the overwhelming majority of data upon which intelligence is borne seems to be open source (OSINT) and freely available. As with so many topics that attract mass media hyperbole, the narrative is often far more frightening than the rather mundane reality!

Moreover, many who depend on, or deploy intelligence, may feel closer to the frontline of a risk scenario than their detractors who may well be more ignorant as to the perceived ground truth. Consumers and producers of intelligence may well perceive themselves and their colleagues as the last defensive line in terms of mitigating a threat. They might even be under clear and present danger themselves. They might also seek to 'get ahead' of unfolding events that will directly impact them. They therefore seek to learn more about their operating environment and developing a better level of knowledge than any market competition. While some or all of this is the case, clients and recipients may not necessarily wish to be too closely associated with the sources of information. One former head of the British domestic security service testified (Rimington: 190) (16):

> *"Ministers for their part, may well have thought that although the intelligence services were essential, they were a potential embarrassment to the government and the less they knew about them the better."*

It is usually stacked against this sensitive, publicity-shy, backdrop that those tasked with directing, collecting, processing and disseminating intelligence must operate.

What is meant by the terms intelligence and espionage?

In a security context, *intelligence* suggests the gathering, collating, synthesising and secure dissemination of information. Intelligence is refined information which is supposedly of an advanced quality, and must fulfil a somewhat abstract criteria of being timely, accurate and relevant. Intelligence products are therefore *actionable* for the client: they stimulate activity and decision making, even if that decision is 'an NFA' in security parlance, no further action.

Espionage is a method of gathering intelligence. This trade involves clandestine and covert spying to gather information which can be processed into intelligence. Espionage is getting information from somebody covertly (17). Despite the end of the Cold War (circa 1947-91), the conduct of economic, diplomatic and military espionage by many governments remains popular. Espionage can conjure up such exciting images as static and mobile surveillance, moles undertaking slow-burn *sleeper* roles whereby companies or public authorities are penetrated over a longer duration of time. Moreover, many cases of espionage are conducted by insiders; usually, but not always, disgruntled or avaricious employees who pass on critical information to adversaries.

Why do organisations gather intelligence?

- To achieve competitive advantage
- Better information can help target scarce resources and/or reduce duplication
- To achieve prior warning around a major incident which could save lives, prevent injuries or huge financial losses
- Identify threats and exposure to risks
- To detect and prosecute criminals and terrorists
- To defend the realm and prevent subversion
- Acquire sensitive knowledge to 'control' the subject and/or carry out blackmail
- Material or financial benefit.

All of these reasons boil down to one single, overall aim for gathering intelligence: to reduce uncertainty.

> ### How is the Intelligence Cycle Organised?
>
> Like most conceptual applications in the security sphere, there is no single, authoritative conceptual model that can be said to illustrate the end-to-end development of an *intelligence product*. Given the kinetic nature of security management scenarios, and vastly different operational conditions from task to task, there simply cannot be a one-size-fits-all approach. But the CIA model outlined below does draw for us a convenient and plausible intelligence model that is often emulated by other organisations:
>
> ### The 'Action-on' CIA Intelligence Model
>
>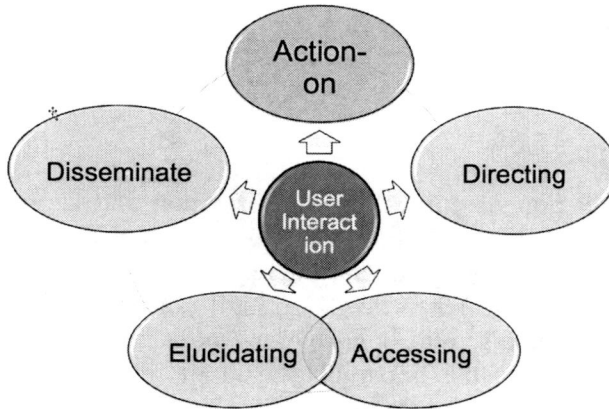
>
> *Source: CIA website (18)*

Intelligence cycles tend to include at least four core components:

Direction: The beginning of the process. The client informs the intelligence manager what they need or wish to know. A recurring challenge is 'information void', whereby decision makers often do not know enough about what they need to know, in order to give clear direction in the first instance. This is because they begin the task with a negligible amount of useful existing intelligence. This stage can also be used to issue feedback and change tactical direction in response to prior intelligence shortcomings.

Collection: Raw data and information is collected from a variety of sources which may help intelligence analysts at the next stage of the cycle. Sources could be: Geospatial (GEOINT), Human (HUMINT), Imagery (IMINT), Intercepted Communications (SIGINT), Measurement and Signature (MASINT) or Open Source (OSINT).

Processing: The human analysis and assessment of available information, collated, synthesised and processed into timely, relevant and accurate intelligence. Successful assessment and interpretation of data by intelligence analysts is akin to correctly piecing together available jigsaw pieces, within a given timeframe, to establish the most accurate situational picture possible for the client. The intelligence product is also sanitised before being disseminated, in order to remove details which may compromise sources or methods used to gather information or expose the client. For example, an intelligence agency may insert aliases to protect the identity of sources, or those under observation.

Dissemination: The process of moving and communicating the actionable intelligence reports to the client and/or any given end-user. This must happen in a secure manner which will not compromise any of the three prior phases of the intelligence cycle.

Information hierarchy

Of course, production of any relevant information and appropriate knowledge sharing can be very useful to business and government decision makers within any security operating environment. But merely gathering useful information, or employing company researchers to do so, still potentially falls far short of the specific benefits that disciplined *business intelligence* processes can usher in. Business intelligence is the impartial pursuit of insightful and highly refined information that will reduce operational uncertainty for organisations. For example, reports from daily newspapers may well tell us that hackers were attacking IT networks run by commercial banks. This will, indeed, be very useful for a security manager in Manhattan but they might not be able to action this information other than to issue a general warning to staff, perhaps to urge them to be more vigilant and report anything suspicious. Yet more specific and insightful knowledge, such as prior methods, trends and timings, the most popular targets, the scale of expertise and research used by perpetrators, or if there was a suspected underlying reason why some banks or staff networks were prioritised as a target, could all be fairly construed as snippets of actionable business intelligence.

As such, intelligence is considered by many to sit at the apex of knowledge management models, see Figure 20.

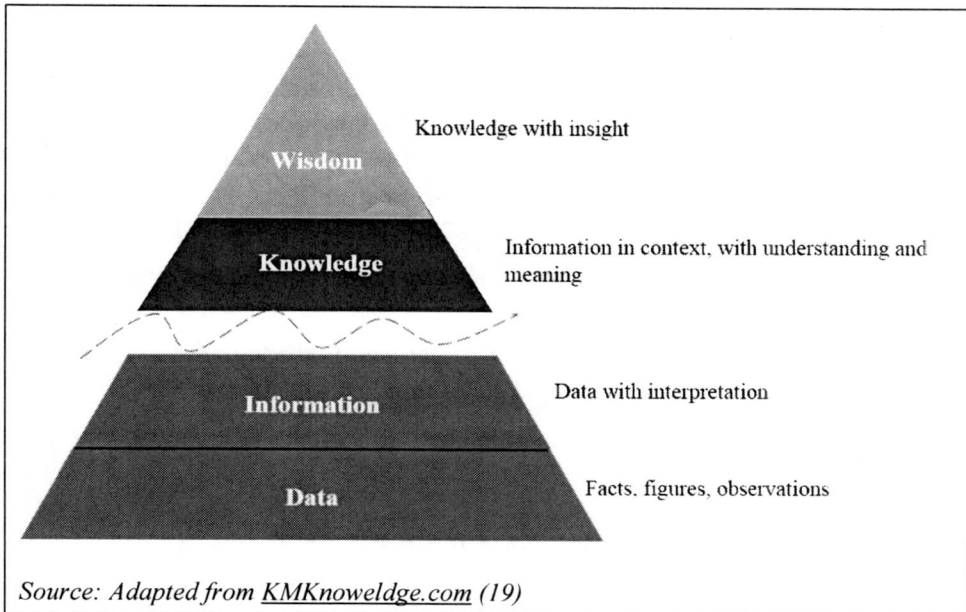

Source: Adapted from KMKnoweldge.com (19)

Figure 20: The knowledge hierarchy

Knowledge hierarchy explained

Data: Raw information gathered or received from a third party which has not been analysed or subject to any form of processing.

Information: This could be data that has been sifted, or been subject to a basic to moderate degree of processing, such as translation, cross-referencing, formatting, comparative analysis and double-checking.

Knowledge: Supporting information, or pre-existing understanding and comprehension, which is required to help assess, evaluate, organise and process incoming data and information into actionable intelligence.

Intelligence outcomes

We have seen that intelligence products are principally designed to provide critical insights into defined 'subjects' or target areas. Demands for intelligence can often come in the form of priority information requests (PIRs) or slightly less urgent information requests.

As we have established, intelligence is information which is refined, assessed and disseminated, usually with the intention to *trigger* or assist certain action by the client/end-user. Conversely, intelligence can also be used to keep a *watching brief* on potential adversaries, or monitor certain threats and risks in order to confirm NFA. Intelligence gathering therefore helps to provide context and clarity to our decision making. It can help to clear a logical pathway through an operating environment riddled with uncertainty; a domain that the great Prussian military strategist, Carl von Clausewitz, famously described circa 1873 as the "fog of war' (20). Forms of intelligence products can include:

- Identify incumbent organisational and personnel weaknesses and courses of action (COA)
- Identifying risks to employees and the organisation through threat assessments
- Target group profiling (TGP) and monitoring
- Issuing early warning to decision makers

Why is business intelligence becoming more popular?

Usually companies are looking to sensibly and proportionately allocate their resources in order to achieve strategic objectives. In striving for their outcomes, against ferocious competition, they may ask for employees and business divisions to work to SMART objectives; these being … specific, measurable, achievable, relevant and time-bound. Management is often implemented by the use of individual employee targets that are established as key performance indicators (KPIs), where specific individual and team targets and performance requests can be measured and recorded. Such methods are used by companies to drive forward momentum, a sense of corporate interoperability and to reinforce quality controls and a sense of fairness; because everybody supposedly fits into one clear system of corporate rules. KPIs and corporate management quantification techniques are on the rise, asserted management author, GT Doran, and that was back in the early 1980s (21)!

The growth of opportunities for security contractors to make extra revenue lines from business intelligence products, corresponds to these increasingly scientific business management cultures. Information research departments are nowadays expected to directly support and align to core business goals in any company. Moreover, there is little tolerance for random 'background briefings' and snippets from in-house subject matter experts which may have impressed and reassured executive boards in the past. Significant reputational loss, punitive legal penalties, market sanctions, and bottom line cash loss, are the consequences that any business can expect if it stumbles haphazardly into a security-related crisis.

Several influencing factors have converged, at the time of writing, which have established a global-market-wide desire for intelligence-led decision making. The quantification of business management approaches, ICT convergence, the expansion of corporate litigation, and the spending squeeze hewn by the latest international financial crisis, are all factors that have driven up demand by executive boards and corporate governance committees to insist that they become equipped for decision making with timely, accurate and relevant information. The idea of an *activity trap* has been posed by crisis management academic, Geary Sikich and others, who carried out isomorphic learning lessons on the 2010 Deepwater Horizon oil disaster, mentioned earlier in this book, caused accidentally by an explosive blow-out of an oil platform owned by a subsidiary of the oil major, BP. Management academics noted that in some large companies, the overall commercial goal becomes eclipsed by an entrenched fulfilment to traditional process. Companies become automated and inflexible, and unable to adapt to changing conditions within their operating environment. Poor ground intelligence has been identified as a contributor in many corporate disasters. But this is often not the case. It's the inability of a big organisation to adapt fast enough to the new information or incoming 'intelligence' that is so often the problem (22).

In response to such concerns, many companies and senior executives now seek specific business intelligence reporting, either in house or contracted in. The Business Innovation Council has adopted "intelligence-led" security approaches, where a blend of "current, estimative and research" intelligence products are woven together to help inform executive decision makers about security strategy and courses of action to take, reports *Computer Weekly* magazine (23). Some CEOs report that their entire corporate agenda setting is *intelligence-led* because they could not possibly fix medium- to long-term objectives without the most appropriate, up-to-date insights, which can help to facilitate the best possible decision-making cultures.

Where does intelligence fit into the risk management process?

Source: Striking Project Management (24)

Figure 21: Risk management model

In contrast to merely utilising intelligence at the beginning of the risk management process (Identify & Analyse Exposures), intelligence activity and reporting can play a critical role throughout the *entire* risk management process and its core five phases (see Figure 21). Organisations will wish to stick to strategy and objectives. But those that are more adaptive – and are therefore able to avoid or mitigate emerging risks, or exploit emerging opportunities – tend to be those that have embraced and embedded business intelligence techniques within their own organisational cultures. Just as people who carry out regular exercise and health checks tend to enjoy a better longevity, in the sphere of organisational resilience, it's precisely the same; active knowledge-gathering of upcoming problems, followed by exercise and adaptive techniques to evade the risk, are also core ingredients for corporate survival and prosperity. "Facts do not cease to exist because they are ignored", the Brave New World author, Aldous Huxley, poignantly wrote (25).

Integrity and compliance

Gathering intelligence is controversial. The integrity of information, source protection and legal compliance are all critical responsibilities that will help safeguard business intelligence functions and an organisation's overall reputation.

If information is gathered or handled illegally, or source identities become compromised, the consequences for a corporate body, or government organisation, can be calamitous. While for individuals directly impacted, intelligence failures can often lead to tragedy. Before undertaking any intelligence function you will need to be aware of different local, regional, national and intergovernmental protocols, rules and legislation which may support or constrain your initiative (*see Chapter 3: Legislation and Regulations*).

In some sectors, such as banking and insurance, business intelligence functions are ubiquitous cantilevers that underpin and influence almost every other sphere of work. Business intelligence functions can include financial risk monitoring, anti-fraud detection and due diligence around new depositors; these measures are warmly welcomed by many consumers and stakeholders, including the media and political decision makers, especially since the 2007/8 banking crash, caused in part by too much bad debt poisoning the wells of the banking sector. However, extra tiers of red tape for customers, and use of private investigators by private companies, has also attracted public ire. Moreover, the term *intelligence* can often provoke unsettling perceptions of sinister Big Brother-esque controls, either in workplace or public domains.

Due to negative connotations which resonate from intelligence gathering functions, terminology used by an organisation to identify its intelligence functions is often different to a straightforward, brazen identification of a particular unit's purpose; namely, 'intelligence'. For example, one security manager explained to me: "The current organisation that I work for is a large retail organisation and we use intelligence gathering and management, often referred to as *horizon scanning*, in a number of ways in order to anticipate future threats and plan the response. The company have a dedicated team of six analysts who look at horizon scanning and the information is then managed by the business continuity and executive protection managers" (26). Conversely, some organisations may prefer to opt for greater transparency, or even a public demonstration of force projection, by stating that they do have intelligence units; it may be that this dissuades and deters various security risks, including fraud, money laundering and cyber attacks. One major bank recently hired a former UK MI5 chief onto its board and remains one of many to operate a 'financial intelligence unit' (27).

Corporate espionage

Corporate espionage, sometimes referred to as *industrial, commercial* or *economic* espionage, is a covert method of business intelligence gathering carried out in order to provide companies with information that they hope will give them competitive advantage over their rivals. This practice, unlawful and unethical in many but not all domains, is usually driven by a desire to reduce research and development costs and time.

Case studies of alleged corporate espionage

Company-on-company espionage
In 2012, manufacturer Dyson took a case to London's High Court and alleged that designs and product assembly information for its high speed motors and microchip technology on brushless vacuum cleaners had been sold by an internal employee to German competitor, Bosch (28). Product research and development reportedly cost Dyson around £100m and the corporate know-how for these valuable products was collected over 15 years. Bosch denied the claims.

During 2008, the US State Department was so concerned that American business travellers would experience the theft of valuable corporate information while visiting the Olympic Games in Beijing, that they authorised the use of formal warning messages from the Overseas Security Advisory Services. In response, Washington DC duly received the diplomatic wrath of China, the US's largest bilateral trading partner, reported *Forbes* magazine (29).

Government-on-company espionage
China is deemed by US defence officials to be the world's biggest state-sponsor in 'economic espionage' according to the Pentagon's annual report on the PRC's military (30). Recent allegations levelled at Chinese State-owned companies for buying trade secrets include Pangang Group allegedly acquiring DuPont's titanium dioxide pigment technology, also known as 'whiteners', reported the *Asia Times* in 2012 (31). Computer security company ESET claim that computer worms that originated in China were targeted at their AutoCAD software which was used by architects and designers in Peru. The company claimed that thousands of technology blueprints were transferred to two China based internet service providers. China's Government-run National Computer Virus Response Centre was reported to have helped ESET by blocking compromised email accounts. But this was not before the company concluded: "From our analysis of all the used email accounts we can derive the scale of the attack and conclude that tens of thousands of AutoCAD drawings (blueprints) were leaked" (32).

Employer-on-employee espionage
Employers appear to be increasingly turning to monitoring practices that could be defined by some as surveillance or espionage.

In the UK and many similar legal jurisdictions, covert spying on employees is lawful so long as specific limitations and conditions are satisfied. Several cases have hit the headlines. In 2002, one British corporate intelligence agency was reportedly employed to monitor the activities of senior staff at law companies to establish if lawyers were working for competitors, and to establish other details, reported the *International Intelligence and Law Gazette* (33). Two European supermarket companies, Lidl and Aldi, were exposed by the *Daily Mail* in 2013 for allegedly deploying secret cameras in staff lockers at some European locations. Staff alleged that personal information was then used to pressurise certain staff to leave their jobs. The companies firmly denied that information relating to private details was sought (34).

Monitoring of employees in the UK may only be carried out for the following given reasons:

- To comply with wider legal requirements, including health and safety, the prevention of violence, or other crimes, including those with a potential corporate culpability lawsuit
- To identify staff training, customer service and productivity improvements

Small business adviser, Lesley Furber, writes that UK employers need to comply with the following laws when they choose to carry out monitoring or surveillance of employees:

- The Regulation of Investigatory Powers Act 2000
- The Telecommunications (Lawful Business Practice) (Interception of Communications) Regulations 2000
- The Data Protection Act 1988 (including the 2003 Code, Monitoring at Work) – Employers must act in accordance with the Act and its eight key principles (*see Chapter 3*).

Nevertheless, the consideration of human rights laws is also crucial. According to Furber: "The [UK] Human Rights Act 1998 also plays an important role here as it gives individuals' a right to privacy and the UK's laws try to recognise that employees may feel that monitoring by their employer at work is intrusive". He continues: "… employers need to find a balance between an employee's legitimate expectation to privacy and the employer's interests when they monitor their staff, in any way" (35).

5.4 Internal risks

The European Network and Information Security Agency reported in 2009 that human *errors* are consistently the most likely reason for a breach of information (36). This feature of self-sabotage is unlikely to alter in the short term. A lack of risk management awareness among non-security minded employees can be a relatively easy business case to make for security managers. This is borne out by a plethora of reports that illustrate ignorance or lassitude toward information management in the approaches of many employees and, indeed, systems access controls. PricewaterhouseCoopers found that 75% of large companies "allow staff to use smartphones and tablets to connect to their systems". According to accountancy company PwC, one public sector organisation found that it was leaking sensitive information through the front door via social media platforms, rather than via any previously-suspected back-door skulduggery (37).

Nevertheless, security community practitioners are hardly immune themselves from perpetrating inadvertent or even *deliberate* losses of critical information. For example, a security guard at weapons-manufacturer BAE Systems, offered to sell research and design secrets from the company's Stanmore centre to a Russian buyer, who actually turned out to be an MI5 investigator. During the 2001 court case, it transpired that documents, reports and printouts had mainly been pilfered from office desks. According to a court reporter: "One document referred to specifications for Prophet Asic, an advanced electronic warfare surveillance system designated a NATO secret. Two documents were marked 'UK Eyes Only'" (38). When the names, addresses, national insurance numbers and personal bank details of 25 million people – kept on disks by UK HM Revenue and Customs – were reported missing in 2007, a leading politician was able to say that the incident was "another blow to people's trust in this government". The organisation's reputation was dealt a further blow when it was revealed by a national newspaper that missing data included both the original and newly assigned names of approximately 350 people sheltered by police witness protection programmes (39).

The risk of failure to comply with strict information protection laws, such as RIPA 2000, or the 1998 Data Protection Act, or historical antecedents, can also bring security practitioners into disrepute. Such cases are not so much attacks upon internal information systems but nevertheless can reasonably be construed as internal threats to information security, due to the grave consequences that any such compromises bring, including the subsequent embarrassment, notoriety, legal punishments and flushing out of that organisation's entire operating processes in a public courtroom. A pre-eminent modern example is the successful prosecution of private investigators and journalists who unlawfully intercepted and listened into voicemail messages on behalf of the now-defunct weekly tabloid *News of the World*. More than 100 reporters, private investigators, security contractors and police officers were arrested for crimes associated with the Computer Misuse Act 1990, payments to public officials, bribery of public officials, conspiracy to intercept communications and, breaches of the Data Protection Act and RIPA laws. At least one investigator illegally accessed subscriber information from telecommunications company databases (40).

History also reminds us about 'pressure cooker' operating environments where internal security functions can be driven into disreputable conduct. In America, President Richard Nixon was forced to resign after ordering a mole hunt to find out who was leaking the *Pentagon Papers*. These documents were detailed defence department accounts from national intelligence estimates and survey reports gathered by US and Vietnamese officials during the Vietnam War (1963-75). Nixon's own chief of staff sanctioned the burglary of several office buildings by private investigators including *Watergate*, home to the opposition Democratic Party National Committee in 1972. This whole saga ended for Nixon's administration as a self-destructive farce, but a salutary lesson for all security professionals who can become consumed by the urgency of here and now. The ultimate irony, being, that the papers were always intended for public consumption.

Several years before, Defence Secretary, Robert McNamara, personally authorised the Pentagon Papers to be compiled in order for future American policy makers to 'learn the lessons' of Vietnam which he hoped would never be repeated (41). Moreover, Nixon was caught out by his own, recently beefed-up, surveillance systems. Just months before, the same President had personally authorised tape-recording within the White House's famous Oval Office and across executive branches in order to catch out any so-called 'moles'. Audio tapes eventually released to the House of Congress revealed that the President sanctioned covert listening operations upon his own staff, elected Congressman and other elected opponents (42). The abuse of power was vast, and Nixon was at his career peak. He had just won re-election in 1972 by a record majority. He established successful negotiations with both the USSR and Communist China which helped to end the Vietnam war. Despite his ascendancy, the President was forced to quit by 1974. It was felt by Congress that he and his team (some of whom were jailed) had clearly broken his own country's constitution and laws; including the prohibition of hostile surveillance on US soil (43). On the eve of Congressional impeachment hearings, Nixon resigned his office. Yet he passionately argued, until his death, that such investigations served a higher purpose, to prevent publication of materials useful for the enemy. This purpose may well, in his view, have been grounded in a genuine moral perspective. The problem was that in terms of legal compliance, Nixon and his team failed to have a lawful defence.

The overweening power of those in authority (or those *without* public permission) to conduct surveillance on organisation's information systems is generating an interesting new line in opportunities for cyber security educationalists and consultants; namely, how to become as anonymous and bulletproof as possible. Invasive information gathering techniques from both government, and less legitimate gatherers of data, is to some extent fuelling a revised approach to online security which is more guarded and less confident in specific or bespoke mitigation counter-measures. At least one organisation has coined this new phenomenon as a 'zero trust' era. IT network management specialists, Cryptzone, say that: "IT today is in the middle of a paradigm shift … It used to be taken for granted that an IT department could draw a line between trusted and untrusted environments. Now those boundaries are becoming blurred – a development that has exposed organisations to countless new cyber attack patterns" (44).

5.5 Cyber security

The US cyber security division, located within the DHS, called it right when the agency wrote that: "Today's world is more interconnected than ever before. Yet, for all its advantages, increased connectivity brings increased risk of theft, fraud, and abuse" (45). The UK Government in its *Cyber Strategy* document speaks in similarly sober tones: "There is a growing realisation that technologies contain vulnerabilities that are being attacked and exploited and as awareness of this problem spreads, the dependence of modern economies and societies on internet technologies has become alarmingly clear" (46). During March 2015, UK police forces arrested more than 50 individuals on charges related to cyber crime. Attempts had been made to attack several prominent websites including Police Scotland, the US Department of Defence and a popular search engine. "Further arrests were made in connection with various cyber fraud campaigns, the theft of intellectual property from a financial services company in London and the purchase, use and distribution of various cyber attack tools (47)." Given that there are more than 200 national police jurisdictions, and two billion internet users in the world, it's a safe bet to assume that the cases above can be fairly described as a visible pinhead on the tip of an iceberg!

In the US, the Secret Service division maintains responsibility for several electronic crimes task forces. The agency runs a cyber intelligence section which it states has, "directly contributed to the arrest of transnational cyber criminals responsible for the theft of hundreds of millions of credit card numbers and the loss of approximately $600 million to financial and retail institutions" (48). This is an impressive track record indeed. But, again, the cases above can fairly be described as the visible tip of an iceberg. Towards the end of this chapter, we take a closer look at mitigation methods and management frameworks for repelling the type of cyber attacks that are fast becoming defined as top priority security risks for corporations, governments and individual citizens alike. Indeed, the British Government's Department for Business, Innovation and Skills, has begun to keep a close eye on cyber-related threats. Its 2013 report, *Information Security Breaches Survey*, found that attacks against small businesses had increased by ten percent in just one year, costing some six percent of turnover (49). US-based financial security experts at *Javelin Strategy and Research* found that identity theft occurred every two seconds in America in 2013 (50). Experts attribute the upward trend in online fraud to several contributors, including a surge in data and money transfers carried out by using applications (apps) and mobile devices. For example, at the London 2012 Olympics, some 50% of web users were using mobile platforms (51). There is a perception, driven by western media organisations, that most cyber threats emanate in the eastern hemisphere and are inflicted upon victims in the western hemisphere. In truth, risks are far more complex and pervasive. For example, in preparing for the 2014 Sochi Winter Games, Russia's finance ministry declared that one in five malware attacks were targeted against financial services. Furthermore, one in five Russian nationals had experienced fraud as a consequence of mobile app usage (52). It's something to bear in mind for security managers who are responsible for operations and personnel in any domain.

So what other types of cyber attack might security managers want to keep an eye out for? Towards the end of 2014, one of the first significant cases of cyber terrorism occurred, as Sony Pictures Entertainment acted as a lightning conductor for alleged North Korean wrath, over plans to air a movie which depicted a plot to assassinate its national leader, Kim Jong-un.

Case study: Sony Pictures entertainment hack and terror alert

On 24 November 2014, a group of hackers calling themselves the 'Guardians of Peace', released confidential data belonging to Sony Pictures Entertainment. The data included personal details including salaries, communications between employees and unreleased film scripts. One news organisation reported that the data hoist also stole some 47,000 social security numbers. Among other uses, these numbers can be used for bank account access verification in the US. One of the most vivid emails leaked was from a movie producer who described actress Angelina Jolie as 'a minimally talented spoilt brat'. After eight tranches of 'data dumps' the scenario took a sinister twist. The Guardians of Peace issued a threat on 8 December 2014:

> *"We will clearly show it to you at the very time and places 'The Interview' be shown, including the premiere, how bitter fate those who seek fun in terror should be doomed to. Soon all the world will see what an awful movie Sony Pictures Entertainment has made. The world will be full of fear. Remember 11 September 2001. We recommend you to keep yourself distant from the places at that time. (If your house is nearby, you'd better leave.) ... Whatever comes in the coming days is called by the greed of Sony Pictures Entertainment. All the world will denounce the SONY."*

This was the first reference to a movie titled *The Interview*, which was a comedy set to depict an attempt to assassinate the leader of North Korea. Two lead actors, Seth Rogan and James Franco, cancelled media appearances relating to the film. Many cinema chains cancelled airing the movie. On 18 December, the White House confirmed that it was treating the hack as "a serious national security matter" (53). Sony set aside $15m to deal with business disruptions that followed. The method of attack was well-planned and took more than one year to accomplish. Malicious software, dubbed *wiper* because it destroys data on a target's hard drive, had been implanted into Sony's network infrastructure. Some computers were rendered inoperable and several related social media accounts were hijacked. Monetary compensation was demanded from the outset but emails had been missed or ignored by executives. Responsibility for the attack is, so far, unproven.

The latest attack upon Sony is an exemplar of just how detailed cyber attack planning can become. After all, cyber crime is a very lucrative business. Researchers at Group-IB in Moscow found that Russian-speaking hackers accounted for one third of the world's cyber crime market in 2011, making some $4.5bn (54). One tenth of this revenue came from mobile internet banking fraud. Spamming campaigns, particularly for counterfeit products, raised a similar amount in revenue. For hackers, who attack both domestic and international markets, and who are often subcontracted by clients via the dark web to target specific institutions or sectors, the risks are far lower and rewards far higher. Cyber crime groups organise into a centralised 'management system' and outsource work to 'specialist teams of hackers', report Group-IB. "This trend leads to the merging of the two criminal worlds with the subsequent resource allocation from the mafia's traditional areas of control – prostitution, drug and arms trafficking and so on – in favour [sic.] of cyber crime (55)." IT services provider, IBM, produces an annual Cyber Security Intelligence Index, which reported in 2014 that US companies were attacked, on average, 16,856 times during the previous year (56). IBM also point to under-reporting issues: "some victims aren't even aware they've been compromised", the report concedes (57). This will certainly be the case with several thousand US citizens during 2014 and 2015 who have had their online tax-return accounts hacked by cyber criminals who have filed inaccurate data on their behalf and pocketed millions in fraudulent tax rebates well before the victim or Inland Revenue Service became aware. Although one in five businesses told IBM that cyber attacks caused them 'lost productivity', many companies, conversely, fear that taking further loss prevention measures to address cyber-related risks might actually harm productivity to an even greater extent, and thus engender a law of diminishing returns (58). Moreover, the case of American, Edward Snowden, an American systems administrator who leaked more than one million classified intelligence documents to a variety of media organisations during 2013, demonstrated that perhaps the biggest single point of failure to any IT system remains the 'insider threat'. Snowden, who remains more famous than his own country's president in virtually every country outside of the US, has caused many to change the way 'we view security' writes American company Panda Security (59). The *Canadian Centre for International Governance Innovation* found in their comprehensive survey of international internet service users that "some 39% of respondents claimed they regularly change their passwords, and that they do so more frequently than in the previous year" (60). A humdinger of a dilemma for the security consultant follows from this feeble statistic: what about the other 61%? How do we wake them up to the clear and present dangers posed by public cyber security inertia?

Insider threats and risks

In Maroochy Shire, Queensland, millions of gallons of raw sewage were pumped into the local environment by a computerised waste management system. "Marine life died, the creek water turned black and the stench was unbearable for residents", reported the Australian Environmental Protection Agency (61). Police later found that a contractor at the sewage plant, Vitek Boden, held software on his hard drive that enabled him to control the sewage management system. According to the UK Centre for the Protection of National Infrastructure (CPNI), Boden had used the internet, wireless radio, and his inside knowledge, to carry out an attack over a remotely controlled SCADA system, which he had attempted 46 times over several weeks beforehand (62). Boden was jailed for two years in 2001 for his crime. His motivation: revenge for being turned down for a permanent job within the city council.

In 2008, five men were jailed for the largest known cash heist in British criminal history. Four gangsters, dressed as police officers and disguised by facial prosthetics, kidnapped the cash depot manager, his wife and young son at gunpoint. They then raided the facility in Tonbridge, Kent, locked up its terrified employees in cages, and escaped with more than £53m in bank notes. Soon attention came to focus upon a security contractor, Emir Hysenaj, who had worked at the depot. CPNI reported that Hysenaj was accused of providing information to the criminal network ahead of the raid, using a hidden camera to film the inside of the deport. Shift patterns and interior protective security arrangements were recorded. It was only after the event that colleagues purportedly recollected Hysenaj's heightened interest in the security arrangements at the depot (63). Hysenaj was sentenced on three criminal charge counts to 20 years' imprisonment.

These two selected cases highlight just how devastating risks from inside security lapses can be. In each scenario, the resilience of entire organisations and human lives were at stake. CPNI carefully define the phrase 'insider risk' as, "The potential damage that can be caused to an organisation from an 'insider' within their workforce who uses their legitimate access for unauthorised purposes ..." (64). Henrik Kiertzner, at QinetiQ, the UK defence research company, explains that managing the risk from information security violations should also consider acts which are not always deliberate. Insider threat can be summed up as the, "Threat of compromise of your internal systems from an internal source ... generally speaking it falls into two categories: malicious and non-malicious" (65).

Network and cyber security specialists have also been working with the concept of insider threats several decades before revelations from Wikileaks (founded 2006) and Edward Snowden exploded into the public domain. The SANS Institute began its mission in 1989 as a co-operative education and research organisation for computer security professionals. It has since grown to be the largest information security certification body in the world. Perhaps some of its most prominent work has been to establish 20 so-called *Critical Security Controls* which were published in 2013 following collaboration meetings of US and international experts, agencies and corporations (66). This menu of information security protections has been particularly useful in assisting American companies and agencies to respond, both in strategy and practice, to the US President's Executive Order 13636 for 'Improving Critical Infrastructure Cyber Security' (67). SANS also offer a clear definition for an internal threat: "An insider is a trusted member of your organisation such as an employee or a contractor who intentionally causes harm ... such as infecting our computers, causing our network to crash or stealing confidential information" (68).

Motivations are almost countless, and this means that the same can be said for the potential amount of targets. For example, Rory Byrne, a security adviser to humanitarian organisations, explains that his, "experience has uncovered that insider threats – like disgruntled employees or paid cover sources like cleaners or security guards – are becoming a common intelligence tactic used against human rights NGOs by governments" (69).

Is there anything we can do to anticipate insider risks?

According to information security specialist, Ramkumar Chinchani, self-taught 'insider' perpetrators are often more difficult to defend against, because the nature of attack is more subtle; the targeting pattern is more often a soft probing of system or personal/organisational vulnerabilities rather than the type of 'brute force' targeting that network defences and modelling may pick up beforehand (70). In order to bring a sense of process control and security strategy for companies and critical infrastructure, dedicated risk assessment processes around specific insider risks are well advised, say government agencies including CPNI (71). Further risk assessment models outlined by this author in Chapter 6 (6.2) will also assist security planners to identify, analyse, evaluate and (hopefully) mitigate internal risks.

When contemplating, addressing and treating insider risks, it is vital to understand that legal, cultural, environmental and situational factors are at all times taken into account. For seldom are the manifestations of insider threats as clearly and neatly cut for airtime production, as newspaper copy writers and prosecutors might have us believe. The lines of distinction between strange practice and malpractice in the office are very often blurred. Security management staff can be at their most vulnerable if they make a bad 'call' about any threat, let alone one from the inside. A falsely accused employee, or clumsily monitored manager, will justifiably feel embarrassment and anguish if they – or others – come to realise they are under suspicion. So before we close this section, let's pause and reflect on the 'grey areas' of insider risk management. Employees and colleagues who may raise alarm bells for various behavioural patterns on network systems, may not be criminals but could be: uncovering malpractice which is not being properly addressed internally; quietly carrying out permitted tasks with senior approval, such as secretly testing business continuity; over-enthusiastic researchers; bored and underworked; suffering from mental health issues, and so on.

5.6 Mitigation: Developing a security policy

"Cyber risk is not so much about the vehicle, but more about the individual using it." – City of London Police Commissioner, Adrian Leppard, to a CSARN business conference, July 2014 (72)

Developing any form of mitigation strategy can seem daunting. Particularly with insider threats, where the identifiable lead-in time (reconnaissance) before any attack is usually minimal to non-existent. The scale of the problem seems so vast, and in most modern civilian workplace environments, there is an employee assumption that access and convenience has commercial primacy over security and controls. Upwards of 80% of adults in your workplace use the Internet every day. On average, an employee uses two to three mobile data devices. More than four out of five employees use smartphones – often their own, or their families – to access work documentation (73). Authorities in the UK estimated that some £27bn was lost from the national economy due to cyber crime which included malicious attacks (74). In relation to global data, Britain's plight is merely the tip of a never-ending iceberg. IT security specialists, MacAfee, reported in 2013 that the world economy was damaged by anything from $300bn - $1tr by cyber-enabled attacks (75). Complexity around data protection policies spawn when one considers an emerging trend of 'remote workers'. By 2009, the UK had seen an upsurge from almost 2.3 million remote workers to 3.7 million over the prior decade (76). Britain's mobile employee culture is similar to dozens of other jurisdictions; in fact the term 'jurisdiction' is almost becoming dormant for many employees and businesses. The growth of international business travel, covered in Chapter 8, and executives who depend on ease of access to company data in order to win new contracts or drive forward new investments, does add at least one extra layer of vulnerability to information security risks.

Therefore, as US-company Cryptzone envisage, an era of risk mitigation based upon zero trust (of anything or anyone) may well be arriving. Security managers will already be aware that some military, police and government environments are already, perhaps, at an advantage when it comes to establishing sensible processes and policies around information security.

This is because there is a keen public expectation that sensitive national information – which can also include one's own personal details, such as medical, tax, criminal and passport records – should be protected. Yet, as we have noted in this book previously, if anything, civilian business environments have become less hierarchical and more relaxed in recent times. Some specific sectors or premises, such as luxury fashion or jewellery retailers, may well be able to enforce so-called 'spot checks' upon employees. But could such random IT testing, which possibly included email and social media scanning, ever become acceptable in a civilian work environment? It may be an inconvenient proposal for future employers and employees to consider together.

Access controls – A fun test of reverse psychology

Perhaps a task of security contractors' is to ask busy fellow colleagues to pause and reflect about rights and responsibilities for a moment. For it may be that we need to reverse the psychology of IT access entitlement pervasive in some work cultures for a minute! If colleagues are so happy for the company to grant them open-ended access to ICT, then, in turn, would they consider enabling their company and executives unlimited access to their own personal devises and data? What do I mean? Well, if you think for a moment that this author has become adversarial, just consider the following case:

During 2014, brute force attacks levelled by hackers against an iCloud provider, enabled the perpetrators to access and distribute very private photos of celebrities, including nude and other deeply personal images. Many victims were unaware that their phone provider automatically backed up their photo albums to the Cloud. (Very helpful, no doubt, if the device gets lost or stolen.) In the first instance, vivid photos were circulated to a controlled audience of gleeful hackers within the dark web. Several days later however they were re-leaked onto a publicly accessible online bulletin board. Thousands of sensitive images immediately went viral. The world woke up to an inconvenient fact; one that many security practitioners grasped a long time ago. Namely, that there is literally no such thing as *private* electronic data. Not in the national security arena. Not in a film star's bathroom. Not anywhere. The question, thus, to put to staff that use their own mobile data devises on workplace systems, or oppose any policy to prohibit such, might be to ask them if they are comfortable with their own most personal files being uploaded for all to see in the workplace domain, or even onto the Internet? Because any Hacker targeting their workplace will hardly have the scruples to differentiate between some bland corporate data stored on the company hard-drive, or the very personal data of employees, who may have inadvisably or inadvertently plugged in a smartphone or a tablet. In fact, they and their online friends may well like your personal photos more!

How do we assess vulnerability?

The risk assessment process for identifying information or cyber security threats is no different to other forms of security risk assessment. Some basic modelling is shown in our next chapter (6.2), including a basic risk management wheel. For business continuity purposes, security practitioners will seek to work with colleagues across the business to both identify the threats and also minimalise (or eradicate) the impact. The core security risk assessment phases involve:

1. Identify the threats and hazards
2. Decide who or what may be harmed and how
3. Evaluate the risks and decide on treatment and/or exposure
4. Implement safeguards
5. Monitor and review

When considering appropriate safeguards, the Institution of Engineering and Technology and the Centre for Protection of National Infrastructure recommend:

Avoidance: perhaps by deciding not to pursue the deployment of a vulnerable piece of equipment

Reduction: take steps to minimalise the likelihood of any risk, or to lessen the impact of a threat scenario

Sharing: spread the risk with other partners, contractors or insurance

Retention: retain the risk in-house but put in place contingency measures, in case it does occur (77)

Mitigation approaches – CIA triad

Ascertaining precisely what key building blocks an information security policy requires, has stimulated widespread debate within the information security sphere. By far the most prominent security model is the memorably named 'CIA triad', and this is not solely because it shares its acronym with a certain famous US-based government agency. The triad is recommended by many experts and the ISO27001 information security management system standard, for its balance and ease of applicability, on the one hand, and rather robust security management framework, on the other. Here's how it works:

Confidentiality: Keeping information stored in a manner that is secure and only accessible by authorised individuals who have permission and purpose to access it. Information is often discretely separated and should in no way be accessible to non-intended parties. Typical examples in HR domains could be health records, personal addresses, and spouse and next of kin details.

Integrity: Information is complete and, so far as possible, is unalterable by unintended or unauthorised parties. Such information could be credit and store card records with retailers, health records held by doctors, and academic achievement records held by schools, colleges and universities. (For example, a university student in the UK was jailed in 2015 for hacking into his departmental academic records and altering his marks from 57% to 73%.)

Availability: Policies to achieve maximum up-time and to thwart power outages, cyber attacks and hard drive failures. Protecting business continuity and access to information that the business may need during periods of downtime.

Security practitioners should also consider the limitations of the CIA model. First, it deals only by providing a framework to protect and safeguard information. It does not consider changes to your specific physical or personnel environment that may well get considered by additional empirical risk considerations and assessments. Furthermore, the CIA framework is a distillation of various information security management models that have been debated and banded about for several decades. In summary, the CIA triad are three great building blocks towards a robust information security policy but they should probably not be considered as the completely finished information security policy product.

Mitigation approaches in medium and higher risk environments

Security contractors will be cognisant of the many features used in secure zones often operated within, or around, government, police and military establishments. Features to promote information security can include: restricted access areas, rigid network information firewalls, 'clean' zones and buildings where electronic devices are prohibited, strict procedures to prohibit entry by outside visitors and provisions to prevent movement of furniture. Moreover, since the 2013 revelations by renegade US defence contractor, Edward Snowden, peer observation for network users on classified materials is being considered writ large across many secure domains. The difficulty is that such cases only become famous because they impact high-profile security establishments, such as the CIA or the US Pentagon. At street level, most employees simply don't absorb how such cases of information insecurity relate to them, as evidenced by a reporter at the *IT Security Blog*:

> *"Many people fail to appreciate that value of the data they have gathered. They fail to appreciate the value of a strict IT policy mainly because all they care about is a workstation to use and opening files (both internal and external) as they please. So if you put all these things together, you can imagine the problems that an IT guy has to work with."* (78)

Another difficulty with location-based protective security arrangements is that such a 'ring of steel' can hardly extend beyond the perimeter walls of any installation. The introduction of such physical information security issues can leave employees much more vulnerable to physical hostile surveillance, burglaries, extortions and even 'honey traps' before and after working hours.

Companies should have little to fear from learning lessons available from other cyber security practitioners who are experienced in operating in complex and higher physical threat environments. In such environments, discipline around data protection does undoubtedly save lives and livelihoods. In the mitigation methods section below, we draw together some cyber and information security mitigation measures which have been deployed by a number of contractors in complex and hostile operating environments:

Technology

Biometrics: Access controls and authentication can be predicated on a range of options: finger and palm prints, DNA swabs, retinal scans, facial recognition and photographing.

Computer and network access: Establish induction and regular training courses, and an internal 'driving permit' for network computer use. From the outset use this process to explain, detail and commit staff (perhaps by way of a users' code of conduct) to acceptable practices and embed the overall cyber security strategy. Be clear on network access firewalls: who has access to areas and why. Explain and regularly reinforce messages as to 'why' data security is so critical (79). Emphasise that all employees own the process and are responsible for its overall success. Start out by issuing equipment where floppy drives and USB ports are either disabled or missing then access has to be granted by the IT or security function (80).

Encryption: By using widely available software, companies are able to codify information so that it cannot be easily understood by unauthorised persons. This process can be made more secure by the use of key code words, known only to those within an organisation, to reinforce data security against outsiders.

E-purge: Reset mobile data devices to factory restore settings before being moved off-site or reassigned.

Radios: Deploy those with frequency jumper capabilities (81).

Notepads and tablets: Prohibit multiple use and mixed social/business use of work-issue mobile devices. No personal mobile devises, including notepads and tablets, should be permitted to record confidential work notes. Use a personal unblocking code (PUC) on every work device.

Passwords: Introduce and embed single use and personal ownership of passwords: devices are not to be shared and default allocated passwords must be changed immediately. Establish dual or triple authentication layers with different, user-unique passwords for: protecting the hard drive, individual network access and various software and databases.

Moving devices between sites: Consider prohibiting the removal of work-based devices and memory sticks (thumb drives) from work premises, except by authorised individuals and in an audited and documented manner.

Thumb drives: Can be signed for on being issued, and encrypted before and after use (82).

People and processes

Clear desk policy: Those who are too busy to keep a tidy desk, are, unwittingly the best friends of others who may be more hostile, equipped with audio bugs, have a penchant for stealing important files, or even placing mini video cameras.

Filing cabinets: Can be locked at all times, with designated employees as key holders. Original documents to be retained within the bureau, with sign-in procedures for access and to make copies. Further security barriers to this information will be locked inner and outer doors within the site.

Interaction: Work topics – including descriptions of the operating environment and access controls – should not be discussed beyond the workplace, particularly in public or social situations.

Hard-copy and paper disposal: Burn bags and shredding devices should be available to all employees, and their daily use should be encouraged to prevent loss of confidential or important documents. Burn bags should be incinerated and also the actions supervised by trained individuals (83).

Shared work and rest areas: Enforce closure of workstations and devices while the employee is away from their desk. Be aware that many data leakages stem from internal sources, accidental and deliberate eavesdropping, and also accidental and deliberate disclosure.

Telephone conversations: If sensitive, take calls in private offices or spaces where doors can be closed. Be aware that in today's highly litigious and voyeuristic working environments, it is not uncommon for people to record phone conversations for all manner of motivations.

Awareness and training

Familiarisation and orientation: From the outset, show employees around accessible zones and actively identify any inaccessible zones where access controls are in place.

Cultural awareness: Help to develop emotional intelligence, team reassurance and knowledge around any cultural differences that may exist among employees. Without clear exposure to them from the outset, work or social cultural differences can nurture difficulties in the longer-run. Such communication gaps may lead to the non-reporting, or misreporting, of security risks.

Personal development: Carry out a skills gap analysis from the outset to fully challenge and examine potential employee weaknesses and vulnerabilities which could expose the organisation to risk. Provide reassurance and training to address any skills gaps.

Values: Explaining and reinforcing the critical importance of collective security: drily put by former UN Secretary General, Kofi Annan, *"We all share responsibility for each other's security, and only by working to make each other secure can we hope to achieve lasting security for ourselves"* (84).

Embed and follow-up: Create an open and inclusive culture where colleagues are allowed to openly and informally provide 'feedback' to other team members, if they believe that they see a lapse in security.

Auditing and testing: Risks can only be minimised by testing in unison all three domains of cyber security: people, processes and technology.

Management mindsets: Information security policy

RAF: Risk management framework for information security controls

The following three core management principles – that conveniently adhere to the mnemonic RAF – can be applied when we aim to devise our information security plan for medium to higher risk environments:

Robust: carry out a thorough assessment of vulnerabilities and design robust, realistic responses that can absorb or repel all threat vectors. Far better to fix the bar high and adjust – if necessary – to a lower notch later.

Awareness: be clear to employees and network users around acceptable rules and processes. Be open and transparent, and provide regular training and reminders for users. Create a positive culture around reporting accidents, risks and misuse. Remind people of the Computer Misuse Act 1990 (85).

Facilitate: "If you don't want to be replaced by a computer, don't act like one", so the saying goes. Remember: the IT network and you are both there to serve the business – not the other way around!

Source: Antoni D Bick and Richard Bingley, 2014

Further learning and support

As we have discovered, cyber and information security planning is one of the key growth areas for security management professionals. Many companies and public authorities have chosen to entirely merge the information technology and security management functions, with either the chief security officer, CIO, or CISO now taking the lead, when bringing the blended issues of security and information protection into any executive boardroom. Increasingly, security practitioners are being asked to manage, or work in close collaboration with, a myriad of information technology job roles including: information security and risk analysts, IT security managers and network security consultants. Those security practitioners that can articulate reasonable information risk management strategies, and also interface proficiently with this sphere's subdisciplines – such as identity theft, network security and cryptography – are perhaps set to become corporate security's new aristocracy. With so much at stake – possibly one quarter of the world's GDP, says leading global management company, McKinsey – there can be little doubt as to the future of security management tasking (86).

Hundreds, if not thousands of websites and recruitment agencies make an income from advertising cyber security related jobs, with such diverse vacancy titles as senior penetration tester, security architect, information assurance lead practitioner, senior information security specialist, information security team leader … the list of cyber pageantry has become endless (87). The expectation by clients upon security contractors to be able to have a *handle* on the brave new world of cyber threats, is emerging as 'desirable' or even 'essential' criteria for employment and contracts. Such is the dependency of people and property upon the security and continuity of their ICT systems that the security sector will continue to move inexorably towards becoming more technologically driven. Therefore, this book will now bring together a series of sources for further information, and support, in order to assist the reader to further develop their knowledge and skills:

> **Academic centres of excellence in cyber security research:** There are 13 universities in the UK that are formally recognised as ACEs by CESG, the UK Government's technical authority for information assurance. At the time of writing these are: University of Bristol, Imperial College London, University of Kent, Lancaster University, University College London, Queen's University Belfast, Royal Holloway – University of London, University of Southampton, University of Surrey, University of Birmingham, University of Cambridge, University of Oxford and Newcastle University (88).

Bruce Schneier website and blog: A chief technology officer and academic, Schneier has been a prolific and prominent author and soothsayer on IT security since his first monthly newsletter went live in 1998 (89).

Buckinghamshire New University: Foundation degrees in cyber security will be delivered from 2015 in classroom taught sessions and with flexible and distance learning options available (90).

CESG: The UK Government's technical authority for information assurance which describes itself as "the Information Security arm of GCHQ". CESG, which is an acronym for Communications-Electronics Security Group, advises government departments on information security but also works "with industry to ensure that appropriately assured products, services and people are available". CESG provides training and awareness briefings, policy and guidance, and other products and services (91).

CPNI: The UK Centre for Protection of National Infrastructure produces various guidance on carrying out due diligence and background checks around 'insider' threats. Among several excellent guides are the *Pre-Employment Screening: A Good Practice Guide* (Edition 5: 2015), *The Secure Procurement of Contract Staff: A Good Practice Guide for the Oil and Gas Industry* (2011), and *Resilience and Cyber Security of Technology in the Built Environment* (2013), produced by the Institution of Engineering and Technology in partnership with CPNI (92).

CREST: CREST is a not-for-profit organisation that serves the technical information security marketplace. According to the organisation's website, "CREST provides organisations wishing to buy *penetration testing* services with confidence that the work will be carried out by qualified individuals with up-to-date knowledge, skill and competence of the latest vulnerabilities and techniques used by real attackers" (93).

Graham Cluley: Cluley is a fast emerging prominent internet security expert that runs a popular newsletter named GCHQ (not to be confused with the British Government's own government communications headquarters). Cluley is independent, topical and well-informed, and offers practical mitigation advice, just like fellow authors, Schneier, Krebs and Hunt (94).

Information asset protection and pre-employment screening group: This influential group of practitioners is run by ASIS, the American Industrial Security Society. The forum advises and produces protection of assets manuals and coined the phrase 'information asset protection' in its 2008 PoA manual (95).

Information Assurance Advisory Council: The IAAC is a non-profit group that brings together UK policy makers, corporate leaders, law enforcement and researchers, in order to create and maintain "a safe and secure information society" (96).

ISO 27001:2013: Is the International Standards Organisation's response to what it describes as the 'plague' of 'cyber threats' against businesses and governments around the world. This excellent guidance document provides a coherent management framework for "assessing and treating risks, whether cyber-oriented or otherwise, that can damage business, governments and even the fabric of a country's national infrastructure", explains lead author and ISO convenor, Professor Edward Humphreys (97).

Krebs on security: Brian Krebs is a former Washington Post reporter who was attacked by cyber criminals in 2001. This incident made him "intensely interested in computer security". Krebbs now runs one of the most successful blogs on cyber crime under the banner 'In-depth security news and investigation' (98).

NIST Special Publication 800-53 (Revision 4) *'Security and Privacy Controls for Federal Information Systems and Organizations'*: published by the National Institute of Standards and Technology, at the US Department of Commerce. This is a comprehensive catalogue of standards for information security professionals to apply in the workplace (99).

Open University: The OU offers a number of undergraduate and postgraduate programmes in computer and network security topics. The institution also offers, at the time of writing, a free 'Introduction to Cyber Security' workshop for those wishing to learn about protecting their 'digital life' at home and work (100).

Troy Hunt: Slightly more technical and with a bent for software developers, Hunt describes his website as "Observations, musings and conjecture about the world of software and technology". Hunt has launched a security-related newsletter *Security Sense* and provides entertaining advice: step into the shoes of your adversary and 'hack yourself first' (101).

UK cyber security: The role of insurance in managing and mitigating the risk, is a report by HMG and Marsh, one of the world's leading insurance companies, which highlights the exposure of companies to cyber risk, including from within their own supply chain (102).

Chapter 5: Wrap-up

In closing this chapter on **Information and Cyber Security**, we reflect on some of the approaches and attributes that will help your company gain the competitive edge. These include:

1. Companies and security contractors are increasingly turning to the information security management system (ISMS) standard ISO27001, in order to introduce proportionate and sensible controls across ICT platforms and the work domains that any high-tech machinery is supposedly there to serve.

2. The *entire* success of a security management function is very much dependent upon its contribution to data protection issues and cultures within any project or organisation. This can only be done by evaluating and anticipating weaknesses and then closing the gaps. Details matter. The loss of a principal's smartphone, or failure to recover an unencrypted memory stick which contains sensitive data, can nowadays be just as embarrassing for a security function as a serious physical security breach might well be.

3. Many security practitioners, business organisations and policy-makers see significant value in supporting and deploying intelligence work and operations. This willingness is, in part, because the overwhelming majority of data upon which intelligence is borne seems to be Open Source (OSINT) and freely available.

4. The risk assessment process for identifying information or cyber security threats is often no different to other forms of security risk assessment. For business continuity purposes, security practitioners will seek to work with all colleagues across the business to both identify the threats and also minimalise (or eradicate) the impact. Because it is not the technology that we need protecting from, but the end-user.

5. Companies should have little to fear from learning lessons available from other cyber security practitioners who are experienced in operating in complex and higher physical threat environments. One software company feels that we are moving into an era of 'zero trust' information security strategies.

6. The expectation by clients upon security contractors to be able to have a *handle* on the brave new world of cyber threats is emerging as 'desirable' or even 'essential' criteria for employment and contracts.

7. Those security practitioners that can articulate reasonable information risk management strategies, and also interface proficiently with this sphere's subdisciplines – such as identity theft, network security and cryptography – are in all likelihood set to become corporate security's new aristocracy.

References

(1)   Shaw, E, (2014), address to the CSARN Corporate Espionage Conference, City of London, 10/07/2014

(2)   Daily Telegraph (20/07/2008), 'Downing Street aide in Chinese Honeytrap sting', accessed and downloaded on 09/03/2015 at: *www.telegraph.co.uk/news/politics/labour/2437340/Downing-Street-aide-in-Chinese-honeytrap-sting.html*

(3)   BBC News (10/06/2011), 'John Terry's car 'had tracking device attached'', accessed and downloaded on 09/03/2015 at: *www.bbc.co.uk/news/uk-england-surrey-13734330*

(4)   BBC News (18/10/2009), 'Enfield comedy show ideas stolen', accessed and downloaded on 09/03/2015 at: *http://news.bbc.co.uk/1/hi/entertainment/8313116.stm*

(5)   CSARN (06-19/02/2015), The Monitor, accessed and downloaded with kind permission from CSARN

(6)   KPMG (2012), 'Data Loss Barometer 2012', accessed and downloaded on 09/03/2015 at: *www.kpmg.com/US/en/IssuesAndInsights/ArticlesPublications/Documents/data-loss-barometer.pdf*

(7)   ISO27001 (2013), accessed and downloaded on 09/03/2015 at: *www.iso.org/iso/home/standards/management-standards/iso27001.htm*

(8)   Calder, A, (2012), 'Implementing Information Security based on ISO27001/ISO27002', Zaltbommel: Van Haren

(9)   Evening Standard (14/09/2006), 'Mourinho's favourite restaurant is bugged', accessed and downloaded on 09/03/2015 at: *www.standard.co.uk/sport/mourinhos-favourite-restaurant-is-bugged-7209704.html*

(10) Deloitte (2013), 'The Connected Workplace: War for Talent in the Digital Economy', accessed and downloaded on 20/03/2015 at: *www2.deloitte.com/content/dam/Deloitte/au/Documents/finance/deloitte-au-fas-connected-workplace-2013-240914.pdf*

(11) Information Assurance Advisory Council can be accessed at: *www.iaac.org.uk/*

(12) Techtarget online (n.d), 'Six Ways to measure the value of your information assets', accessed and downloaded on 09/03/2015 at: *http://searchcio.techtarget.com/feature/Six-ways-to-measure-the-value-of-your-information-assets*

(13) Ibid.

(14) OP. Cit., Shaw

(15) Kirkwood, (n.d.), 'Chapter 3: The Value of Information', accessed and downloaded on 20/03/2015 at: *www.public.asu.edu/~kirkwood/DAStuff/decisiontrees/DecisionTreePrimer-3.pdf*

(16) Rimington, S, (2002) Open Secret: The Autobiography of the Former Director-General of MI5, London: Random House

(17) Leppard, A, (2014) Keynote address of CSARN Corporate Espionage Conference, City of London; 10/07/2014

(18) CIA website (2014) teaching Intelligence Analysts in the UK, accessed and downloaded on 14/11/2014 at: *www.cia.gov/library/center-for-the-study-of-intelligence/csi-publications/csi-studies/studies/vol-52-no-4/teaching-intelligence-analysts-in-the-uk.html*

(19) Knowledge Management (KM.com), accessed and downloaded on 13/06/2013 at: *www.skyrme.com/kmbasics/ktypes.htm#hierarchy*

(20) Von Clausewitz, C, 1973, On War, London: N. Trubner, accessed and downloaded on 02/03/2013 at: *www.clausewitz.com/readings/OnWar1873/TOC.htm*

(21) Doran, GT (1981), 'There's a S.M.A.R.T. way to write management's goals and objectives'. Management Review, Volume 70, Issue 11(AMA FORUM), pp. 35-36

(22) Sikich G, (2010), 'Enterprise risk management lessons from the BP Deepwater Horizon catastrophe': Continuity Central: *www.continuitycentral.com/feature0790.html*

(23) Wenham, P, 'Security Think Tank: Intelligence Led Security is About Risk Management', Computer Weekly: downloaded on 9 November 2012 at: *www.computerweekly.com/opinion/Security-Think-Tank-Intelligence-led-security-is-about-risk-management*

(24) Striking Project Management, Qualitative Risk Analysis, accessed and downloaded on 11/11/2014 at: *http://strikingprojectmanagement.com/qualitative-risk-analysis/*

(25) Huxley, A, (1932) Brave New World, London: Chatto & Windus

(26) Interview with Security manager at leading UK retailer conducted on 25/11/2014

(27) International Business Times (31/05/2015), 'HSBC Hires ex-MI5 Spy Jonathan Evans to Help Fight Financial Crime', accessed and downloaded on 24/03/2015 at: *www.ibtimes.co.uk/hsbc-jonathan-evans-mi5-spy-money-laundering-473324*

(28) Daily Telegraph, (24 October 2012), 'Vacuum maker Dyson claims a spy was selling secrets to a German rival', downloaded from: *www.telegraph.co.uk/finance/newsbysector/retailandconsumer/9631492/Vacuum-maker-Dyson-claims-a-spy-was-selling-secrets-to-German-rival.html*

(29) Forbes Magazine online (04/08/2008), 'Commercial espionage 'Travelers Beware': 4 August 2008 downloaded from: *www.forbes.com/2008/04/08/viator-corporate-espionage-oped-cx_slw_0408viator_print.html*

(30) FT.com: 'China linked to 'industrial Espionage'', downloaded from: *www.ft.com/cms/s/0/92d6032a-a108-11e1-9fbd-00144feabdc0.html#*

(31) Asia Times online, 'China Tangled up in industrial espionage', 11 February 2012, downloaded from: *www.atimes.com/atimes/China/NB11Ad01.html*

(32) Zweinenberg, R, in 'Helpnet Security Online', (21/06/2012), 'AutoCAD worm steals blueprints, sends them to China', accessed and downloaded on 14/11/2014 at: *www.net-security.org/malware_news.php?id=2153*

(33) International Intelligence article on UK law firms employing corporate intelligence agency was accessed and downloaded on 12/11/2012 at: *www.international-intelligence.co.uk/media/law-gazette-september-2002/*
And: Law Gazette, Law Firm Call in ex-SAS Personnel: 5 September 2002 was accessed and downloaded at: *www.international-intelligence.co.uk/media/law-gazette-september-2002/*

(34) Mail Online (06/01/2013), 'Aldi hid cameras to spy on staff', accessed and downloaded on 14/11/2014 at: *www.dailymail.co.uk/news/article-2258161/Aldi-hid-cameras-spy-staff-Detective-claims-company-wanted-details-employees-relationships-finances.html*

(35) Furber, L, in Crunch Love Accounting (2014), 'Workplace surveillance: can your employer spy on you at work?', Accessed and downloaded on 14/11/2014 at: *www.crunch.co.uk/small-business-advice/2012/10/31/workplace-surveillance-can-your-employer-spy-on-you-at-work/*

(36) European Network and Information Security Agency (2009), Information security awareness in financial organisations guidelines and case studies: Luxembourg: Luxembourg publications office. Full report accessed and downloaded on 03/09/2014 from: *www.enisa.europa.eu/publications/archive/ar-book-09/at_download/fullReport.*

(37) Potter C, and Waterfall, G, (2012) Information Security Breaches Technical Report: London: Pricewaterhouse Coopers. Full report accessed and downloaded on 03/09/2014 from: *www.pwc.co.uk/audit-assurance/publications/uk-information-security-breaches-survey-results-2012.jhtml*

(38) Norton Taylor, R, (2001) 'Guard stole secret weapons papers', The Guardian (18/12/2001), accessed and downloaded on 03/09/2014 from: *www.theguardian.com/uk/2001/dec/18/richardnortontaylor*

(39) Porter, A. (2007) 'Lost data discs 'endanger protected witnesses'', The Telegraph (05/12/2007), accessed and downloaded on 03/09/2014 from: *www.telegraph.co.uk/news/uknews/1571536/Lost-data-discs-endanger-protected-witnesses.html*

(40) The Wire, (2011), 'A complete list of the arrests and resignations in the News Corp. scandal', accessed and downloaded on 21/03/2015 at: *www.thewire.com/global/2011/07/complete-list-arrests-and-resignations-news-corp-scandal-so-far/40082/*

(41)   McNamara, R (1996) 'In Retrospect: The tragedy and lessons of Vietnam', New York: Vintage Books: ISBN-10:0679767495

(42)   Bernstein, C, and Woodward, B (2014) 'All the President's Men', New York: Simon & Schuster reissue edition: ISBN-10 1476770514

(43)   Gaddis, J, L, (2007) 'The Cold War: The deals, the spies, the lies, the truth', London: Penguin: ISBN-10 0141025328

(44)   Cryptzone (2015), 'Preventing Cyber Attacks with a Layered Network Security Model: Risk mitigation based on the principles of Zero Trust', can be accessed by applying via the organisation's website at: *www.cryptzone.com/forms/preventing-cyber-attacks-layered-network-security-whitepaper*

(45)   US DHS online, Cyber Security division, accessed on 26/03/2015 at: *www.dhs.gov/combat-cyber-crime*

(46)   UKTI (2012), 'UK Cyber Security: A Strategic Approach to Exports', UK HMG Stationery Office.

(47)   CSARN Monitor: 5: 12: (20/03/2015)

(48)   Op. Cit., US DHS online

(49)   BIS (2013), 'Information Security Breaches Report', accessed and downloaded on 26/03/2015 at: *www.gov.uk/government/publications/information-security-breaches-survey-2013-technical-report*

(50)   Javelin Strategy and Research, (2014), 'A New Identity Fraud Victim Every Two Seconds in 2013 According to Latest Javelin Strategy and Research study', accessed and downloaded on 26/03/2015 at: *www.javelinstrategy.com/news/1467/92/A-New-Identity-Fraud-Victim-Every-Two-Seconds-in-2013-According-to-Latest-Javelin-Strategy-Research-Study/d,pressRoomDetail*

(51)   Bingley, R, (08/02/2014) 'Information Security Threat Assessment' for client at Sochi Winter Olympics, redacted from wider publication

(52)   Ibid.

(53)   Entertainment Weekly, (18/12/2014), 'White House is treating Sony hack as 'serious national security matter'', accessed and downloaded on 26/03/2015 at: *www.ew.com/article/2014/12/18/white-house-sony-interview-north-korea*

(54)   Bloomberg Business, (24/04/2012), 'Russian hackers Gain Third of Global Cybercrime Market, IB Says', accessed and downloaded on 26/03/2015 at: *www.bloomberg.com/news/articles/2012-04-24/russian-hackers-made-4-5-billion-last-year-vedomosti-says*

(55)   Ibid.

(56)   IBM Security Services, (2014), 'Data Breach Statistics', accessed and downloaded on 26/03/2015 at: *www-935.ibm.com/services/us/en/it-services/security-services/data-breach/*

(57) Ibid.
(58) Ibid.
(59) Panda Security (18/12/2014), 'The Snowden effect: Has cyber-espionage changed the way we view security?', accessed and downloaded on 26/03/2015 at: *www.pandasecurity.com/mediacenter/security/snowden-effect-cyber-espionage-changed-way-view-security/*
(60) Ibid.
(61) The Register (31/10/2001), 'Hacker jailed for revenge sewage attacks: Job rejection caused a bit of a stink', accessed and downloaded on 26/06/2015 at: *www.theregister.co.uk/2001/10/31/hacker_jailed_for_revenge_sewage/*
(62) CPNI: THE SECURE PROCUREMENT OF CONTRACTING STAFF: A GOOD PRACTICE GUIDE FOR THE OIL AND GAS INDUSTRY: April 2011. Downloaded on 13/3/2013 from: *www.cpni.gov.uk/documents/publications/2011/2011012-gpg_contracting_staff-oil_and_gas.pdf?epslanguage=en-gb*
(63) Ibid.
(64) Ibid.
(65) Kiertzner H, (26/3/12), 'Qinetiq Cyber Security Industry Expert Insights' downloaded on 14/03/13 from: *www.youtube.com/watch?v=5XbSNeVsQYc*
(66) SANS Critical Security Controls – Version 5: was accessed and downloaded on 26/06/2015 at: *www.sans.org/critical-security-controls/*
(67) Executive Order 13636 (12/02/2013), 'Improving Critical Infrastructure Cybersecurity', was accessed and downloaded on 26/06/2015 at: *www.gpo.gov/fdsys/pkg/FR-2013-02-19/pdf/2013-03915.pdf*
(68) SANS 'Insider threats and Need for Fast and Directed Response' can be accessed and downloaded at: *www.youtube.com/watch?v=GQnueERQ31c*
(69) Byrne, R, (2014) in 'Communications Technology and Humanitarian Delivery: Challenges and Opportunities for Security Risk Management', (EISF: p.16), can be accessed at: *www.eisf.eu/library/communications-technology-and-security-risk-management/*
(70) Ramkumar Chinchani et al., (2005), 'A Target-Centric Formal Model For Insider Threat and More', Department of Computer Science and Engineering State University of New York at Buffalo
(71) Op. Cit., CPNI. For an example risk assessment matrix please read p.29
(72) Leppard, A, (2014) Keynote address of CSARN Corporate Espionage conference, City of London; 10/07/2014
(73) Cisco and Forester (2013), Enterprise IT Guide, Managing your mobile devices: accessed and downloaded on 11/09/2014 from: *www.enterpriseitguide.com/connectivity/managing-your-mobile-devices/*
(74) Op. Cit., Leppard

(75)   Ibid.

(76)   Office of National Statistics (2009), 'Labour Force Survey' and UK National Crime Agency (2014) Presentation at the CSARN Corporate Espionage conference, City of London; 10/07/2014

(77)   CPNI and IET (2013), 'Resilience and Cyber Security of Technology in the Built Environment', was accessed on 28/03/2015 at: *www.cpni.gov.uk/ documents/publications/2013/2013063-resilience_cyber_security_ technology_built_environment.pdf?epslanguage=en-gb*

(78)   IT Security Blog (2010), accessed and downloaded on 20/03/2015 at: *www.it-security-blog.com/it-security-basics/implement-a-strict-it-policy/*

(79)   Bick, A (2013): 'Information Security' formative paper, Buckinghamshire New University (redacted)

(80)   Op. Cit., IT Security Blog

(81)   Op. Cit., Bick

(82)   Ibid.

(83)   Ibid.

(84)   Kofi Annan, quoted from: *www.quotationsource.com/q-52-Collective-responsibility.htm*

(85)   Computer Misuse Act (1990), to find out more about this UK act go to: *www.legislation.gov.uk/ukpga/1990/18/contents*

(86)   Op. Cit. IHLS

(87)   Cyberjobstite.com,   was   accessed   on   20/03/2015   at: *www.cybersecurityjobsite.com*

(88)   A full list and contact details of Academic Centres of Excellence in Cyber Security Research can be accessed via the CESG website at: *www.cesg.gov.uk/ awarenesstraining/academia/Pages/Academic-Centres.aspx*

(89)   Bruce Schneier's website was accessed at: *www.schneier.com/*

(90)   Wood P, (09/07/2014), Buckinghamshire New University Cyber Security Foundation Degree, was accessed on 25/03/2015 at: *https://buckssecurity. wordpress.com/2014/07/09/new-foundation-degree-in-cyber-security/*

(91)   CESG's website was accessed on 20/03/2015 at: *www.cesg.gov.uk/ Pages/homepage.aspx*

(92)   CPNI, (2015), 'Pre-Employment Screening: Good Practice Guide', was accessed on 28/03/2015 at: *www.cpni.gov.uk/documents/publications/ 2015/pre-employment%20screening%20edition%205%20-%20final.pdf? epslanguage=en-gb*
        CPNI, (2011), 'The Secure Procurement of Contract Staff: A Good Practice Guide for the Oil and Gas Industry', was accessed on 28/03/2015 at: *www.cpni.gov.uk/documents/publications/2011/2011012-gpg_contracting_ staff-oil_and_gas.pdf?epslanguage=en-gb*

CPNI and IET (2013), 'Resilience and Cyber Security of Technology in the Built Environment', was accessed on 28/03/2015 at: *www.cpni.gov.uk/ documents/publications/2013/2013063-resilience_cyber_security_ technology_built_environment.pdf?epslanguage=en-gb*

(93) CREST website was accessed on 20/03/2015 at: *www.crest-approved.org/*

(94) Graham Cluley's website and newsletter can be accessed at: https://grahamcluley.com/

(95) The Information Asset Protection and Pre-Employment Screening Group website was accessed on 20/03/2015 at: *www.asisonline.org/Membership/ Member-Center/Councils/iapps/Pages/Members.aspx?rpage=1&k=*

(96) Information Assurance Advisory Council website was accessed on 20/03/2015 at: *www.iaac.org.uk/*

(97) Humphreys, E, (09/10/2013), 'The new cyber warfare', accessed and downloaded on 26/03/2015 at: *www.iso.org/iso/home/news_index/ news_archive/news.htm?refid=Ref1785*

(98) Krebbs on Security was accessed at: *http://krebsonsecurity.com/*

(99) NIST Special Publication 800-53 (Revision 4) 'Security and Privacy Controls for Federal Information Systems and Organisations': was accessed and downloaded on 26/06/2015 at: *http://nvlpubs.nist.gov/ nistpubs/SpecialPublications/NIST.SP.800-53r4.pdf*

(100) Open University Cyber Security introductory information and courses can be accessed at: *www.futurelearn.com/courses/introduction-to-cyber-security*

(101) Troy Hunt's website was accessed at: *www.troyhunt.com/*

(102) UK Cabinet Office and Marsh (March 2015), 'UK Cyber Security: the role of insurance in managing and mitigating the risk', was accessed and downloaded on 28/03/2015 at: *www.gov.uk/government/news/cyber-security-insurance-new-steps-to-make-uk-world-centre*

CHAPTER 6: PROTECTIVE SECURITY

6.1 Context

"In business, if we don't gain insights from foresight, we risk learning from hindsight—and a lot more expensively. The life and death of our business can depend upon it." – Former US Navy SEAL Commander, Bob Schoultz (1)

This chapter aims to dig beneath the surface of protective security functions; job roles often glamorised and misunderstood by those who have not been privy to the many opportunities presented by the protective security sector. Associated with the more muscular domains of physical security – such as ship security and close protection – the protective security field has become professionalised at a rapid pace across many environments in recent times. Much successful tradecraft within protective security management is discreet, behind-the-scenes planning, and also an increasing reliance on soft skills that are compatible with corporate environments and tasks which may involve de-escalating conflict situations. Several sub-chapters have been devised in order to help the reader understand the planning and protocols that govern this sphere of security operation. These sub-sections are:

6.2 Methods of risk assessment

6.3 How to conduct a person-focused threat assessment

6.4 The ethos and expectations of protective security roles; 'adaptive practitioners'

6.5 Anti-piracy; market, countermeasures and agencies

6.6 Firearms

6.7 Management of 'action-oriented' individuals

6.8 Protective security management standards

6.9 Wrap-up: what can give consultancies the competitive edge in fast emerging markets?

Protective security refers to the domain of security most associated with guarding persons, or assets, of high national or organisational value. The word *protection* derives from a Latin term meaning *cover in front*. During their working life, protective security agents can experience a ludicrous diversity of roles. A pal of mine spent the best part of a year accompanying a pop star's pooch around the world. This was an important role, "because if the dog was happy then the principal was happy", explained the agent (2). Some jobs can be quite static in nature. Such as maintaining a presence at, or monitoring, various residences. Or spending weeks at sea, guarding valuable cargo. Many females with law enforcement or military backgrounds are particularly well placed to chaperone prominent middle and far eastern families around the world to the most luxurious shopping and financial districts. Protective security roles can often be highly dynamic, kinetic and changeable and demand a large degree of patience, physical fitness and personal discomfort. This is because the job follows the threat, which is usually a highly mobile person, known in security parlance as *The Principal*. Such severe operational stresses demand that protective security specialists do retain continued situational awareness, adhere to peak levels of self-discipline, and are able to consider, or anticipate, an almost-immeasurable range of risks that may possess the potential to fell any principal. Unlike organisations (which are groups of people and teams that can transfer or tolerate risk), the ultimate safety of one principal human being does mean that much of the close protection operative's role is about avoiding big risk in the first place. This may appear in contrast to Hollywood, and now Bollywood's, conveyor belt of depictions about glamorous bodyguards.

Nevertheless, such artistic licence from film-makers, is perhaps a significant plus point for our industry. Such an aura of excitement does undoubtedly help to attract a huge amount of enthusiastic recruits into a growing reservoir of employment and business opportunities. But it does tend to be the more mundane business approaches, including decent research, presentational and networking skills that provide protective security agents with the competitive edge, as we shall read from various interviews conducted and related later in this chapter.

Team leaders and all protective security agents should be well versed in local crime, kidnap and terrorism data. In deciding how to allocate resources, they should be able to distinguish between high-profile media stories that may temporarily seize popular attention on one hand, and the granular ground-truth facts, which may be a whole lot different on sober reflection. For example, although terrorism has been on the increase since 2000, *The Global Terrorism Index* concludes that the phenomenon is "… relatively small when compared to the 437,000 people killed [globally] by homicides in 2012, this being 40 times greater" (3).

Protective security operatives should know where and what is safe, and where and what is less so, in any domain. Moreover, making sweeping judgements about a locality based upon simplistic, and often dormant, national data, can cause reputational damage for any ill-prepared protective security company. More often than not, expertise and proactivity with the client around managing more mundane risk scenarios, provides the real service value. Knowing local routes to hospitals, airports, train stations … and knowing contacts at each. Or carrying tissues and deodorants, mouth mints, pocket torches, first aid kits, a couple of decent up-to-date newspapers, weather reports, spare phones and chargers … are all handy attributes and items that will endear a security agent to their client. (These plus points will sometimes embarrass the client's own full-time support staff in the process!) Expertise and prior planning around evacuation and other emergency planning – in order to mitigate big ticket risks, such as severe weather, personal confrontations, political disturbances and natural disasters – is clearly a must-have skill for protective security professionals. The capacity and capability of a security agency to provide calm leadership and viable solutions in a crisis, may well be the very reason that a client has chosen a specific company rather than their main competition. "Reliability and dependability are among the most important attributes of a protective security agent", says Paul Brown, an experienced UK-based close protection trainer and former Royal Household police bodyguard (4).

Case study: Examples of government-run protective security agencies

The US Secret Service may well be the most pre-eminent protective security division in the world. It is tasked with protecting the POTUS, vice presidents, former presidents and presidential families. The Secret Service also carry out criminal investigations and reviews, such as the 2008 inquiry with the US Department of Education into the 1999 Columbine High School atrocities. In the United Kingdom, the London Metropolitan Police Service's Specialist Protection Branch (SO1) is responsible for providing security to prime ministers and prominent Members of Parliament including ministers, opposition leaders and higher-risk ex-ministers. SO1 also protects some visiting dignitaries and ambassadors. It is a duty under the 1961 *Vienna Convention on Diplomatic Relations* for countries to provide safe passage for visiting foreign leaders and diplomats, and this responsibility falls in the UK to SO1. At present, Specialist Operation Branch SO6 provide armed protection to static sites, such as overseas embassies in the United Kingdom. SO14 branch is the Royalty Protection Branch tasked with securing the British Royal Family and their residences. Armed with Norinco submachine guns and Taurus pistols, it is reported that more than 8,000 officers based across 36 squadrons within the *Central Guard Unit*, or *Central Security Bureau*, provide protection to China's president and senior government members (5).

Anecdotal accounts suggest that there are more protective security sector jobs, often referred to as *close protection*, or *executive protection*, within the private sector compared to public-owned authorities, such as police or military institutions. This pattern has been augmented by wide-scale moves by large government customers to turn to private contractors and consultants in order to provide solutions; often in hostile environments. For example, in Iraq, for the several years that followed US-led military operations, one publication reported that some 30,000 close protection roles were available (6). In the UK House of Commons, then Metropolitan Police Head of Specialist Operations, John Yates, told a Parliamentary Committee that, "Protection cannot be immune from the current fiscal climate", which could be a pointer that even domestic protective security agencies in some countries will soon be opened up to private sector providers. In the UK, taxpayers were funding budgets of some £130 million per year, for providing official protection to the Royal Family and some high-profile Members of Parliament (7). The UK is not the only country where such increased costs for protective security were said to be becoming unsustainable by many influential police and political leaders.

6.2 Methods of risk assessment

This book will not dwell too much upon hazards that protective security agents and their clients face in the line of duty. Suffice to say, hostile and fragile environments do provide for extremely dangerous working environments. Therefore, anticipating threats and risks posed to workers and organisations in such environments is both business-critical and life-saving. Private security contractors are, at times, under more threats than regular soldiers or armed combatants. Recently in Afghanistan, the *Congressional Research Service* found that private contractors were 2.75 times more likely to be killed than US armed forces personnel. This figure rose exponentially, to around eight times, for security agents working more 'mobile' patterns (8). In many operating environments, political, economic and legal domains can be treacherous too, in addition to the physical security environment. Popular protective security recruitment markets – including Afghanistan (8/100), Libya (15/100), Iraq (16/100), South Sudan (14/100), Nigeria (25/100), The Ukraine (25/100) and Russia (28/100) – fall within the world's most corrupt operating environments, according to Transparency International's *Corruption Perceptions Index 2013* (9).[*]

Drawing such in-country threats and risks together is an inordinately difficult and long exercise. Certain types of threat-assessment work will also demand that security managers and consultants integrate their own company's risk analysis with the other pre-existing organisational resilience strategies that may already be firmly embedded by the client, and thus familiar to some of the client or principal's own team. The merger of different risk assessment approaches can often create the most difficult hurdles for any security contractor who knows what the client has to do to improve security, but is often hitting a cultural wall with the client, or their support team, because the new suggestions destabilise existing resilience structures or emergency plans that a client is comfortable with. Security consultants therefore "should push as

---

[*] *To explain, the bracketed marks above indicate a score out of 100 based on 'how corrupt their public sector is perceived to be'. 100 is the highest possible score for public finance probity. Denmark came the closest with 91/100. A zero score would illustrate the highest possible level of corruption. Somalia, achieving just 8/100, was perceived to be the most corrupt state in the world out of 177 countries measured overall.*

much as possible to develop a close and effective partnership with the senior corporate security or resilience director at headquarters level", says Jon Hill, Managing Director of Operations Group, a UK-based close protection training and deployment company. "It may be that consultants have the local or technical expertise, and would have been specifically recruited for these attributes. But they still must ensure that their proposed risk assessment and mitigation plans are accepted and integrated by the client or principal before an operation. A difficult conversation or two to set out parameters beforehand can save several megawatts of tension and recriminations at a later date, especially after a crisis (10)."

It is this author's firm view that, at the time of writing, it is impossible to see into the future. Therefore, as a corollary, it remains impossible to predict the size, scale and type of a risk. Despite this rather inconvenient fact, a risk assessment process is *the* critical ingredient to any successful protective security operation. Security management guru, John Fay, wrote: "A good deal of the analytical input comes from knowing the current nature of the threat, tapping into one's base of experience and applying good old-fashioned common sense" (11). A plethora of security risk assessment models exist to help us process, and even calculate, Fay's sound advice. Moreover, the range and ingenuity of so many risk models does rather pay testament to the security industry's professionalisation in recent times. But now there is also fair criticism from within the industry that some protective security functions are becoming over-planned, or micro-managed, by a surge of well-intended guidance and standards documents on related issues, such as crisis management or organisational resilience. This is a moot point. But, undoubtedly, the kinetic and unpredictable nature of protective security operations does often lead security operators to abandon (or not even begin) the cool-headed, neutral, monitoring and analysis of threats and risks. Time and opportunity for background research may well be scarce but if some do lapse into this unfortunate mode of unthinking 'autopilot', then how will they be able to see any major risks emerging and, thus be prepared to put in place various treatments to counter or avoid them?

A further dilemma may be to what extent security consultants, including close protection operatives, should enter the sphere of health and safety operations within their assessments? For the successful functioning of both security and safety remits, it is far better for there to be *overlap* rather than *underlap*. Even if this does mean figuratively 'stepping on a few toes' within the client and/or principal's sphere. In the aftermath of a serious safety glitch, such as a principal being caught up in a house fire, or slipping and cutting their head badly, to pithily argue a job demarcation line could well lose a security practitioner the prospect of repeat business!

In order to bring some sense of control and structure to assist in the pre-planning for risk-based scenarios, this book will now outline five simple risk assessment models that seem to be favoured by those interviewed for this publication:

Model 1: HSE five step risk assessment

Step 1: Identify the hazards
Step 2: Decide who might be harmed and how
Step 3: Evaluate the risks and decide on precaution
Step 4: Record your findings and implement them
Step 5: Review your assessment and update if necessary
Source: UK Health and Safety Executive, 2014 (12)

Such a hazard identification process does begin to propel an organisation into a risk consideration culture, without necessarily demanding that the likelihood and severity of risks be much debated or calculated. In environments where risk analysis and risk management approaches may not yet have matured (such as civilian environments, or in some emerging markets), the HSE hazard identification tool may be an ideal starting point to engage local customers. Some security companies have been known to offer a free initial, basic risk assessment.

Model 2: Quantitative risk assessment matrix

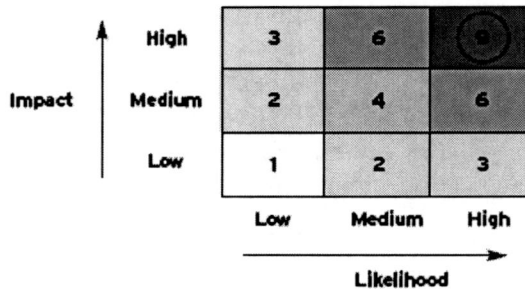

Source: The Scottish Government, 2014 (13)

This type of risk assessment matrix enables assessors to allocate simple scored ratings to the likelihood of threats occurring. They then estimate any potential impact that will 'hit' the victim organisation. Ratings out of three, five, or seven, are most common-place with quantitative risk calculations. Colour codes are then usually deployed into the matrix, in order to illuminate what risks should be prioritised (or passed over) for treatment. A shade of red will usually indicate a high or major risk. Yellow to amber may indicate a medium/moderate risk. While a light yellow or green background shading often indicates a negligible/low risk. This model provides a more visible and memorable matrix for team members and influential managers/directors. It is, in essence, a scorecard with ratings. But it can lead to internal organisational pontification and sign-off issues, as fellow colleagues sometimes become too absorbed in debating the scoring and challenging the scorers!

Model 3: Qualitative risk assessment matrix

RISK ASSESSMENT MATRIX				
SEVERITY PROBABILITY	Catastrophic (1)	Critical (2)	Marginal (3)	Negligible (4)
Frequent (A)	High	High	Serious	Medium
Probable (B)	High	High	Serious	Medium
Occasional (C)	High	Serious	Medium	Low
Remote (D)	Serious	Medium	Medium	Low
Improbable (E)	Medium	Medium	Medium	Low
Eliminated (F)	Eliminated			

Source: Advanced Diving Systems website, 2014 (14)

Again, with this model, results are colour coded, with green indicating a lower and possibly acceptable risk. Yellow/amber indicates a medium risk which is usually acceptable to an organisation *provided* that some mitigation measures are put into effect. Red indicates an unacceptable level of risk and tangible action should be immediately taken. This method again provides a clear visualisation of whether additional measures should be taken.

Model 4: Swiss cheese model

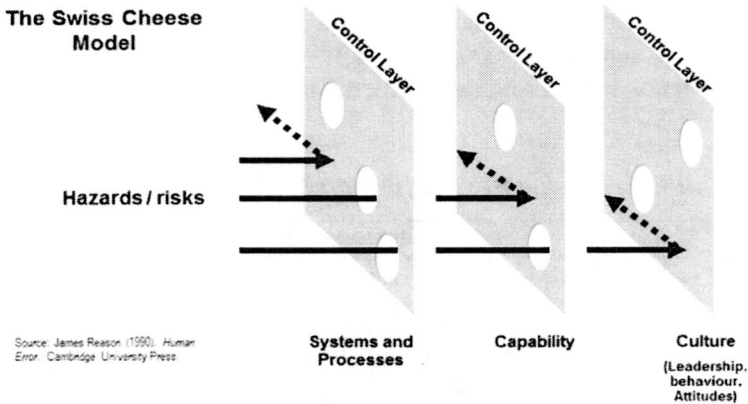

The Swiss Cheese Model

Control Layer   Control Layer   Control Layer

Hazards / risks

Source: James Reason (1990). Human Error. Cambridge University Press

Systems and Processes   **Capability**   **Culture** (Leadership, behaviour, Attitudes)

Source: Risk Management Magazine, Australia (15)

Each safety barrier, or defence mechanism that is in place to mitigate any particular hazard, is represented by a slice of Swiss cheese. The model was developed by Dr James Reason in order to provide reflective learning evaluation of major accidents. Reason showed, through isomorphic lessons, that crises tended to develop from untreated multiple, smaller failures, leading up to the actual major scenario. Reason's model is often used in the aviation sector. Reason's focus was to look at business intangibles – perhaps most crucially – the culture of a workplace and the approach to risk-based activities. According to risk analysis authors, Pearce and Flavell, who also deployed this model: "The Chernobyl disaster in 1987 triggered an acceleration of thinking about the role of culture in managing workplace risk" (16).

Model 5: Bow tie model

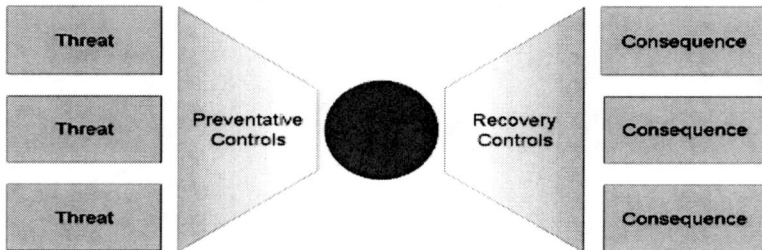

Threat | Preventative Controls | Recovery Controls | Consequence
Threat | | | Consequence
Threat | | | Consequence

The bow tie method is popular within the oil and gas sector and enables users "to conceptualise the interaction of causes, controls and consequences of a risk" (Bow

Tie Pro website: 2014) (17). According to an industry website dedicated to bow tie risk modelling, three steps are needed to undertake a risk assessment:

1. Of all possible consequences resulting from the risk (these are the orange boxes above), identify which is the most foreseeable, as opposed to the worst-case.
2. Identify the consequence level of the most foreseeable consequence.
3. Identify the likelihood level of the risk occurring and resulting in the consequence identified in Step 1 (18).

How and why should I choose a particular risk management approach?

There are no hard and fast rules in relation to what risk assessment model to adopt for your project or organisation. There are thousands of methods to choose from, which very much indicates that it is the prerogative of an organisation or individual to either select or devise a system that works best for them. Outlined above are merely the most basic frameworks, provided for the reader as baseline toolkits, in order to help you visualise, or develop, a risk assessment model that may work best for your company, within your operating environment. The core components will tend to be:

- Research, identify and assess the security threats and risks
- Calculate the likelihood
- Record the results in a living document and treat the risks
- Monitor existing and new threats and risks
- And so on …

Your risk assessment model, and the calculations imposed within it, can never be perfect. Such written processes are living reports that are designed – as their priority objective – to keep your company, and its clients, safe and secure. In essence, they serve to keep your team warned and informed. They also serve to outline and establish you or your client organisation's *Risk Appetite,* which can be defined as the amount of risk judged to be tolerable and justifiable. An organisation's appetite for risk will be decided by the nature of tasks undertaken and resources available. According to Scott Brant: "Risk management should be embedded within the daily operations of a security project. Through understanding risks, decision-makers will be better able to evaluate the impact of a particular decision or action on the achievement of the organisation's objectives. Risk management strategy does not focus upon risk avoidance but on the identification and management of an acceptable level of risk" (19).

6.3 How to conduct a person-focused threat assessment

It can be exciting to devise and deliver a risk assessment for a static building or a multi-sited business, using some of the models outlined above. Yet much of the protective security function is related to the security of a moving person, or group of moving people. For any protective security team, it is usually good practice to provide a formal, documented, risk assessment of each location visited by your principal person under protection. Thus, a common-sense approach is advised, whereby regular locations, such as residences and routine journeys, may indeed require their own specific layers of risk assessment and controls.

However, in theoretical terms, just as in the field of surveillance, close protection agents will throw an imaginary 'net' around the life of the principal. They will seek to build in different layers of protection at various pressure points and potential points of failure, such as getting into a family car each morning.

Many different approaches to devising a person-focused risk assessment are taught. Common approaches across all decent training courses are that the security team are able to build in planning, adaptability and emergency evacuation options. Agents will seek to ensure that they monitor, review and integrate latest intelligence feeds with existing risk management processes. Despite all of this hard work, a people-focused risk-assessment of the principal/s should be carried out by a protective security team. This will help them to figuratively 'step into the shoes' of any adversaries, and to systematically identify, and address, the most likely areas of vulnerability that a protected person may be susceptible to. One assessment method now widely taught in UK close protection circles, and originally outlined by the British Standard BS8507-1-2008, became memorably dubbed as *The Seven Ps*. The method of risk calculation involves a protective security agent carrying out prior research to compile a *Personal Profile* of the principal:

Case study: The Seven Ps that make a personal profile

PERSON: Who are they? What do they do? What did they do?

PLACES: Where do they go? What are their routines, including routine ingress and egress points? What places are they perceived to have strong links to?

PREJUDICES: Do they have any clear prejudices? Are they perceived to be prejudiced in any way?

PERSONALITY: What is their attitude with people? How are they perceived to internal employees and outsiders?

POLITICAL VIEWS: Any perceived or actual political or religious controversies lurking?

PERSONAL HISTORY: Medical history? Career background? Any grudges held against principal or family? Who also has access to any phones, computers and legal documents, such as trusted lawyers and accountants?

PRIVATE LIFESTYLE: Business and love-life including possible background vulnerabilities? Behaviour and attitude in private sphere?

Sources: BS8507-1 2008 and author interview with Hill, J, and Brown, P, 2014. (20)

At first glance, the model above undoubtedly raises as many questions as it answers. "The key is to not get hung up over purity", says Jon Hill, managing director of a protective security agency in the UK. "Sure, some threats and risks will overlap, but the Seven Ps are just a very decent way to conceptualise and calculate risk around a person (21)." Ex royal protection officer, Paul Brown, added: "Protecting individuals and groups can become very complex as they often do not behave predictably or even rationally. But the best protective security agents anticipate and map out both risks and responses well before an operation. Otherwise they will become awfully exposed in front of the client". The demonstration of both strategic and tactical control before any client, during any job, as well as "an uncanny ability to access the most useful intelligence feeds, will also guarantee the competitive edge", asserts Brown (22).

Case in point: Calculating risk levels under the Seven Ps method

The imaginary football club manager at a UK Premier League team was rated as follows:

Risk Type	Notes	Risk Rating
PERSON	Long serving football manager of League Winners Milkchester United. US National. In Britain's Top 200 'Rich List'. Former national football coach for US and Finland. Very high global public profile.	2/3

PLACES	In UK: attends boxing gym for Boxing and Muay Thai lessons twice per week. Same hairdressers every two weeks. Favourite restaurant with wife weekly in Milkchester City Centre. Daily trips to HQ and training ground. Holiday villa in Sandbanks, Dorset, once per month. Attends St Mary's Catholic Cathedral Milkchester, every Sunday morning. Outside UK: Visits family burial plots in Boston on average once per month. Visits child cancer charity in Russia every quarter, with wife. This is off-record. Drives 4x4 Range Rovers with tinted windows and generic plates, but refuses security in-vehicle.	2/3
PERSONALITY	Quiet and friendly, sober. Lively after alcohol but rarely drinks. Generous and kind to staff; even those he has sacked remain friendly. Very generous to close staff and friends.	2/3
PREJUDICES	Perceived to be very tribal to the 'United' and once called fans of the neighbouring team 'Nazis' on a live TV broadcast. Refuses to do BBC interviews, without explanation.	2/3
POLITICAL	Public supporter and donor of the US Republicans. Strong Irish Catholic family heritage and, as a student, was reported to have supported a 'United Ireland', although principal is on record as not commenting on domestic politics in UK.	2/3
PERSONAL	Aged 57. Media reports of a mini-stroke, aged 39, but denied as 'nonsense' by Principal and Milkchester's backroom staff. Close friend Anthony Diamond-Everidge (ADE), celebrity lawyer, is principal's best friend and attorney in UK. ADE was convicted for assault and burglary as a teenager and is a publicly reformed character but is widely reported to have links with serious and organised criminals via various lucrative loophole defences. Principal uses an old mobile phone, has no smartphone, and all social media is conducted through the FC.	2/3
PRIVATE LIFE	On second marriage, to Russian model and TV news anchor, Lydia Lechberg (1999). First marriage ended bitterly in 1995; ex sister-in-law on record as saying principal should suffer a 'slow and painful death' after 1995 divorce hearing. Comments retracted in ex-wife's biography in 1999. One business insolvency – Abercloth Capital Investments – around 1998. One investor, London businessman, boxing promoter, Frank Sherbert, claimed he was owed £1m by principal; but High Court found in principal's favour (2002). Media sometimes try to get two to clash. Two children with wife, Aleksandr (14) and Katya (12) both attend boarding school in the US. No known behavioural problems. Firearms licences held by principal and wife. Family perceived to be happy and functional. In 2006 secretary-turned-model, Lynn Franks Dietrich, alleged a brief affair with the principal.	2.5/3

	Media surveillance footage was unclear. Both subsequently called the scenario a 'media wind-up'. Wife is gadget-obsessed and runs live social media feeds on phone, often publicising upcoming trips.	
Overall risk rating		14.5/21*

Overall risk ratings

   0-7: Low Risk

   8-14: Medium Risk

   15-21: High Risk

Personnel profile risk assessments can be enhanced by adding numerical scores into a matrix, see above. Ratings out of three are allocated to each of the seven 'P' risk categories. This scoring helps to provide an overall risk rating, but assists agents by highlighting specific pinch-points of vulnerability, where extra controls may be needed, that may never have been considered without carrying out cold, hard, analysis of the principal beforehand. The imagined example, provided above, does show that this risk assessment method is even more dynamic and prone to necessary revision than others, including those shown previously. With all risk assessments, a cut-off point is ill-advised. Risk assessments and the effective updated communication of them, are live operational organisms; the very heartbeat to a successful protective security operation. Moreover, when it comes to protecting high-profile people, you will notice through your research just how much public information is wildly inaccurate in relation to the principal. Seek to corroborate information, particularly from internet sources. A protective security agent's job is, therefore, far more cerebral than relying on deterrent and muscle power. They seek to understand who the principal actually is, their likes and dislikes, and the nuts and bolts of what they do. Their skills are extended into domains of research and prediction. A security agent needs to quickly understand how others might perceive the protected principal. Understanding the causes of attack enables them to prevent, and evade, the risk in the first place.

Often, close protection operations are spread across more than one high-asset individual or group. Such risk rating systems that we have shown above, do help team leaders and managers to decide upon a fair allocation of resources in what can be very stretched and intractable working conditions. It does show true

---

*Please note that it is recommended that these highly personalised details would be encrypted and key identifier phrases should be codified to protect the identity of the principal, other key individuals and organisations.

professionalism and task commitment to carry on with the risk assessment process during times of acute stress or task overload. Former Navy Seal Commander, Bob Schoultz, reminds us that US Navy "SEALs are masters of chaos. They specialise in creating chaos and disruption within the enemy's organisation, getting inside its strategy and decision-making cycle, anticipating plans and striking where least expected" (23). Close protection officers often must feel that some of their own clients and principals were trained by the SEALS, such can be the nature of orders, counter-orders and disorder on many protective security jobs!

6.4 Ethos and expectations of protective security roles; 'adaptive practitioners'

Mullins (2008) defined management as "the process through which efforts of members of the organisation are coordinated, directed and guided towards the achievement of an organisational goal" (24). It would be trite to say that 'no two protective security roles are the same'; often they can be, and work can be extremely dull and monotonous. Conversely, most roles do, at some point, demand a calm head, a great deal of training and operational experience, and an almost innate ability to juggle the management of several competing risks, whilst appearing to regally float like a swan on the surface. Protective security agents can find themselves tracking lost property in foreign airports, shepherding pets or movie stars to far-flung precincts of the world, or trying to enjoy a rest day, yet fidgeting because they don't quite know when the next call of duty will come in. Those who survive and prosper in this environment are *adaptive practitioners*. People who can comfortably while away numerous hours during peace time. Yet, they are consistently alert, can activate and organise themselves, or groups, very quickly and can also apply crystal clear logic in any potential crisis.

In corporate domains of protective security management, softer skills, such as deportment, style and attitude, become equally, or more important than certifications in firearms and jiu jitsu. The acquisition of potential agents with so-called *soft skills* has been a priority for many protective security recruiters and training companies in Europe and the US for several years. This is, in part, due to an increasingly interventionist legal, public health and work safety environment, imposed by national authorities. On protective security training programmes, conflict management modules have become much more about evading and mollifying risk, rather than actively handling a physical risk scenario.

In UK territory, close protection operatives (CPO) are lawfully required to hold security licences, issued by the UK Home Office's Security Industry Authority. However, many non-UK recruiters, especially in Europe and other more developed security markets, also expect to see this accreditation as a minimum standard to demonstrate a CPO's employability. At present, the UK SIA requires CPO students to study for a minimum of 138 hours across 14 'core competencies' (which began their life some years ago as National Occupational Standards). An additional two days of conflict management training and first aid (three days) is required. In the civilian sector, the role is unarmed within UK territories, therefore no firearms training is formally required by examination assessors. Neither is a driving licence. The 14 core competencies and conflict management sessions are listed by the SIA as:

SIA close protection specialist modules

- Session 1: Roles and responsibilities of the close protection operative
- Session 2: Threat and risk assessment
- Session 3: Surveillance awareness
- Session 4: Operational planning
- Session 5: Law and legislation
- Session 6: Interpersonal skills
- Session 7: Close protection teamwork and briefing
- Session 8: Conduct reconnaissance
- Session 9: Close protection foot drills
- Session 10: Route selection
- Session 11: Close protection journey management
- Session 12: Search procedures
- Session 13: Incident management
- Session 14: Venue security

Conflict management module

- Session 1: Avoiding conflict and reducing personal risk
- Session 2: Defusing conflict
- Session 3: Resolving and learning from conflict
- Session 4a: Application of communication skills and conflict management for security guarding and close protection (25)

Such a range of skills were designed to provide a baseline of competencies for a lower risk civilian environment, such as the United Kingdom. This view is very much reinforced by former royal personal protection officer and author, Geoffrey Padgham, who goes on to emphasise an array of soft skills that protective security agents should be coaching themselves in if they want to be successful in this area within corporate and/or other civilian environments (26). Additional skills, such as, speaking the language of business, fitting into the client's corporate culture, a familiarity with any intended operating environment, possessing in-country language and navigational expertise, enhanced defensive driving, first aid proficiency and decent interpersonal and presentational attributes, were all identified as essential in the eyes of private sector close protection recruiters interviewed for this book. One close protection advisory company explained it well when they said: "Personal qualities within the industry are good communication skills and the ability to plan and work well within a team. Good close protection officers [who] can maintain attention to detail perform well under stress at short notice" (27).

My own preferred addition to this expert advice could be summed up in one word: leadership. In the tight-knit, high-pressure environment of close protection tasks, there is a double responsibility that falls upon the shoulders of each security agent. First, an inherent duty for all agents to successfully carry out their own tasks. Yet agents should also be actively and consistently aware of their team's overall objectives and vulnerabilities. Your survival – either contractual or otherwise – lives and dies with the team. An overdependence on the designated team leader by bodyguards (BGs) and personal escort sections (PES) is unfair and unacceptable. Sulkers, skulkers, slackers and those who prefer radio silence, should beware: there are now more than 13,000 agents licensed with a UK close protection licence, thus contractors and corporations can pick and choose who they hire next time around. Protective security agents are advised to follow Padgham's advice and develop their own skills portfolio by being mindful of softer, interpersonal requirements from industry. "To be a manager means sharing in the responsibility for the performance of the enterprise", asserts Drucker (28). But because protective security is so rooted in collective team responsibility, each CPO should take on board this group leadership mindset.

More kinetic and operational drills are embedded to a much greater effect via police and military CPO courses, such as the National Protection Officers Course run by UK police services, or the world-renowned UK Royal Military Police eight-week training at Longmoor. Such career backgrounds will undoubtedly provide reassurance to any client that any attack or evacuation scenario can be handled in the most professional and safe manner. As world champion British boxer, Carl Froch, said about an opponent: *"He knows I'm brutal. He's knows I can punch hard. He knows if I connect on his chin, at any one moment, 12 three minute rounds, he's going to be in serious trouble. If he's not on the floor, his legs will do a funny dance" (29)*. Quite amusing and suitable ringside language. But for all the Kung Fu qualifications in the world, a corporate client won't want to hear this type of chatter near their business!

6.5 Anti-piracy; market, counter-measures and agencies

Formed in 2009, Washington DC-based maritime security company, AdvanFort, soon became a fixture within global anti-piracy operations. The company produced excellent weekly piracy threat analysis reports for clients and the wider marketplace. Its website news updates are topical and relevant to the whole maritime security community. In October 2013, a crew of 35 (ten civilians and 25 armed guards) aboard Advan's own vessel, *MV Seaman Guard Ohio*, drifted slightly in extreme winds. They were arrested and charged by India's Attorney General for entering territorial waters while being in possession of firearms. Following an exhausting campaign, led by the company's CEO, Sam Farajallah, 33 of 35 guards were released on strict bail conditions. They were ordered to remain in-country and attend a police station in Chennai each day. The ship's captain and tactical deployment officer remained incarcerated. Eight months later, in July 2014, all charges were eventually dropped and Advant's sailors were free to go home (30).

It was the hijacking of US-registered vessel, *MV Maersk Alabama*, during 2009, which re-established popular awareness of piracy, particularly around the Indian Ocean and Horn of Africa. Four armed teenage hijackers had targeted *Alabama* using a skiff. They attempted to control the vessel and its 23-strong crew and sought to redirect the ship to Somalia. They failed after the crew retaliated. After the bungled attempt to seize the main vessel, the pirates then kidnapped the ship's master and took him aboard a lifeboat, hoping to escape. Intervention by the US Navy ended a four-day hostage ordeal for Captain Richard Phillips. Three hijackers were shot dead by US SEALS after they were viewed pointing guns into the captain's back. The hijacking failed due to the crew's courage. Moreover, their rigorous professionalism beforehand in carrying out security drills and anti-hostage training had served them well. *Captain Phillips,* the movie, casting Hollywood A-list star, Tom Hanks, in the lead role, was inspired by the tenacious and calm leadership shown by *Alabama's* crew.

This perilous set of events preceded a second tragedy on *Maersk Alabama*. In 2014, two former US Navy SEALS, who were subsequently working as ship security guards for a US-based maritime security company, were found to be dead in cabins in the Port of Victoria, Seychelles. No external suspects were sought. The case was recorded by Indian police authorities as inadvertent, self-inflicted harm; respiratory problems caused by toxic substances. Family and colleagues rejected the official in-country investigation findings. They point to training and mandatory drug and alcohol tests undertaken by all on-board privately contracted armed security personnel (PCASP). The US coastguard's office launched its own investigation. This was not concluded at the time of writing. This tragic case does, nevertheless, demonstrate a range of undoubted health and well-being risks to personnel in high-risk environments (31). The two individuals had reportedly told friends that "boredom ... was the real enemy of the open sea" (32). The 500-foot vessel had successfully repulsed two attacks since the attempted 2009 hijacking. Yet, it appears, all too often human frailties brought the operator an equally stern test to her resilience. At the time of writing, she remains at sea, although her bullet-ridden 5-ton fibreglass lifeboat was donated to the National Navy UDT-SEAL Museum in Florida, US, several years ago.

Case study: Somalia's pirates

Armed with assault rifles, rocket propelled grenades, pistols and knives, Somalia's elongated coastline has become one of the world's most familiar and feared zones prone to piracy. Yet Somali-based pirates cast their net far wider, famously ensnaring leisure sailing couple, Paul and Rachel Chandler, from Royal Tunbridge Wells in England, as they blissfully cruised around the Seychelles in the Indian Ocean, several hundred nautical miles away. Seized from *Lynn Rival* in October 2009, they were held for 388 days. The following table shows the torrid rise and recent fall of Somali-based piracy; a phenomenon that has subsequently seen European Union Naval Forces (EU NAVFOR), US Navy Seals and the US Office of Naval Intelligence (ONI) combine forces in the region, in order to repel and degrade a maritime threat which proliferated gravely between 2009-11.

Area	2007	2008	2009	2010	2011	2012	2013
Gulf of Aden	7	19	100	33	20	13	4
Red Sea	0	0	0	14	18	12	2
Somalia	17	5	44	51	125	44	4
Arabian Sea	4	0	1	2	0	0	0
Indian Ocean	0	0	1	0	0	0	0
Oman	2	0	1	0	0	0	0
Total	30	24	147	100	163	69	10

Source: International Maritime Bureau 2012 and 2013 (33)

**Figure 22: Actual attempts and reported attacks on vessels
by Somali-based pirates**

Rules and regulatory bodies

The *Security in Complex Environments Group* (SCEG) is a special interest group within the large defence industry association, ADS. SCEG members "represent the vast majority of the UK industry, delivering security in challenging environments on land and at sea" (34). The group is the accepted UK Government's industry partner for the regulation of private security companies (PSCs) and providers. The group provides a continuous forum for government and industry to exchange views, shape policies, enhance and embrace best practice and regulation. Membership of SCEG is conditional upon signing up to the International Code of Conduct for Private Security Service Providers (ICoC), and also the UN Guiding Principles on Business and Human Rights (further details below).

Some 58 private companies originally signed up to *The International Code of Conduct for Private Security Service Providers* (ICoC) back in 2010, and momentum kicked in soon afterwards. A Swiss Government inspired initiative, ICoC, was established to improve oversight and accountability of private security providers principally operating in 'complex' and/or hostile environments (35). By 2013, some 708 companies from 70 countries were ICoC signatories. In the words of ICoC:

> *"The Code sets-out human rights based principles for the responsible provision of private security services. These include rules for the use of force, prohibitions on torture, human trafficking and other human rights abuses, and specific commitments regarding the management and governance of companies, including how they vet personnel and subcontractors, manage weapons and handle grievances internally."*

The *UN Guiding Principles on Business and Human Rights* refers to the "corporate responsibility to protect human rights" in its 2011 publication and codification. The accompanying guide goes on to say that: "States do not relinquish their international human rights law obligations when they privatise the delivery of services that may impact the enjoyment of human rights" (36).

The *Security Association for the Maritime Industry* (SAMI) is a business membership organisation for companies working within maritime environments and acts as a "focal point for maritime security matters" (37). Through its forums, training, guidance and events, SAMI works with national and international shipping organisations, flag states, regulatory bodies, insurance and legal professionals, in order to ensure that vessels and private security providers are equipped with the best possible knowledge, networks, technology and training to ensure safe passage for maritime staff and cargoes. On a quarterly basis, SAMI publishes its digital magazine called *The Bridge*. The organisation's website carries lots of news and updates on business risks and threats. SAMI's website, and *World Maritime News*, a separate publication, provide daily news and information bulletins for risk management practitioners. For example, during 2014, SAMI provided important information and guidance around chartered vessels and the West Africa Ebola outbreak.

International standards and maritime security rules

ISO 9001:2008 sets out the criteria for a quality management system and is the only one of the ISO9000 series that can be certified.

ISO 28000:2007 points out the requirements for a security management system and looks at those aspects that are critical to the security assurance of the supply chain.

ISO/PAS 28007:2012 is an additional set of guidelines aimed at private maritime security companies (PMSCs) who provide privately contracted armed security personnel (PCASP) on-board ships. To be certified ISO/PAS 28007:2012, organisations must show proof of being ISO 28000:2007 certified. At the time of writing, the international maritime authority had not endorsed ISO28007. Yet this has not stopped shipping owners signing a pro-forma contract with PMSC on the rules for the use of force policy (see below).

100 Series: Rules for the use of force (RUF): In 2013, due to concerns of legal and reputational damage for companies, alongside a sense that clarification was needed in the delivery of force interventions at sea, a group of industry associations and influential 'flag states' met together to draft an *International Model Set of Maritime Rules for the Use of Force (RUF)* that became commonly known by the report's headline: *100 Series*. At one point, the Code departs from its measured prose to shout at its readers, using emboldened, red capital letters:

> **NOTHING IN THESE RULES SHALL BE INTERPRETED IN ANY WAY WHATSOEVER AS LIMITING AN INDIVIDUAL'S RIGHT OF SELF-DEFENCE AS UNIVERSALLY RECOGNISED AND PROVIDED FOR UNDER APPLICABLE AND RELEVANT NATIONAL AND INTERNATIONAL LAWS. (38)**

The 100 Series provide for a legal, graduated and proportionate response to a violent attack, or the perception of a violent attack, and are credited with reducing further a number of potentially inflammatory incidents. Under the rules, the ship Master's authority under SOLAS, *The International Convention for the Safety of Life at Sea,* remains absolute. The Master can order the cessation of firing by PCASP at any point. Under SOLAS (Chapter V 'Safety of Navigation',

Regulation 34-1) the "Master's discretion in decision making [must] not be compromised" (39). SOLAS was inducted in 1974 after previous incarnations, which dated back to the aftermath of the 1912 Titanic disaster. SOLAS requires that flag states ensure that their vessels comply with minimum safety standards in construction, equipment, navigation and operation.

According to Jason Layton (2014), a maritime security specialist interviewed for this book, "many organisations such as SAMI, ICoC, ASIS, Baltic International Maritime Company (BIMCO) and The Maritime Security Committee of the International Maritime Organisation (IMO), are all involved in multiple certification schemes to create a level of oversight and legitimacy within the maritime security sector. Sadly, it is clear that in spite of these efforts, regulations will not be effective until they are clearly defined and enforced by legitimate authorities" (40).

The *International Maritime Organisation,* a United Nations agency, was founded in 1959 and adopted SOLAS, which the IMO describe as "the most important of all treaties dealing with maritime safety" (41). According to the IMO, shipping is one of the world's most dangerous industries. Following the United States' 9/11 terrorist atrocities, and increasingly audacious terrorist and piracy attacks (principally around the Horn of Africa), a more comprehensive and obligatory "security regime entered into force … which contains detailed security-related requirements for governments, port authorities and shipping companies in a mandatory section", known as the *International Ship and Port Facility Security Code.* The ISPS Code, Section A, is a series of non-mandatory guidelines. Section B relates as to how best to meet these requirements (42). The Code is implemented through the 1974 SOLAS treaty (Chapter XI-2).

The code's 13 "special measures to enhance maritime security" are as follows:	
Regulation 1	Definitions
Regulation 2	Application
Regulation 3	Obligations of contracting governments
Regulation 4	Requirements for companies and ships
Regulation 5	Specific responsibility of companies
Regulation 6	Ship security alert system
Regulation 7	Threats to ships
Regulation 8	Master's discretion for ship safety and security
Regulation 9	Control and compliance measures
Regulation 10	Requirements for port facilities
Regulation 11	Alternative security arrangements
Regulation 12	Equivalent security arrangements

Regulation 13	Communication of information
Source: IMO website, 2014 (43)	

Figure 23: International ship and port facility code provisions

In 2011, the IMO produced guidance for private ship owners who deploy private security contractors with firearms into high-risk areas, such as off the Horn of Africa. In this region particularly, the fusion between piracy and sub-state terrorism became almost endemic during the noughties. The UN and IMO are keen to note that such guidance is not an endorsement of private companies turning to private sector armed guards. But the regular physical threat to crew and cargo from attacks consisting of, sometimes, dozens of armed pirates travelling at speed in attack boats (skiffs), has ensured that a raft of practical advice for private companies has now been issued and this book can only really skim the surface of it all. In 2014, the *UK Maritime and Coastguard Agency* produced a *Code of safe working practices for merchant seamen.* The UK Government say: "the UK COSWP is of a safety-critical nature. You're strongly advised to refer only to the official Maritime and Coastguard Agency version" (44). Copies should be made available to all on-board, and specifically the master, safety officer and any members of a safety committee.

Thought to be the world's largest membership association representing ship owners who cover a large chunk of the world's seafaring tonnage, the *Baltic and International Maritime Council* (BIMCO) is a leading stakeholder and contributor to international maritime training and regulations. Linked to BIMCOs' website is the popular *Shipmaster's Security Manual*, a must-have read for most maritime security professionals (45). BIMCO has also produced guidelines to help ship owners, and their employees, with security risk management in the form of its *Ship and Voyage Specific Risk Assessment Guide.*

From the early 1990s, based from Kuala Lumpur, Malaysia, the *International Maritime Bureau* (IMB) has run a 24-hour *Piracy Reporting Centre*, and acts as a first point of contact for the ship's master to report any type of potential piracy incident. According to the IMB, the central function of the reporting centre is two-fold:

1) "To be a single point of contact for ship masters anywhere in the world who are under piratical or armed robbery attack. The information received from the masters is immediately relayed to the local law enforcement agencies requesting assistance.

2) The information received from the ship master's is immediately broadcast to all vessels in the Ocean region – thus providing vital information and increasing the master's domain awareness (46)."

In partnership with the International Chamber of Commerce, the IMB's Reporting Centre has become increasingly sophisticated. It produces a *Live Piracy Map*, which over recent years have shown the world's piracy prone hotspots to be found around South East Asia and the Indian subcontinent, East Africa and the Red Sea, including the Horn of Africa, West Africa, and South and Central America and the Caribbean waters (47).

Led by the *Maritime Security Centre Horn of Africa*, with several other influential signatories and endorsers, a coalition of groups produced the *Best Management Practices for Protection Against Somalia Based Piracy – Version 4*. This is a powerful set of voluntary guidelines which detail advice for private security companies operating in high-risk areas. This guide provides readers with risk assessment procedures, threat identification advice, ship protection measures, what to do if pirates 'take control', and advice 'in the event of military action' (48).

Most flag states also produce their own national guidance. Some do formalise extant domestic legal obligations that security practitioners should ensure they are up to date with. For example, the US Coastguard Office, an agency of the Department of Homeland Security, issues Security Directives to American-flag vessels. One notable and helpful guide for consumption is the 2012 *Guidelines for US Vessels in High Risk Waters* (49).

6.6 Firearms

The use and carrying of firearms are governed by national and, in some countries, sub-national laws. This can restrict or empower private security contractors in a variety of ways depending on the domain. In some environments, and perhaps when off-duty, or off-site, protective security agents may not be eligible to carry firearms. In many environments, where firearms ownership can be said to be more liberal, it follows that security agents might actively seek to be *carrying* in order to achieve a sense of reassurance, or to be equipped with a practical tool for survival, for both self and client. The purpose of this section is to highlight some common legal vulnerabilities and risks that may regularly interface with the conduct of security tasks. Moreover, we shall explain and embed the critical importance of human rights laws, firearms legislation and the compliance to such fundamental rules of civil liberty, by way of case studies and isomorphic learning.

Incidents that cause risk to principals, organisations and protective security personnel, are not merely confined to deliberate, pre-planned, plots of assassination, extortion or terrorism. In countries and cultures where access to firearms is easily obtained, scuffles and celebrations can also quickly morph into lethal threat scenarios. For example, in trying to suppress a troublesome gang, an armed security guard drew fire and seriously injured a woman in a McDonald's restaurant in Washington DC in 2014 (50). In September 2013, Wazir Akbar Khan, the main diplomatic quarter of Kabul, Afghanistan, experienced a full-scale security alert when an outburst of crackling gunfire was heard nearby. The noise spread alarmingly. Afghanistan's national football team had beaten neighbouring India 2-0, to qualify for the 2014 FIFA Football World Cup (51). The *Centers for Disease Control and Prevention* raised concerns about celebratory gunfire in Puerto Rico where two citizens are killed, and some 25 injured, each year, "from celebratory gunfire on New Year's Eve" (52).

The way that laws are written and *interpreted* can vary massively between jurisdictions in scenarios related to self-defence. Indeed, judges and juries within those jurisdictions can fundamentally disagree on interpretations when the stated law can appear relatively straightforward. Some famous cases involving firearms related offences do provide some important lessons for protective security professionals. We observe a few here:

Famous cases: Firearms and the law

Although verdicts from each of these cases became controversial, readers are asked to suspend any value-judgements that they may have about each case. Instead, security practitioners are requested to absorb the clear lessons that we can derive from looking at each of the five cases below:

Case 1: In 2014, South African athlete, Oscar Pistorius, discharged several shots through his bathroom door, killing his girlfriend. The judge found that Pistorius was 'negligent' but that he had shot his partner by 'mistake' in the genuine belief that an intruder lurked behind the door. Pistorius was found guilty of culpable homicide (manslaughter). His actions were therefore 'negligent', but the judge found no proof of an 'intention' to kill. In South Africa, such a conviction carries a maximum sentence of 15 years' imprisonment (53).

Case 2: Tony Martin, a farmer and isolated lone resident, in Norfolk, Great Britain, shot two burglars in August 1999 with an unlicensed pump action shotgun at his premises. The younger perpetrator, 16 year-old, Fred Barras, died of his wounds at the scene. Shooting into the dark, as the two attempted to escape out of Martin's home, the elderly farmer later found himself convicted (10-2) by a jury for murder and sentenced to life imprisonment, a minimum of nine years. He claimed to have been burgled up to ten times previously, including by the same pair. The prosecution claimed, however, that

Martin had in fact laid in wait for the perpetrators. Martin was also charged with attempted murder upon Barras' accomplice, Brendon Fearon. For this, he was sentenced to a ten-year term, to run concurrently. On appeal, Martin's murder conviction was reduced to manslaughter, due to being diagnosed with paranoid personality disorder caused by depression. Thus, the Appeal Court had again rejected his main plea, which was that he acted out of self-defence. Martin's prison sentence was reduced to five years. He served three years before being released in 2003. It was subsequently reported that Martin lives in hiding with, reportedly, a £60,000 bounty upon his head. By the time of the infamous 1999 burglary, Fearon and Barras had dozens of convictions between them. Fearon was later jailed for a subsequent burglary on Martin's farm, whilst the farmer served his prison term, and also for illegal drugs dealing a couple of years later (54).

Case 3: During September 2007, in Nisour Square, Baghdad, private security contractors from a US-owned company, Blackwater, were chaperoning a convoy. A Kia sedan car, driving erratically on the wrong side of the road, travelled towards them. Ignoring the policeman's whistle, and subsequent warning shots, a female driver and her adult son continued to make a beeline straight toward the Blackwater convoy. Believing the car to be a vehicle borne improvised explosive device (VBIED), some Blackwater security guards began to discharge lethal fire. The car kept moving. An Iraqi policeman ran across to the vehicle but was gunned down too. A firefight between Iraqi police officers and Blackwater contractors broke out. The PSCs believed that – as was sometimes the case in Iraq – they were under sustained armed attack from Iraqi insurgents disguised in official police uniforms. They radioed the phrase enemy 'contact' several times. One contractor, however, kept to a sustained level of firing, despite colleagues ordering him to ceasefire. 17 Iraqi civilians were killed and 20 wounded. The following day, Blackwater's licence to operate in Iraq was reportedly revoked. After several official investigations, including a condemnatory 2007 UN report, and legal cases brought against some of the PSCs by the US military and FBI, four Blackwater employees were convicted in a US Federal court: one for murder. Another three were indicted for voluntary manslaughter and firearms offences (55).

The 2007 UN report criticised the US military for allowing PSCs to carry out military tasks, which was a breach of the 1989 UN Mercenary Convention, although the US is not a domestic signatory to this piece of international law. The Convention prohibits the use of private sector individuals taking part in 'hostilities' for 'private gain' (56). The Report noted: "The trend toward outsourcing and privatising various military functions by a number of member states in the past ten years has resulted in the mushrooming of private military and security companies" (57). This may not be bad news for security contractors seeking jobs and contracts in emerging markets but the tight oversight of the UN, and domestic law-enforcement and media agencies, does mean that risk management consultants, and their employers, must be absolutely clear on precisely what the parameters of local laws allow or prohibit.

Case 4: The arrest in 2013 by Indian police officers, of 35 crew members (including 25 security contractors) on vessel MV Seaman Guard Ohio, owned by AdvanFort security company in Washington DC, was touched upon earlier in this chapter. The crew were seized for carrying semi-automatic guns and 5,000 rounds of ammunition, allegedly within Indian waters, but without necessary licenses. Their plight more than exemplifies the difficulties and huge disruptions that can emanate by involving the necessary firearms provision within your security capability. After months of legal wrangling, AdvanFort's team were released and cleared (58). The maritime security threat in India is judged as severe. Particularly following the 2008 terrorist atrocities in Mumbai, which saw a team of Lashkar-e-Taiba-trained Pakistani militants travel by boat and dock at Colaba, before causing carnage during a four-day murderous siege.

Case 5: Trafficking firearms in between international borders can also be legally perilous. Especially for former British SAS officer, Captain Simon Mann. He was seized after being, reportedly, double-crossed by airport border officials in Zimbabwe's capital, Harare. Mr Mann was supposedly co-ordinating the transfer of $180,000 to pay for an arms cache and leading a 60-strong mercenary group. The team was tasked to accompany Mr Mann into neighbouring Equatorial Guinea in order to topple President Teodoro Obiang Nguema. Mann was jailed for three years by Zimbabwe's courts, before being extradited to Equatorial Guinea to serve a very lengthy prison sentence. After confessing guilt and regret, Mr Mann was pardoned by Nguema after just one year. On his return to the UK, Mann subsequently appealed against his Zimbabwe conviction. He argued that he was employed by a South African company which did possess a license to deal with firearms in Zimbabwe (59). However, as with all of these cases, most of the damage had already occurred and was irreversible.

UK police provisions in use of force and firearms

Private companies and workplace domains will undoubtedly need to have their own strict protocols and procedures if they require tasks to be carried out that may involve firearms. Nevertheless, a decent written example of legal, moral and operational guidelines is provided by the UK National Policing Improvement Agency and the Association of Chief Police Officers. Therefore, a thorough read and comprehension of the 2011 *Manual of Guidance on The Management, Command and Deployment of Armed Officers* is advised, even for private sector contractors engaged with use of firearms (60). This booklet serves well as a blueprint for any security contractor or services provider wishing to develop the highest professional and ethical approaches which are absolutely essential when dealing with firearms.

Fundamental to sensibly handling and deploying firearms, is a pro-active appreciation of civilian human rights obligations. Across European signatory states, the European Convention on Human Rights (ECHR) enshrines each human being with the 'right to life' (Article 2). ECHR upholds "the prohibition of torture, inhuman and degrading treatment or punishment" (Article 3). ECHR provides for the "right to a fair trial" (Article 6) and underlines the "respect for family and private life" (Article 8). "When determining whether the level of force used in any particular instance was lawful, the courts will take account of the ECHR provisions", states the ACPO/NPIA manual (61). In the UK, the ECHR was enshrined into the Government's 1998 Human Rights Act, and is therefore considered statutory law.

Personal responsibility is paramount when utilising firearms: The manual states that: "All [police] officers have an individual responsibility for ensuring that they are aware of relevant legislation and are informed about the extent of their legal powers and the context within which those powers can be properly exercised. Forces should constantly identify any relevant legislation for the continued professional development of firearms commanders and AFOs" (62). In private sector domains, such rules, as well as the embracing of a human right's ethos, should be similarly viewed as essential.

Legal provisions: Use of firearms and force

Other legal provisions related to the use of firearms and force for UK companies include the *2007 Corporate Manslaughter and Corporate Homicide Act* and also the 1974 Health and Safety at Work Act, outlined in more detail in this book's Chapter 3: Security Legislation and Regulations, and Chapter 8: Safer Business Travel.

In the UK legal system, from which so many other judicial systems originate, the right to self-defence, as it relates to the use of force and firearms, is provided for both in common law and by the 1967 Criminal Law Act (63):

> *A person may use such force as is reasonable in the circumstances in the prevention of crime, or in effecting or assisting in the lawful arrest of offenders or suspected offenders or of persons unlawfully at large.*

Common law provides that a person may use necessary or reasonable force to protect themselves or another. One case (Griffiths in Beckford v The Queen, 1998) upheld that a person does not need to wait to be attacked: "circumstances may justify a pre-emptive strike" (64).

The law was clarified by Section 76 of the Criminal Justice and Immigration Act 2008, following concerns that many victims of burglaries and assaults were, themselves, becoming indicted, when attempting to defend themselves and family members. Subsection 5(a) permits householders to use "disproportionate force when defending themselves against intruders in the home". Taken into consideration is the "personal circumstances of the householder" and the "perceived threat" to them (65). In other words, did they sincerely believe that they, or others, were under grave physical threat?

The 2014 UK Home Office *Guide on Firearms Licensing Law* states that "gun ownership is a privilege, not a right". This is in stark contrast to the United States which declares that "the right of the people to keep and bear Arms, shall not be infringed" in its Constitution's Second Amendment and the 1791 *Bill of Rights*. Within Europe, similar constitutional rights are conferred upon Swiss citizens. The Czech Republic, Italy, France and parts of Eastern Europe are also regarded as quite lax permit regimes, although this does appear to be changing. Firearms cultures in some of these nations are similar, but somewhat lighter versions of the liberal US and Switzerland pro-gun environments; where a fear of marauding 'big government', and also a love of hunting, tend to thwart various civil society attempts to more tightly regulate firearms ownership.

The UK's gun ownership laws, where most types of firearms, including shotguns and rifles, require a licence, are generally held to be among the toughest in the world. Handguns are altogether banned. At present, UK police forces are the licensing authority for firearms certificates. Each constabulary decide upon whether somebody is a threat to public safety and if they have a "good reason to own a firearm" (66). This 'reason' does not stretch to a 'self-defence' argument. As one UK Home Office guide states: "In general, applicants should be able to demonstrate that they 'use' their firearm on a regular, legitimate basis for work, sport or leisure (including collections or research)" (67). The guide clarifies the 1968 Firearms Act in many areas and emphasises that it should be fully understood and absorbed by UK-based practitioners. As should any relevant domestic in-country laws, or impending legal changes, that apply to international readers of this book, operating beyond UK shores.

International dimensions and protocols

With gun crime and terrorism much more visible, and a risk from mass casualty attacks using firearms methods generally on the increase, it is possible that previously quite relaxed domestic arms control regimes – such as those in Italy and France – do become tightened. It is mission critical, therefore, to stay abreast of related news items and possible impending legal changes in any country; radical alterations to law can often be enacted into local and national laws following big headline-grabbing atrocities. According to EU Home Affairs Commissioner, Cecilia Malmström, during 2011, more than 5,000 murders within the EU (about 20%) were committed using firearms (68). France is just one major EU state that is under pressure to further tighten gun ownership rules, following a series of massacres and attempted mass casualty gun killings in urban environments. Recent atrocities include the Lille Theatre and Bertry Nightclub shootings (2012), Mohamed Merah's Jewish school shooting rampage in Toulouse (2012), and the execution of workers by terrorists at the Paris-based satirical magazine, Charlie Hebdo, in January 2015.

Although, at the time of writing, it remains principally within the power of national governmental authorities to set the legal criteria for acquiring and selling firearms, the EU has established two Directives to address the inconsistent level of national controls. This is a big challenge given the EU's fundamental reason-for-being: to guarantee an 'internal market' based upon a core 'freedom of movement' principle (69). According to EU law expert, Theresa Papademetriou, Directive 2008/51/EC "requires EU Members to ensure that any firearm or part thereof is marked and registered prior to entering the market". It also requires EU members "to establish a register of firearms, to which only designated authorities will have access. Dealers are also required to maintain a register of firearms" (70).

A second Directive (91/477/EEC) deals "with the transfers of firearms for civilian use within the EU territory" (71). It transposes into European law, some clear and unequivocal provisions set out by governments to counter intractable and very harmful small arms proliferation, articulated within the 2001 *UN Protocol Against the Illicit Manufacturing of and Trafficking in Firearms*. More than 50 countries are now signatories to this UN Protocol and have enshrined, either partially or fully, its provisions into domestic law (72).

To be clear then, civilian-sector-use firearms and ammunition, or their parts and components thereof (including dual-use parts), do *not* enjoy the privileges of free movement under either EU provisions. Domestic laws within member states, such as the UK's own Export Control Act (2002), which governs the international transfer of UK-based weapons, do also usually provide for very clear rules. They also empower prosecutors by equipping them with severe legal sanctions for offenders. These include jail terms and/or extensive fines and reputational damage for those convicted. Those accused of illegal arms trafficking are likely to also be extradited to overseas jurisdictions. Ignorance as to the intended end-use of such equipment is not tolerated by any legal domain, as evidenced in the case of British businessman, Christopher Tappin. Mr Tappin's company reportedly sold zinc/silver oxide reserve batteries to Iran; allegedly for use in an air-defence missile system, according to US prosecutors. The directors were extradited to the US and jailed in 2012 (73). In conclusion, declarations at borders, and to all necessary public authorities, remain an order of the day. As does the conduct of rigorous due diligence checks around all paperwork, and monitoring the end-use of any exported firearms equipment. For the security management team who find themselves legally responsible for picking up the pieces of any shoddy background work, anything less could be more hazardous than the equipment itself (74).

Wrap-up lessons

- *Know the law:* A thorough understanding and education in firearms-related legislation, including rules around carrying, national and international human rights laws, and arms export licensing, should be provided by employers to everyone expected to hold arms – not just the team leader.

- *Cost benefit analysis of carrying:* Cases involving security personnel and the discharge of firearms are matters of heightened public interest in any domain. As such, cases are of acute interest to media organisations. Security contractors caught up in such controversies seldom feel that cases are covered in a fair and balanced manner. Nevertheless, becoming convicted of firearms breaches, or merely facing allegations, could be ruinous to your reputation and imperil your future viability as a security contractor. Therefore, think very carefully before you decide to carry or ask others to do so.

- *Life on hold:* Do expect prosecutors and official authorities to take many years, possibly decades, in order to carry out investigations and inquiries related to firearms incidents.

- *Respect human rights – lead by example:* Profoundly understand and ensure respect for individual human rights at all times, both for self, and in your conduct with other colleagues.

6.7 Managing people in protective security environments

"When we are recruiting, we are looking for a sense of self-discipline ... "
– Jon Hill, Close Protection Operative trainer and manager (75)

Protective security environments are often highly kinetic, involve close team work, and tend to bring together individuals who may well share similar action-oriented attributes. Notwithstanding, the same hum drum human resource-related issues extant in other industry sectors do also crop up within security management realms. Such as, how to carry out a fair recruitment process? How to resolve conflicts and rivalries? How to break down silos? Alternatively, in some environments, organisations might need to constrict the flow of information and communication; how can this be carried out fairly and lawfully?

Within protective security domains, it is essential for all team members to possess very decent interpersonal communications, including conflict management skills. Particularly so, for team leaders. After all, a mistake in approach or timing can lead to tragic consequences in protective security scenarios. For instance, over-caution could delay an essential evacuation. Conversely, an over-reaction, perhaps by a PES team intervening in too robust a manner, could cause significant personal harm to an innocent victim who was merely caught up in the wrong place at the wrong time. Maybe a jogger or smartphone-obsessed teenager, who accidentally passed within close proximity to a heavily guarded principal, might be straying into danger if they crossed the path of an over-exuberant CPO.

In precincts where firearms ownership is liberal and private security guards may be armed, conflict resolution skills using non-violent means does become even more crucial for the health and well-being of all those around. "When we are recruiting, we are looking for a sense of self-discipline, innate balance, and also a clear indication of potential ability for our agent to instinctively take control in a deteriorating situation", asserts Jon Hill (76).

Resolving conflict situations

Although timescales on many protective security projects may be shorter-term, and perceivably more intense than many other work cultures, looking out for personal and organisational psychological well-being issues is just as important to the security enterprise as the actual service delivery function.

The excuse that 'we didn't have time' to sort out a row between A and B will ring hollow if, a couple of weeks later, a communications gap between those very same two sulkers leads to loss of high-value assets or human life. (See the later *Charge of the Light Brigade* case study.) The University of California, who specialise in HR management, via their HR management company, *Berkeley HR*, publish advice around resolving conflict situations. "To manage conflict effectively you must be a skilled communicator", states Berkeley, which has published useful guidance on all related matters (77).

- Don't brush problems and disputes under the carpet – acknowledge that they exist and acquaint yourself with the problem
- Let individuals express their feelings – emotions, including hurt and anger, should be expressed and acknowledged
- Define the problem – meet with each party separately, understand personalities, and get to the root of the problem
- Determine underlying need – don't decide who is right or wrong, "the goal is to arrive at a solution that everyone can live with" (78)
- Identify mutual areas of agreement – agree on the problem/s; agree on procedures to pursue; "agree on some small change to give an experience of success" (79)

Source: Berkeley HR, University of California, 2014

Figure 24: Top tips on conflict management from Berkeley HR include

Avoiding an issue or clash of personalities, which can turn into a living sore within the team and spawn a conflict in the first instance, is a modus operandi that serves healthily functioning protective security teams well (80). Harvard professor, Robert Fisher, a lawyer by profession, who then became a globally respected negotiator and political advisor, found modest fame through one of his final books, *Getting to Yes*, co-authored with Bill Ury (81). Fisher and Ury emphasised four core approaches to avoiding misunderstanding. These are:

1) Active listening: Understand the other person/side as well as you understand yourself. Keep close attention to what they are saying. If necessary repeat back what you think they have said, this shows you are seeking to understand them (though, not necessarily agreeing with them).

2) If possible, speak directly to the other person. Avoid being diverted and distracted by others.

3) Use 'I' statements, rather than 'You' statements, to speak about situations. For example, 'I felt exposed and isolated on that street the other night', rather than 'you left me like a sitting duck near that slum gang the other night'. (There may have been a very good reason why they didn't appear to help you at that given time.) 'You' messages are automatically accusative and will prompt defensiveness, and possibly a deterioration in dialogue.

4) Speak for a purpose: too much communication can appear like a rant, excessive self-interest, a demonstration of poor focus or prolonged defensiveness. The

line from Shakespeare's play Hamlet (1602): "The lady doth protest too much, methinks ..." rings true several centuries later (82).

Case study: Miscommunication of the highest order:
The Charge of the Light Brigade

In 1853, Russia invaded the Balkans. Soon after, following hyperbolic media coverage, Britain and France deployed forces into The Crimea in order to protect Turkey, with whom they held Treaty obligations. There were strong fears about access to important surrounding sea-routes. After a series of skirmishes with Russia, the British Army and her Allies were generally thought to have gained the upper hand during the Battle of Balaclava in 1854. That was until the ill-fated order for the Charge of the Light Brigade, commanded by the 7th Earl of Cardigan, straight into a phalanx of Russian artillery in Autumn 1854. Out of 674 soldiers who loyally followed seemingly inexplicable orders to attack Russian gun positions, 247 perished or were wounded (83).

Cardigan was euphorically welcomed back into Britain as a war hero by crowds of enthusiasts and awarded an audience with Prime Minister, Benjamin Disraeli, and Queen Victoria. But doubts soon began to surface in relation to the kamikaze nature of the Light Brigade's operation. Moreover, suspicion also grew around the truth of Cardigan's self-aggrandising claims. Harsh accounts from returning ground troops, and critical reflections from fellow senior officers, opposition Russian officers and war correspondents (William Russell and George Ryan), finally amalgamated into a new, rather inconvenient truth: The Charge of the Light Brigade had been one of Britain's largest military leadership disasters of all time.

How could this have happened?

The interesting fusion of personal feuds, rivalries and deficient decision making, all prevalent in this military debacle, have caused gallons of ink and thousands of printer cartridges to be spent ever since. Military and business coaches alike have tried to make sense of these traumatic events that occurred in a location dubbed the 'valley of death' by poet, Alfred Lord Tennyson.

The Earl of Raglan was appointed overall commander of British armed forces, principally because he had served as military secretary to the Duke of Wellington. Wellington was widely held to be a pre-eminent strategic military genius since his pivotal leadership at Waterloo in 1815. Although Raglan was a decent political operator in British circles, he had no practical experience of military leadership in the field. Four decades later, it was hoped that some of Wellington's strategic military genius might have rubbed off on his successor.

The Cavalry Brigade at Balaclava was made up of a Light and Heavy Brigade, commanded overall by Lord Lucan. Earl Cardigan, who was in charge of the Light Brigade, was subordinate to Lord Lucan. However, by a twist of coincidence, both men were brothers-in-law to one another. Cardigan believed that Lord Lucan mistreated his sister. He

---

therefore barely spoke with Lucan. Instead, he preferred to liaise directly, and wherever possible, with the conciliatory personality of the overall British commander, Lord Raglan.

Fully aware of bad blood between his commanders, yet keen to keep the peace, Raglan implored both men to bury their differences and work together. Neither showed any prospect of being able to do so. On 25 October 1854, large numbers of Russian units began to threaten British supply lines down in the valley. On a hilltop alongside his staff officers, Raglan's team looked down onto a ridge and spotted some Russian soldiers who began to remove British artillery guns from the scene. Believing that this incident disgraced the British Army's good name, Raglan sent four orders via messengers downhill in quick succession to Lucan, stipulating that the Cavalry Brigades should stop the guns being taken away from the ridge and therefore attack the Russian positions. Raglan failed to appreciate the physical ground-view that Lucan and Cardigan, and also their troops, were experiencing.

From lower down, in the valley, the order's final recipient, Lucan, could only see another Russian gunnery position. Confused, but not pressing the messenger for certain clarifications, Lucan passed the messages down to Cardigan, the Light Brigade commander in the valley. From his position, his team could not see the guns upon a ridge being removed by Russians. They just saw the Russian artillery guns pointing at them. They assumed, incorrectly, that the somewhat suicidal order, related to the visible gunnery positions inside the valley. Lucan was also reportedly irked that he had been criticised by Raglan's team for being too cautious in the past (84).

Perhaps too proud to ask his hated brother-in-law for clarification, and aware that he may look like a coward, Cardigan failed to vent his fears and ask for clarification. He prepared his men to attack a line of Russian guns, that, ultimately Lord Raglan could not see from the hills.

The messenger from Raglan to Lucan who carried the fourth order was one Captain Louis Nolan, staff officer to Lord Raglan. Nolan was a precocious young cavalry officer who had developed deep-seated frustration in Balaclava towards the conduct of aristocratic British commanding officers in Crimea. Safely on the hilltop working alongside his boss, and also guilty of not seeing any direct threat from Russian gunners upon the Light Brigade, Nolan galloped down to the ridge and curtly gave Raglan's order to Lucan: attack the guns. When asked for clarification by Lucan, Nolan was reported to have brusquely waved his arms in the general direction of the Russians and said: "There are your enemy. There are your guns, my Lord" (85).

Lucan did not demur this time. He relayed the fourth and final order onto his brother-in-law, Cardigan. This time Cardigan did reply that, "I shall never be able to bring a man back", before launching his regiments forward directly towards Russian gun positions without any further delay.

Private Thomas Dudley of the 17th Lancers wrote in his account of the scene: "When we received the order, not a man could seem to believe it ... Not a word or a whisper. On – on we went! Oh! If you could have seen the faces of that doomed 800 men at that moment; every man's features fixed, his teeth clenched, and as rigid as death, still it was on – on!" Another described the attack as a "perfect madness". Captain William Morgan, also of the

17th Lancers, wrote to his father the charge had been "gallant, brilliant (but, as all add, useless)". He said the order arrived "as we must believe, by mistake" (86).

The main protagonists in this error-strewn operation, Raglan, Cardigan and the 3rd Earl of Lucan, all survived the infamous Charge. Lucan was subsequently promoted to Lieutenant General and then Field Marshal. Cardigan's war hero status became slightly dented, although Queen Victoria made him a Knight in the Order of Bath. He spoke irregularly on politics from his House of Lords seat.

All expressed concern at the poor communication of Raglan's orders by his staff officer, Captain Nolan. But Nolan did not survive to defend his reputation falling with his comrades that very same afternoon.

Sources: London Daily Telegraph and BritishBattles.com

Resolving communication gaps

A fun way to underline the difficulty of team and organisational communications is to conduct a version of the telephone game. Organise for a team member to receive a simple set of instructions via the telephone. Then, without writing them down, convey these instructions to the next colleague, and so on, along a chain of individuals. The end-result is often very much at odds with those original orders.

Book author and communications expert, Naomi Karten, writes: "A common misconception is that communication gaps are caused by too little communication. Some are, certainly. Often, however, the problem is the reverse: too much communication. Often, too, the problem isn't simply the quantity of communication but the kind: Gaps are frequently caused by misdirected, one-way, poorly timed, or badly worded, communications" (87). In a world of rapid, and possibly much more public communications, poor written communications can wreak a lot of damage upon workplace relationships and the overall process of team and organisational communications. Brianna Davis, an author for the popular *Lee Hopkins* communications sector blog, describes a sensible remedy: "Taking a minute to review your work can save you tons of apologising time later" (88). Nevertheless, this is easier said than done. A layer of peer reviews upon important communications is advised.

Failure to review: don't let spellchecker and autocorrect do all the work, computers still aren't quite up to the task of editing messages and memos the way that people are.

Too many words: The sheer volume of communication hitting us means that time can't be spent … reading anything that is too long. … If you just need an approval on a request, send the simple request.

Appropriate-ness – You may be really mad about a setback, but the words you use to express your anger can be remembered long after the setback is corrected. Act, react, and speak appropriately, or forever be remembered as 'that guy who goes crazy'.

Failure to praise – If someone is doing something right, let them know. This can boost the self-esteem and productivity of whoever is hearing it, and also ensure that the thing you like is done the way you like it, time after time.

Criticism –If someone is doing something incorrectly, it is important to [carefully] highlight it as soon as possible to ensure it is done correctly in future.

Say what you mean, mean what you say – Being taken at your word is still [very] important. The only difference is that instead of a handshake, there are now emails and much more to prove what you said.

Being closed off – Having others fear communicating with you – or that communication with you is a pointless process – can hinder you far more than help you.

Source: This is an abridged version of Brianna Davis's 'Top Ten Business Communications Mistakes' (89)

**Figure 25: Brianna Davis's top tips to avoid
communications mistakes**

Using or avoiding certain types of body language is also critical in avoiding or defusing conflict. Body language expert, James Borg, states that: "More communication is conveyed through the eyes than any other part of the body" (90). Borg points out that the lowering of eyes might be perceived as untrustworthiness or submissiveness. Conversely, over-zealous eye contact may appear aggressive or even convey sexual attraction. Unfocused and flitting eye contact – particularly repeated glances over the shoulder, to the wrists (where a watch may be), or towards a phone – explicitly suggests a lack of focus and attention to the person and conversation in motion. This is not a good message to convey if one is trying to engage, motivate, or even pacify an aggressive or hostile person.

The seminal work of Dale Carnegie, *How To Win Friends And Influence People*, is literally an encyclopaedia of business protocols. The book has an enduring and pervasive relevance to most, if not all, business activity. One passage will serve entrepreneurs and business managers very well indeed:

Why talk about what we want. That is childish. Absurd. Of course, you are interested in what you want. You are eternally interested in it. But no one else is. The rest of us are just like you: we are interested in what we want.

So the only way on earth to influence other people is to talk about what they want and show them how to get it. (91)

Chapter 6: Wrap-up

In closing this chapter on **Protective Security**, we reflect on some of the approaches and attributes that will help your company gain the competitive edge. These include:

1. Lives and livelihoods depend on protective security contractors. Such severe operational stresses demand that protective security specialists do retain continued situational awareness, adhere to peak levels of self-discipline, and are able to consider, or anticipate, an almost-immeasurable range of risks facing the Principal.

2. It does tend to be the more mundane business approaches, including decent research, presentational and networking skills that provide protective security agents with the competitive edge, as we witnessed from various interviews conducted in this chapter.

3. Ex British Royal Family protection officer, now a private sector CP contractor, Paul Brown, added: "Protecting individuals and groups can become very complex as they often do not behave predictably or even rationally. But the best protective security agents anticipate and map out both risks and responses well before an operation. Otherwise they will become awfully exposed in front of the client".

4. In corporate domains of protective security management, softer skills, such as deportment, style and attitude become equally, or more important than certifications in firearms and jiu jitsu. The acquisition of potential agents with so-called *soft skills* has been a priority for many protective security recruiters and training companies in Europe and the US for several years.

5. Know the law when it comes to everything security-related, but even more so with the use of force and firearms. A thorough understanding and education in firearms-related legislation, including rules around carrying, national and international human rights laws, and arms export licensing, should be provided by business owners to *everyone* expected to hold (or come in to contact with) firearms – not just the team leader.

6. Talk about what your customer wants, not about what you want, says management guru, Dale Carnegie.

References

(1) Schoultz, B. and Richardson, M., (2013), Risk Management Online, 'Managing Risk like a Navy Seal', accessed and downloaded on 02/12/2014 at: *www.rmmagazine.com/2013/08/27/managing-risk-like-a-navy-seal/*

(2)   Interview with an UK-based Close Protection Operative, carried out in London on 27/11/2014.

(3)   Institute for Economics & Peace (2014), 'Global Terrorism Index 2014', accessed and downloaded on 26/11/2014 at: *http://economicsandpeace.org/research/iep-indices-data/global-terrorism-index*

(4)   Author interview with Paul Brown conducted on 11/11/2014

(5)   Information accessed and downloaded on 25/11/2014 at: *www.militaryphotos.net/forums/showthread.php?238405-China-paramilitary-police-use-PT709-pistol&p=7200050#post7200050*

(6)   Close Protection website (2011), information accessed and downloaded on 25/11/2014 at: *www.close-protection.org/Resources.html*

(7)   The Telegraph (2010), 'Met Police spends more than £350,000 a day on VIP protection', accessed and downloaded on 27/11/2014 at: *www.telegraph.co.uk/news/uknews/law-and-order/7986977/Met-police-spends-more-than-350000-a-day-on-VIP-protection.html*

(8)   Nobes, F., (2011) 'Licensed To Be Killed: The hidden cost of war'. INSS Dynamic Dialogue. [online], p.8. Accessed and downloaded on 27/11/2014 at: *http://inssblog.wordpress.com/2011/07/05/licensed-to-be-killed-the-hidden-cost-of-war/*

(9)   Transparency International (2013), Corrupt Perceptions Index 2013, accessed and downloaded at: *www.transparency.org/cpi2013/results*

(10)   Author interview with Jon Hill, Managing Director at Operations Group, London, conducted on 11/11/2014

(11)   Fay, J., (2006), 'Contemporary Security Management', – Second Edition, Oxford: Elsevier

(12)   Health and Safety Executive (2014), 'Five Steps to Risk Assessment', and 'A Brief Guide to Controlling Risks in the Workplace', accessed and downloaded on 01/12/2014 at: *www.hse.gov.uk/risk/controlling-risks.htm*

(13)   The Scottish Government website (2014), 'Planning and Priority Setting', accessed and downloaded on 01/12/2014 at: *www.scotland.gov.uk/publications/2005/09/27134643/46478*

(14)   Advanced Diving Systems website (2014), Risk Assessment, accessed and downloaded on 01/12/2014 at: *www.advanceddivingsystems.com/RiskAssessment.aspx*

(15)   Pearce, A., and Flavell, D., (2013), Risk Management Magazine Australia online, 'Risk culture, all talk and no action?' Accessed and downloaded on 01/12/2014 at: *www.riskmanagementmagazine.com.au/opinion/risk-culture-all-talk-and-no-action-126516.aspx*

(16)   Pearce, A., and Flavell, D., (2013), Ibid.

(17)   Bow Tie Pro website, 'Frequently Asked Questions', accessed and downloaded on 02/12/2014 at: *www.bowtiepro.com/btp_faq_Simple.asp*

(18) Ibid.
(19) Brant, S., (2013), 'Risk Management Assessment Model', accessed and downloaded from Bucks New University Certificate in Security Management Journal (13/11/2013)
(20) Interviews with Jon Hill and Paul Brown, Close Protection trainers, conducted on 11/11/2014. BS 8507-1-2008 can be accessed at:
(21) Ibid.
(22) Ibid.
(23) Op. Cit., Schoultz, B. and Richardson, M., (2013).
(24) Mullins L.J (2007), 'Management and Organisational Behaviour' – Eighth Edition, Harlow: Pearson
(25) Security Industry Authority website (2014), Close Protection Training, accessed and downloaded on 08/12/2014 at: *www.sia.homeoffice.gov.uk/pages/training-cp.aspx*
(26) Padgham., G., (2006), 'Close Protection – the softer skills', Cambridge: Entertainment Technology Press Ltd.
(27) Close Protection.org website (2014), accessed and downloaded on: 08/12/2014 at: *www.close-protection.org/Resources.html*
(28) Drucker, P., (1974), 'Management: Tasks, Responsibilities, Practices'. New York: Harper and Row.
(29) Froch., C., Accessed and downloaded on 08/12/2014 at: *www.mightyfighter.com/carl-froch-quotes/*
(30) AdvantFort press release (11/07/2014), 'Charges Against MV Seaman Guard Ohio Crew & Guards Quashed by Indian HC', accessed and downloaded on 10/12/2014 at: *www.advanfort.com/Charges-against-MV-Seaman-Guard-Ohio-Crew-Guards-Quashed-by-Indian-HC.pdf*
(31) CNN (20/02/2014), Police ID 2 Americans Found Dead on Maersk Alabama – 'Captain Phillips Ship', accessed and downloaded at: *http://edition.cnn.com/2014/02/19/world/asia/seychelles-maersk-deaths/*
(32) New York Times (25/02/2014), 'Hired to Fight Pirates, but Doomed by Boredom', accessed and downloaded on 14/12/2014 at: *www.nytimes.com/2014/02/26/world/africa/hired-to-fight-pirates-but-doomed-by-boredom.html?_r=0*
(33) IMB (1 Jan. to 30 June 2012), 'Piracy and Armed Robbery Against Ships', London: ICC International Maritime Bureau, and also, IMB (2013), 'Piracy and Armed Robbery Against Ships, London: ICC International Maritime Bureau'
(34) Security in Complex Environments Group (SCEG), accessed and downloaded on 09/12/2014 at: *www.adsgroup.org.uk/pages/24204653.asp*

(35) International Code of Conduct for Private Security Providers website, accessed and downloaded on 10/12/2014 at: *www.icoc-psp.org/About_ICoC.html*

(36) Guiding Principles on Business and Human Rights (2011), 'Implementing the United Nations 'Protect', 'Respect' and 'Remedy' Framework', Geneva: United Nations Office of the High Commissioner, accessed and downloaded on 09/12/2014 at: *www.ohchr.org/documents/publications/GuidingprinciplesBusinesshr_en.pdf*

(37) Security Industry for the Maritime Industry (SAMI) website, and 'The Bridge' Digital Magazine was accessed and downloaded on 09/12/2014 at: *www.seasecurity.org/*

(38) The Hundred Series Rules: An International Model Set of Maritime Rules for the Use of Force (RUF) (2013), was accessed and downloaded on 09/12/2014 at: *https://100seriesrules.com/uploads/20130503-100_Series_Rules_for_the_Use_of_Force.pdf*

(39) SOLAS Regulations, accessed and downloaded on 09/12/2014 at: *https://mcanet.mcga.gov.uk/public/c4/solas/solas_v/Regulations/regulation34_1.htm*

(40) Written interview conducted with Jason Layton, Maritime Security Specialist, conducted on 09/12/2014

(41) International Maritime Organisation (IMO) website, 'Maritime Safety', accessed and downloaded on 10/12/2014 at: *www.imo.org/OurWork/Safety/Pages/Default.aspx*

(42) International Maritime Organisation (IMO) website, 'Maritime Security and Piracy', accessed and downloaded on 10/12/2014 at: *www.imo.org/OurWork/Security/Pages/MaritimeSecurity.aspx*

(43) Ibid.

(44) Her Majesty's Government (2014), Code of safe working practices for merchant seamen, accessed and downloaded on 15/12/2014 at: *www.gov.uk/government/publications/code-of-safe-working-practices-for-merchant-seamen-coswp*

(45) BIMCO website, security section, was accessed and downloaded on 10/12/2014 at: *www.bimco.org/Security.aspx*

(46) International Maritime Bureau (IMB), ICC Commercial Crime Services website, accessed and downloaded on 10/12/2014 at: *www.icc-ccs.org/piracy-reporting-centre*

(47) IMB Piracy and Armed Robbery Map 2014, was accessed and downloaded on 10/12/2014 at: *www.icc-ccs.org/piracy-reporting-centre/live-piracy-map*

(48) Maritime Security Centre Horn of Africa (2011), Best Management Practices for Protection Against Somalia Based Piracy (Version 4), accessed

and downloaded on 10/12/2014 at: *www.mschoa.org/docs/public-documents/bmp4-low-res_sept_5_2011.pdf?sfvrsn=0*

(49) U.S. Coastguard Office (2012), 'Guidelines for U.S. Vessels in High Risk Waters', accessed and downloaded on 10/10/2014 at: *www.maritimedelriv.com/Port_Security/USCG/USCG_Files/FR_Guidelines_US_Vessels_High_Risk_Waters.pdf*

(50) NBC Washington (20/10/2014), 'Woman Accidentally Shot by Security Guard During Scuffle at McDonald's', accessed and downloaded on 06/01/2015 at: *www.nbcwashington.com/news/local/Woman-Accidentally-Shot-by-Security-Guard-during-Scuffle-279702422.html*

(51) Hudson, G., (2014), 'Celebratory gunfire and its impact in Kabul, Afghanistan', Buckinghamshire New University Department of Security and Resilience (Restricted)

(52) Centers for Disease Control and Prevention (24/12/2004), New Year's Eve Injuries Caused by Celebratory Gunfire, accessed and downloaded on 12/02/2014 at: *www.cdc.gov/mmwr/preview/mmwrhtml/mm5350a2.htm*

(53) BBC News Africa (12/09/2014), 'Oscar Pistorius found guilty of culpable homicide', accessed and downloaded on 09/01/2015 at: *www.bbc.co.uk/news/world-africa-29149581*

(54) The Telegraph (27/07/2003), 'Tony Martin is "going to get it", warns cousin of the boy he shot, accessed and downloaded on 09/01/2015 at: *www.telegraph.co.uk/news/uknews/1437256/Tony-Martin-is-going-to-get-it-warns-cousin-of-the-boy-he-shot.html*

(55) New York Times (22/10/2014), Blackwater Guards Found Guilty in 2007 Iraq Killings, accessed and downloaded on 12/01/2015 at: *www.nytimes.com/2014/10/23/us/blackwater-verdict.html?_r=1*

(56) USA Today (17/10/2007), US Rejects UN Report, accessed and downloaded on 12/01/2015 at: *http://usatoday30.usatoday.com/news/world/2007-10-17-3392316246_x.htm*

(57) Ibid.

(58) CBS News (18/10/2013), 'India Arrests 35 from U.S. Security Firm Advan Fort's well-armed anti-piracy mother ship', accessed and downloaded on 12/01/2015 at: *www.cbsnews.com/news/india-arrests-35-from-us-security-firm-advanforts-well-armed-anti-piracy-mother-ship/*

(59) The Telegraph (26/01/12), 'Simon Mann appeals against Zimbabwe gun conviction over Equatorial Guinea plot', accessed and downloaded on 12/01/2015 at: *www.telegraph.co.uk/news/worldnews/africaandindianocean/equatorialguinea/9042303/Simon-Mann-appeals-against-Zimbabwe-gun-conviction-over-Equatorial-Guinea-plot.html*

(60) National Policing Improvement Agency, ACPO & ACPOS (2011), Manual of Guidance on The Management, Command and Deployment of Armed

Officers (Third Edition), accessed and downloaded on 09/01/2015 at: *www.acpo.police.uk/documents/uniformed/2011/201111MCDofAO3.pdf*

(61) Ibid. pp.16-17

(62) Ibid.

(63) Her Majesty's Government website, accessed and downloaded on 12/01/2015 at: *www.legislation.gov.uk/ukpga/1967/58*

(64) NPIA/ACPO Op. Cit., p.14

(65) Crown Prosecution Service Online, 'Self-Defence and the Prevention of Crime', accessed and downloaded on 12/01/2015 at: *www.cps.gov.uk/legal/ s_to_u/self_defence/#Reasonable_Force*

(66) Home Office (October 2014), 'Guide on Firearms Licensing Law', accessed and downloaded on 08/01/2015 at: *www.gov.uk/firearms-licensing-police-guidance*

(67) Ibid. P.103

(68) Malmstrom., C., EU Commissioner for Home Affairs, Speech at the Conference on the Fight Against Arms Trafficking: Where Do We Stand? at 2 (Nov. 19, 2012), *http://europa.eu/rapid/press-release_SPEECH-12-841_en.htm*

(69) Her Majesty's Government Report (2014), 'Review of the Balance of Competences between the United Kingdom and the European Union: Single Market: Free Movement of Goods', London: Crown Copyright, accessed and downloaded on 13/01/2015 at: *www.gov.uk/ government/uploads/system/uploads/attachment_data/file/288194/2901479_ BoC_SingleMarket_acc5.pdf*

(70) Papademetriou., T., (2013), Firearms Control Legislation and Policy: European Union, Washington D.C.: Library of Congress: accessed and downloaded on 13/01/2015 at: *www.loc.gov/law/help/firearms-control/eu.php*

(71) Ibid

(72) United Nations website, accessed and downloaded on 13/01/2015 at: *https://treaties.un.org/pages/viewdetails.aspx?src=ind&mtdsg_no=xviii-12-c&chapter=18&lang=en*

(73) The Guardian (01/11/2012), 'Christopher Tappin pleads guilty to selling batteries for Iranian missiles', accessed and downloaded on 13/01/2015 at: *www.theguardian.com/law/2012/nov/01/christopher-tappin-pleads-guilty-extradited*

(74) Her Majesty's Government website, Export Control Act, briefing and full text accessed and downloaded on 13/01/2015 at: *www.gov.uk/export-control-act-2002*

(75) Author interview with Jon Hill, Managing Director at Operations Group, London, conducted on 11/11/2014

(76) Ibid.
(77) Berkeley HR (2014), Resolving Conflict Situations, accessed and downloaded on 06/01/2015 at: *http://hrweb.berkeley.edu/guides/managing-hr/interaction/conflict/resolving*
(78) Ibid.
(79) Ibid.
(80) Burgess, H., (2013), Beyond Intractability: Misunderstandings, accessed and downloaded on 05/01/2015 at: *www.beyondintractability.org/essay/misunderstandings*
(81) Fisher, R., Ury, B., (1981). Getting To Yes: Negotiating Agreement Without Giving In. Boston: Houghton Mifflin.
(82) Ibid.
(83) British Battles.com, Crimean War/Balaclava, accessed and downloaded on 19/03/2015 at: *www.britishbattles.com/crimean-war/balaclava.htm*
(84) Ibid.
(85) Ibid.
(86) Copping, J., (20/04/2014), The Daily Telegraph: New accounts emerge of Charge of Light Brigade, accessed and downloaded on 06/01/2015 at: *www.telegraph.co.uk/history/10776275/New-accounts-emerge-of-Charge-of-the-Light-Brigade.html*
(87) Karten, N., (2013) 'Mind the Gap: Communication Gaps and How to Close Them', accessed and downloaded on 05/01/2015 at: *www.informit.com/articles/article.aspx?p=2122831*
(88) Davis, B., (2014) 'Top Ten Communications Mistakes – A Guide for Gen Y', accessed and downloaded on 05/01/2015 at: *www.leehopkins.net/2011/11/14/top-ten-business-communication-mistakesa-guide-for-gen-y/*
(89) Ibid.
(90) Borg, J. (2008), 'Body Language', p.28, Harlow: Pearson
(91) Carnegie, D., (1936), 'How To Win Friends And Influence People', p.37, Chancellor Press, ISBN 1 85152 576 9

CHAPTER 7: SAFE BUSINESS TRAVEL

7.1 Context

"To travel is to discover that everyone is wrong about other countries." –
Aldous Huxley, English writer and philosopher.

The world is a strange place. Millions of CCTV cameras scan and record much of our movement. PIN numbers and ATM cash machines track each and every money transaction; sometimes in order to prohibit fraudulent access of our bank accounts. Digital media devices report many of our movements, record our photos to an iCloud, and publish our GPS position to whomever, or whatever, wishes to know. We can use mobile phones on civilian aircraft. We can take our pets around the world as our travel companions and they are entitled to their own biometric passport. We can check out possible holiday locations using satellite imagery. Parish councils use Google Earth nowadays to check that planning applications by residents to alter their homes were submitted accurately, or that garden trees were not unlawfully felled in a family's private garden to create the space for a building extension. When we travel, visas are often requested that demand a whole range of personal contact details, to be processed by in-country consular services and embassies.

How is it then that so many business travellers continue to suffer difficulties when they travel overseas?

Although growth of digital media and VOIP platforms, such as Skype and Jitsi (formerly SIP Communicator), have provided far greater and cheaper facilities for telephone conferencing, business travel volume does appear to have significantly increased since the millennium. The World Travel and Tourism Council report that business-related travel does yield a return on investment worth ten times the initial investment (1). One hotel sector online news blog stated that the business travel sector was worth around $1.2tn and had expanded during the latest global recession (2). As most world markets become more accessible, and traditional markets decline, the opportunity to identify and develop investment strategies within emerging markets (that may have more volatile security situations) has driven a surge of corporate protective security work. Those security management companies that have the foresight and local knowledge to exploit the fundamental global economic changes that we visited in Chapter 1, will surely lever themselves into a position of competitive advantage over those companies that sit tight in traditional markets waiting for the phone to ring.

One growth area for protective security practitioners is around the provision of security and safety-related services for net-high-worth business travellers to medium or higher security risk environments. Such jobs are, sometimes, more akin to executive chaperoning: being the eyes and ears on the ground. Typical environments might once have been fraught with dangers, so much so that they may have dissuaded potential investors. But now they have picked themselves up, offering more opportunities than threats. Nevertheless, there will still remain a strong reason to carry out detailed planning before travel is undertaken. This should include the conduct of a risk assessment beforehand, to establish whether protective security personnel should accompany the individual or group. Some common errors crop up time and again in news reports and case studies of business travel itineraries which ended in a horror story. This chapter is therefore designed to outline basic support and planning techniques available to those tasked with securing the safe and enjoyable passage of colleagues to either overseas or home country domains which can pose risks to travellers from a plethora of security, legal or culturally-related causes.

7.2 Government help and basics

Passports

Keep your passport valid for at least six months well in advance of your travel. Those applying for a passport for the first time need to leave at least six weeks, for enhanced security checks and possible face-to-face interviews.

You can renew your passport at any time before it runs out, and the UK Identity and Passport Service (IPS) will carry over up to a maximum of nine months validity from your existing passport. Allow up to three weeks for posted standard renewals. Businesses sometimes pay for a fast-track service (up to one week, including appointment; current cost: £112.50) or for a one-day premium service including an appointment (current cost: £129.50) in an emergency.

Make sure your next of kin is up to date and clearly articulated on your passport.

Make a note of your passport number, date, place of issue and nominated next of kin. Keep these records separately and/or take a photocopy.

If you lose your passport on location, please report it to the local police immediately, followed by the local British Consulate (3).

Money

Before you leave, make a note of bank card details, or take photocopies, and leave them at home. Check that your bank and credit cards are well within their dates of validity.

Always try to keep a few banknotes and coins easily accessible in your pocket, rather than visibly rummaging through areas on your person where you may store valuables.

In the developing world, US dollars to hand are almost always useful, particularly in emergencies.

European Health Insurance Card (EHIC)

If you are going on a business trip, you should apply for the EHIC card (a replacement of the old E111) which entitles you, a spouse and siblings, if you register them also, for reduced cost or free medical care within the European Union and Switzerland. This should not prevent you from taking out sensible business travel insurance.

The online application for EHIC takes just under five minutes but the coverage lasts for five years. The EHIC card must be presented before, or shortly after, medical treatment for full entitlement to be recognised.

Register with EHIC, keep your card with you, but take a photocopy and leave with friends/family.

According to the UK National Health Service, the following healthcare is covered:

- It will cover any medical treatment that becomes necessary during your stay because of either illness or an accident.
- The card gives access to reduced cost or free medical treatment from state healthcare providers.
- It allows you to be treated on the same basis as a resident of the country you are visiting. Therefore, you may also have to pay a patient contribution, also known as a co-payment. For UK citizens, you may be able to seek reimbursement for this when you are back in the UK, if you are not able to do so in the other country.
- It includes treatment of a chronic or pre-existing medical condition that becomes necessary during your visit.
- It includes routine maternity care (not solely illness or accident), provided the reason for your visit is not specifically to give birth. However, it does cover the

cost of all medical treatment, for mother and baby, which is linked to the birth where that occurs unexpectedly.

- It includes the provision of oxygen, renal dialysis and routine medical care.

What won't the EHIC cover me for?

- The EHIC is not a substitute or replacement for private travel insurance. You should always take out an appropriate private policy in addition to carrying your EHIC.
- It will not cover the costs of private healthcare or services that are not part of the state healthcare system.
- It will not cover the costs of being brought back to the UK.
- It will not allow you to go abroad to specifically receive treatment, including going abroad to give birth.
- The card may not be used in some regions, as there may be no state provided healthcare available (4).

Foreign and Commonwealth Office alerts

The UK Foreign and Commonwealth Office (FCO) publish lots of advice online to link UK nationals to consular crisis services and regional information alerts in the event of a major incident overseas. A prior system known as 'LOCATE', whereby UK nationals registered their email and phone details, so that they could be located in a crisis, was dropped in 2013 after poor take-up (5). Nevertheless, travellers can register via the FCO website for regional and social media updates (6). Select the country or places that you are travelling to on the FCO website, click on 'Email Alerts' and enter your email address. A small but dedicated team within the FCO and the Trade and Investment Department (UKTI) have formed a joint enterprise to provide an overseas business risk service for UK-based business heading overseas. According to its increasingly informative website, this service aims to provide "British business with information relating to the security related risks which companies face when operating overseas" (7). Online guidance from this service includes briefings on: bribery and corruption; businesses operating in high-risk environments; protecting your intellectual property abroad; crime and fraud prevention; and emergency assistance measures provided to UK nationals caught up in terrorist attacks. This is particularly important because many UK travel insurance policies fail to cover terrorist incidents. Security practitioners are advised to double-check travel insurance provisions of themselves and clients well before any planned travel.

Overseas Security Advisory Council

The US State Department, Bureau of Diplomatic Security, runs OSAC, perhaps the most comprehensive and successful government-administered travel safety forum on the planet. OSAC was established by the 1985 Federal Advisory Committee Act to "promote security cooperation between American private sector interests worldwide and the US Department of State," which leads on federal government foreign relations (8). Various services include:

- Daily newsletter, covering geo-political issues, protests, evacuation 'warden' message alerts, security incidents and information security risks
- Daily afternoon digest that covers all of the above and constituency invites to chapter meetings
- Crime and safety reports covering all manner of countries and cities, and providing insightful briefings on street-crime and safety issues, terrorism, kidnappings and other serious, organised crime, natural hazards, industrial accidents, public transportation disruptions, driving conditions, *inter alia*

Although much OSAC information is from open sources, its written briefings are succinct and logically structured. It is therefore well worth taking the time to subscribe and attend in-country chapter meetings, should your company or organisation satisfy the registration criteria. However, it is well worth corroborating any governmental advice with online travel forums, such as *TripAdvisor,* which has a travel forum blog section for most conceivable travel locations that routinely discuss crime and safety concerns (9). Moreover, expat forums in-country, such as *InterNations* can provide crucial travel security information (10). Do bear in mind though, that any information you might post, is also likely to be scanned in some quarters by those who do not necessarily have the best interests of your personal security at heart!

Consular help

Government embassies or consulates are often deluged with hundreds or thousands of requests for assistance, so it is right only to make contact in emergency or potentially very serious circumstances. If travellers get into dire straits, consular services can often – although, not always – assist with the following:

- Replacement passports
- Provide information about transferring funds to you/family

- Provide details of local lawyers, interpreters, doctors, hospitals (do not guarantee quality)
- Attempt to contact you within 24 hours of being told you are detained
- Contact friends and family for you
- Offer support in a range of traumatic cases, such as abductions, deaths and missing people
- Make special arrangements in cases of terrorism, civil disturbances or natural disasters

Consulates cannot, and do not tend to, provide the following help:

- Get involved in private disputes over property, employment or other matters
- Get you out of prison, better conditions in prison, or prevent deportation
- Investigate crimes or give you legal advice
- Help you enter a country or interfere with another country's immigration procedures
- Get you better treatment in hospital or prison unless international standards are undermined
- Pay bills for you, or any money from the public purse
- Make travel arrangements for you, or find you accommodation
- Provide compensation if you are affected by a major catastrophe or terrorist attack (11)

Case study: FCO crisis response to Japan disaster 2011

The following case provides an insight into the volume and demand for resources upon governmental services in the aftermath of a major crisis or natural disaster. Security practitioners are therefore advised to plan, rehearse and allocate all necessary resources that will provide for the personal safety of all employees travelling. Security practitioners are also responsible for considering holistic planning issues around group security and wider organisational resilience, such as evacuations, back-up evacuation routes and other contingencies. The following case is an extract from the speech of a UK Foreign Minister to Parliament, following a devastating earthquake, tsunami and consequent meltdown of nuclear reactors at Fukushima Daiichi, in Japan, 2011:

In the immediate aftermath of the disaster we set up an emergency helpline for those concerned about British nationals in the affected areas. As of 27 March, we have received over 9,000 calls to our helpline and can confirm that some 970 people reported to our missing person's hotline have been confirmed safe. There are, to date, no confirmed British fatalities. We continue to work to locate British nationals whom we have been unable to contact. There are now a small number

---

about whom we remain very concerned. We are making every effort to track them down. It is important to stress that in these difficult circumstances, it is likely to take some time for the Japanese authorities formally to identify those who may have lost their lives or been injured and to notify next of kin.

Within 48 hours of the earthquake and tsunami, our Ambassador to Japan led the first British team deployed to Sendai, one of the main cities affected. In the following days, we deployed over 60 specialist consular staff drawn from across the FCO's global network to north east Japan to provide consular assistance and established a 24 hour consular response centre in Sendai. Our rapid deployment teams visited reception centres, hospitals and other locations to trace British nationals. They assisted more than 170 British nationals.

We reinforced our Embassy in Tokyo, which worked around the clock on the crisis response including the provision of consular assistance to those in need. We stationed staff at both of Tokyo's airports, provided consular help at our Consulate-General in Osaka, and staffed a temporary desk at Kansai International Airport. We continue to provide assistance from our Embassy in Tokyo and our Consulate in Osaka.

In light of the severity of the disaster, the government decided to provide a higher level of consular assistance and support for those directly affected. This included help with transport out of the immediate danger zone, from Sendai to Tokyo, financial support for people who needed essentials, such as food and clothing, telephone calls home and accommodation in Tokyo. This support was delivered by the FCO's consular teams on the ground in north east Japan and Tokyo. We supplemented the available commercial capacity with charter flights to help those British nationals leave Japan who wished to do so.

In addition:

Events at the Fukushima Dai-Ichi nuclear plant have been of serious concern. On Thursday 17 March, we advised British nationals currently in Tokyo and north east Japan to consider leaving the area. We also joined the US in advising nationals to remain outside a broader 80km zone around Fukushima. As a precautionary measure, we also began issuing iodine tablets to British nationals from locations in Sendai, Niigata and Tokyo. We are now distributing iodine tablets solely from our Embassy in Tokyo. We have explained the circumstances in which people should take this medicine, who are the priority recipients (children and pregnant and breastfeeding women), and how we will advise people further on this if the situation changes.

Source: Foreign Office Minister, Jeremy Browne, MP to Parliament on 27 March 2011 (12)

7.3 Before you go: Safety and security tips

Before undertaking business travel, the FCO and other security advice groups, such as CSARN and ASIS, recommend that all employees carry through several elementary health, well-being and security preparations. According to CSARN CEO, Brett Lovegrove, who is a retired head of counter-terrorism for the City of London Police, health, well-being and basic pre-planned security measures should be absorbed into "the corporate muscle memory because it should be 'business as usual' for employees and responsible companies who travel overseas for work purposes" (13).

Health and well-being tips

Dehydration: it is important to drink six to eight glasses of water per day to ensure that you stay hydrated and help your body get rid of toxins. If you are exercising, or the weather is warm, you will need to drink more and include an isotonic drink (e.g. Lucozade Hydro Active).

Eat breakfast: 'break the fast' as you've just gone for six-eight hours without food and liquid. A solid breakfast, with clean water, gives you extra energy needed to catch-up and begin the day productively.

Tiredness>disorientation>vulnerable; the more fatigued that you become, the more absent minded and disoriented you can become, which increases your vulnerability to crime, poor 'activation' in an emergency, and more commonplace mistakes, such as misplacing keys, wallets, phones and even hotel locations!

Medication: keep original packaging and copies/photocopies of doctor's note/s.

Hygiene: use hand wipes, wash your hands regularly, especially after handling money.

Alcohol and ice: steer clear wherever possible of alcohol or simultaneously hydrate with bottled water. Remember local ice cubes are usually sourced from local water taps, so avoid ice in areas where tap water may be disagreeable.

Drugs: almost half of all UK nationals detained abroad are imprisoned on drugs-related charges. Most EU countries fix severe penalties for offences (particularly Greece). Many developing countries impose extremely severe penalties for possession. China, Vietnam, Thailand, Malaysia, Singapore, Indonesia and Iran can impose the death sentence for some drugs charges. Drugs related incidents are likely to invalidate insurance and deter Consular help.

Vaccinations and anti-malarials: check what vaccinations you will need with your GP at least six weeks before travel. Cases of Malaria in people living in Britain have risen by almost a third in two years, reported the UK Health Protection Agency in April 2011 (14). High risk areas are North Latin America, Sub-Saharan Africa, South and South East Asia.

Symptoms of malaria: Flu-like including a high temperature, sweats, chills and aches. As in the case of pop star Cheryl Cole, who did take anti-malaria pills before she visited Tanzania, malaria can still develop. Therefore, if you suffer these symptoms after travelling to at-risk malaria regions, please inform and visit your GP immediately.

The charity *Medecins Sans Frontieres International* provides some comprehensive advice online in relation to particular health risks prone to specific locations (15).

Security planning

The *International Federation of Journalists* is a non-profit organisation that publishes a lot of useful information in relation to safety and security for reporters and support crews who regularly travel to the world's least desirable hotspots, often when organisations are fleeing in the opposite direction. Nonetheless, several years ago, the IFJ produced an excellent pamphlet entitled: *Danger: Journalists at Work*, supporting the safety of news hacks on their travels. Some of their tremendous advice is provided below:

Before

Understand the region: ask who hates whom and why?

Research country/region/area thoroughly

Access and print off maps and transport maps

Learn the basic language

Keep cover letters with you

Leave controversial docs at home

Carry out a wallet purge of any perceivably offensive material

If necessary, hire an interpreter – but carry out lots of due diligence around the person first

On location

Stay in contact (leave details)

Comply if violently confronted: not worth you/your colleagues' life

Leave if threatened

Think about clothing: colours, legends and labels

Avoid bias

Avoid crossing sides

Hold conversations first/notes on permission

Permission for photos

Avoid interest in police and military equipment and sites. Be aware of everything that is in the photo before you click away

Satellite phone

Spare cash

Neighbouring countries visas

Full tank of fuel (16)

7.4 Reporting and responding to crime in-country

Report crime and lost passports: to local police and obtain a written statement and reference from them for insurance and consular purposes. Then report lost passports immediately to your national consulate/embassy.

Sexual assaults: should be reported in-country and as soon as possible afterwards, as many countries will not open an investigation in the longer term. It is the remit of in-country national authorities where the crime occurred to investigate suspected offences. Nevertheless, the UK police can link victims to specialist experts on their return. The Metropolitan Police Service run Project Sapphire aimed at improving rape investigation and victim care (17). Project Sapphire can at least put you in touch with local police and support services back home.

Advice in a violent scenario

- 'Activate' – don't be inert, your best chance to escape is immediately (18)
- Stick close to walls and barriers; head down
- Do as you are told by armed person
- Be polite and respectful
- Attempt to shake your brain into a functional, non-emotional mode. The fact they haven't killed you means that they prefer to keep you alive and want something from you
- Try to obtain written receipt when handing over equipment
- Memorise potential access points or egress routes with good cover (19)

Preventing harassment: Lone or at-risk travellers

CSARN, the FCO, IFJ and other organisations, offer the following tips around lone business travel, which could also be practical for lone females:

- Wear sunglasses – avoid unnecessary eye contact
- Wear a pseudo wedding band
- In a group taxi, get dropped-off first and send follow-up text to nominated person
- Caution around 'announcing' or publicising travel plans and accommodation, particularly in cafés, bars, hotel foyers and online
- Avoid going anywhere with a stranger/unknown quantity

General security tips

- Orientate – print off maps, key locations and transport maps for days out or new locations
- Avoid political demonstrations
- Tune in and/or read BBC World Service (20)
- Beware of unattended bags
- Sit well away from glazing or behind a protective wall
- Take seating with views and exits
- Research scams – don't trust easily, see *Safe from Scams* website (21)
- Research known quantities – don't trust easily (tip: research the case study of journalist Tony Lloyd, who was betrayed and kidnapped by his trusted minder in Syria)
- Taxis – don't allow for more than one driver or passenger
- Stay in regular and scheduled contact with home or point of contact
- Give copy of planned itinerary to friends or family
- Beware of cultural *faux pas* – see case studies from *Detained in Dubai* (22)

Case studies: Respecting local cultures

How could you be perceived? The following two cases provide significant warnings that business travellers in any domain should retain an awareness of dominant local cultural practices at all times:

Case of Roxanne Hillier: Sharjah, UAE:
Miss Hillier was a diving instructor in Sharjah, the neighbouring Emirate to Dubai in the UAE. Leaving her apartment while it was renovated, she stayed over in the upstairs room of her male boss's dive shop. He was fixing equipment downstairs when police arrived and arrested the pair. Then aged 21, Miss Hillier signed a confession under duress that she had shared a room with her married boss, which is prohibited under Sharjah law. She undertook various invasive medical tests to prove that no sexual relationship existed between the two. The tests proved Miss Hillier's innocence. Nevertheless, Hillier was sentenced to three months imprisonment, and her manager, a local man, received a six month's jail term (23).

Case of Sun McKay, Dubai airport, UAE:
Sun McKay from Adelaide, Australia, was a seasoned traveller. But he ended up being incarcerated in solitary confinement in a Dubai prison cell for seven weeks. McKay was grabbed roughly at an ATM machine and said in his defence that he turned around instantaneously and offered the rejoinder: 'what the fuck?' It soon transpired that McKay's cashpoint antagonist was an undercover Dubai police officer. McKay apologised profusely and explained the situation. McKay's passport was seized. He was interrogated and held in prison for several months on charges of insulting and inappropriate language to a police officer (24).

7.5 Business travel insurance

A whole host of medical and insurance companies provide business travel related insurance premiums. The fact that many list among their headline benefits emergency medical and evacuation benefits is telling: it tells us that many don't! Even when they claim to, check the small print carefully. For example, one major online insurer does reassure us that "in the unlikely event that you fall victim to a terrorist act, our insurance includes emergency medical treatment, personal accident and hospital benefit at no extra cost" (25). Nevertheless, on further reading, so-called *general exclusions* do mean that a customer is not covered by disturbances that are "caused by a nuclear, chemical or biological attack", or events that are "underway at the beginning of your trip" (26). Often major events, such as coups and insurgent attacks, can take several months or years to come to fruition, so it really is worth reading insurance policy definitions and terms and conditions. Alternatively, phone a broker, or company, for clarifications that are relevant to the operating environment into which you are travelling. Moreover, at the time of writing, authorities in the UK and US were mooting the placement of restrictions, or a complete ban, on companies based in those domains being able to pay out kidnap for ransom insurance (27). The overriding rule-of-thumb for security practitioners is to double-check policy inclusions and exclusions once you have carried out a country risk analysis (CRA), then to apply treatment to each gap in insurance coverage. Several of the larger private sector risk consultancy companies, and most large insurance houses, specialise in supporting insurance provision and contingency planning for larger companies that regularly send dozens of employees and invest heavily in medium-to-high risk environments. Clients may not expect their security contractors to deploy a personal army at times of crisis but they will fairly expect that all security practitioners possess at least some live contacts on speed-dial within larger risk consultancy companies and specialist insurance houses.

General advice

Keep a copy of your travel insurances and email to next of kin/family/friend.

Be realistic and do the maths beforehand. Some easy-to-access online travel insurance policies generally offer very low levels of cover in relation to the overall costs of a major incident.

Get the basic requirements right. For example, it is little use buying cover for expensive medical treatments overseas, if the insurance cover excludes certain 'disruptions', such as acts of terrorism or suspected kidnap scenarios.

In summary, security planners are advised to be realistic and to actively consider worst possible scenarios when advising clients in relation to business travel insurance. A cheap and easily accessible premium can be a much more costly option in the longer run. For instance, if an executive is caught up in an armed attack while away visiting another hemisphere, and they then require significant surgery, followed by weeks of convalescence, then an escorted flight home, as did happen with several survivors of the 2008 Mumbai terrorist attacks, the very last thing a survivor and/or employer needs is the added impact of severe financial loss, as they attempt to rebuild their lives.

Thus, before beginning any work trip, check that the company's business travel insurance covers the following:

- Acts of terrorism and political violence
- Non-business related activities, such as outdoor pursuits, excursions, during or after the business trip
- Kidnap for ransom, hijacking, carjacking, employee detention and extortion

- Specialist and tailored insurance needs that cover pre-existing medical conditions
- Property and intellectual property loss
- Liability cover – you and your company may be *accused* of, or proven to have caused, harm to another party while overseas

It may be that a company cannot reasonably provide comprehensive travel insurance, or they are not required to do so under domestic laws. In most domains, companies do tend to provide insurance because they are held to be legally responsible for incurred expenses if an employee is injured or falls ill, while carrying out work assignments (28). If a company does not wish, or cannot provide insurance cover for the entire trip (perhaps because the employee is working for a few days, then taking leave while on the same trip), then a clear understanding of personal and company insurance cover should be established between both parties. Otherwise, in the event of an emergency, a legal quagmire beckons. It is also not unusual for some employees to keep existing medical conditions hidden from employers, for a variety of understandable reasons. Again, this can provide some jeopardy to any responsible employer who acts reasonably to provide insurance cover to all travelling staff. Security practitioners can add tremendous value by acting as a bridge between employees and management on such sensitive issues. Some security functions in major corporates have run drop-in centres for concerned employees and have also carried out an audit of corporate travel arrangements and personal employee profiles in order to ensure that all identified risks (whether around people, property or assets) are covered by a suitable insurance provider and portfolio of inclusions (29).

Case study: How do we get home? Medical emergency travel costs

£50,000 - £100,000: Treatment, flight upgrades, medical accompaniment and air ambulance support for a remote worker with a kidney infection in sub-Saharan Africa

£30,000 - £50,000: Air ambulance from east coast US to the UK

£15,000 - £20,000: Economy class flights with medical escort from Australia and South East Asian countries

£5,000: Scheduled flights, in economy seating, accompanied by a doctor within the EU

Sources: FCO and CSARN (30)

7.6 Kidnap for ransom, kidnap and countermeasures

Kidnap and ransom scenarios (K&R) may appear too farfetched to consider for many companies spreading their operations internationally, but are an increasing risk beyond the traditional kidnap hotspots of, principally, Latin America, Nigeria and South East Asia.

It is still likely that most K&R cases do not make it into the wider public domain. Certainly, this was the case before the social media revolution when the *Wall Street Journal* reported back in 2002 that up to 90% of kidnappings remained unreported (31). According to Aon Insurance, an estimated 70% of overseas business kidnap cases led to some form of litigation taken out by the victims and their families against employers who sent them abroad in the first place (32).

According to global risk management company, *Control Risks*, the top 20 kidnap countries in the world are: 1) Mexico 2) India 3) Nigeria 4) Pakistan 5) Venezuela 6) Lebanon 7) Philippines 8) Afghanistan 9) Colombia 10) Iraq 11) Syria 12) Guatemala 13) Yemen 14) Libya 15) Egypt 16) Brazil 16) Kenya (tied) 18) Nepal 19) Malaysia 19) South Africa (tied) (33).

Some of the above are tough environments, yet also some of the world's most promising emerging markets for business executives. The cost of ransom can fluctuate wildly from case to case. Some of the following locations have become notorious in recent years for producing environments where kidnap and ransom trends have flourished:

Somalia and coast: around 2,000 employed in piracy. Ransoms between $2m to $5m are usually dropped by cash onto a boat after an average six months of negotiations.

Mexico: 75% of all kidnappings go unreported. The number of K&R cases has surged by 317% in the past five years, with US companies and families turning to private security. Ransoms are typically lower than other K&R 'markets', dependent on the victim's profile. Some police and military have been involved in abductions, therefore be vigilant even with 'officials'.

Philippines: 41 cases of K&R in 2010, a 10% drop from previous year. Kidnapping is prevalent and used by Islamist insurgents and criminal gangs to raise funds.

Trinidad and Tobago: three K&R cases during 2011, including the seizing of a new émigré and restaurant owner. A text was sent a day later asking for $4m.

Nigeria: most kidnappings traditionally occurred in the Niger Delta and Port Harcourt region: approximately 200 in the past couple of years, with three suspected fatalities. Nevertheless, K&R has soared in recent times due to the spawning of Islamist insurgency and terror group Boko Haram (which stands for 'western education is forbidden') (34).

Figure 26: Kidnap for ransom hotspots

The human factor: Kidnap for ransom

Julie Mulligan, a Canadian national, visited Nigeria to carry out humanitarian work, but was kidnapped by armed gunmen as she returned to her accommodation. A machine gun was held against her back and a pistol to her head during the abduction. They dragged her to a car, pushed a gun into her back, and took her to an unfamiliar city. She was held for two weeks during Spring 2009 by a group of five and her two permanent guards were aged 19 and 22. A ransom of some $880,000 was demanded. Mrs Mulligan chose to get along with her captors –helping to clean the house and by attempting to form a bond with those holding her. "I knew it was for my own good – and partly because I just needed to." She slept on a board outside the house, kept to a diet of white rice, and remained free of malaria and disease, despite receiving bites from mosquitoes and bugs. Mulligan was eventually found by Nigerian secret service agents after one of the kidnappers was apprehended (35).

Our second case will be of keen interest for security practitioners who keep a keen eye on industrial relations. Eclipsed by a period of relative calm in France's industrial sectors, the 'boss-knapping' of Luc Rousselet, the director of 3M's French operations, was met by mirth by much of the media. Mr Rousselet was held for two days and nights by angry workers who were fighting redundancies. "It is our only remaining bartering tool", one union leader said. During the 1960s and 1970s boss-knapping became frequent; chief executives were barred from leaving the premises until they wilted under the pressure of demands. In Rousselet's case, militant staff soon softened, bringing him trays of beverages, plates of mussels and chips, and permitting him regular toilet breaks (36).

Our third case used a scam to lure a Brazilian businessman to South Africa. Although the businessman survived, he was held captive and tortured, during the summer 2010 period when South Africa hosted the FIFA Football World Cup, by a Nigerian gang, in the Johannesburg suburb of Kensington. The businessman ran an international timber company, and became the second known victim to fall into the gang's clutches. Prior to that, a South Korean businessman, and president of an international shipping company, was released only after his company paid a ransom fee to his captors under the guise of a business deal. "He was badly burnt on his stomach, chest and feet by his captors, who used a hot iron to inflict the pain. He believed his days were numbered and his captors threatened to kill him", said an investigator with South Africa's Hawks, a specialist priority crime directorate. "These men thought they were coming here to conclude legitimate business deals. The man from South Korea thought that he would be meeting with another businessman to ship concrete to Iraq", he said. Other businessmen swindled by business scams in South Africa include the 2008 case of Osamai Hitomi who was lured under the false impression that he would become a partner of a fake investment company called Jeffdon Properties. Hitomi was robbed and held hostage, and his captors demanded a $5 million ransom. Seven people were arrested, six were Nigerian and one South African. The modus operandi is to establish a front company to lure the men to the country. Once in South Africa, they are kidnapped, tortured and held for ransom (37).

Our final case to note is that of a 39-year-old Israeli businessman who was abducted from his home in the Nigerian city of Port Harcourt, during August 2008. No group claimed responsibility for the Israeli's abduction. The kidnapping occurred just days after Nigeria's Counter Terrorism Bureau issued a rare worldwide travel advisory warning of possible attempts by armed group, Hizbullah, to kidnap Israelis abroad, in revenge for the assassination of Imad Mughniyah in Damascus, Syria (38/39).

Escape and evasion: Tips to prevent kidnappings

Kidnap prevention advice can be some of the most fun, but important, security training for employees. It is well worth practicing some of the following training drills for all employees that travel to medium and high risk kidnap environments. Some of the best practice advice was published by the Police Service of Northern Ireland (PSNI), in order to assist at-risk individuals to carry out their own prevention techniques against so-called 'Tiger kidnappings' (short-term hijacking to access cash and valuables), or terrorism:

Vehicle travel

- Be alert, especially when leaving or entering your home/premises
- Vary your routes and times of journeys
- Travel with company where possible
- Report any suspicious vehicles or people
- If you think you are being followed, contact police immediately and avoid becoming isolated
- Be suspicious of anyone trying to get you to stop or leave your vehicle
- If possible, keep windows closed and doors locked
- When stopping, do not allow yourself to be boxed in, leave enough room to manoeuvre

- When parking, do not leave anything in your vehicle that may identify you or your business
- Try to avoid parking anywhere that may become dark or isolated before your return
- Keep a full tank of fuel and limit your fuel stops in riskier locations (40)

Walking and jogging

- Keep to busy, brightly lit areas where possible
- Avoid short cuts across waste ground, deserted parks, underpasses and alleys
- Be alert to your surroundings
- Approach and have a good view of your destination, from the opposite side of the path/road, to give a wider viewing angle. Approach accommodation or meeting points behind any useful cover. For example, use vehicles or wear a 'hoody', or cap and sunglasses, to block a view of your face
- Be aware of vehicles, particularly parked vehicles, with people inside, near to you and your destination (41)

Reading people and personalities

Be mindful of some of the following red flag warnings from prior kidnapping cases which, when taken in isolation, may not confirm a high-risk scenario. Nevertheless, when the overall pattern of the entire business engagement process is considered, the following traits may point us to heightening our awareness and caution. Some clues could be:

- Person provides inconsistent information about age, interests, appearance, marital status, profession, employment, inter alia
- Person appears anxious – possibly looking around a lot, or studying clocks/watches
- Person demonstrates a particular keenness to meet in a remote, strange, or quiet location with few external witnesses
- Person appears disoriented themselves, because they may not be quite as local as they pretend
- You become quickly and inexplicably outnumbered and harassed or cajoled into visiting a new or one specific location

- Your contact appears significantly different in person from his/her online persona
- The person never introduces you to close professional associates or family members
- If you meet more than person, the personal chemistry may not be developed well between the other parties which suggests that their relationship is new or stage managed
- Be careful with what you say. Do you feel that the person is trying to lure or trick you into saying something embarrassing, perhaps overtly political or critical? If so, be aware with smartphone and micro-camera equipment, that you may be being recorded, scammed or being made susceptible to blackmail

Meet in a safe place

- When you choose to meet, always tell somebody precisely where you are going and when you will return. Better still, ask somebody to accompany you
- Leave your meeting contact's details and telephone number with your friend or colleague
- Provide your own transportation. Meet in a public place – such as a popular café, restaurant or hotel – during a time when many people will be around
- When the meeting is over, find an excuse to leave on your own
- If you decide to move to another location, take your own car

Accommodation

- If you are flying in from another city, arrange for your own car and hotel room
- Change your hotel room, or hotel location, after a couple of days
- Do not disclose the name of your hotel and don't allow your new business contact to make the arrangements for you
- Hire a taxi or car at the airport and drive directly to your hotel. In medium to high risk areas, your hotel or security agent should pick you up
- Call your meeting contact from the hotel, or meet at the location you have already agreed to. If the location seems inappropriate or unsafe, go back to your hotel and make an excuse
- Always make sure a friend or family member knows your plans and has your contact information. Carry a fully charged cell phone, and a small, fully charged back-up, in a secreted location on your person, at all times

Escape and evasion

Never do anything you feel unsure about. If you have gotten yourself, or your client, into a position or location that you feel uncomfortable about, then don't hesitate to activate and evacuate.

Good excuses for quick movement include:

- Feigning illness and leaving instantaneously while you apologise
- Receiving an important SMS message about a work or family emergency and departing instantaneously, while you apologise
- Embarking on a conversation with the waiter or establishment staff member, then follow them away from the table in continued conversation, while signalling to your guests that you will return in a moment. One good excuse may be that you are concerned that you've left your jacket or wallet elsewhere in the premises
- Pretending to see a colleague pass by the window. Rush into the street to say 'hello', then quickly moving away from the scene
- Pretending to see a temporary situation on the street outside, such as somebody who may need assistance. Rush out but signal you will come back

Golden rule to remember: Never, ever feel embarrassed about quickly disengaging from a threatening situation. Activate immediately, and if necessary, apologise later. Your safety is much more important than what an unknown group of people might think of you.

Wrap-up: Lessons from K&R cases

- Fixed accommodation locations provide extra vulnerability
- Beware of wider events and news stories that might impact your locality/region
- Thoroughly vet and research potential new business acquaintances and partners
- Carry out reconnaissance on meeting locations, noting exits and emergency routes, and take the initiative to suggest neutral and safer venues
- Recommend the use of travel tracking and panic-alarm technology for employees, but be aware that if Bluetooth is enabled, your location, movements and messages may be hacked by adversaries
- Do not at any point publish your travel plans on social media, or allow others to

- Beware of the legal consequences for employers if it can be proved *on the balance of probabilities* (civil case) or *beyond all reasonable doubt* (criminal case) that they were insufficient in their duty of care

7.7 Corporate liability laws and business travel

To be found guilty of a gross breach, the organisation's conduct must have fallen far below what could have been reasonably expected. This is an opportunity for employers to think again about how risk management, or the lack of it, can be interpreted by a legal system. For consistency, we have again used the British legal domain to illustrate examples of legislation. Although, to an extent, the following passages do reprise some content of Chapter 3: Security Legislation and Regulations, it is important to take a fresh look at some laws in relation to corporate litigation, in order to discuss how they might be applied to the process of delivering security management for business travellers. The **Health and Safety at Work Act (1974)** states that if a health or safety offence is committed with the consent or connivance of, or is attributable to any neglect on the part of, any director, manager, secretary or other similar officer of the organisation, then that person (as well as the organisation) can be prosecuted under section 37 of the Act.

Recent case law has confirmed that directors cannot avoid a charge of 'neglect' under section 37 by being 'ignorant', or arranging themselves to be ignorant, of circumstances which would trigger their obligation to address health and safety breaches. This includes the deployment of direct employees and contractors overseas. Those found guilty are liable for fines and, in some cases, imprisonment. In addition, the **Company Director's Disqualification Act 1986**, section 2(1), empowers the court to disqualify an individual convicted of an offence in connection with the management of a company (42). Gross negligence manslaughter (criminal) is proved when individual officers of a company (directors or business owners), by their own grossly negligent behaviour, cause death. This offence is punishable by a maximum of life imprisonment.

The **Corporate Manslaughter Act 2007** replaced weaker laws from the 1960s which lacked the teeth to prosecute senior organisational decision makers for the death of an employee. Hugh Martin, travel security expert, and Founder of Boiling Frog travel app, suggests: In large organisations there is sometimes the belief that no one person can really be blamed for events or accidents that lead to an employee being injured or killed. However, the new act has been phrased in such a way that the head of HR in a large company may be just as culpable as the owner of a small private company – both can be sent to prison and/or fined (43). The act's first prosecution occurred in Gloucestershire in February 2011, when a junior geologist was inspecting a pit which collapsed on top of him. He suffocated and died. The company, Geotechnical Holdings Ltd, was prosecuted and fined £385,000. An individual director was also charged with common law 'gross negligence manslaughter' and another offence under section 37 of the HASAW Act (44). London Law Company, Eversheds, point out that the act has, at its core, the concept of a 'gross breach of a duty of care by senior management', and covers business, public sector organisations, and also third sector employers too, including partnerships and trade unions (45). An organisation to which this section applies is guilty of an offence if the way in which its activities are managed or organised – (a) causes a person's death, and (b) amounts to a gross breach of a relevant duty of care owed by the organisation to the deceased (46). Only in defined situations of 'emergencies' does the act *not* cover first responders, the military, and other crown authorities. Nevertheless, overall in relation to everyday business activities, all organisations, particularly boards and senior managers, appear to be responsible under the act for their employees, property, equipment, and the processes of supplying their goods and services (47). Part of the Corporate Manslaughter Act gives courts the power to issue an additional publicity order that requires a guilty organisation to publish that it has been convicted, the specified particulars of any case, and legal penalties imposed upon them. In addition, companies then could be liable to prosecutions in the country where an incident occurred, or back in the UK for 'manslaughter on the grounds of gross negligence'.

Case studies: Gross negligence manslaughter

Case 1: "We acted for a young man working for a charity which took physically and mentally disabled children abroad for a holiday and to provide their families with some respite. During once such trip and [sic] severely disabled boy was tragically run over by a reversing coach and killed. Our client was interviewed at length by police investigating this as gross negligence manslaughter. Our client was co-operative and provided a detailed account following which he was not charged with any offence."

Source: Birds Solicitors (48)

Case 2: The managing director of a manufacturing company with around 100 workers was sentenced to 12 months' imprisonment for manslaughter following the death of an employee who became caught in unguarded machinery. The investigation revealed that, had the company adequately maintained guarding around a conveyor, the death would have been avoided. The judge made clear that whether the managing director was aware of the situation was not the issue: he should have known as this was a longstanding problem. An area manager also received a custodial sentence. The company received a substantial fine and had to pay the prosecution's costs.

Source: Health and Safety Executive online (49)

Employer in the dock

Mark Scoggins is a Solicitor Advocate and London-based environmental law barrister, called to the Bar in 1983. His principal practice is the defence of individuals and organisations in the construction, chemical, transport, waste and water sectors in regulatory and civil cases, particularly in health and safety, corporate manslaughter and environmental domains (50). Scoggins is a popular and entertaining presenter for the Terrorist Information New York Group (TINYg), a leading corporate and law-enforcement networking forum. Mr Scoggins outlined seven major lines of inquiry for companies that may find themselves in court accused of breaches of health and safety-related laws. These are:

What was your job on the day?

Were you relevantly trained to do it?

Did you have a clear plan and procedures?

Did you exercise such emergencies regularly?

Did you get all the support and resources you needed?

Did you do your job properly?

Can you prove it? (51)

Tips for responding to an official investigation

- Make an assumption that you cannot, and should not, hold anything back. It will be found eventually. Moreover, legal delays cost more. You could also be accused of 'contempt of court', which could scupper your case and reputation.

- Media criticism around a slow response can be particularly virulent. It shows that – perhaps – you or your company have something to hide. Excessive caution can also lead to further civil claims or prosecutions, and will certainly demoralise other employees, clients and stakeholders.

- During and after a major incident, do ensure that all actions and responses are recorded and officially logged. Keep logs and charts of actions taken and alternatives rejected. Keep them in a safe and retrievable place.

- There can be no excuse for lack of preparation; if something goes wrong, excuses won't make a reasonable defence. Contact the HSE if you have any questions or require any clarification (52).

- According to travel safety expert, Hugh Martin, "Employees should be given simple procedures to follow from the moment planning a trip starts, right through to whenever they return home. They then have a duty to follow those procedures to ensure that contingency plans work in times of crisis" (53). Enough said.

7.8 Protective security approaches to travel security

Not all security executives that are tasked with providing travel safety measures will have formal close protection training. Moreover, not all companies will employ security practitioners to manage staff travel plans. This is even the case when companies are organising major events, such as annual general meetings, in new and riskier locations. We have therefore outlined some of the basic principles of safe travel management in this subsection, for those organising such activities to consider. The following advice has been compiled from analysis of various terrorist and natural disasters that have befallen overseas business travellers. The recommendations are geared principally to security practitioners and organisations that may be taking groups overseas, or running events abroad. But, equally, lone travellers would also benefit from some or all of this preparation.

Routes and transport

Carry out a risk assessment on the location/s beforehand: what is the crime data showing? What are the safer or riskier districts and why? What natural hazards have occurred in the past? What is the road traffic accident rate?

Airports protocol: make sure that the pick-up and/or taxi drivers are NOT holding up executives' or organisational names – agree a different moniker beforehand.

Rehearse primary, alternative and other emergency evacuation routes. Vary routes if you have VIPs or at-risk groups in transit.

Carry out lots of due diligence and vetting on contract staff, such as in-country drivers and chaperones.

If you are responsible for travel safety, arrive into your location a few days early. Orientate by walking around or taking over-ground transport. Read in-country newspapers to catch daily news and social context. Make a note of, and visit, any medical facilities that you may need to use. Check that they still exist.

As you travel about, make a record of landmarks and potential safe havens.

If you are self-driving, always keep as full a tank of fuel as possible.

Collect business cards of trusted and untrusted individuals.

Accommodation and hotel security

Due diligence: has the hotel been named as a target before? Who runs it and where is the parent company based? Does it have fire 'sprinkler' systems? Does it have clearly articulated and practical emergency plans?

Room position: in medium to high risk terrorism environments, consider using a hotel room above the first and second floor level, or above a hotel foyer.

Evacuation and emergency planning: after you check in make yourself and all team members familiar with <u>functioning</u> entrances, exits, and potential evacuation routes, as well as secure internal positions known as *invacuation* points. Agree a safe and sensible muster point well beyond the location's periphery, in case of an emergency. Wear clothes suitable for an evacuation scenario at all times, or keep them with you. (Trainers/sneakers will be much more useful than flip-flops in an emergency evacuation.)

In room: lock your door with all possible bolts. Lock your windows and all external doors, particularly if you are on the ground and first two floors, or if you have a balcony.

Social life: be aware of *honey traps* or people who may try to entice you into a vulnerable situation or location. Be cautious around leaving your drinks unattended in a bar or accepting drinks from a stranger.

Connectivity: keep a fully-charged working mobile phone with you at all times. Consider the benefits of switching off Bluetooth and location trackers in a suspected terrorist or siege scenario.

Information security: leave laptops, mobile phones and work bags fully clean of sensitive data, particularly if you are going to leave them in your hotel room safe.

Counter-terrorism: conduct meetings well away from unprotected glazing. Move away from suspicious groups, individuals or unattended bags, as soon as possible.

Situational awareness: try to sit away from the entrances of bars and restaurants, but retain them in view. Make yourself actively aware of all evacuation points in cafés, bars and restaurants, as soon as possible.

Event and venue security

Reconnaissance: physically visit and check out your visit locations. Verify and decide your movements and routes on the sites beforehand. Be aware of the GEEBS! Avoid being near to unprotected **glazing**; draw room plans, record and physically test **entrances and exits** and other **evacuation** points. Know the whereabouts of **bathrooms** and *holding rooms*.

Holding rooms: these are separate rooms for special guests, such as speakers, event chairpersons or other VIPs. They should usually be opaque and not be visible to passing delegates or hotel guests. Ensure that these have ease of access to an evacuation point.

Room bookings: conference, meeting and bedrooms can be booked out a day or two before to *seal* your location. If you are nervous that your organisation booking rooms may cause undue attention, it is always worth booking the room under another brand name, especially if the audience is by invite only.

Prior notification to the outside world: is it really necessary to tell various adversaries that several dozen wealthy industrialists are going to be bobbing about at a specific public venue (such as a hotel conference centre) at a particular date and time? If you face any sort of risk, consider whether you really do need to publicly advertise your event beforehand? Perhaps let modesty prevail and carry out the great publicity work afterwards.

Empathise with local adversaries: set into the shoes of a local militant group. How do they view your presence? Moreover, is there anything about your company or senior executives' approach that might have antagonised any local groups? Think laterally. For example, has anybody at the company ever said or written anything that could be construed as offensive in the area that they are visiting? Is their private life likely to increase their risk in this area?

Use technology to assist: Google Earth is an interactive, virtual globe that enables you to find and explore just about any location on our planet and beyond.

7.9 Due diligence

A number of legal background checks are available for security practitioners and all employers, in order to establish the credentials of support staff that they may be wishing to recruit. In the UK, a Standard level *Disclosure and Barring Check* (formerly known as a Criminal Records Bureau or *CRB check*) will detail every conviction, including spent convictions, cautions, warnings or reprimands that have been recorded in central police records; or it will state that there is no such information held. An enhanced level check will detail all criminal information, as above, as well as any information which, in the opinion of a Chief Police Officer, might be relevant for the purpose and ought to be included in the certificate. Additionally this level of disclosure will provide clarification as to whether the applicant is banned from working with children or vulnerable adults (54). International criminal checks can also be conducted, usually within three weeks.

Costs are a little more expensive, usually between £100 and £200 per case (55). Driver reports are available from the DVLA for a small cost at the time of writing (56). Some companies can be employed to carry out further background checks, perhaps in order to establish enhanced levels of vetting for security operators that may become hired to protect at-risk facilities or persons. Security and counter-terrorism clearance can take around one month to process and may be a requirement for some security sector jobs. The Baseline Personnel Security Standard (BPSS) is defined by HMG, Cabinet Office. "The standard covers Civil Servants, Armed Forces, temporary staff and government contractors", writes the UK Cabinet Office (57). The BPSS level of screening is required before an individual may be submitted for further CTC, Security Clearance or Developed Vetting. The British Standard for vetting staff who work within the security industry was the *BS 7858:2006* but this was replaced by the *Security Screening of Individuals Employed in a Security Environment, BS 7858:2012* (58).

IPS' Passport Validation Service (PVS) began in 2006 to support the business community in preventing fraud. The service is now widely used. According to its website: "Financial services organisations and government departments have benefited significantly from PVS. The service has prevented many fraudulent transactions since its inception and the saving to business has been millions of pounds. It is now a business-critical tool for any organisation where UK passports are presented as proof of identity". To give some context around the scale of the problem, in 2007, some 290,996 UK passports were reported stolen. PVS is offered to government and private sector organisations that require definite proof of identity. The PVS customer base in the private sector includes high street retail banks, insurance services and mortgage intermediaries (59). Other useful data is freely available online: the US Transport Security Administration produces a long list of several thousand passengers barred from flying on civilian aircraft due to terrorism concerns under a published *No Fly List* (60).

Chapter 7: Wrap-up

In closing this chapter on **Safe Business Travel**, we reflect on some of the approaches and attributes that will help your company gain the competitive edge. These include:

1. Although growth of digital media and VOIP platforms has provided far greater and cheaper facilities for telephone conferencing, business travel volume does appear to have significantly increased since the millennium. This provides excellent new prospects for security entrepreneurs to offer chaperoning, travel management and advisory services.

2. Clients may not expect their security contractors to deploy a personal army at times of crisis. But they will fairly expect that all security practitioners possess at least some live contacts on speed-dial within larger risk consultancy companies and specialist insurance houses.

3. Ensure that clients are fully aware of the range of legal inquiries, sanctions and penalties that are now in place to punish those employers who do not offer a 'duty of care' approach to staff who travel overseas on business.

4. Provide briefings and advice drawn from prior lessons of business travel incidents, in order to inform clients about the tangible risks of business travel, and various risk mitigation options open to them.

5. Familiarise yourself with the vast array of decent quality FREE open-source information from government websites, trade bodies and private sector experts, to help your own organisation's bottom line.

References

1) Newman, R., (2014), 'THE RISKS FACING INTERNATIONAL BUSINESS TRAVELLERS AND THEIR EMPLOYERS; IN PARTICULAR, WHETHER BUSINESS TRAVELLERS SHOULD BE TRACKED'

2) Ibid.

3) HMG Passport Office online was accessed on 10/03/2015 at: *www.gov.uk/renew-adult-passport*

4) EHIC online was accessed via the UK NHS online on 10/03/2015 at: *www.nhs.uk/NHSEngland/Healthcareabroad/EHIC/Pages/about-the-ehic.aspx*

5) Wanderlust Travel Magazine online (30/04/2013), 'British FCO to drop Locate service', accessed and downloaded on 10/03/2015 at: *www.wanderlust.co.uk/magazine/news/fco-to-drop-its-locate-service*

6) FCO online 'Travel Abroad' section was accessed on 10/03/2015 at: *www.gov.uk/foreign-travel-advice*

7) FCO and UKTI Overseas Business Risk website was accessed on 10/03/2015 at: *www.gov.uk/government/collections/overseas-business-risk*

8) OSAC's website was accessed on 10/03/2015 at: *www.osac.gov/Pages/Home.aspx*

9) Tripadvisor, Moscow Travel Forum, was accessed and downloaded on 10/03/2015 at: *www.tripadvisor.co.uk/ShowForum-g298484-i718-Moscow_Central_Russia.html*

10) InterNations, Expat Guide Moscow for working and living in Moscow was accessed on 10/03/2015 at: *www.internations.org/moscow-expats/guide*

11) FCO (2014), 'Support for British Nationals Abroad', accessed and downloaded on 10/03/2015 at: *www.gov.uk/government/uploads/system/uploads/attachment_data/file/317474/FCO_Brits_Abroad_2014.pdf*

12) Jeremy Browne MP (2011), Speech accessed and downloaded on 10/03/2015 at: *www.publications.parliament.uk/pa/cm201011/cmhansrd/cm110330/wmstext/110330m0001.htm*

13) Interview with Brett Lovegrove, CEO of CSARN, undertaken by the author on 10/03/2015 via email

14) Cited in Patient.co.uk, accessed and downloaded on 10/03/2015 at: *www.patient.co.uk/doctor/malaria-pro*

15) **Médecins Sans Frontières (MSF) online was accessed on 10/03/2015 at:** *www.msf.org.uk/*

16) International Federation of Journalists (n.d): 'Danger: Journalists at Work': Provides advice to reporters around global hotspots, personal safety and crisis responses. Website accessed on 12/04/2012 at: *www.ifj.org*

17) Project Sapphire - the Metropolitan Police Service run Project Sapphire aimed at improving rape investigation and victim care. Project Sapphire can put you in touch with local police and support services back in the UK: *www.met.police.uk/sapphire*

18) Author interview with Dr Nicole Lipkin, CEO of Equilibria, Philadelphia, on 16/09/2014

19) Op. Cit. IFJ

20) BBC World Service programmes can be accessed at: *www.bbc.co.uk/worldservice/programmeguide/*

21) Safe from Scams website (2013) was accessed on 13/04/2013 at: *www.safefromscams.co.uk/TravelScamsCategory.html* and: *www.safefromscams.co.uk/NigerianScamsCategory.html*

22) Detained in Dubai, support group for alleged victims in the UAE: *www.detainedindubai.org*

23) Telegraph online (09/06/2009), 'British engineer's daughter jailed in UAE for sleeping with boss', accessed and downloaded on 10/03/2015 at: *www.telegraph.co.uk/news/worldnews/middleeast/unitedarabemirates/5486730/British-engineers-daughter-jailed-in-UAE-for-sleeping-with-boss.html*

24) Open Australia online (19/09/2012), accessed and downloaded on 10/03/2015 at: *www.openaustralia.org.au/senate/?id=2012-09-19.67.1*

25) EssentialTravel.co.uk, accessed on 10/03/2015 at: *www.essentialtravel.co.uk/travelinsurance/terrorism-travel-insurance/*

26) Ibid.

27) Commercial Risk Europe (27/11/2014), 'UK government plans to ban kidnap insurance and ransom payouts', accessed and downloaded on 10/03/2015 at:

www.commercialriskeurope.com/cre/3799/15/UK-government-plans-to-ban-insurance-kidnap-and-ransom-payments/

28) Insurance QnA online (2015), 'Does my employer have to provide travel insurance?', accessed and downloaded on 10/03/2015 at: *www.insuranceqna.com/travel-insurance/does-my-employer-have-to-provide-travel-insurance.html*

29) Interview with anonymised corporate security director at a global investment bank conducted in the City of London on 23/10/2014 by this author

30) City Security and Resilience Networks (CSARN) 'Security Risk Monitor', can be accessed via subscription at: *www.csarn.org* and FCO booklet 'Support for British National Abroad'

31) Reuters (2011), 'Kidnap and ransom: negotiating lives for cash': interview with John Chase at AKE, risk advisory firm in London, accessed and downloaded on 13/04/2015 at: *www.reuters.com/article/2011/02/17/us-crime-kidnap-ransom-idUSTRE71G3U520110217*

32) Cited by AON Insurance speaker at CSARN Safer Business Travel Briefing in City of London on 04/11/2010, accessed and downloaded on 10/03/2015 at: *www.csarn.org/nov4saftrv.html*

33) 33) Perlberg, S., (12/12/2013), 'The 20 Countries Where People Get Kidnapped The Most', Business Insider online, accessed and downloaded on 10/03/2015 at: *www.businessinsider.com/top-20-countries-by-kidnapping-2013-12*

34) Havoscope Black Market database: kidnap and ransom, accessed and downloaded on 11/12/2012 at: *www.havocscope.com/black-market/human-trade/kidnap-and-ransom/*

35) Interview with kidnapped Canadian businesswoman Julie Mulligan, accessed and downloaded on 10/03/2015 at: *www.journalpioneer.com/Living/People/2009-08-17/article-1382758/Despite-ordeal,-Julie-Mulligan-believes-in-Rotary-mission/1*

36) The Guardian (27/03/2009), Desperate French workers resort to kidnapping bosses to force redundancy negotiations', accessed and downloaded on 10/03/2015 at: *www.guardian.co.uk/world/2009/mar/27/bossnapping-france-workers-fight-layoffs*

37) News story was accessed and downloaded on 10/04/2012 at: *www.nairaland.com/nigeria/topic-459085.0.html*

38) InfoLiveTV (27/08/2008), 'Israeli Businessman Abducted at Gunpoint in Nigeria', accessed and downloaded on 10/03/2015 at: *www.youtube.com/watch?v=Zy1EllQX*

39) USA Today (27/08/2008), 'Israeli businessman kidnapped in Nigeria', accessed and downloaded on 01/03/2015 at: *http://usatoday30.usatoday.com/news/world/2008-08-27-9814701_x.htm*

40) PSNI (2012): Kidnap prevention advice from the Police Service of Northern Ireland, accessed and downloaded on 12/04/2012 at: *www.psni.police.uk/advice_tiger_kidnap.pdf*

41) Ibid

42) Health and Safety Executive and IOD: 'Leading Health and Safety at Work: leadership actions for directors and board members', accessed and downloaded on 12/04/2012 at: *www.hse.gov.uk/corpmanslaughter/ about.htm*

43) Martin, H., (2012), 'The Corporate Manslaughter Act', accessed and downloaded on 12/04/2012 at: *www.apbusinesscontacts.com/ the_people_bulletin-pb_4/disaster.aspx*

44) Eversheds (2011), 'Gloucestershire firm fined £380,000 over trench death', accessed and downloaded on 12/04/2012 at: *www.eversheds.com/ uk/home/articles/index1.page?ArticleID=templatedata\Eversheds\articles\da ta\en\Industrial_engineering\Cotswold_Geotechnical_Holdings_Limited_ sentenced*

45) Ibid.

46) Ibid.

47) Ibid.

48) Birds Solicitors online (2012), 'Gross Negligence Manslaughter', accessed and downloaded on 12/04/2012 at: *www.birds.eu.com/serious_crime/ corporate_manslaughter*

49) Health and Safety Executive online

50) Fisher, Scoggins, Waters online (2015), 'Mark Scoggins, Leader in Health and safety and Environmental law', accessed and downloaded on 13/03/2015 at: *www.fisherscogginswaters.co.uk/about-the-team/ mark-scoggins*

51) Cited from Mark Scoggins speech to TINYg conference, London, on 08/10/2012, agenda can be accessed and downloaded at: *www.tinyg.info/ Tinyg%20London%20brochure%202012%20small%20(8).pdf*

52) HSE can be contacted at: *www.hse.gov.uk/contact*

53) Op. Cit., Martin, H.

54) CRB Screening was accessed and downloaded on 12/04/2015 at: *www.cbscreening.co.uk/enhanced-crb-check*

55) CRB international criminal checks was accessed and downloaded on 12/04/2015 at: *www.cbscreening.co.uk/international-criminal-checks*

56) DVLA Reports are available from: *www.cbscreening.co.uk/dvla-reports*

57) HMG (2014), 'Baseline Personal Security Standard', accessed and downloaded on 15/03/2015 at: *www.gov.uk/government/publications/ government-baseline-personnel-security-standard*

58) Agenda Security Services (2013), BS7858 has changed', accessed and downloaded on 16/03/2015 at: *www.agendasecuritynews.co.uk/bs-7858-has-changed-are-you-aware/*
59) HM Passport Office website was accessed and downloaded on 16/03/2015 at: *www.ips.gov.uk/cps/rde/xchg/ips_live/hs.xsl/563.htm*
60) Transport Security Administration (2015, 'No Fly List', was accessed on 16/03/2015at: *www.no-fly-list.com/index.php*

CHAPTER 8: PERSONAL AND ORGANISATIONAL RESILIENCE

8.1 Context

"It may sound strange but many champions are made champions by setbacks." – Bob Richard, two-time Olympic Pole Vault champion.

As advanced security professionals, there is an expectation that your specific personal value to the organisation will probably be at its premium, and most visible, during major incidents and acute organisational challenges. In prior chapters we examined effective ways to carry out business planning, networking, investigations, communications and compliance. Now is the time to draw our prior learning together: how we can nurture our personal preparedness for crisis management and also develop our own contribution to the wider mission of a business organisation's resilience? (We briefly touched upon what was meant by 'organisational resilience' in Chapter 2.)

The aim of this chapter, therefore, is to provide sharper focus upon several approaches to individual, and also organisational, resilience. Individual and organisational initiative towards individual and team development is investigated in this chapter's first half. We establish how personal and group resilience tactics can, ultimately, act as a very useful contributor to overall organisational resilience. This chapter's second half will familiarise the reader with commonly deployed strategic crisis management and continuity concepts and techniques. We will refer to several eminent studies that have taken place since the 9/11 terrorist atrocities. This concluding chapter will:

- address issues of personal fitness, health and well-being, teamwork and intellectual development
- provide context for crisis management studies
- explain some conceptual frameworks that enable us to understand a crisis, and its attendant phases
- provide lessons and techniques in crisis management and longer-term organisational recovery from communications management professionals beyond the security industry sphere
- wrap-up: what will give your company the competitive edge before, during and after a crisis?

8.2 Personal resilience

"That which does not kill us makes us stronger." – (Friedrich Nietzsche)

Do levels of individual physical fitness matter in respect of contributing directly to an organisation's overall resilience? President John F Kennedy thought so: "Our growing softness, our increasing lack of physical fitness, is a menace to our security", he said of American society in the early 1960s, as he launched a National Council of Fitness.

Fast-forward four decades from Kennedy's Camelot presidency and we see that four small groups of people could seize control of four civilian passenger jets and direct them into crowded buildings; armed with just bolt cutters and knives. A few weeks later in 2001, other cabin crew staff and passengers were luckier. They physically suppressed and stopped terrorist, Richard Reid, from detonating an onboard bomb. Reid had explosives tucked in a shoe-heel and was travelling upon a crowded Boeing jet running from Paris to Miami. Tragically, almost 100 commercial airliners have been attacked by bombs, a third by identifiable terrorist groups, with the loss of some 3,000 passengers since 1933, reports *Aerospaceweb* (1). In reality then, individual physical fitness and resilience can only take us so far along a path of delivering a resilient 'culture' or organisation.

In fact, it is fair to say that the root causes of insecurity during modern times have little connection to personal fitness and resilience. The industrialisation of weapons technology and the continued proliferation of weapons of mass destruction, continues to threaten humanity, or vast portions of it. For each year, between 2004 and 2011, the world spent $60 to $80 billion dollars each year on buying arms and defence products, stated the website of *Global Issues* in 2014 (2). Moreover, investment by public authorities and private companies in cyber security management has burgeoned. Companies have had servers and Cloud accounts hacked, bank accounts plundered and research and development blueprints stolen and counterfeited. Customers have had their ATM cards cloned, tax records destroyed and compromised, PIN numbers and passwords scanned and stolen. Governments and their military systems have been comprehensively breached by outsiders and insiders committing physical and information attacks upon their colleagues and countries.

Why then should we be worried by individual fitness and personal resilience issues, at all? How can physical fitness or personal resilience training help larger organisations become more 'resilient'? Moreover, as Diana Coutu from the *Harvard Business Review* puts it: "Why do some people and some companies buckle under pressure? And what makes others bend and ultimately bounce back? (3)" The following sections will show us that President Kennedy, a decorated

World War Two combatant in his own right, was more than justified to make his claim; improved personal resilience is an important contributor to organisational and societal sustainability and drive.

What is personal resilience?

Author of *Positivity* (2009), Dr Barbara Fredrickson, suggests that resilience is predominantly achieved by psychology and perspective management. Due to in-built survival mechanisms, human brains are naturally wired to give more attention to negative events than positive ones. But in all likelihood, we experience many more positive events than negative ones. One essential ingredient to building resiliency, reports Fredrickson, lies in "noticing and appreciating those positive experiences whenever and wherever they occur" (4).

In researching for her article 'The 5 best ways to build resilience', Jessie Sholl examined, by way of first hand interviews, how some people appear to flourish during a crisis, while others seriously stumble. Scholl carried out a series of qualitative interviews with people who, it would be fair to describe, had experienced significant personal adversities. Scholl also carried out a copious literature review of materials from psychologists who had also examined, or sought to identify, the key personal ingredients to an emerging notion of *resiliency*. Scholl arrived at her conclusion that 'good physical conditioning' was a significant enabler to the personal resilience shown at later, and more traumatic, life trajectories (5).

8.3 Personal resilience initiatives in the workplace

Private sector companies are fast adopting fitness and personal resilience programmes in order to hopefully enhance overall organisational resilience. *Equilibrium* is Deloitte's wellness programme, aimed at "improving employee wellness and well-being" (6). Accountancy company, Deloitte, say that such an initiative "addresses the physical and psychological components of well-being by offering information sessions and programmes covering fitness, health, diet, alternative and complementary therapies, yoga classes, etc. throughout the year on a subsidised basis" (7). The company has a strong tradition in advocating employee wellness and gives the following reasons for this:

- It provides a strong incentive for employees to remain with their current employers
- It reduces absenteeism due to injury, illness or burnout from heavy workloads
- It improves working relationships and increase attitudes to productivity

- It helps manage stress
- It increases job satisfaction (8).

Research by diet advice company, *Weight Watchers*®, found that overweight employees have twice as many health-related absences and "higher levels of presenteeism": defined as remaining on the job but not functioning at full capacity (9). In the US, a lot of data suggests that stress management and obesity-related illness account for a vast majority of employee health issues. Researchers at the *American Institute for Stress found* that some 80% of employees felt stress at work, while more than 55% of absences are caused by family-related issues (10). Moreover, due to soaring insurance costs for employers, the past two decades have witnessed a large upsurge in workplace well-being programmes across the US. According to Philadelphia-based health assistance company, *Health Advocates*: "80% of these [workplace impacting] diseases are lifestyle-related … and having a wellness program on-board that helps employees adopt healthier habits can significantly reduce illness, accidents, absences and medical claims. Increased productivity is a further hard-to-ignore benefit" (11). Much evidence on this and related concerns has been gathered by the US Department of Health and Human Services and an NGO called *Partnership to Fight Chronic Disease*. Other corporate success stories include *The Bank of America* which introduced health risk assessments (HRAs) alongside educational materials. The following year, the bank then reported a ten percent *decrease* in healthcare costs. Biometric screenings that include blood cholesterol tests were offered in addition to HRAs by US communications company, Cadmus. Reported results are significant: employees spent half as much time in hospital after the initiative compared to before. Cadmus's healthcare bill was reportedly reduced by 75% (12). Another large company, *Caterpillar Inc,* reports that it has reduced workplace insurance premiums by $75 per employee since introducing HRAs (13). Other companies, including furniture maker *Wi*, pharmaceutical giant *Johnson & Johnson*, and insurance company, *Florida Blue,* also publicly endorse and offer employee's fitness programmes and outcome-based incentives reported the *Wall Street Journal*. Thus, a whole range of American companies sense that they receive great, untapped, extra value, from promoting personal fitness and resilience strategies at work.

Some US public authorities have taken a more persuasive approach. Houston city authority staffers reportedly received a $25 payroll 'surcharge' if they did not fulfil mandated personal fitness tasks. Obligations included taking part in HRAs, biometric testing, meetings with health coaches, and signing up for a fat reduction programme (14).

Nevertheless, organisations and managers may wish to be aware of possible negatives. With outcome-incentive schemes, there is an increased likelihood of false or embellished reporting on self-reporting HRAs. Moreover, disproportionate or random high-intensity activity bursts, or peer pressure to undertake such, may be hazardous to an individual. (Or a company balance sheet, if they get sued.) As could poor vetting or lax recruitment processes around so-called personal fitness and self-help coaches. Furthermore, many employers and employees in the civilian sphere might feel very uncomfortable that corporate decision making, such as promotions and incentives, are being based around performance in workplace physical resilience initiatives. In some domains, pressures upon employees (even within police and army domains) to conform to physical resilience initiatives may attract rebuke from interest groups, or even feel the full force of legislation that seeks to protect human rights and eradicate workplace discrimination. Following criticism of some British police forces, a report published by Sir Tom Winsor during 2012 claimed that some 52% of Metropolitan Police Service officers were 'overweight'. In another force "barely one in four male officers was normal weight", the *Daily Mail* reported (15). A 'bleep test' system was introduced, with the bar set much lower than other comparable police forces around the world. But a year later, a female Chief Constable of Cleveland scored just 4.2 reported the *Northern Echo*, some 1.2 lower than the minimum pass grade (16). Some cases of discrimination have been brought against UK police service employers. The attempt to improve personal fitness performance has floundered in the UK temporarily. It was firmly critiqued by the UK Police Federation, a body that represents beat police officers:

> *"Physical fitness is just one aspect of a police officer's role. In some roles it is more important than in others and officers who undertake those roles should have an appropriate fitness test. Health and well-being is equally important and officers should get regular health screening and help to keep in shape. But to value physical prowess above all other things has the potential to change the whole culture of the service and devastate diversity."* (17) (18). Food for thought indeed.

8.4 Developing team resilience from personal resilience techniques

In their 2013 study *Defining and characterising team resilience in elite sport*, eminent team sports psychologists, Morgan, Fletcher and Sarkar, make clear connections between successful individual and team sporting activity and implications for entrepreneurs and companies that may wish to learn from such practices. Security practitioners thus might wish to note:

The structural aspects of team behaviour, such as shared interpretive responses, role systems, rules, and procedures, enable these groups to organise themselves during a crisis. "These aspects appear to allow team members to co-ordinate their responses to stressors through agreed patterns of behaviour and the subsequent creation of collective sense making", assert Morgan, Fletcher and Sarkar (19). The analysts continue: "Research has suggested that resilience at an organisational level is more likely to occur when rich social capital exists" (20). 'Social capital' has been usefully defined as "the goodwill available to individuals, groups, and organisations that lies in the structure and content of their interpersonal relationships" (21).

Shared experience and collective processing of adversity is critically important to develop team resilience, suggest Morgan et al. "… resilient teams regard setbacks as a natural part of their development" (22). From their significant study, the group conclude that, "Team resilience was defined as a dynamic, psychosocial process which protects a group of individuals from the potential negative effect of the stressors they collectively encounter. It comprises of processes whereby team members use their individual and collective resources to positively adapt when experiencing adversity" (23).

Other researchers have also focused on identifying key ingredients to team resilience. The US-based *Search Institute* found that "resilient inner-city youth often have talents, such as athletic abilities that attract others to them". These kids had "an uncanny ability to get adults to help them out" (24). In another important academic study, *Develop Resilience – lessons learned from Olympic Champions,* produced after London's 2012 Olympics, Sarkar and Fletcher interviewed 12 Olympic champions "from a range of sports regarding their experiences of withstanding pressure during their sporting careers". They found that athletes demonstrated a "number of key psychological attributes" (25). The pair then developed a *personal resilience framework* – core personality components that were demonstrated by each of the athletes. There appear to be five common traits for success: "positive personality, motivation, confidence, focus and perceived social support", the researchers concluded (26). The following quote illustrates just how the quality of team confidence and collective, optimistic consciousness, can influence an individual evaluation of pressure:

> *"We were playing against (country) in our last game … and I looked at my opposite number and I thought 'I'm going to give you a hard time today kid' … Now if I had that internal thought 18 months ago, I would have thought I was being schizophrenic or something, because if you're going to lose to anybody it's (country), but I just felt I had such confidence in … my team's ability."* (27)

Imagine, for a moment, propelling that type of undefeatable corporate mindset against your competitors! Furthermore, an ability to focus with intensity on the incumbent task was also found to be a critical aspect of personal resilience practiced by the world's best athletes. Each was able to focus on themselves and tasks (challenges) that they had to achieve in order to win the greater prize. They did not permit themselves to be distracted by others. Gold medallists also learned to focus on overarching process, rather than specific event outcomes. Each could 'switch' their focus on and off to suit demands that they faced (28). This author is probably not alone in betting that our top entrepreneurs have only reached the peaks of enterprise by deploying precisely the same intensity of focus at key junctures in their working lives.

Military team-building techniques and resilience

Dr Martin Seligman's *Building Resilience* model is instructive in the manner that it develops physical fitness values into a mental health well-being strategy for one of the most kinetic, high-risk security job roles: the modern day soldier. Seligman is one of a group of leading psychologists who have worked with the US military to develop the Comprehensive Soldier Fitness (CSF) programme. This consists of three 'components':

1. A test for psychological fitness
2. Self-improvement courses following the test
3. Master resilience training for drill sergeants.

According to Seligman, who has been regularly dubbed the 'father of positive psychology', the core components are based on the mnemonic, PERMA: positive emotion, engagement, relationships, meaning, and accomplishment. Seligman calls these, "the building blocks of resilience and growth" (29). A 'spiritual fitness module' within a CSF self-improvement course "… refers not to religion but to belonging to and serving something larger than the self". This component is of particular relevance to corporate leaders argues Seligman: "… it begins with the ancient wisdom that personal transformation comes from a renewed appreciation of being alive, enhanced personal strength, acting on new possibilities, improved relationships, or spiritual deepening" (30).

Case study: Seligman's 'positive psychology':
The ingredients of post-traumatic growth

Seligman wrote that five elements were known to contribute to post-traumatic growth, these are:

1. Understanding the response to trauma (read failure), which includes shattered beliefs about the self, others and the future. This is a normal response, not a symptom of PTSD or a character defect.
2. Reducing anxiety through techniques for controlling intrusive thoughts and images.

---

3. Engaging in constructive self-disclosure. Bottling up trauma can lead to a worsening of physical and psychological symptoms, so soldiers are encouraged to tell their stories.

4. Creating a narrative in which the trauma is seen as a fork in the road that enhances the appreciation of paradox – loss and gain, grief and gratitude, vulnerability and strength.

5. Articulating life principles. These encompass new ways to be altruistic, crafting a new identity, and taking seriously the idea of the Greek hero who returns from Hades to tell the world an important truth about how to live. (31)

8.5 Crisis management and personal resilience

When we dig among the plethora of well-researched and documented work in fields of 'organisational resilience' – perhaps by taking isomorphic lessons from company survival strategies – we can see *prima facie* that little comment is made around levels of personal fitness being an enabler to survival.

Case study: Rick Rescorla – 9/11 planning 'genius'

Morgan Stanley President and COO, Robert G Scott, paid testament to the work of security director, Rick Rescorla, who brought in strict evacuation drills and contingency preparations for the investment bank and its employees after the New York World Trade Center was initially bombed by terrorists affiliated to Al-Qaeda in 1993.

Rescorla, who was sadly killed while trying to evacuate staff members from Tower 2 on 11 September 2001, was a military veteran who forced staff to practice emergency evacuation drills. Led by Rescorla on a 'bullhorn', the vast majority of employees survived during 9/11, and the bank's operations were transferred to three contingency back-up sites.

Scott commented afterwards: "Multiple back-up sites seemed like an incredible extravagance on September 10 ... but on September 12, they seemed like genius".

Source Diane Coutu, Harvard Business Review, 2002 (32)

During many other cases of mass casualty terrorism, or natural disasters, including the Mumbai 2008 terrorist bombings and siege, a key survival strategy was quick mental activation, followed by the physical ability to evacuate safely and cover long distances on foot away from the danger zone. For example, the full impact of a fully-loaded vehicle borne improvised explosive device may well be felt over several thousand metres. The 2008 hotel bombing carried out in Islamabad by drivers of a dumper truck laden with explosives, reportedly caused injuries more than two kilometres away, due to the direction of explosive blast and limited barriers within its path. 54 people were killed and several hundred badly injured, and a deep earth-crater was left to the Marriott Hotel's frontage (33). Furthermore, first responder resources are very limited in any domain and must attend to priority cases, if indeed they can access the incident at all. Physical and group self-preservation is the order of the day in most emergency scenarios, in any environment, at least to begin with.

The late resilience expert, Dr Al Siebert, stated: "highly resilient people are flexible, adapt to new circumstances quickly, and thrive in constant change. Most important, they expect to bounce back and feel confident that they will. They have a knack for creating good luck out of circumstances that many others see as bad luck" (34). It therefore seems entirely logical that the stamina and strength of each individual is of direct material significance for the team, and organisation, which they contribute their physical, emotional and intellectual matter to.

8.6 Crisis management and communications

"While not all crises can be foreseen, let alone prevented, all of them can be managed far more effectively if we understand and practice the best of what is humanely possible." – Professor Ian Mitroff, 2001 (35)

Case study: Tylenol poisonings: 'Be the boring guy, not the bad guy'

Professor Ian Mitroff is broadly associated with leading the foundation of the academic field of *crisis management* (CM). Mitroff reported on, and analysed, the response by companies caught up in the infamous 1982 Tylenol poisonings, which occurred in and around Chicago. The response by the parent company, Johnson & Johnson, was deemed so professional by journalists that it became a benchmark for emerging crisis management analysts. The Tylenol response is held by some subject matter experts to be a formative case which turned crisis management into an academic discipline. Pharma company, Johnson & Johnson, speedily admitted that products were contaminated. They immediately recalled the products and offered large rewards for information to catch the culprit/s. They worked with media agencies to guide the public away from Tylenol to alternatives. On his popular and informative blog, Mitroff observed that several lessons emerged from the company's response: "Be proactive to identify 'latent defects': move from 'if it ain't broken don't fix it' to 'fix it beforehand'. Be the boring guy, not the 'bad' guy", the professor urges. Mitroff also argues that employees should "challenge 'denial' cultures that can be found within most organisations" (36).

Corporate communications techniques

High-profile organisations and people attract lots of media attention. Major incidents and crises attract a whole lot more. However, the responsibility for dealing with such a volcanic eruption of public interest can fall on the shoulders of employees and executives that are often unfamiliar with professional media management techniques and inexperienced in crisis management. Dynamic and multifaceted media management strategies have been practiced by government institutions and agencies since the advent of mass media, and they provide some lessons for security and emergency planners.

The brutally honest and professional memoir by President Bill Clinton's former communications director, George Stephanopoulos, *All Too Human: A Political Education* (1999), provides a valuable insight into how any major organisations can understand crisis communications management (37). Stephanopoulos' isomorphic-style work provides a frank assessment of public relations mistakes made by the White House in the early 1990s. Four key lessons that I've identified spring out from the book for corporate leaders:

1. The near-simultaneous occurrence of multiple crises – often with interconnected causes, and lethal proximity to 'contagion' – that can impact one organisation, and one team. Lesson: Overall strategy is critical.

2. The relationship between sustained crisis management, employee mental health well-being, and how decision making can become skewed into supporting narrow, inward-looking agendas. Lesson: Look after your own staff.

3. Dealing with several simultaneous official investigations and subpoenas, for cases with serious implications for employees and executives. Lesson: Get expert advice and be transparent.

4. Develop processes in order to establish feedback on performance of the media operation. Lesson: Don't alienate reporters and ask friendly reporters for feedback.

Crisis communications: Process and stages

According to crisis communications author, RL Dilenschneider, a crisis can create three related threats: public safety, financial loss and loss of good reputation. Another academic in this sphere, W Timothy Coombs, wrote in his prominent 2007 article *Crisis Management and Communications* that, "effective crisis management handles the threats sequentially". Timothy Coombs adds: "The primary concern in a crisis has to be public safety. A failure to address public safety intensifies the damage from a crisis" (38). Barton's (2001) report *Crisis in*

Organisations II and Coomb's own report *Code Red in the Boardroom* build on prior research from other CM academics who suggest that, in practice, crisis management can be more effective if it is divided into three tangible phases:

1. **Pre-crisis:** Crisis management plans are developed; a designated CM team appointed; CM plans are practiced regularly; public messages can be 'pre-drafted' as much as possible.

2. **Crisis response:** How management actually respond to a crisis. Barton (2001) recommends that the CMT include the following business functions: finance, legal, human resources, public relations and security.

3. **Post-crisis:** Investigate and implement improvements for next CM response; fulfil commitments made during crisis; wind down intensity – no longer CM mode but drop down a gear, yet still maintain strategic CM controls (39).

Instructing information

Speed, accuracy and efficient audience targeting will be critical tasks for the communications teams and public-facing executives during a crisis. Leaders and spokespeople will not want to face the wrath of media and stakeholders without being armed with key facts, pledges and an option to carry out news briefings from secure and appropriate locations. In scenarios involving public safety, incorrect information can be fatal to an organisation's reputation. For public authorities, getting baseline information disseminated to the general public may well be their mandated responsibility. Public 'warning and informing' duties often involve the dissemination of *instructing information*. Such notices, via broadcasts or electronic communications, can help to publicise evacuation and shelter points, safe routes and diversions, public health information and other useful messages. Speed and reach of communications are critical at the beginning of a crisis. However, police or security agencies may be worried that extra security risks could be posed by too widely disseminating certain public safety arrangements. Many business communities (and individual companies) have responded since 9/11 by developing their own, fast-time notification systems, such as the popular i-modus SMS and email alerts that get disseminated to registered City of London-based security managers. This initiative, and many similar ones, can deliver specific, relevant and *actionable* information to trusted individuals and subscriber organisations. Wherever security practitioners operate in the world, they are recommended to research and join such useful information notification networks (40).

Verbal crisis responses

Expressions of regret and sympathy by any culpable organisation can, of course, lessen the damage to its waning reputation. Nevertheless, research demonstrates that expressions of sympathy can bring unintended consequences. Here's the good news: Cohen (1999) evaluated some legal cases and discovered that early expressions of concern did actually help to lessen the volume of claims made against an organisation that was *perceived* to be responsible for a crisis (41). However, Tyler's prominent research (1997) demonstrated that lawyers may try to suggest expressions of concern are admissions of guilt (42). Another communications analyst, Hearit (2007), cautions that regular expressions of sympathy and concern can begin to appear routine, suggesting a loss of emotional intelligence by company representatives. Without delving too much into psychology as a discipline, an informed awareness of Kubler-Ross's model, popularised as the 'five stages of grief', published in his magnum opus, On *Death and Dying* (1969), would serve any CM or crisis communications planners well (44).

Argenti's study into companies responding to the 9/11 attacks in America emphasised the importance of turning attention internally after any major crisis or disaster. By interviewing managers and assessing survivor responses following conversations some time after the Manhattan disaster, Argenti recommends: "employees need to know what happened, what they should do, and how the crisis will affect them" (45). One institution which lost several hundred colleagues allocated surviving staff volunteers to act as unofficial liaison with families of co-workers who had not survived the atrocities (46). In the aviation industry, trauma teams are immediately despatched to support staff and families of victims. Such psychological support services are now routinely made available across several sectors including major banks to support robbery victims, usually their own employees. As mordant as it may be, news organisations and social media platforms are inundated with macabre, microscopic and unreasonable, cynical examinations in relation to the conduct of organisations, leaders and employees during times of major organisational and personal turmoil.

W Timothy Coombs has devised and developed various crisis response frameworks. With fellow crisis communications expert, Bill Benoit, Timothy Coombs has developed a *Master List of Reputation Repair Strategies*. However, before we plough ahead and report headline best practice, it is worth reflecting that not every substantial incident does require a formalised crisis management response. A well-intended overreaction can sometimes create more harm than good. That said, we finish this section by offering an easy-to-use crisis communications checklist.

Crisis communications checklist: W Timothy Coombs's crisis response best practices

1. Be quick and try to have initial response within the first hour

2. Be accurate by carefully checking all the facts

3. Be consistent by keeping spokespeople informed of crisis events and key message points

4. Make public safety your number one priority

5. Use all of the available communications channels including the Internet, intranet and mass notification systems

6. Provide some expression of concern/sympathy for victims

7. Remember to include employees in the initial response

8. Be ready to provide stress and trauma counselling to victims of the crisis and their families, including employees.

Source: W Timothy Coombs (2007), 'Crisis Management and Communications', Institute for Public Relations (47)

8.7 Social media and crisis management

In 2011, the journalist, Eric Berto, wrote poignantly on his blog: "The *state of journalism* is in flux. It is either morphing into a free-for-all landscape where anybody with internet access is a journalist. Or, the true journalists still exist in the form of somebody willing to conduct interviews, challenge the information given and work to gather facts not normally accessible" (48). Berto may well be correct. But as security practitioners, we have to treat and respond to the risks of the world as we find them. And, undoubtedly, although social media platforms may be the root cause of a major security incident, or add rocket fuel to a crisis, they do also provide a tremendously influential tool for problem solvers and security solutions innovators. Bad communications cause crisis; good communications can fix them.

At the time of writing, the number of people registered to use social media continues to rise. Where people are online, around seven out of ten use a social media platform. In the US, seven out of ten online users have a Facebook account (though up to three out of four might not regularly use it). One in four use LinkedIn, Pinterest, Twitter and Instagram. For many years, governments, businesses and NGOs have attempted to research and identify methods to use social media platforms to communicate during a major incident or crisis.

Case study: Social media exposure … can Russell Brand and Miley Cyrus do anything to help?

In its 2011 evidence to Congress, the US Federal Emergency Management Agency stated it had 33,000 Facebook followers. By November 2013 the agency had 155,003 'likes'. This compares to comedian Russell Brand with 2,010,089 'likes' and pop princess Miley Cyrus who scored nearly 34 million 'likes' (33,910,019) around the time of her 21st birthday – during November 2013. Cyrus herself 'likes' America's Red Cross, and promoted the organisation on the front page of her Facebook account. Within one click we can visit the American Red Cross on Facebook and join their own community that attracts 569,019 'likes' – a substantial online support footprint that would be the envy of most small and medium sized companies. 16 months later, as I came to the end of writing this book, America's Red Cross Facebook page attracted almost 90,000 new 'likes' (651,174). But Cyrus had added ten million 'likes' (47,062,528), by March 2015, leaping ahead of President Obama scoring at around 42 million (42,821,901).

Both Brand and Cyrus dwarf the Facebook presence of UK Prime Minister, David Cameron, who registered 202,354 'likes' with his 10 Downing Street account. Calculations for these comparisons were taken by the author in November 2013, at the end of a week which saw the emergence of nuclear materials negotiations with Iran which the British Government was pitching itself to have played a key role in. PM Cameron was promoting the Disasters Emergency Committee response to Typhoon Haiyan in the Philippines. Former President George W Bush's Facebook was recorded with just under 3 million (2,850,741) 'likes'. Bush himself 'likes' the US Military Facebook page which scored 305,574 in November 2013.

However, whether frantic celebrity and political social media activity and endorsements actually influence an upward curve in material support for charities and good causes remains a moot point for many. During November 2013, British comedian and self-confessed political revolutionary, Russell Brand, gave a 'like' to an important Long Island charity, *The Pulmonary Hypertension Support Group*. The group had 382 'likes' back in November 2013. Five days later the charity had gained just two more. Perhaps celebrity endorsement via social media is not always as influential as some of us like to imagine (49).

Governments and public authorities turn to social media to both get messages out around major incidents and also to receive critical information. A study commissioned by the Red Cross found that social media is the fourth most popular source to access emergency information (50). It also found that around half of all respondents would sign up for emails, text alerts, or social media alert applications for emergency information if services were offered. Private companies, such as BP in responding to the 2010 Deepwater Horizon explosion and oil spill disaster in the Gulf of Mexico, have become proficient at using social media as a frontline communications tool in emergency recovery scenarios. Although criticised for widespread mishandling of the broadcast media following this disaster, BP were able to publicise emergency contact details and offer direct contact with financial relief schemes via its Facebook pages. This conversation loop did assist some impacted companies and communities to access compensation. The ability for companies, NGOs and governments to communicate directly via social media with audiences, especially during periods of intense mass media hostility, has provided a literal lifeline and significant tool of organisational resilience for many under-fire enterprises.

The business security advisory group, CSARN, produced a mini-report explaining how organisations can use social media to support emergency response and recovery (51). Some of the headline scenarios identified by CSARN include:

- Social media is now very frequently used by individuals, companies, community groups and public authorities to warn others of unsafe areas or situations, to contact friends and families of those injured and rescued, and also to raise vital funds and materials for disaster relief missions.

- Facebook, the world's largest social network, supports many emergency-related organisations, including the Information Systems for Crisis Response and Management (ISCRAM) initiative, The Humanitarian Free and Open Source Software (FOSS) Project, as well as numerous university-based disaster programmes.

- Social media has played an influential role during a wide range of emergency situations. Sometimes for better or for worse. For example, in 2009, the US Army used its twitter account to provide coverage and updates during the Fort Hood shooting. The American Red Cross uses its social media platform in a similar way to issue alerts of potential disasters. Yet terrorists, for example during the 2008 Mumbai sieges and other mass casualty attacks, do often use social media to identify where visitors and guests may be hiding.

- Social media can be used to help update communities on response and recovery actions, and to keep communities informed of developments. It can help alleviate the pressure and diversion that can sometimes be contributed to by excessive or unreasonable broadcast and print press media demands.

- According to FEMA's Craig Fugate, social media helps government to communicate in a crisis because it is interactive and enables two-way, 'backchannel communication' with those impacted, or those with better information. Fugate also identified a disadvantage for government and victims of violence. US Armed Forces were effectively tied into a race against social media platforms when it came to the sad duty of informing service personnel families of their deaths (52) (53).

- People in disaster impacted areas have started to use social media to alert the authorities to their needs, especially when telecommunication networks go down. Researchers studying the 2011 Japanese earthquake and tsunami found that individuals 'tweeted' for assistance when they could not use a phone. This also posed a problem for emergency services as tweets for assistance were often 'retweeted' after the victims had already been rescued. This presents the problem that social media could add to the confusion and misinformation that often arises from emergencies and disasters (54).

- One major concern, though, are threats and risks caused by the deliberate provision of inaccurate information (misinformation) to confuse or harm response efforts.

8.8 Crisis management standards and guidance

Enterprise risk management academic and practitioner, Geary Sikich, is one of many commentators who – without dismissing the role of industry guidance – does illustrate the real world limitations of abstract manuals which provide us with instructions for supposed standards and best practices. High-profile incidents and organisations are susceptible to intensely hostile and resource-sapping scrutiny. In his reflective article, *Lessons from the BP Deepwater Horizon Catastrophe*, Sikich (2010) states that some organisations are stuck in an "activity trap; dominated and controlled by internal process and outdated controls. Such constrained business practices could run contrary to changes in the operating environment or developments in technology". From his isomorphic studies, Sikich observed that, "Risk and non-risk management professionals are so enmeshed in following risk-management protocols promulgated by financial and non-financial regulatory and oversight entities that they cannot see the risk for what it really is. They get caught in the 'activity trap'" (55). One particular company failure attracted Sikich's ire. In his critique of BP's response he found that: "… eventually, procedures become a goal in themselves – [they were] doing an activity for the sake of the activity rather than what it accomplishes" (56).

Nevertheless, guidance reports and national and international standards are exceedingly important to access for security and emergency planners. Security and emergency planners may themselves be newcomers to various corporate crisis scenarios, but this won't prevent their non-security colleagues carrying a realistic expectation that they are, de facto, the first port of call in a crisis! Published and emerging BSI and ISO standards and guidance documents available to support crisis management and incident management are given below.

Business Continuity Institute: Good Practice Guidelines (2013) are, according to the BCI, "the independent body of knowledge for good Business Continuity practice worldwide. They represent current global thinking in good

Business Continuity (BC) practice and now include terminology from ISO 22301:2012, the International Standard for Business Continuity management systems" (57).

PAS 200:2011: *Crisis Management – Guidance and good practice* was published in September 2011. PAS 200 is a Publicly Available Specification (PAS) sponsored by the UK Government's Cabinet Office and developed in partnership with the British Standards Institution. It is aimed primarily at top managers and aims to inform the development of a strategic crisis management capability within an organisation (58). The PAS differentiates between the terms *incident* and *crisis* and refers to the *BS 25999 Business Continuity Management* standard for incident management guidance and requirements.

ISO 22320:2011: *Societal Security – Emergency management – Requirements for incident response*, was published in 2011. ISO22320 includes requirements for integrated and cooperative aspects of incident response between organisations at international, national and regional levels. This includes, for example, creation of command and control structures that facilitate information flows and inter-operability between organisations. Prof Ernst-Peter Döbbeling, convener of the working group that developed the standard said: "ISO22320 is a valuable tool that all types of organisations can use to improve their capabilities in handling incident response in any crisis" (59).

ISO 22301:2012: the International Standard for *Business continuity management systems – Requirements* was published midway through 2012. According to its ISO sponsor: "ISO22301 provides a framework to plan, establish, implement, operate, monitor, review, maintain and continually improve a business continuity management system (BCMS). It is expected to help organisations protect against, prepare for, respond to, and recover when disruptive incidents arise" (60).

BS 25999: This British Standard for business continuity management systems was replaced by *ISO 22301:2012* above. It was withdrawn in 2013, but remains well-known. In the BSI document, the practice of business continuity management was defined as the: "*... holistic management process that identifies potential threats to an organisation and the impacts to business operations those threats, if realised, might cause, and which provides a framework for building organisational resilience with the capability of an effective response that safeguards the interests of its key stakeholders, reputation, brand and value-creating activities*" (61).

Chapter 8: Wrap-up

In closing this chapter on **Personal and Organisational Resilience**, we reflect on some of the approaches and attributes that will help your company gain the competitive edge. These include:

- As advanced security professionals, there is an expectation that your specific personal value to the organisation will probably be at its premium, and most visible, during major incidents and acute organisational challenges.

- Due to in-built survival mechanisms, human brains are naturally wired to give more attention to negative events than positive ones. But in all likelihood, we experience many more positive events than negative ones. One essential ingredient to building resiliency lies in "noticing and appreciating those positive experiences whenever and wherever they occur", reports resiliency expert Barbara Fredrickson.

- Shared experience and collective processing of adversity is critically important to develop team resilience, suggests Dr Paul Morgan, Head of Sport at Buckinghamshire New University. He adds that, "resilient teams regard setbacks as a natural part of their development".

- Many national and city public authorities run 'Warn and Inform' message alert systems for businesses and security managers in their area. Bulletins send out 'instructing information' in the occurrence of a major incident. These crisis communications initiatives can deliver specific, relevant and *actionable* information to trusted individuals and subscriber organisations. Wherever security practitioners operate in the world they are recommended to join such useful information notification and peer-support networks.

- Be prepared to get proficient with using social media! The ability for companies, NGOs and governments to communicate directly via social media with audiences, especially during periods of intense mass media hostility, has provided a literal lifeline, and significant tool of organisational resilience for many under-fire enterprises.

- National and international standards are exceedingly important to access for security and emergency planners. Security and emergency planners may themselves be newcomers to various corporate crisis scenarios, but this won't prevent their non-security colleagues carrying a realistic expectation that they are, de facto, the first port of call in a crisis! Security practitioners should familiarise their teams with all guidance and standards documents and requirements that are made available to support crisis management and incident management.

On a closing note, it is the aforementioned 'holistic' process of business continuity that, ultimately, clients are now asking security consultants to protect. Traditional threats and risks have by no means gone away. It's just that the role of a modern security practitioner has shifted from being a predominantly protective site and assets person, into emerging as a leading contributor towards overall organisational resilience. The definition of an *entrepreneur* is somebody who sets up a business, taking on financial risks in the hope that they make a profit. I very much hope that this book has helped you thrive in taking risks and decisions as a business entrepreneur; whether in your own company or somebody else's. But I also sincerely wish that this edition has helped you to better protect other entrepreneurs and businesses as they too seek to turn a profit in our uncertain and remarkable world.

References

1) Aerospaceweb (2014), 'Commercial Airline Bombing History', accessed and downloaded on 06/05/2014 at: *www.aerospaceweb.org/question/planes/q0283.shtml*

2) Global Issues.org (2014), 'The Arms Trade is Big Business', accessed and downloaded at: *www.reuters.com/article/2014/02/05/us-usa-retailers-cybersecurity-idUSBREA1409H20140205*

3) Coutu, D., (2002), 'How Resilience Works', Harvard Business Review, May 2002

4) Fredrickson, B., (2009), 'Positivity', Crown Archetype

5) Sholl, J., (2011), 'The Five Best Ways to Build Resiliency', Experience Life Magazine online, September 2011. Accessed and downloaded on 16/05/2014 at: http://*experiencelife.com/article/the-5-best-ways-to-build-resiliency/*

6) Deloitte website (2006), 'Workplace initiatives', accessed and downloaded on 12/05/2014 at: *https://mycareer.deloitte.com/ie/en/students/life-at-deloitte/workplace-initiatives*

7) Ibid.

8) Deloitte website (2006), 'Workplace wellness: Organised wellness', accessed and downloaded on 12/05/2014 at: *www.deloitte.com/view/en_gb/uk/6ef976787e090310VgnVCM3000001c56f00aRCRD.htm*

9) Miller-Kovach, K., (2007), 'Weight and the Workplace', accessed and downloaded on 12/05/2014 at: *www.weightwatchers.com/images/1033/dynamic/GCMSImages/weight_workplace.pdf*

10) The American Institute of Stress, (2007), 'Job Stress', accessed and downloaded on 12/05/2014 at: *www.stress.org/archives/*

11) Health Advocate (2007), 'Guide to workplace wellness: healthy employees, healthy bottom-line', accessed and downloaded on 12/05/2014 at: *www.healthadvocate.com/downloads/whitepapers/WorkplaceWellnessGuide.pdf*

12) McQueen, M., (05/12/2006), 'The Road to Wellness is Starting at the Office', Wall Street Journal, 5,

13) Wieczner, J., (08/04/2013), 'Your Company Wants to Make you Healthy', Wall Street Journal, accessed and downloaded on 12/05/2014 at: *http://online.wsj.com/news/articles/SB10001424127887323393304578360 252284151378*

14) Ibid.

15) Doyle, J., (2012), 'Fat cop crackdown: Police officers too unfit for the beat face pay cut... and later retirement looms to current head', Daily Mail, 15/03/12: accessed and downloaded on 16/05/2014 at: *www.dailymail.co.uk/news/article-2115335/Fat-cop-crackdown-Police-officers-unfit-beat-face-pay-cut--later-retirement-looms-current-head.html*

16) Northern Echo (23/07/2013), 'Chief Constable fails fitness test', accessed and downloaded on 14/04/2014, and subsequently redacted, at: *www.thenorthernecho.co.uk/news/10704384.Chief_constable_fails_fitness_ test/?action=complain&cid=12028487*

17) Police online (2014), Winsor Part 2 Update: Why an annual fitness test is not a 'one size fits all' solution. April 2014: accessed and downloaded at: *www.policemag.co.uk/editions/349.aspx*

18) Police UK.com (2014) Police Fitness, accessed and downloaded on 16/05/2014 at: *http://policeuk.com/ fitness_test.php*

19) Morgan, P., Fletcher, M., Sarkar, M., (2013). 'Defining and characterizing team resilience in elite sport', Elsevier Psychology of Sport and Exercise

20) Ibid.

21) Lengnick-Hall and Beck (2005), 'Adaptive Fit versus robust transformation', accessed and downloaded on 12/12/2014 at: *http://jom.sagepub.com/content/31/5/738.short*

22) Op. Cit., Morgan et al

23) Ibid.

24) Op. Cit., Coutu

25) Sarkar, M., Fletcher, D., (2012), 'Developing Resilience - Lessons learned from Olympic Champions', The Wave Lane 4, Issue 4 October 2012

26) Ibid.

27) Ibid.

28) Ibid.

29) Seligman, M., (2011), 'Building Resilience', Harvard Business Review April 2011

30) Ibid.

31) Ibid.

32) Op. Cit., Coutu

33) 33) Telegraph online (21/09/2008), 'Islamabad Marriott Hotel bomb killed 52', says Pakistan, accessed and downloaded on 31/03/2015 at: *www.telegraph.co.uk/news/worldnews/asia/pakistan/3041148/Islamabad-Marriott-hotel-bomb-killed-52-says-Pakistan.html*

34) Berrett-Koehler, Siebert, A. (2005), 'The Resiliency Advantage', New York, Practical Psychology Press

35) Mitroff I, with Anagnos, G., (2001), 'Managing Crises Before They Happen', New York: Amacam Books

36) Ibid.

37) Stephanopoulos, G., (1999), 'All Too Human: A Political Education', Boston, Little Brown

38) W. Timothy Coombs (2007), 'Crisis Management and Communications', Institute for Public Relations

39) Ibid.

40) The City of London i-modus scheme is run by the communications firm, Vocal, on behalf of the City of London Police

41) Cohen, J.R. (1999), 'Advising clients to apologize', S. California Law Review, 72, 10009-131

42) Tyler, T., (1997), 'Liability means never being able to say you're sorry: Corporate guilt, legal constraints, and defensiveness in corporate communication'. Management Communication Quarterly, 11(1), 51-73

43) Hearit, K. M., (1994) 'Apologies and Public Relations Crises at Chrysler', Toshiba, and Volvo', Public Relations Review, 20(2), 113-125

44) Kubler-Ross, (1969), 'On Death and Dying', Routledge, ISBN 0-415-04015-9

45) Argenti, P., (2002), 'Crisis Communication: Lessons from 9/11', Harvard Business Review, 80(12), 103-109

46) Author interview with senior director of corporation impacted by 9/11 conducted in New York during September 2014.

47) Op. Cit., W. Timothy Coombs

48) Berto, E., (02/08/2011), 'Crisis communications lessons from the News of the World scandal', was accessed and downloaded on 31/03/2015 at: *http://blogs.waggeneredstrom.com/thinkers-and-doers/tag/journalist/*

49) Facebook George W. Bush page was analysed and accessed on 27/11/203 at: *https://en-gb.facebook.com/georgewbush* Facebook FEMA page was analysed and accessed on 27/11/2013 at: *www.facebook.com/FEMA*. Facebook Long Island Pulmonary Hypertension Support Group was analysed and accessed on 27/11/2013 at: *www.facebook.com/LongIsland PHSupportGroup*
Facebook Miley Cyrus page was analysed and accessed on 27/11/2013 and 31/03/2015 at: *https://en-gb.facebook.com/MileyCyrus*

Facebook Barack Obama page was analysed and accessed on 27/11/2013 and 31/03/2015 at: *www.facebook.com/barackobama* Facebook Russell Brand page was analysed and accessed on 27/11/2013 at *www.facebook.com/RussellBrand*
Facebook US Military page was analysed and accessed on 27/11/2013 at: *www.facebook.com/USMilitary*
Facebook 10 Downing Street page of David Cameron was analysed and accessed on 27/11/2013 at: *www.facebook.com/10downingstreet*

50) Red Cross (2012) The American Red Cross and Dell Launch First-Of-Its-Kind Social Media Digital Operations Center for Humanitarian Relief, accessed and downloaded on 31/05/2012, available at: *www.redcross.org/ portal/site/en/menuitem.94aae335470e233f6cf911df43181aa0/?vgnextoid= 1cc17852264e5310VgnVCM10000089f0870aRCRD*

51) CSARN (2012), Security Viewpoint (1) 'The role of social media in emergencies', downloaded from the CSARN.org website on 02/12/2013 from: *http://news.csarn.org/2012/07/csarn-security-viewpoint-1-the-role-of-social-media-in-emergencies.html*

52) Department of Homeland Security (2011) Written Statement of Craig Fugate, Administrator, Federal Emergency Management Agency, before the Senate Committee on Homeland Security and Governmental Affairs, Subcommittee on Disaster Recovery and Intergovernmental Affairs: 'Understanding the Power of Social Media as a Communication Tool in the Aftermath of Disasters', accessed on 31/05/2015 at: *www.dhs.gov/ynews/ testimony/testimony_1304533264361.shtm*

53) Sutton, J. Palen, L. Shklovski, I. (2008) Backchannels on the front lines: Emergency uses of social media in the 2007 Southern California Wildfires. Colorado: University of Colorado

54) Lindsay, B. (2011) Social Media and Disasters. Washington DC: Congressional Research Service

55) 55) Sikich. G., (2010), 'Enterprise Risk Management Lessons from the BP Deepwater Horizon catastrophe', Continuity Central website, accessed and downloaded on 23/11/2013 from: *www.continuitycentral.com/feature0790.html*

56) Ibid.

57) BCI (2013), 'Good Practice Guidelines', can be accessed via the BCI website at: *www.thebci.org/index.php/resources/the-good-practice-guidelines*

58) PAS 200:2011 Crisis Management (2011), 'Guidance and good practice', London: BSI, can be accessed via the BSI shop at: *http://shop.bsigroup.com/ en/ProductDetail/?pid=000000000030252035*

59) ISO News (21/12/2011), 'New ISO standard for emergency management', was accessed and downloaded on 01/04/2015 at: *www.iso.org/iso/home/ news_index/news_archive/news.htm?refid=Ref1496*

60) ISO 22301:2012 (2012), 'Business continuity management systems - Requirements', was accessed and downloaded on 01/04/2015 at: *www.iso.org/iso/news.htm?refid=Ref1587*

61) ISO 22301 World (n.d), 'BS25999 and ISO 22301 Introduction', accessed on 01/04/2015 at: *www.25999.info/*

ITG RESOURCES

IT Governance Ltd sources, creates and delivers products and services to meet the real-world, evolving IT governance needs of today's organisations, directors, managers and practitioners.

The ITG website (*www.itgovernance.co.uk*) is the international one-stop-shop for corporate and IT governance information, advice, guidance, books, tools, training and consultancy. On the website you will find the following pages related to the subject matter of this book:

www.itgovernance.co.uk/infosec.aspx

www.itgovernance.co.uk/iso27001.aspx.

Publishing Services

IT Governance Publishing (ITGP) is the world's leading IT-GRC publishing imprint that is wholly owned by IT Governance Ltd.

With books and tools covering all IT governance, risk and compliance frameworks, we are the publisher of choice for authors and distributors alike, producing unique and practical publications of the highest quality, in the latest formats available, which readers will find invaluable.

www.itgovernancepublishing.co.uk is the website dedicated to ITGP. Other titles published by ITGP that may be of interest include:

- Once more unto the Breach

  www.itgovernance.co.uk/shop/p-985.aspx

- Information Security: A Practical Guide

  www.itgovernance.co.uk/shop/p-1701.aspx

- Nine Steps to Success: An ISO27001:2013 Implementation Overview

  www.itgovernance.co.uk/shop/p-963.aspx.

We also offer a range of off-the-shelf toolkits that give comprehensive, customisable documents to help users create the specific documentation they need to properly implement a management system or standard. Written by experienced practitioners and based on the latest best practice, ITGP toolkits can save months of work for organisations working towards compliance with a given standard.

To see the full range of toolkits available please visit:

www.itgovernance.co.uk/shop/c-129-toolkits.aspx.

Books and tools published by IT Governance Publishing (ITGP) are available from all business booksellers and the following websites:

www.itgovernance.eu   *www.itgovernanceusa.com*

www.itgovernance.in   *www.itgovernancesa.co.za*

www.itgovernance.asia.

Training Services

Staff training is an essential component of the information security triad of people, processes and technology, and of building an enterprise-wide security culture. IT Governance's ISO27001 Learning Pathway provides information security courses from Foundation to Advanced level, with qualifications awarded by IBITGQ. Many courses are available in Live Online as well as classroom formats, so delegates can learn and achieve essential career progression from the comfort of their own homes and offices.

Delegates passing the exams associated with our ISO27001 Learning Pathway will gain qualifications from IBITGQ, including CIS F, CIS IA, CIS LI, CIS LA, CIS RM and CIS 2013 UP.

IT Governance is an acknowledged leader in the world of ISO27001 and information security management training. Our practical, hands-on approach is delivered by experienced practitioners, who focus on improving your knowledge, developing your skills, and awarding relevant, industry-recognised certifications. Our fully integrated and structured learning paths accommodate delegates with various levels of knowledge, and our courses can be delivered in a variety of formats to suit all delegates.

For more information about IT Governance's ISO27001 learning pathway, please see:

www.itgovernance.co.uk/iso27001-information-security-training.aspx.

For information on any of our many other courses, including PCI DSS compliance, business continuity, IT governance, IT service management and professional certification courses, please see *www.itgovernance.co.uk/training.aspx*.

Professional Services and Consultancy

ISO 27001, the international standard for information security management, sets out the requirements of an information security management system (ISMS), a holistic approach to information security that encompasses people, process, and technology. Only by using this approach to information security can organisations hope to instil an enterprise-wide security culture.

Implementing, maintaining and continually improving an ISMS can, however, be a daunting task. Fortunately, IT Governance's consultants offer a comprehensive range of flexible, practical support packages to help organisations of any size, sector or location to implement an ISMS and achieve certification to ISO27001.

We have already helped more than 150 organisations to implement an ISMS, and with project support provided by our consultants, you can implement ISO27001 in your organisation.

For more information on our ISO27001 consultancy service, please see:

www.itgovernance.co.uk/iso27001_consultancy.aspx.

For general information about our other consultancy services, including for ISO20000, ISO22301, Cyber Essentials, the PCI DSS, Data Protection and more, please see:

www.itgovernance.co.uk/consulting.aspx.

Newsletter

IT governance is one of the hottest topics in business today, not least because it is also the fastest moving.

You can stay up to date with the latest developments across the whole spectrum of IT governance subject matter, including; risk management, information security, ITIL and IT service management, project governance, compliance and so much more, by subscribing to ITG's core publications and topic alert emails.

Simply visit our subscription centre and select your preferences:

www.itgovernance.co.uk/newsletter.aspx.

CPSIA information can be obtained
at www.ICGtesting.com
Printed in the USA
FFOW01n1349231015
17984FF